The American Catholic Voter

Other Works by George J. Marlin

The Quotable Chesterton (1986)

More Quotable Chesterton (1988)

The Quotable Fulton Sheen (1989)

The Quotable Ronald Knox (1996), with Richard Rabatin and Jack Swan

The Guidebook to Municipal Bonds

The History, the Industry, the Mechanics (1991), with Joe Mysak

The Quotable Paul Johnson (1994), with Richard Rabatin and Heather
    Higgins

*The Politician's Guide to Assisted Suicide, Cloning and Other Current
    Controversies* (1998)

Fighting the Good Fight: A History of the New York Conservative Party
    (2002)

Squandered Opportunities: New York's Pataki Years (2006)

General Editor of *The Collected Works of G.K. Chesterton*

Other Titles of Interest from St. Augustine's Press

Winston S. Churchill, *The River War: An Historical Account of the
    Reconquest of the Soudan* (in two volumes, slipcased)

Bernard J. O'Connor, *Papal Diplomacy: John Paul II and the Culture of
    Peace*

E. Michael Jones, *The Slaughter of Cities: Urban Renewal as Ethnic
    Cleansing*

George A. Kelly, *The Second Spring of the Church in America*

Kenneth D. Whitehead, ed., *The Catholic Citizen: Debating the Issues of
    Justice*

Richard Peddicord, S.J., *The Sacred Monster of Thomism: An Introduction to
    the Life and Legacy of Reginald Garrigou-Lagrange, O.P.*

Servais Pinckaers, O.P., *Morality: The Catholic View*

John F. Harvey, OSFS, and Gerard V. Bradley, eds., *Same-Sex Attraction: A
    Parents' Guide*

Teresa Wagner, ed., *Back to the Drawing Board: The Future of the Pro-Life
    Movement*

Josef Pieper, *Leisure, the Basis of Culture*

Roger Scruton, *The Meaning of Conservatism* (revised 3rd edition)

Roger Scruton, *An Intelligent Person's Guide to Modern Culture*

Ralph McInerny, *The Defamation of Pius XII*

C.S. Lewis and Don Giovanni Calabria, *The Latin Letters of C.S. Lewis*

John Lukacs, *Confessions of an Original Sinner*

The American Catholic Voter

200 Years of Political Impact

George J. Marlin

Introduction by Michael Barone

ST. AUGUSTINE'S PRESS
South Bend, Indiana
2006

Library of Congress Cataloging in Publication Data
Marlin, George J., 1952–
   The American Catholic voter: 200 years of political impact /
George J. Marlin; introduction by Michael Barone.
      p.   cm.
   Includes bibliographical references and index.
   ISBN 1-58731-023-6 (hardbound: alk. paper)
   1. Catholics – United States – Political activity – History.
   2. Voting – United States – History. 3. Elections – United States
   – History. I. Title.
E184.C3M37 2004
324.973'0088'282 – dc22   2004013933

Paperbound edition ISBN: 1-58731-029-5

∞ *The paper used in this publication meets the minimum requirements of the
American National Standard for Information Sciences – Permanence of
Paper for Printed Materials, ANSI Z39.48-1984.*

ST. AUGUSTINE'S PRESS
www.staugustine.net

My efforts are dedicated to

Richard P. Rabatin

and

The next generation of
Catholic Voters

Lindsay Crofton
Aidan Crofton
Augustine Crofton
Aquinas Crofton
Aloysius Crofton
Alicia Dyson
Briana Dyson
Caitlin Foye
Heather Foye
Olivia Foye

Table of Contents

Preface

I am a Catholic. I was born in Greenpoint, Brooklyn, into a family of "Al Smith" Democrats, who were socially conservative, supportive of New Deal programs, and critical of the Great Society's largesse. Growing up in the fifties and early sixties, most of my friends and neighbors had similar backgrounds and outlooks. They were second- and third-generation blue-collar ethnics committed to family, church, discipline, loyalty, and hard work. The parish neighborhood of my youth was a microcosm of the political culture of America's Catholic working class.

My parents and grandparents survived the Depression thanks to the parish and the local political clubhouse. These institutions helped to prevent the emergence of a rebellious underclass during the 1930s by serving as social and educational centers. Priests and nuns instilled the moral direction necessary to maintain civility, while local pols gave helping hands, although not handouts.

In *The American Catholic Voter*, I attempt to describe the impact Catholics have had on the electoral process during the past two-hundred years. I argue that for most of our country's history, the Catholic bloc has been a pivotal swing vote that determined outcomes in numerous national, state, and local elections.

I subscribe to the belief that most Catholics voters, who were loyal to family, church, and neighborhood, cast their ballots according to cultural standards determined by their faith. With political analyst Michael Barone, I believe that "The voting bases of the traditional Democratic and Republican Parties were primarily cultural; both drew allegiance from Americans who saw them not as promoters of their economic status, but as a protector of their way of life." The party label of "protectors of Catholic blue-collar values" has been claimed at different times by both Democrats and Republicans. But over time just one of the political parties has embraced the elitist notion that the best political structure is an efficiently engineered society where the individual is rendered meaningless. The other party has been the defender of the neighborhood and has adopted the concept of subsidiarity (long championed in Catholic social thought) which, to quote Michael Novak, "maintains that human life proceeds most intelligently and creatively when decisions are made at the local level closest to concrete reality."

During the nineteenth century and the early decades of the twentieth, the Democratic Party endorsed the concept of subsidiarity. Mr. Barone asserts that "the Democrats, drawing on their past, called themselves Jeffersonian and took care to respect local mores and idiosyncrasies, from segregation in the South to the saloon in the North. . . . The Democracy was a party of White southerners and northern Catholics, of Southern Baptist prohibitionists and immigrant imbibers, of nativists and those who spoke no English, of teeming eastern cities and the wastelands of the Great Basin."

Catholic voters overwhelmingly supported the presidential ambitions of Andrew Jackson, Samuel Tilden, Al Smith, Franklin D. Roosevelt, Harry Truman, and John F. Kennedy. In the late 1960s, however, political analysts began to detect a shift in the Catholic vote. Many Catholics voters felt unwanted in a changing Democratic Party whose leadership now frowned upon Catholic values. As a result, Catholic voters began to embrace politicians who portrayed themselves as antagonistic to cultural liberalism. Tired of being ridiculed by social engineers, Catholics gave their support to Richard Nixon and Ronald Reagan, because those candidates viewed the local defenders of traditional values as America's real heroes. Reagan paid tribute to them when he praised the "parents who sacrifice long and hard so their children will know a better life then they've known; church and civic leaders who help to feed, clothe, nurse, and teach the needy; millions who have made our nation and our nation's destiny so very special – unsung heroes who may not have realized their own dreams themselves, but then who reinvest those dreams in their children."

But by the end of the twentieth century, many political pundits were writing obituaries about the Catholic voter, whose influence these commentators claimed was declining and marginalized in a nation dominated by secular humanism. I address these claims and analyze the potential impact of the Catholic voter on the evolving political process in the twenty-first century.

I hope I have done justice to the story of millions of ethnic Catholics who arrived on America's shores with only the clothes on their backs, who worked through their parishes and neighborhoods to overcome nativist bigotry, and who became a significant voice in local, state, and national political affairs.

I am most thankful to my wife, Barbara, for once again putting up with me during the forging of this work. Without the untold hours she put into the assembling of the manuscript, this book would never have been completed.

I also want to thank Brad Miner, J. Freedley Hunsicker, and Pat Foye for their critiques of the manuscript. Their comments and suggestions made this a much better book.

I am also grateful to Michael Barone for writing the introduction. He was kind enough to take on the task even as he was facing the publication of his new book, *Hard America, Soft America*. Mr. Barone's 1990 work, *Our Country: The Shaping of America from Roosevelt to Reagan* has had a great impact on my thinking.

Heartfelt thanks as well to the following friends: Rev. John Bonnici, Michael Uhlmann, Mike Long, Robert Royal, Austin Ruse, Allen Roth, Paul Atanasio, Nelson Warfield, John McLaughlin, Msgr. Michael Wrenn, Rev. Gerald Murray, Steven and Cynthia Marlin, Tim and Mary Marlin, Pat and Larry Azar, Jim Kelly, Jim Gay, Joe Darden, and Charles Woram.

I also want to thank Templeton Prize Winner Michael Novak and Kevin Phillips. Reading their respective works, *The Rise of the Unmeltable Ethnics* and *The Emerging Republican Majority*, in the early 1970s spurred my interest in the political and cultural demography of inner-city Catholic neighborhoods.

My thanks to my colleagues at The Philadelphia Trust Company for their patience: Michael G. Crofton, Richard Sichel, Jerry Yandoli, Mary Walker, Barbara Civitella, Matthew Walker, Ray Teatum, Joel Harpel, Tom Praiss, Thomas Kelly, Marilyn Novak, Tom Clancy, Zach Thomson, Lindsay Lombardi, and Bill Lamb.

I am indebted to all my friends, and I hope their kindness is vindicated by this present work. I alone am responsible for any errors, inaccuracies, or follies in what follows.

George J. Marlin
New Hyde Park, New York
June 2004

Introduction

In 1776, fifty-five Protestants and one Catholic signed the Declaration of Independence: Roman Catholics have been part of America and American politics from the beginning. And often a controversial part. The colonists who came over from England in the seventeenth century were coming from a society which was convulsed with religious conflicts. Puritans vied to change the ways of the Anglican Church in the 1620s and 1630s, and some of them came to New England colonies to seek refuge. In the Civil War of the 1640s Presbyterians fought against Anglicans. In the 1650s the soldier-led government of the Commonwealth disestablished the Church of England, and sects of all kinds flourished. With the return of the King in 1660, the Church of England was reestablishment, and public office and the vote were denied to those who refused to take an oath upholding strict Anglicanism. In a stormy three-year reign the Catholic King James II offered toleration to Dissenting Protestants and Catholics and prosecuted Anglican bishops, then reneged; he was forced to flee the country in the Glorious Revolution of 1688. That brought to the throne the Dutch Protestant William III, who saw as his great mission the containment of King Louis XIV of France, whose military expansionism and intolerant Catholicism seemed a threat to English liberties. After the Glorious Revolution, Dissenting Protestants were more tolerated and Catholics allowed to worship only at home.

Through all these struggles and shifting tides, the large majority of Englishmen saw the Roman Catholic Church as a threat. It was a church, they were taught, which persecuted martyrs in the reign of "Bloody Mary" in the sixteenth century, a church which would take away English liberties, a church which supported England's vastly larger and richer continental enemies, Spain and then France. It was a church whose Jesuit order, it was said, allowed Catholics to take oaths as Protestants without sinning if they had a "mental reservation": you could not count on Catholics telling the truth. These fears about Catholicism had reverberations through much of American history. The vice president's oath, specified by the First Congress, requires him to swear that he has no "mental reservation."

There were few practicing Catholics in seventeenth-century England, and few in the colonies; but there were some. George Calvert, Lord Baltimore, a

Catholic, got King Charles II to grant him a charter for the colony of Maryland. Maryland became the first colony to tolerate all Christians, with freedom of religion and "the free exercise thereof" – language copied in the First Amendment in 1790. But the charter was revoked and after the Glorious Revolution, Catholics were no longer allowed to hold office. Other colonies, notably Pennsylvania, were more tolerant. But Catholics were less than 1 percent of the population when the thirteen colonies launched their Revolution against Britain.

The Revolution transformed Britons into Americans, and transformed their attitudes toward Catholics as well. Prominent Catholics supported the cause, including Charles Carroll of Maryland, perhaps the richest man in the colonies, who was the one Catholic signer of the Declaration of Independence, and Philip Mazzei, immigrant from Italy and neighbor and friend of Thomas Jefferson. "All men are created equal," Jefferson wrote in the Declaration, and the successful Revolutionaries decided this applied to Catholics as well as Protestants. The Constitution specified that there would be no religious test for office, as there still was in Britain, where Catholics were not allowed to hold office until 1829. The First Amendment provided that "Congress shall make no law respecting an establishment of religion, or prohibiting the free exercise thereof."

This does not mean that Catholics were equally tolerated: Protestant churches were established in states as late as the 1830s, and prohibitions on Catholics holding state office as late at the 1840s. Nevertheless, Catholics immigrated to the United States in large numbers, so that the Catholic percentage of the total population rose from 1 percent in 1790 to 2 percent in 1820, 5 percent in 1840, 12 percent in 1860, 14 percent in 1880, 19 percent in 1900, and 21 percent in 1920. This inevitably meant that Catholics became involved in politics, and involved often as a distinctive group – and sometimes a target group. The suspicion that Catholics were subject to a hostile foreign power persisted and flared during periods of heavy Catholic immigration. Conflict was particularly sharp over education, immigration policy, and (because of Irish Catholic hostility to British policy in Ireland) relations with Britain.

As they became more numerous and public schools became more common, Catholics began to object to the use of the King James Bible and other Protestant writings in public schools. New York Governor William Seward, a Whig, proposed in 1838 state support for Catholic schools, but this was rejected by the legislature. In time, New York's Bishop John Hughes decided to set up a separate system of Catholic schools – a system which continues to exist today. In the 1850s, a decade with sharply increasing immigration, including large numbers of Irish and German Catholics, the American or Know-Nothing Party called for longer periods of naturalization for immigrants and won big electoral victories for a few years. But the Know-Nothing movement collapsed, and the new Republican Party sought immigrant support. One of the reasons that the Republican National Convention in 1860 settled on Abraham Lincoln was that he had opposed anti-immigrant measures, and Lincoln ran well in German Catholic, though not in Irish Catholic, precincts: immigrants may have provided his margin of victory.

Despite Seward's efforts in New York and Lincoln's appeal in 1860, American Catholics tended to give large majorities to Democratic candidates through most of the nineteenth century. In those years the Democrats were the laissez-faire party, opposing road- and canal-building projects and subsidization of railroads, standing for free trade rather than tariffs, tolerating local customs from slavery and segregation to the saloon. They tended also to oppose religious tests for state office where they were in effect. These stands tended to appeal to members of a minority group who wanted tolerance for their own religion and social customs.

The Catholic bishops took care to be neutral on slavery and, in the Northern states where the large majority of Catholics lived, urged Catholics to support Lincoln's administration in its attempts to suppress the rebellion in the South. But that did not prevent Irish Catholics from opposing the Civil War. In 1863 Irish Catholics were numerous in the mobs during the New York draft riots; they were suppressed in large part because of the intervention of the by-now-elderly Bishop Hughes.

The thirty years after the Civil War were years of close competition between the two parties, and Catholics cast large majorities for the Democrats. But their large numbers, especially in New York, one of the few states where the division between the parties was close, meant that they were the target of appeals from both parties. It is generally believed that Republican James G. Blaine lost the 1884 election because a Protestant minister at a Republican rally denounced the Democrats as the party of "rum, Romanism and rebellion." It is also believed that Democrat Grover Cleveland lost New York and hence the election in 1888 (despite winning a popular vote plurality) because of Irish backlash against his policy toward Britain. In any case, the large number of Catholics in New York, the nation's largest state and usually one closely contested between the parties from 1860 to 1960, meant that Catholics had leverage in presidential politics disproportionate to their numbers.

The years from 1896 to 1930 were years of Republican majorities in most elections. One reason was that the Democrats of that period had little appeal to Catholic voters. Predominantly urban, they distrusted the agrarian politics and Protestant piety of William Jennings Bryan and went over in large numbers to William McKinley, Theodore Roosevelt, and William Howard Taft. Irish Catholics disliked Woodrow Wilson's partiality toward Britain, and many German Catholics opposed his decision to go to war with Germany. Wilson may have gained some credit with Polish Catholics for his support of a new independent Poland, but Italian Catholics were unhappy with his rebuffs of Italy at the Paris peace conference. These were years when many in the Protestant elites were calling for immigration restriction and for eugenic policies preventing the reproduction of supposedly inferior people of immigrant stock. But the importance of the immigrant vote was great and may have prompted Taft and Wilson to veto immigration restriction legislation.

In these years when Catholics were unusually partial to Republicans in presidential contests, they were also the mainstays of the Democratic political organizations – machines – that grew up in almost every large Northern city and which were usually headed by and largely manned by Irish Catholics. (There were also some Republican machines, notably in Philadelphia, also with heavy Catholic participation.) As Daniel Patrick Moynihan pointed out, the hierarchal structure of the machines, like the hierarchical structure of the Roman Catholic Church, appealed to Irish Catholics, who were content to wait their turn for eventual reward as their ancestors had in rural Irish villages. And although the Church set up ethnic parishes and the machines courted new immigrant groups, leadership was largely reserved for the Irish: it was not until the 1950s, six decades after heavy Italian immigration began, that the Church appointed its first Italian bishop and Manhattan's Tammany Hall had its first Italian leader.

Probably the greatest Tammany leader of them all was Charles F. Murphy, leader from 1902 to 1924, who took care to promote promising young men of modest background, like Governor Al Smith and Senator Robert Wagner (a German Protestant who married a Catholic; his son, New York Mayor Robert Wagner, was a Catholic). Smith, of Irish, German, and Italian descent, was the first great national politician of immigrant stock. In 1928 the Democrats could not deny him their nomination for president but, in a time of peace and prosperity, he lost to Republican Herbert Hoover. He would probably have lost in any case, but his Catholicism hurt: many Protestant leaders argued that he would take dictation from the Vatican, and many Protestant voters believed a Catholic should not be president. Smith lost many ordinarily Democratic Southern and border states because of his Catholicism – Florida, Kentucky, Missouri, North Carolina, Oklahoma, Tennessee, Texas, Virginia, West Virginia – and ran poorly in Midwestern and Western states with few Catholics. The seventeenth-century religious struggles still had reverberations in twentieth-century America.

But Smith also ran far better than the Democratic candidates of the preceding thirty years in urban states with large Catholic populations. He carried Massachusetts and Rhode Island, hitherto Republican bastions, but with large and fast-growing Catholic populations. He came within 3 percent of carrying New York. Smith's showings in these areas were almost as good as Franklin

Roosevelt's in his landslide victories four and eight years later. While Smith himself rejected the New Deal and opposed Roosevelt in 1936 and 1940 (they reconciled before Smith's death in 1944), Smith had established part of what would become Roosevelt's New Deal coalition: the Catholic masses in the big cities.

To that Roosevelt added the solidly Democratic (for a Protestant) South and the old progressive Northwest from the Great Lakes to the Pacific Coast

Roosevelt's relations with Catholics were, however, fraught with difficulty. He had opposed Tammany Hall early and often in Democratic politics, and caused the removal from office of Tammany Mayor Jimmy Walker in 1932. He supported Fusion Mayor Fiorello LaGuardia over Tammany's favorites. He always had uneasy relations with the New York archdiocese and conducted diplomacy with the Church through Chicago's Cardinal Mundelein. In 1940 his support of Britain antagonized Irish and German Catholics, and his disparaging remarks about Mussolini's Italy stabbing its neighbor in the back antagonized Italian Catholics as well. Roosevelt's share of the Catholic vote dropped sharply in 1940 and 1944.

After World War II American Catholics moved rapidly up the economic ladder and also found themselves opposed on cultural issues by other Democrats: both developments frayed their attachment to the Democratic Party. The biggest cultural issue was federal aid to education, a key plank in the postwar Democratic platform: Catholics would not support it unless it included Catholic schools; Catholic Southerners would not support it if it did.

This blocked the passage of federal education aid from 1949 to 1965. Catholics did not deliver their old Democratic percenatges for the diffident patrician Adlai Stevenson in 1952 or 1956. Roosevelt had already weakened the political machines by delivering aid to the poor through government rather than machine wheelhorses. Now Catholic leaders of political machines found themselves targets of mostly Protestant and Jewish reformers in the 1950s and 1960s.

Into this setting came the presidential candidacy of John F. Kennedy. It was the product of the ambition of his father, Joseph P. Kennedy, one of the few Irish Catholic multimillionaires, who made fortunes in several businesses, shewdly backed Franklin Roosevelt in 1932 (he was one of his few $50,000 contributors that year), and was appointed first head of the Securities and Exchange Commission and then Ambassador to Great Britain. This was a post of immense significance to Irish Catholics, and Kennedy became a political celebrity – and had hopes of running for president in 1940. These were frustrated by Roosevelt's third term bid and by Kennedy's own support of appeasement in Britain. But after 1940 Kennedy began promoting his son's candidacy. He courted media barons and won great publicity for John Kennedy's rather dubious record as a war hero; he stage-managed his successful campaigns for the House in 1946 and for the Senate in 1952; he got *Life* magazine to run a cover story on his children, "The Fabulous Kennedys," in 1957.

At forty-three, Kennedy seemed too young for the presidency in 1960 (no one else has ever been elected that young), and his legislative record was skimpy. But he was articulate, handsome, self-assured, and exceedingly well-financed. Despite continuing fears that a Catholic could not be elected, he won most of the primaries and was nominated in 1960.

Kennedy was exceedingly popular with Catholic voters and was rejected by many Protestants who ordinarily voted Democratic. But his performance in assuring a meeting of Protestant ministers in Houston that he would not let his faith affect his performance in office reassured many. His performance against incumbent Vice President Richard Nixon in debates assured many that he was mature and knowledgeable enough for the office. Yet at a time when analysts believed in a natural Democratic majority, he was elected by the narrowest of margins in the popular vote though by a wider margin in the Electoral College. According to the Gallup Poll, he won the votes of 78 percent of Catholics but only 37 percent of white Protestants. That meant higher Democratic percentages in northern industrial states and lower Democratic percentages in Southern, border, and rural states. The seventeetnth-century religious struggles still reverberated.

But they would cease to do so because of two developments over the next several years. The first was the fact that Kennedy was an unusually well regarded president, with job approval ratings around 70 percent during most of his term (that dropped after he endorsed the civil rights bill in June 1963, but all the drop occurred in the South, and he was headed for reelection by a margin similar to that won by his successor Lyndon Johnson in 1964). Kennedy's assassination cemented in, seemingly forever, the high regard with which he is held. Even in the twenty-first century, more than forty years after his assassination, and despite his somewhat skimpy accomplishments in office, he is still rated one of America's great presidents. The other development was rapid change in the Roman Catholic Church. The reforms of the Vatican II conference and the papacy of Pope John XXIII changed the image of the Church and made Catholics far less distinctive in American society. The Latin mass was abolished; Catholics were no longer required to eat fish on Friday. At the same time American Catholics' behavior changed. Young Catholic married couples in the 1950s, enjoying postward prosperity, had very large numbers of children; then quite suddenly in the early 1960s, coinciding with the introduction of the birth-control pill, Catholic family size dropped sharply. It was at this same time that the number of vocations, of young Catholics choosing to become priests and nuns, dropped suddenly too. Now Catholics seemed much more like other Americans.

In politics this proved true as well. Catholics gave Lyndon Johnson as large a share of the vote as they had given Kennedy, but since he won 61 percent of the total vote that was not a greatly distinctive response. In later years, Catholic presidential voting ceased to be very much different from that of other Americans. Nor did the lure of a Catholic on the ticket prove very strong. Republicans in 1964 and Democrats in 1968 and 1972 nominated Catholics for vice president, but all three tickets lost, two by wide margins. You can only elect the first Catholic president once; then the candidate's religion does not matter very much, and no party nominated a Catholic for president or vice president again until 2004.

Meanwhile, Catholic voters, increasingly affluent and suburban, moved to the right and started voting Republican – or even Conservative, as they did when they supplied most of the votes for New York Senator James Buckley, elected as the Conservative Party nominee in 1970. In the late 1960s and early 1970s, the Democratic party moved sharply to the left on foreign and cultural issues, opposing the Vietnam war, opposing tough law enforcement, supporting hugely generous welfare benefits and school busing. All these positions were opposed by most Catholic voters. In addition abortion became a central national issue. Between 1968 and 1972, sixteen states liberalized their abortion laws, over the vehement opposition of the Catholic Church. Other states would probably have followed, but instead the Supreme Court nationalized the issue in January 1973, when its *Roe v. Wade* decision overturned the abortion laws of every state and in effect created a regime of abortion on demand. To this the Catholic Church and many Catholic voters were strongly opposed.

In the 1970s both major parties were split on the issue: in some state legislatures, opposition to abortion was strong among Democrats representing districts with many Catholic voters, while supporters of abortion rights included Republican governors; in the 1976 election Democrat Jimmy Carter seemed more anti-abortion than Republican Gerald Ford. But in the 1980s the Democrats became mostly (as abortion rights supporters put it) "pro-choice" and the Republicans mostly (as abortion opponents put it) "pro-life." By the 1990s, positions on abortion had become central planks of both parties: the Democrats refused to allow the pro-life governor of Pennsylvania to speak at their convention while a pro-life position became essential for anyone seeking the Republican presidential nomination. To be sure, some Catholics opposed the Church's position on the issue, or considered it less important than other issues on which they favored Democrats. But for many Catholics, opposition to abortion remained strong, and these tended to move toward the Republicans. Some Catholic politicians, notably New York Governor Mario Cuomo, argued that, though anti-abortion themselves, they must take a pro-choice position in public life and not impose their moral views on others. But most Italian Catholics voted against Cuomo in his one close election, in 1982, either on the abortion issue or for other reasons. In the same period, Catholic voters supported Ronald Reagan in great numbers, as he carried 93 of a possible 100 states in 1980 and 1984 – including Massachusetts, Rhode Island, and New York both times.

By the twenty-first century America had developed a politics based on cultural identity in which religion correlated with voting behavior more than any other demographic variable. But religion not just in terms of denomination but in degree of observance. In that environment, Catholics overall ended up voting just about the same as the nation as a whole. In the exceedingly close election of 2000, Catholics were just about equally split between George W. Bush and Al Gore. Observant Catholics, those who attended church once a week or more, who tended to agree with the Church's teachings on abortion, gave Bush a majority. Less observant Catholics, those who attended church less often than once a week or not at all, who tended to disagree with the Church's teachings on abortion, gave Gore a majority.

We are a long way from the seventeenth century now. There are still issues on which Catholics, or at least observant Catholics, are an identifiable voting bloc, but there are fewer of them than there once were. Education is no longer a key issue, as bishops have allowed the number of places in Catholic schools to greatly diminish (and many of those places go to non-Catholics) and have made it clear that they will not enlarge the system if school vouchers are passed. Immigration, an important issue to the growing number of Latino Catholics, is of little interest to the still-far-more-numerous non-Latino Catholics. Specific foreign policy issues are no longer of any serious interest to Catholics descended from pre-1924 immigrants (except in a few cases to Irish Catholics). In 1988 I was covering a Republican state convention, and got to talking with a Catholic woman who had been caucusing with Evangelical Protestants. "We were talking about issues, and I realized these Evangelicals believed the same things I do," she said. A moment has passed, I thought, a long moment that goes back to the seventeenth century and its memories of the sixteenth. American Catholics are as numerous as ever, more prosperous than ever, more diverse in their opinions than ever; but they are less of an identifiable bloc than they were well within living memory, when America had not elected a Catholic president.

But let George Marlin, who knows political history and Catholic politics as well as anyone I know, tell the story.

Michael Barone
Washington, D.C.
June 2004

Chapter 1
"The Free Exercise Thereof . . ."

By the time the first English-speaking Catholics arrived in North America, the Roman Catholic Church had a hundred-year presence in the New World. European Catholics such as Christopher Columbus, Jacques Cartier, Hernan Cortez, Hernando DeSoto, Ponce DeLeon, and John and Sebastian Cabot had explored and conquered huge tracts of land for their respective sovereigns. The Jesuit Black Robes, among them St. Isaac Jogues, Jacques Marquette, Louis Hennepin, and the Franciscan Brown Robes led by Junipero Serra and scores of martyrs preached to the faithful settlers and converted Native Americans throughout New Spain and New France.

English Catholics crossed the Atlantic not to seek conversions, to conquer, or to seek adventure and riches. Traveling across a hostile North Atlantic in miserable shipboard conditions, they risked their lives simply to attend mass without fear of punishment.

After Henry VIII broke with Rome and consigned the Church to royal control, British Catholics who remained faithful to Rome were often severely persecuted. Although there were benign periods, particularly during the Stuart reigns, when Catholics were tolerated, there were long years in which fanatics suppressed and slaughtered faithful Catholics. Archbishop Thomas Cranmer, Queen Elizabeth I, and Lord Protector Oliver Cromwell were responsible for the deaths of thousands of Catholics.

When the tyrannical Cromwell assumed the title of Lord Protector of England after the beheading of King Charles I, he declared war on "Roman harlots." Dedicated to "purifying" the old church, Cromwell abolished Christmas, theater, and the arts, and confiscated the property of both Catholic churches and practicing Catholics. Because the Church of England was Britain's established church, Cromwell and his Puritan allies tried Catholics as traitors, declaring that professions of faith or oaths of allegiance to the Pope were acts of treason.

The Lord Protector's invasion of Catholic Ireland was particularly brutal. At the Battle of Droghedan in 1649, he ordered his forces to massacre every one of the nearly 3,000 Irish defenders. Just thirty Catholics survived. The reign of terror that resulted led to the slaughter or starvation of more than 600,000 Irish Catholics—which was one-third of the population of Ireland.

In 1652, an Act of Parliament confiscated the lands of Ireland's surviving Catholics and awarded the property to Puritan soldiers, veterans of Droghedan and the brutal suppression that followed. Ireland was ransacked and its remaining "Popish" population was impoverished. Educating Catholics was a criminal act; reading and writing were forbidden. The lucky Catholic survivors became tenant farmers on lands they had previously owned.

This poisonous atmosphere prompted Catholics to leave Britain and Ireland and seek religious liberty in the New World. In 1584, Sir Hubert Gilbert, the first to sail for America, led a small fleet of 260 Catholics on an expedition of settlement to Maine. The excursion was a disaster. Midway across the Atlantic, the ship containing food supplies foundered. The expedition reversed course, but while sailing back to England most of the passengers were lost in a storm in the vicinity of the Azores. A second attempt to colonize Maine was made by Thomas Arundel in 1605, but his expedition also ended in failure.

Although Catholics had no presence in the first English settlements in America, this did not stop the Puritan and Anglican colonists from establishing anti-Catholic ordinances. In Massachusetts and Virginia, for instance, Roman Catholics were banned outright. In 1647, although not one English-speaking Catholic cleric lived on New England soil, an anti-priest law was passed, stipulating that any priest who dared to appear in the region would be deported and, if he returned, executed.[1]

It was the English convert Sir George Calvert (first Baron of Baltimore) who established a Catholic colony in Britain's New World. A favorite of James I, Calvert managed to remain friends with the King after his conversion to Rome. Shocked by anti-Catholic penal laws, Calvert used his powers of persuasion and his friendship with the king to improve the lot of his fellow religionists. Still, his hopes were focused on the New World. In 1627 he failed in an attempt to establish a settlement, which he called Avalon, in Newfoundland: the colonists were driven out by the French and the inclement weather. But Calvert was a determined man.

He looked further south. Although a charter financial investor in the Virginia Company, Calvert was bluntly informed by his business partners that he and his Catholic friends were forbidden to settle in Jamestown unless they took the "oath of supremacy," whereby they accept the King as the head of the Church in England.

Desperate to find a home in which Catholics could have both religious and political rights, Lord Baltimore left his family in the New World and sailed back to England to appeal to King Charles I, the son of his late friend and mentor. Calvert convinced his monarch to grant him a charter for land north of Virginia. The land grant, which was to be named Maryland in honor of King Charles's Spanish-Catholic wife, Queen Henrietta Maria, was situated along the Chesapeake Bay, northeast of the Potomac, west of the Appalachian Mountains and south of the Pennsylvania border.

It should be noted that it was not Lord Baltimore's intention to institute a strictly Catholic colony. Influenced by Thomas More's *Utopia* and the martyr's descendent, the Jesuit Henry More, he envisioned Maryland as a place where people could live in political equality and freely practice religion – regardless of denomination.

In 1632 Calvert crafted a unique charter that he persuaded the King to sign. It contained language that actually evaded Britain's anti-Catholic penal laws. Although Maryland would be a haven of religious tolerance, Calvert thought it prudent to assure Catholic rule. And so the colonial charter he negotiated permitted the proprietor, Lord Baltimore himself, to appoint the colonial governor. Such appointments had always been a royal prerogative.

Those who believe that Roger Williams was the first to create a colony that permitted religious liberty are mistaken. When King Charles approved Lord Baltimore's charter, Maryland became the first tolerant colony under British rule. Williams and his fellow Baptists had left Puritan Massachusetts to escape persecution, and the Rhode Island charter they received stated that settlers had "full liberty in religious discernments" and that no person could be "molested, punished, disquieted or called in question for any difference in matters of religion." But in 1664 Rhode Island passed a law that made one notable exception:

> That all men professing Christianity and of competent estates and of civil conversation who acknowledge and are obedient to the civil magistrate, though of different judgments in religious affairs (Roman Catholics only excepted), shall be admitted freemen, and shall have liberty to choose and be chosen officers in this colony, both military and civil.[2]

William Penn, Quaker founder of Pennsylvania, is also credited with promoting freedom of religious expression for his colony's citizenry, and many persecuted Catholics flocked to Pennsylvania because of language in Article XXXV of Penn's 1682 charter: ". . . all persons living peaceably in the colony should in no way be molested or prejudicial for his religious persuasion or practice in matters of faith or worship, nor shall they be compelled at any time to frequent or maintain any religious worship place or ministry whatever."[3] But like Williams, Penn succumbed to pressure and approved an ordinance that prohibited people from holding office who would not deny the real presence of Christ in the host nor declare the Mass idolatrous.[4] The law also held that "only Protestants were permitted to be naturalized in the colony or to hold lands whereon churches, schools, and hospitals might be built."[5]

Only Maryland was a truly welcoming home for Roman Catholics. Sad to say, the first Lord Baltimore did not live to implement his vision of tolerance. Grief-stricken that his wife and children, who had followed him to England, were lost at sea, he died prematurely in 1632 at the age of fifty-two. His eldest surviving son, Cecil, the second Lord Baltimore, with his wife, Ann Arundel, inherited the Charter. Cecil appointed his brother, Leonard, as governor, and directed him to lead twenty colonials and three hundred laborers on an expedition to the New World on November 22, 1633.

To avoid clashes over religion, Lord Baltimore urged Catholics who joined the voyage to celebrate Mass privately and directed "that the said Governor and Commissioners treat the Protestants with as much mildness and favor as justice will permit."[6]

Two English Jesuits, Fathers John White and John Altham, celebrated the first Masses on March 24, 1636, when they landed off the coast of Maryland on an island they named St. Clement's. In his journal Father White recorded that while Protestants were performing their own service, Catholics marched in a procession and "erected a trophy to Christ the Savior, humbly reciting on our bended knees the litanies of the sacred cross, with great emotion."[7]

It was not just toleration that made Maryland unique among the colonies. Maryland was also the first to permit all free men, not just landowners, to vote for its assembly, and that assembly exercised far greater self-government than the legislatures in the other colonies, because Maryland was so much more removed from the King's direct authority, due in large measure to the "proprietary" appointment of governor. The monarch's authority became positively remote, which gave the settlers a deeper passion for the freedom they happily exercised.

Royal governors and trading companies were notorious for grabbing most of a colony's land and resources. In contrast, Maryland aided its settlers, Catholic and Protestant alike. A Catholic gentleman who brought five laborers to the colony was granted 2,000 acres, and when his indentured servants, many of whom were Protestants, had served their time they were permitted to purchase and cultivate their own land in Maryland.

As the colony grew and prospered, Protestant laborers were invited to immigrate. Puritans who suffered in Virginia and Anglicans who were mistreated in Massachusetts joined the Catholics and worked side-by-side with them.

There were conversions: the Brooke and Taney families, who were to play major roles in American history, came over to Rome. The future Chief Justice of the United States, Roger Taney, was a descendant of the Maryland family.[8]

With the coming of the 1642 English Civil War, Maryland settlers feared the loss of their liberties. Hearing of Catholic persecutions in the motherland,

Protestants became unruly and voiced resentment against the power held by Leonard Calvert and his Catholic colleagues.

While it was Lord Baltimore's policy not to flaunt his Catholicism and to allow true religious liberty in Maryland, he decided to head off any trouble by appointing a Protestant, William Stone, governor after Leonard Calvert died in 1647. When King Charles I was beheaded in 1649, the Maryland assembly hoped to circumvent trouble by introducing the Tolerance Act. Passed with the votes of Catholics and Protestants, the act contained this key clause:

> And whereas the inforceing of the conscience in matters of Religion hath frequently fallen out to be a dangerous Consequence in those commonwealths where it hath been practiced. . . . Be it Therefore . . . enacted . . . that noe person or persons whatsoever within this Province . . . professing to believe in Jesus Christ, shall from henceforth bee any waies troubled, Molested or discountenanced for or in respect of his or her religion nor in the *free exercise thereof.*[9]

One hundred and forty years later, the phrase "*free exercise thereof*" was to so impress America's founding fathers that they incorporated it into the United States Constitution's Bill of Rights.

As a result of these efforts, migration to Maryland continued, with three hundred Puritans arriving in 1649. They settled on the land that would become known as Annapolis.

But there was not always amity between Catholics and Protestants. During the protectorate of Puritan Oliver Cromwell, Maryland Protestants frequently clashed with Catholics. In 1645 several Jesuit priests were abducted and shipped back to England for trial. In 1651 Puritan soldiers invaded Maryland, booted Catholics out of the Assembly, and demanded that the remaining Protestants repeal the Tolerance Act.[10] Governor Stone led forces against the Puritans and was defeated near Annapolis at the Battle of Severn. The victors enacted a new law which stated: "No one who professed and exercised the Papistic, commonly known as the Roman Catholic religion, could be protected in the Province."[11]

It was not until 1658, with the restoration of Charles II to the throne, that Lord Baltimore's proprietary rights were also restored. Cecil Calvert's son, Charles, was appointed governor with the mandate to restore the Tolerance Act.

Charles, who was to become the first Lord Baltimore to reside in Maryland, found the Protestant population resented not only his presence but the rebirth of "Popery." And when the Catholic King, James II, was dumped during the 1688 Glorious Revolution in favor of his Protestant daughter Mary, and her husband, William, Duke of Orange, Maryland Protestants believed their time had come to revolt against Calvert rule.

In 1690 Protestant forces invaded and conquered the City of St. Mary's. Lord Baltimore's proprietary charter was repealed and in 1691 the anti-Catholic penal laws were enacted. Sir Lionel Copley was named the first royal governor of the colony of Maryland, which now recognized the King as the head of the state-sanctioned religion.[12]

> Faithfully reflecting the laws of England, which forbade Catholics the right to bear arms, to vote, to argue law, to inherit or own land or even to ride a horse worth more than five pounds, and which made all priests liable to life imprisonment, Maryland also put her Catholics to the ban. They were forbidden to hold public services, denied priests, fined for educating their children as Catholics or for importing Catholic servants, excluded from office, forbidden to vote, denied parental rights, for a time afflicted with double taxation, and finally, after the capital had been transferred from Catholic St. Mary's City to Protestant Annapolis, their old chapel at St. Mary's was demolished to efface the last visible vestiges of Catholicism from the Maryland earth.[13]

Although America's first experiment in religious liberty was thus crushed, Maryland's 1,600 Catholics held on to their faith throughout the "Penal Age." In fact, census figures revealed in 1708 that the Catholic population had not only endured but had grown to 3,000.[14] And this tightly knit group stayed united and influenced the body politic, particularly when revolution was in the air.

*   *   *   *   *

Throughout most of the eighteenth century, English Catholics were persecuted in all the colonies. In New Hampshire, Massachusetts, and Connecticut the Congregational Church was sanctioned as the official church, and taxpayers (including Catholics) were obligated to give financial support.[15] Maryland joined eight other colonies that recognized Anglicanism as the established religion.[16]

The revised charters granted to New England by William and Mary included language that reinforced the ban on Catholics: "That forever, hereafter shall there be liberty of conscience allowed in the worship of God to all Christians (except Papists) inhabiting on which shall inhabit or be resident within our said province or territory."[17]

In 1704 the Maryland Assembly passed the "Act to Prevent the Growth of Popery." Catholic clergy were fined fifty pounds and imprisoned for six months if they converted children or said Mass, even in private. Families caught sending their children to Europe for a Catholic education were fined one hundred pounds. Employers were fined for hiring Irish Catholics as laborers or servants.

In 1715, Maryland Catholics were stripped of their right to vote and hold office when the Oath of Allegiance was enacted. Any Catholic interested in entering public life would have to sign a declaration condemning the Pope, denying belief in transubstantiation, and agreeing to forfeit office if he attended Mass.[18]

In 1701 and again in 1737 the New York Assembly voted to deny Catholics and Jews the right to vote.[19] In 1741 New Yorker John Ury was tried, convicted, and hanged for being a priest. Connecticut's General Assembly forbade Catholics to own land, or any posts "of honor, trust or profit."[20]

When the English assaulted the Fort at Louisburg during the French and Indian War, their standard was "Nil Desperandum, Christo Duce."[21] In victory, they ransacked Roman Churches and destroyed all reminders of Catholic presence. When the war ended in 1754 and the British had routed the French, Maryland's Governor Sharpe imposed a tax on Catholics to pay for defense that was twice the Protestant assessment.[22]

In the midst of the war fervor, John Adams denounced the Roman Catholic Church, asserting that "the influence of ignorant and wicked priests had made it an article of faith that no one could be saved outside their church."[23] Writing in the *Boston Gazette* (1765) Adams complimented the early Puritan founders for "curbing the power of Monarch and Priest lest government become the man of sin, the whore of Babylon, the mystery of iniquity."[24] His cousin, Sam Adams, was more extreme in expressing his anti-Catholic sentiments: "I did verily believe and I do still, that much more is to be dreaded from the growth of popery, than from the Stamp Act or any other destructive of civil rights. . . ."[25]

Even though the Catholic presence in New England was miniscule (less than a hundred people) this did not stop Massachusetts Attorney General and Chief Justice, Paul Dudley, from endowing an anti-Catholic lecture at Harvard. His will provided his alma mater with one hundred pounds sterling for an annual lecture that in every fourth year was dedicated to "detecting, convicting and exposing idolatry, errors and superstitions of the Romish Church."[26] John Adams publicly approved of the lectures and was known to attend them.

In the 1765 lecture, John Mayhew of West Church in Boston concluded his address, to an audience dominated by Harvard's student body, with the hope that "this seminary of learning . . . the people, ministers and churches of New England be preserved from popish and all other pernicious errors."[27]

And in the 1773 lecture, Brattle Street Church pastor Samuel Cooper told his audience that "Popery is, in a true and proper sense, anti-Christian."[28]

While the vast majority of the Catholics in the English Colonies continued to reside in Maryland, by 1682 significant numbers migrated to the region around Lancaster, Pennsylvania, believing that William Penn's "Holy Experiment" guaranteed them religious liberties. As described earlier, the Quakers had succumbed to pressure from the Crown and in 1705 Pennsylvania had enacted anti-Catholic oaths and legislation. In 1729, additional legislation was passed that forbade the import of "popish" servants.

During the French and Indian War, Pennsylvania's 200,000 Protestants, fearful that the Commonwealth's 1,000 Catholics would side with the enemy, had insisted that civil authorities order all Catholics to turn in their guns and ammunition. And, since Catholics were not permitted to join the militia, they were assessed a defense tax of twenty shillings. Suspicion and fear of the Catholic minority was so widespread that when British General Braddock's forces were annihilated by the French at the Battle of Fort Duquesne, it took armed guards to prevent mobs from burning the few Catholic churches in Philadelphia.

The high watermark of eighteenth century colonial anti-Catholicism was reached in the aftermath of the Seven Years War. Victorious Great Britain absorbed French Canada under the 1763 Peace of Paris accords. To assimilate hundreds of thousands of Canadian Catholics, the British Parliament crafted the "Quebec Act" which contained this clause concerning the practice of religion:

> And, for the more perfect security and ease of the minds of the said province, it is hereby declared, That his Majesty's subjects, professing the religion of the Church of Rome of and in the said province of Quebec, may have, hold, and enjoy the free exercise of the religion of the Church of Rome, subject to the King's supremacy, declared and established by an Act made in the first year of the reign of Queen Elizabeth, over all the dominions and countries which then did or thereafter should, belong to the imperial crown of this realm; and that the clergy of the said church may hold, receive, and enjoy their accustomed dues and rights with respect to such persons only as shall profess the said religion.[29]

Approved by the House of Lords after weeks of heated debate, the Quebec Act passed the House of Commons on June 13, 1774. Tory MP Edmund Burke worked furiously to secure approval of the Act. On the floor of the house, he told his colleagues:

> You have got a people professing the Roman Catholic religion,
> and in possession of maintenance, legally appropriated to the cler-
> gy. Will you deprive them of that? Now that is not a question of
> establishment; the establishment was not made by you; it existed
> before the treaty; it took nothing from the treaty; no legislature has
> a right to take it away; no governor has a right to suspend it. This
> principle is confirmed by the usage of every civilized nation in
> Europe. In all our conquered colonies, the established religion was
> confirmed by them; by which I understand, that religion should
> receive the protection of the state in those colonies; and I should
> not consider that it had received such protection, if their clergy
> were not protected.[30]

When word spread to America in 1773 that Parliament was considering a bill
that would give Canadian Catholics full rights as British subjects, there were
hysterical outcries. The press in Boston and New York published vicious articles condemning the "hellish plan." The Boston Globe reported that 4,000
Catholic Canadians were drafted into the British Army to force with pointed
gun the passage of the act.[31]

Pope Day – the equivalent of Guy Fawkes Day in Britain – took on new
meaning on November 5, 1774. "Charleston, South Carolina, revived the celebration to show 'abhorrence of Pope and Pretender;' Newport outdid itself in
featuring two large effigies of the pope. In Boston, Pope Day had degenerat-
ed into a bitter free-for-all between North End and South."[32] Ezra Stiles,
future President of Yale University, gave a vicious anti-Catholic sermon titled
"Nature and the Danger of Popery in this land, from the opera of the Quebec
Bill for the Establishment of the Romish religion over two thirds of the British
Empire."[33] In New York, a crowd marched on the Stock Exchange with banners that read "George III Rex and the liberties of America. No Popery." On
Pope Day communities throughout the thirteen colonies united in their oppo-
sition to the Quebec Act.

The Continental Congress in late 1774 adopted verbatim a resolution that
Suffolk County, Massachusetts had passed two weeks earlier: "That the late
Act of Parliament for establishing the Roman Catholic religion and French
laws in that extensive country now called Canada, is dangerous in an extreme
degree to the Protestant religion, and to the civil rights and liberties of all
Americas; and therefore as men and Protestant Christians, we are indispensa-
bly obliged to take all proper measures for our security."[34]

Alexander Hamilton, when a student at King's College (later Columbia
University), defended the actions of the Continental Congress in a pamphlet
called "A Full Vindication of the Measures of Congress." In it he queried:

"Does not your blood run cold to think that an English Parliament should pass an Act for the establishment of arbitrary power and Popery in such an extensive country. . . . Your lives, your prosperity, your property, your religion are all at stake."[35]

The reaction was so virulent that even Protestant children at play would chant:

> Abhor that arrant whore of Rome
> And all her blasphemies
> And drink not of her cursed cup,
> Obey not her decrees.[36]

But as threat of revolution against the motherland began to spread throughout the colonies, cooler heads prevailed – particularly in the Continental Congress.

* * * * *

To pay off the debt accumulated during the Seven Years War, the British government imposed a series of taxes on the colonies. The Sugar Act (1764), Stamp Act (1765), Townsend Act (1767), and Tea Act (1773) all received an icy reception. In fact, they were viewed as intrusive and tyrannical. Patrick Henry's reaction to the Sugar and Stamp Act summed up the views of many American colonists: "Targuin and Caesar had his Brutus, Charles the First, his Cromwell and George III . . . may profit from the example." Informed he had spoken treason, Henry replied, "If this be treason, make the most of it." "Taxation without representation" became the battle cry throughout the colonies.

Reacting to the colonists' defiance, Parliament passed four bills known as the Coercive Acts in 1774. These laws closed Boston Harbor to all shipping, revoked Massachusetts charter powers to appoint magistrates, abolished local jurisdictions to try crown judges, soldiers, and revenue officers indicted for murder, and permitted billeting of troops in any home in Massachusetts.

Labeling them the "Intolerable" Acts, the Continental Congress refused to submit and the American colonies moved inexorably toward independence.

Throughout their careers, many of the Founding Fathers openly expressed objections to the Roman Catholic Church. John Jay ran up a "No Popery" flag at his home on Guy Fawkes Day.[37] Benjamin Franklin in his "Plain Truth" pamphlet alerted Pennsylvanians "to the threat to their security in the presence of a number of Catholics."[38] Eminent members of the Continental Congress, including John Adams, Philip Livingston, and Richard Henry Lee all made extremely unfriendly comments about the Church and its membership.

But as the Continental Congress grew closer to breaking with England, there was a change in attitude toward Catholics. The reasons for the softening were both practical and philosophical.

One practical reason was the fear that colonial Catholics might side with the British and become guerilla warriors.

The Catholic population in 1775 represented about 1 percent of the American population – 25,000. Although small in number, they were strategically located. Almost all of the Catholics resided in the Chesapeake Bay area or around the City of Philadelphia. If they sided with the Tories, the Catholics could seize eastern shoreline ports and provide the British Army an entry point to invade Pennsylvania and capture the seat of government.

The Continental Congress also realized that they lacked the necessary resources (i.e., money, guns, soldiers) to defeat the most powerful army in the world. They would have to seek financial and military aid from longtime Catholic rivals of Great Britain – France and Spain. And it would also be wise, they concluded, to neutralize or, better yet, to ally themselves with the citizenry of Britain's latest acquisition, Canada.

In October 1774, Congress blessed an "Address to Inhabitants of the Province of Quebec" authored by Thomas Cushing, Richard Henry Lee, and John Dickinson. The statement expressed the Congress's high regard for the Canadians and their religious beliefs. "It argued that since liberty of conscience is from God and a natural right of men, it was theirs long before it was guaranteed by the Quebec Act."[39] The address concluded that a united front was the best way to confront Britain. The Canadians, however, appalled by American hypocrisy, rejected an alliance with the thirteen colonies. They were shocked that in the same month Congress expressed its virulent hatred of Canadians by portraying them as depraved, they could extend the hand of friendship.

Not to be discouraged, the Congress decided to send a delegation to negotiate an alliance with the Canadians. For this task, they turned to America's leading Catholic family, the Carrolls.

Founded by Maryland's first attorney general, Charles Carroll, the family went on to acquire and develop tens of thousands of acres and was recognized as the richest Catholic clan in the colonies.

Courageous and clever, they often challenged and confounded the Protestant establishment. The first Carroll was described this way: ". . . in spite of the tremendous odds against him, he usually managed to make fools, single-handed, of the entire House or the entire Governor's Council. He was a magnificent fighter because he never knew when he was beaten."[40] His heirs continued the family tradition of eluding Anglican attempts to destroy their fortune and faith.

The Continental Congress turned to the third generation of Carrolls for aid in the Canadian mission: Charles Carroll of Carrollton and his cousin Father John Carroll. In making this decision to send a Catholic priest, John Hancock, president of the Congress, followed the advice of his friend, Charles Lee: "I should think that if some Jesuit or Religious of any other order (he must be a man of liberal sentiments, enlarged mind and a manifest friend of Civil Liberty) could be found out and sent to Canada, he would be worth battalions to us."[41]

In February 1775 the Continental Congress appointed Benjamin Franklin, Samuel Chase, and Charles Carroll to the Canadian Commission. Father John Carroll agreed to accompany the delegation as an unofficial observer.

Commenting on the delegation, John Adams wrote: "We have empowered the Committee to take with them, another gentlemen of Maryland, a Mr. John Carroll, a Roman Catholic priest, and a Jesuit, a gentleman of learning and ability."[42] Of Charles Carroll, Adams pronounced "A Roman Catholic but an ardent patriot."[43]

The Commission ultimately failed because the Canadians were content with British rule. The Ordinary of Canada, Bishop Briand, familiar with the American anti-Catholic outburst against the Quebec Act, concluded it was in the best interest of his flock to continue living under British Rule.[44]

Father John Carroll had predicted exactly this outcome. Before the delegation left, he wrote that the Canadians "have not the same motives for taking up arms against England, which renders the resistance of the other colonies so justifiable."[45]

One happy consequence of the delegation's journey to Canada was Benjamin Franklin's growing fondness for the Carrolls. When Franklin fell ill, Father John took on the duty of restoring his health. Franklin wrote of their time together: "I find I grow daily more feeble, and I think I could hardly have got along so far, but for Mr. Carroll's friendly assistance and tender care of me."[46] Father John recalled the time spent with Dr. Franklin as "one of the most fortunately and honourable events of my life."[47] Historians agree that in later years, John Carroll was chosen as the first native-born Catholic Bishop in America because of Franklin's influence in European circles.

Charles Carroll also impressed his colleagues. Upon accepting the job of commissioner, Carroll humbly observed: "My abilities are not above the common level, but I have integrity, a sincere love for my country, a detestation of tyranny. I have perseverance, and the habit of business and I therefore hope to be of some service."[48]

Charles Carroll was of great service in Canada. He dealt effectively with the French and with the American forces in Canada under the command of General Benedict Arnold. When it became evident that the commission had failed to achieve its goal, Charles Carroll and Samuel Chase remained with

American troops during the long retreat back to America's border. To aid the troops, Carroll and Chase took on numerous responsibilities, serving as "generals, commissaries, justices of the peace, in short to act in twenty different capacities."[49] Carroll's dedication was noted and it increased his prestige within the Congress and his home assembly in Maryland.

The other significant reason for Catholics to align themselves with the revolutionaries was of a philosophical nature.

The Carrolls and other educated Catholics, familiar with the political thought of Aquinas, Montesquieu, and Suarez, grasped that the principles of the revolution were consonant with Catholic philosophy.

Dr. James Walsh, in his definitive 1935 study, *Education of the Founding Fathers of the Republic*, establishes that the eighteenth-century curriculum of Harvard, William and Mary, Yale, Princeton, Pennsylvania, Columbia, and Brown Universities was scholastic in nature. The courses of grammar, logic, rhetoric, and moral and natural philosophy were of a scholastic character.

> The Founding Fathers of our republic, then, were educated according to the academic traditions which had been formulated in the earlier Middle Ages by Boëthius, sometimes hailed as the father of Scholasticism, developed under St. Anselm in the eleventh century, reaching their culmination in the mind of Aquinas and the group contemporary with him in the thirteenth century when there came the conciliation of Scholastic doctrines with Aristotle, thus welding together the whole course of philosophic thought.[50]

As the sole Catholic member of the Continental Congress to sign the Declaration of Independence, Charles Carroll understood that the American Credo was rooted in the tradition of the natural law and the common good. Carroll was also the only member or signer of the Declaration to give his address; he signed his name "Charles Carroll of Carrollton," saying that if the British wanted to hang him, they would know exactly where he was. At the time of the signing, Carroll was likely the richest man in America. He died in 1832, the last signer of the Declaration to die.

From the very birth of our republic, the American credo has been rooted in the tradition of natural law, has been imbued with the belief that there is a higher standard by which all man-made rules must be measured. In the original draft of the Declaration of Independence, Thomas Jefferson justified the American case for separation from Great Britain with a classic appeal to the natural law:

> When in the course of human events it becomes necessary for a people to advance from the subordination in which they have hith-

> erto remained & to assume among the powers of the earth the
> equal & independent station to which the *laws of nature & of
> nature's god* entitle them, a decent respect to the opinions of
> mankind requires that they should declare the causes which impel
> them to change.
>
> We hold these truths to be *sacred & undeniable;* that all men
> are created equal & independent, that from the equal creation they
> derive *rights inherent and inalienable,* among which are the
> preservation of life & liberty, & the pursuit of happiness . . .[51]
> [Italics added]

In Jefferson's view, the American Revolution did not break lawful ties to a sovereign realm, but reclaimed transcendent liberties from an illegitimate and corrupt monarchy.

Just six years later in his *Notes on the State of Virginia*, Jefferson wondered what *disbelief* in natural law might mean for America's future. "Can the liberties of a nation be secure," he asked, "when we have removed a conviction that these liberties are the gift of God?"[52] Jefferson insisted that liberal, natural-law philosophers, with ethical systems premised on man's selfish desires, should subordinate their theories to the realities of man's social nature which derived from the God-given moral sense.

Jefferson was certainly influenced by John Locke who subscribed to the social-contract theory. But unlike Thomas Hobbes, Locke believed that man is naturally social and that a natural law exists that confers rights. Locke wrote: "God, having made man such a creature that in his own judgment it was not good for him to be alone, put him under strong obligation of necessity, convenience, and inclination to drive him into society, as well as fitted him with understanding and language to continue and enjoy it. The first society was between man and wife, which gave beginning to that between parents and children . . ."[53]

Jefferson was also familiar with the writings of other proponents of the natural law. He read, among others, Robert Filmer, Algernon Sidney, Francisco Suarez, William Blackstone, and Edward Coke.

He was also influenced by a Virginia Catholic neighbor, Italian immigrant Philip Mazzei. Born in Tuscany in 1730, Mazzei studied medicine in Florence, and immigrated first to England where he met Benjamin Franklin. It was Franklin who convinced Mazzei to move to Virginia to raise grapes and olives. Mazzei settled on 2,000 acres next door to Jefferson. The two men hit it off and spent hours discussing their concepts of liberty. Siding with the American colonies, Mazzei wrote and distributed pro-American pamphlets and articles. A statement he made in a 1774 edition of the *Virginia Gazette* certainly influenced Jefferson's Declaration of Independence prose:

> . . . all men by nature are created free and independent. Such
> equality is necessary in order to create a free government. It is
> necessary that all men be equal to each other in natural law. A true
> Republican government cannot exist unless in their natural
> rights.[54]

The author of the Declaration of Independence was not the only
Founding Father to view the natural law as the fulcrum of society. Alexander
Hamilton wrote this defense of the legality of actions by the Continental
Congress:

> There are some events in society to which human laws cannot
> extend, but when applied to them lose their force and efficacy. In
> short when human laws contradict or discountenance the means
> which are necessary to preserve the essential rights of any socie-
> ty, they defeat the proper end of all laws and so become null and
> void. . . . The sacred rights of mankind are not to be rummaged for
> among old parchments or musty records. *They are written as with
> a sunbeam in the whole volume of human nature, by the hand of
> Divinity itself and can never be erased or obscured by mortal
> power.*[55] [Italics added]

For Hamilton "no tribunal, no codes, no system can repeal or impair the law
of God, for by his eternal laws it is inherent in the nature of things."[56]

George Mason's *Declaration of Rights* (1787), which was adopted as the
preamble of the Virginia Constitution, refers to the natural law and to the common good:

> 1. That all men are by nature equally free and independent, and
>   have certain *inherent right*, of which, when they enter into a
>   state of society, they cannot, by any compact, deprive or divest
>   their posterity; namely, the enjoyment of life and liberty, with
>   the means of acquiring and possessing property, and pursuing
>   and obtaining happiness and safety.
> 2. That all power is vested in, and consequently derived from,
>   the people; that magistrates are their trustees and servants,
>   and at all times amenable to them.
> 3. That government is, or ought to be, instituted for the *common
>   benefit*, protection, and security of the people, nation, or com-
>   munity.[57] [Italics added]

The vast majority of Catholics sided with the revolutionaries because they
considered themselves American, not British. "They saw, more clearly than

anybody else, that despite the screaming denunciations of the Quebec Act, the winning of political liberty would also mean the winning of religious liberty. They understood the genius of America and its destiny. Without hesitation – they threw in their lot with Congress."[58]

American Catholics distinguished themselves throughout the war. John Barry was named the "Father of the American Navy." General Stephen Moylan of George Washington's staff was the highest-ranking Catholic in the Army.

> Daniel Carroll served as a member of Congress from Maryland and Thomas FitzSimons sat as a representative from Pennsylvania; Captains Roger Kean and John Walsh served with distinction; a volunteer fighting unit was raised by George Meade of Philadelphia; and when George Rogers Clark led his expedition to the West, his success was in great part due to the help given him by Father Pierre Gilbault, an ex-Jesuit trained in the seminary at Quebec. Another French priest who dared the wrath of the anti-American Bishop Briand, Father Louis Eustace Lotbiniere, joined the American invasion of Canada and ultimately became the first Catholic chaplain to be enrolled in the armed services of the United States. The record of European Catholics such as Lafayette, Pulaski, Kosciusko and others, to say nothing of the French army and fleet under Catholics such as Rochambeau and d'Estaing.[59]

Out of respect for the Catholic presence in his army, George Washington ended the observance of the anti-Roman holiday known as "Pope's Day." In his directive he declared:

> As the Commander-in-Chief has been apprised of a design formed for the observance of that ridiculous and childish custom of burning the effigy of the Pope, he cannot help expressing his surprise that there should be officers and soldiers in this army so void of common sense as not to see the impropriety of such a step at this juncture; at a time when we are soliciting, and have really obtained the friendship and alliance of the people of Canada, whom we ought to consider as brethren embarked in the same cause – the defense of the liberty of America. At this juncture, and under such circumstances, to be insulting their religion, is so monstrous as not to be suffered or excused; indeed instead of offering the most remote insult, it is our duty to address public thanks to these our

brethren, as to them we are indebted for every late happy success over the common enemy in Canada.[60]

Throughout the Revolution it was the American Tories who pursued a "no-popery" strategy to place a wedge between Catholic allies and Catholic patriots and Protestant-revolutionaries. But as so often happens in war, American soldiers became more tolerant of the men who fought and died beside them. Bishop Carroll, after a trip to Boston, expressed amazement at the change in attitude: "It is wonderful to tell what great civilities have been done to me in this town, where a few years ago a popish priest was thought to be the greatest monster in creation. Many here, even of their principal people, have acknowledged to me that they would have crossed to the opposite side of the street rather than meet a Roman Catholic some time ago. The horror which was associated with the idea of a papist is incredible; and the scandalous misrepresentations by their ministers increased the horror every Sunday."[61]

In the war's final major confrontation, the Battle at Yorktown, it is estimated that 70 percent of the total American and French forces were Catholic.[62] No one could deny that American Catholics "contributed to the common cause far in excess of their ratio to the total population."[63]

With freedom came the responsibilities of governing and Catholics had an impact on the constitutional structure of the infant nation.

* * * * *

In 1776, Charles Carroll served on the Maryland legislative committee mandated to draft a state constitution. Influenced by the Catholic thinkers Aquinas, Nicholas of Cusa, and Montesquieu, Carroll argued for a mixed government based on the natural law and dedicated to the common good. He designed the legislature of which a lower house of delegates would be elected by the people and a senate chosen by an electoral college. He called for three branches of government – executive, legislative and judicial – "forever separate and distinct from each other."[64]

At the 1787 U.S. Constitutional Convention, the founding Fathers adopted parts of the Maryland Constitution. The creation of the U.S. Senate and presidential selection by the Electoral College were inspired by Charles Carroll's ideas. Alexander Hamilton, in the sixty-third federalist paper praised Carroll's work: "The Maryland Constitution is daily deriving, from the salutary operation of this part of it, a reputation in which it will probably not be rivaled by that of any State in the Union."[65]

Two Catholics, Daniel Carroll (cousin of Charles) and Thomas FitzSimons of Pennsylvania, were among the framers of the Constitution who promoted the belief that power was derived from God and the people. And John Adams agreed. "Our Constitution," he wrote, "was made only for a religious and moral people. It is wholly inadequate for the government of any other."[66]

Catholics who sided with the revolution as the best way to achieve religious liberty were not disappointed by the Constitutional Convention's final product. Article Six permitted Catholics to be part of the government: "But no religious test shall ever be required as a qualification to any office or public trust under the United States." Finally, the first amendment, which was ratified in 1791, adopted the words of Lord Baltimore and guaranteed Catholics equal footing within an impartial governmental structure: "Congress shall make no law respecting an establishment of religion, or prohibiting *the free exercise thereof . . .*"

Knowing that Catholics would now have the opportunity to freely and publicly profess their faith, Charles Carroll happily admitted: "To obtain religiously as well as civil liberty I entered zealously into the Revolution . . ."[67]

The leaders of the U.S. Catholic Church wrote a letter of congratulations to George Washington upon his election as America's first president: "Whilst our country preserves her freedom and independence, we shall have a well-founded title to claim from her justice equal rights of citizenship, as the price of our blood spilt under your eyes . . ." In his reply, Washington described his belief in equality for all and closed with this hope: "And I presume that your fellow-citizens will not forget the patriotic part which you took in the accomplishment of their Revolution, and the establishment of their government; nor the important assistance which they received from a nation in which the Roman Catholic religion is professed."[68]

Chapter 2
First Stirrings:
The Catholic Voter and the Election of 1800

Even as Catholics were celebrating the religious freedom granted to them by the U.S. Constitution, they still faced serious obstacles throughout the new nation. They understood that they were not on an equal footing with other Americans, because the federal right to freely practice the Catholic religion did not necessarily guarantee legal, social, or political acceptance on the state level by Protestant citizenry.

Throughout the Revolution and during the early years of the republic there were fear and distrust of Catholics, including some instances in which Catholics were treated as the enemy. During the War of Independence, for example, Philip Schuyler, a member of the distinguished New York Mohawk Valley Dutch family, forcibly drove to Canada a small group of Scottish Catholics who tried to settle along the Hudson River.

It was only in 1784 that the New York legislature repealed the law that forbade priests from residing in the state. At the state's constitutional convention in 1777, John Jay (who later served as New York governor and as first U.S. chief justice) tried to amend a religious tolerance clause and exclude those who believed in "the wicked and damnable doctrine that the Pope has power to absolve men from sins."[1] Thanks to the efforts of Gouverneur Morris, the measure was defeated. The victory, however, was not complete and the law that did pass included this language introduced by John Jay:

> And this Convention doth further, in the name and by the authority of the good people of this State, ordain, determine and declare that it shall be in the discretion of the Legislature to naturalize all such persons and in such manner as they shall think proper, provided all such of the persons so to be naturalized, as being born in parts beyond the sea and out of the United States of America, shall come to settle in and become subjects of this State, shall take an oath of allegiance to this State *and abjure and renounce all allegiance and subjection* to all and every foreign King, prince, potentate and State *in matters ecclesiastical* as well as civil.[2]

In post-revolutionary New England, the Catholic population was sparse, and the first Catholic Church was not built in Massachusetts until 1788. Because of later immigration, especially from Ireland into Boston, we think of the Bay State as among the most Catholic in the nation, but the total Catholic population in 1790 was only two hundred. In Maine, Vermont, Connecticut, New Hampshire, and Rhode Island, the Church had no visible presence until the early nineteenth century. There were 1,000 Catholics in Rhode Island in 1820, but the first record of Catholics in New Hampshire does not appear until 1822, and their numbers had grown to just 720 by 1835. In 1825 Connecticut had a mere 150 Catholics.

While the Catholic presence was miniscule, that did not stop many of the state legislatures and local constitutional conventions from "prohibiting the free exercise of" the Catholic faith or from insisting on a "religious test" as a qualification "to any office or public trust."

Until 1877, the New Hampshire constitution recognized Protestantism as the state's official religion.[3] The Massachusetts constitution, principally authored by John Adams, recognized religious diversity but still permitted local municipalities to raise taxes "for the institution of the public worship of God and for the support and maintenance of public Protestant teachers of piety, religion and morality in all cases, where such provisions shall not be taken voluntarily."[4] To hold office one also had to take an oath "to abjure all obedience to a foreign ecclesiastical power."[5] These requirements were to remain in force in New Hampshire and Massachusetts until 1833 and 1821, respectively.[6]

In Connecticut, Congregationalism was the state's established religion until 1818, and in New Jersey, Article XIX of its Constitution, which forbade Catholics from holding office, was not repealed until 1844.

North Carolina's Constitution stated that "No person who shall deny . . . the truths of the Protestant religion . . . shall be capable of holding any Office or Place of Trust or Profit in the Civil Department within this state,"[7] and to serve as governor or senator one had to be Protestant. These restrictions were not lifted until 1835.[8]

In 1788, South Carolina adopted anti-Catholic constitutional clauses that read: "No person shall be eligible to a seat in the senate . . . [or] to sit in the house of representatives unless he be of the Protestant religion . . ."[9] and "The Christian Protestant shall be deemed and is hereby constituted and declared to be the religion of this State. That all denominations of Christian Protestants in this State, demeaning themselves peaceably and faithfully, shall enjoy equal civil and religious privileges." It was also provided that no church should be incorporated unless it subscribed to five articles, including "justification by faith only, and the Scriptures as the sole rule of faith." This clearly established some form of Protestantism by law.[10] Unlike other states, however, South Carolina did abolish these restrictions as early as 1790.

Pennsylvania, Delaware, Virginia, and Maryland were the only states that abolished all anti-Catholic penal laws. Thanks to the leadership of James Madison, George Washington, and Thomas Jefferson, Virginia approved a Statute of Religious Freedom in 1786. The statute reasoned that a person's right to freely practice one's religious beliefs is rooted in natural law. The key clause stated:

> That no man shall be compelled to frequent or support any religious worship, place, or ministry whatsoever, nor shall be enforced, restrained, molested, or burdened in his body or goods, nor shall otherwise suffer on account of his religious opinions or belief; but that all men shall be free to profess and by argument to maintain, their opinion in matters of religion, and that the same shall in no wise diminish, enlarge, or affect their civil capacities.[11]

The various restrictions notwithstanding, Catholics were active in public life, and managed to balance their convictions with the political realities, and if they were wary about some decisions made in the newly formed United States, the Carrolls and other leading Catholic families involved in government were unabashedly happy to support the unanimous choice of George Washington as president. They knew that he was a man whose commitment to tolerance could not be doubted.

The president tried to govern in a non-partisan fashion, but conflicts quickly evolved among his key cabinet members. Secretary of State Thomas Jefferson and Treasury Secretary Alexander Hamilton clashed on the use of federal power and on economic and foreign policies.

Hamilton took a broad view, asserting that the Constitution had implied powers that permitted the establishment of a federal bank, the assumption by the national government of the state's Revolutionary War debt, and the establishment of credit and excise taxes. "If the *end* be clearly comprehended within any of the specified powers, and if the measures have an obvious relation to the *end*, and is not forbidden by a particular provision of the Constitution," he wrote, "it may be safely deemed to come within . . . the national authority."[12]

Jefferson, who vigorously opposed these policies, believed that the use of implied powers for the convenience of the moment was wrong. He feared that before long there would be no government actions "which ingenuity may not torture into a convenience . . . to some one of so long a list of enumerated powers."[13] Jefferson agreed with the analysis of his close friend, James Madison, who derailed in Congress many of Hamilton's proposals: that if the Hamiltonian view prevailed, "Everything from the highest object of state legislation to the most minute object of policy would be thrown under the power of Congress."[14]

To promote a national debate on these conflicting visions, the supporters of Hamilton and Jefferson began organizing America's first political parties. Those who supported a strong central government with an active chief executive called themselves Federalists. Their staunchest members included Hamilton, John Adams, and John Marshall. The opposition, known as Republicans, supported a limited national government and championed state's rights. Republican membership included Jefferson, Madison, and James Monroe.

The leader of America's Catholic landed gentry, Charles Carroll, supported the Federalist platform. As a member of the first United States Congress, Senator Carroll chaired the Finance Committee that reported favorably on Hamilton's proposal for federal assumption of war debt. Carroll argued that this was the best policy for establishing sound national credit.

Carroll also sided with the Federalist's skeptical view of the French Revolution and its aftermath. Carroll agreed with the thesis of Edmund Burke's *Reflections on the Revolution in France* that the upheaval could only lead to political chaos and tyranny. According to Carroll, "no real freedom can be enjoyed in France under the existing system. . . . If the different factions distract and afflict that unhappy country would lay aside their animosities and unite in establishing a limited government under the guidance and wisdom and law. . . . France might yet be saved from the destruction to which she seems doomed."[15] Carroll opposed alliance with French "Jacobins" and supported Washington's middle way that steered clear of entanglements with Britain and France.

Carroll was so highly regarded within Federalist circles that in 1792 when it was rumored that Washington would not stand for another term, Carroll's name was suggested by Secretary of War James McHenry as the president's successor.[16] Even Hamilton, who was known for anti-Catholic sentiment, viewed Carroll "as one of the two top who are to fill the two great offices [of president or vice president]."[17] Carroll, knowing it was too early for a Catholic to reach for one of the nation's top offices, dissuaded such talk just as he had in 1778 when he was seriously mentioned for the presidency of the Continental Congress.

*   *   *   *   *

When the British were fighting France for control of the high seas and began seizing neutral America's trading ships, Washington sent John Jay to London to negotiate a settlement. In November 1794, the fruit of his efforts, "Jay's

Treaty," was sent to the Senate for ratification. Its terms included the withdrawal of British troops still stationed within America's northwestern boundaries, the establishment of commissions to arbitrate pre-revolutionary British citizen and ship owner claims, and boundary disputes between Maine and Canada. The treaty also established that trade between Britain and America would be on a most-favored basis and clearly defined the rights of neutral nations.

Federalists embraced the treaty while Republicans were hostile. They denounced it as a betrayal of France, our revolutionary ally, and the Republicans sought to cripple enforcement of the treaty by halting its funding. To initiate the Republican campaign, the Virginia House of Delegates passed a series of "Resolves" urging Congress to withhold all financial support. When Maryland introduced Resolves identical to those supported in Virginia, Carroll was appalled. He not only supported the treaty but vociferously opposed the Congressional usurpation of power implicit in the denial of financing for an approved treaty. To President Washington he wrote: "I am totally at a loss to account for the motives of the majority [in Congress]. Do they wish to engross all power to themselves, to destroy the checks and balances established by the Constitution?"[18] Washington agreed with Carroll and expressed his dismay of the House of Representatives' "assumption of power." To show his support for the president, Carroll led the fight in his state legislature and defeated Maryland's "Resolves."

More than any other event in the early years of the republic, the battle over "Jay's Treaty" hastened the development of political parties. The Federalists, who were often perceived as pro-British and aristocratic, found their strength in New England, while the "States' rights" Republicans dominated the rural south.

Thomas Jefferson, who retired to Monticello after resigning from Washington's cabinet in 1793, was so appalled by Federalist policies that he permitted himself to be persuaded to run in the 1796 presidential race against his old friend John Adams.

Although Charles Carroll viewed Adams as obnoxious, he kept Maryland's Catholics in line for the Federalist candidate. He might have disliked Adams, but he feared Jefferson. Carroll confided to James McHenry: "The friends of the government dread the election of Jefferson . . . [they] want revolution and war. . . . A man must be blind indeed not to see through the designs of their party."[19] Jefferson carried Pennsylvania and all the Southern States while Adams carried New England, New Jersey, and what was considered a swing state, New York. Adams squeaked by with 71 electoral votes to Jefferson's 68.

This was America's first election campaign. Partisans employed cruel and vicious techniques that included inflammatory rhetoric. In speeches on street

corners and in town halls and public houses, each side denounced the other as
enemies of the young republic. Adams was accused of being an "avowed
friend of monarchy" while Jefferson and his supporters were labeled "cut-
throats who walk in rags and sleep amidst filth and vermin."[20]

Between 1796 and 1800, the ideological gulf further widened.
Throughout his term Adams not only had to deal with internal party squabbling, disloyal cabinet members, and a growing opposition party, but constant
international problems. The war between France and England, the "XYZ"
affair, and the Alien and Sedition Acts polarized the country. And Adams's
popularity did not increase in Catholic circles when the first person prosecuted under the Sedition Act was an Irish-Catholic named Matthew Lyon.

There were constant anti-French and anti-British protests. Jefferson, a
French sympathizer, was labeled a Jacobin. Adams, perceived as pro-British,
was called a "Royal" and was accused of wanting to lead a "Prigarchy."

Jefferson and his Republican supporters feared that bankers and investors
– "money changers" – would rule the country by means of financial manipu-
lation, and that their dominance of the nation's fiscal resources would lead to
aristocratic rule. They believed it was only a matter of time before the financial elitists would award themselves royal titles and declare the most powerful
of the lot "monarch." The Jeffersonians viewed themselves as the sworn enemies of the haughty and the defenders of the common man: of his rights and
his ability to make sound decisions.

The Federalists, on the other hand, found support among the wealthy
urban and commercial classes, among whom there was strong support for a
national economic policy. The Federalists viewed themselves as an enlightened group who put aside narrow self-interest in favor of expansive growth.
They were "the wise, the rich and the well born."

> Federalists included a disproportionate number of gentry; in vir-
> tually all states except Virginia the established elites seem to have
> been Federalist. If a person was born into a family of old wealth,
> of respectable calling and of college education, the chances of his
> identifying himself as a Federalist were high. Federalists had often
> been among the more moderate Whigs during the Revolution; as
> we have seen, the nucleus of the party had been Nationalists in the
> early 1780's. Those who were attached to the social order as it
> existed, fearful of change and of religious dissent, usually counted
> themselves Federalists. It was possible to see in the party a hedge
> against novelty, an implied promise that membership in the gentry
> would be equated with a right to be there.[21]

To ensure order and stability, the Federalists believed that the nation had to be led by educated, virtuous men. They feared that too much democracy would lead to mob rule. Their snobbery and distrust for the common man was best expressed by Federalist Timothy Pickering: "If we should fail . . . the Americans can only blame their own negligence, avarice and want of almost every public virtue."[22]

The election of 1800 was a watershed in the early history of the nation. It was the first election in which two organized, ideologically opposed political parties fought for control of the executive and legislative branches of the national government. Two "kindred spirits" who were primarily responsible for the creation of the Declaration of Independence were now bitter enemies, each believing that the other had each betrayed the fundamental principles they had both espoused in 1776.

Adams was elected president in 1796 with the pledge that he would continue George Washington's policies. By 1800, Adams had a record of his own, and it split not only the nation but his own party as well. New York's leading Federalist, Alexander Hamilton, despised the president.

Believing that Adams had failed as a Federalist, Hamilton decided he had to be evicted from the executive mansion. "If we must have an enemy at the head of the government," Hamilton concluded, "let it be one whom we can oppose and who will not involve our party in the disgrace of his foolish and bad measures."[23] Reacting to Hamilton's intrigue, Adams denounced him as "an intriguant, the greatest intriguant in the world – a man devoid of every moral principle – a bastard."[24] As the 1800 campaign heated up, Adam's campaign was jolted when a letter written by Hamilton to a friend was leaked to the press. The correspondence said that the president "does not possess the talents adapted to the administration of government . . . there are great intrinsic defects of his character which unfit him for the office of chief magistrate."[25]

But there was plenty of mudslinging on both sides. Jefferson was charged with cheating creditors and stealing from widows. "Murder, robbery, rape, adultery and incest will be openly taught and practiced . . ." declared the *Connecticut Courant.* A Federalist pamphlet asked: "Can serious and reflecting men look about them and doubt that if Jefferson is elected, and the Jacobins get into authority, that those morals which protect our lives from the knife of the assassin – which guard the chastity of our wives and daughters from seduction and violence – defend our property from plunder and devastation, and shield our religion from contempt and profanation, will not be trampled upon and exploded?"[26]

For their part, Jefferson partisans called Adams "a fool, hypocrite, criminal, tyrant," and they spread the rumor that to create an American dynasty, the president was prepared to marry one of his sons to George III's daughter.[27]

Charles Carroll was disgusted with the intra-party political battling. He feared the political tactics being employed would enrage the mob and lead to the forcible overthrow of the Federalists. In April of 1800 he wrote to Hamilton: "We have strange reports circulated among us concerning the prevalence of Jacobinical principles in your state."[28] Carroll feared New York could go for Jefferson, who, he decided, "is too theoretical and fanciful a statesman" to lead the nation.[29] He was convinced that Jefferson's "fanciful tricks would dissolve the Union."[30]

America's leading Catholic Federalist politician did not grasp that the election of 1800 was not only a watershed election for the nation, but significant for the budding Catholic population. Carroll represented the Anglo-Catholic population that was declining in numbers and influence as Irish-, French-, and German-Catholic immigration to the United States began to grow in the late eighteenth century. And even though the total population of Catholic immigrants eligible to vote was small in number, they were helpful in swinging the closely contested 1800 election to the Jeffersonians.

In 1790, the Catholic population represented approximately 1 percent of the nation. Most of the Church membership was Anglo-Catholic and residing in Maryland, Pennsylvania, and New York.

Historians estimate that in the decade leading up to the election (no accurate numbers were compiled until 1820) the Catholic population grew by over 30 percent to about 47,000. Significant portions of this increased population were immigrants, many of whom settled in New York, which was then part of the Diocese of Baltimore. Although New York did not receive Rome's recognition as a diocese until 1808, it was nevertheless a hotbed of Catholic activity. In 1785 the state legislature incorporated St. Peter's Church in Manhattan, which became the first Catholic Church to be built in New York City. It was built on five lots purchased from Trinity Church at the corner of Church and Barclay Streets, and on October 15 the cornerstone was laid by Don Diego Gardoqui, ambassador to the United States from Spain. French, German, and Irish clerics arrived to tend to the growing ethnic flocks. As early as 1787, a Catholic students' club was founded at Columbia College. Churches began to be built throughout the state, and although few in number, many became active members of their respective communities and helped their immigrant parishioners become citizens and voters.

As the election of 1800 drew near, both political parties began to form grassroots organizations particularly in those states where political sentiment was evenly divided. One state that all agreed was pivotal was New York, with its dozen Electoral College votes. (New York had the third largest of the sixteen electoral blocks. Virginia was the largest with 22.)

New York's Federalists were led by its landed gentry – the Schuylers, the Van Rensselaers, the Van Der Heydens, and the Knickerbockers. These Hudson Valley "Patroons" believed they and the members of their caste were the only people qualified to manage the affairs of their state. They agreed with their fellow party member, John Jay, who in a letter to a friend wrote: "It is not a new remark that those who own the country are the most fit persons to participate in the government of it."[31]

While the influx of Catholic immigrants in the last decade of the eighteenth century was small, their growing presence was noticed and frowned upon by the Patroons. To prevent these lower classes from gaining political influence, the New York Federalists enthusiastically supported the 1798 Alien Act, which decreed that immigrants had to reside in the United States fourteen years, instead of five, before they could apply for naturalization. New York's Federalists opposed suffrage extension because they believed only freeholders possessed proper motivation and virtues necessary to cast a vote and protect individual liberties. As early as 1787, Gouverneur Morris warned: "Give the votes to the people who have no property and they will sell them to the rich who will be able to buy them."[32] Federalist congressman Harrison Gray Otis was even more blunt: "If some means are not adopted to prevent the indiscriminate admission of wild Irishman and others to the right of suffrage, there will soon be an end to liberty and property."[33]

But there was another reason for opposing the extension of the franchise to the immigrant: fear that their votes would contribute to Jeffersonian-Republican success at the polls. The Federalists could not imagine these people who "were different in race, religion and political tradition, but uncouth, unclean, ignorant, unskilled and frequently immoral," deciding the outcome of a presidential election.[34]

Sensing that many of Irish and French descent who resided in New York City were offended by the crass political actions of Federalist "anglomen and monocrats,"[35] the Republicans began to cultivate these ethnics voters.

The Republicans declared that their party supported "freedom of religion and opposition to all manoeuvres to bring about a legal ascendancy of one sect over another."[36] They also urged enactment of liberal naturalization laws. When propaganda was circulated urging Catholics to vote against Jefferson, one Irish Catholic made this sarcastic reply: "We presume the . . . reason to be that it was owing to Mr. Jefferson that the Catholic priest was saved from being hanged for going into . . . Virginia . . . and that to his toleration law it was owing that the Catholics can now build Churches and adore God without incurring the penalties of fine and imprisonment."[37]

Upon hearing the harsh immigrant reaction to President Adams's Sedition Act, Aaron Burr, New York City's leading political operative, sensed an opportunity for his Republican Party. He directed members of the state party committee and the Tammany Society to reach out, cultivate, and organize the Irish downtrodden.

Founded in 1787, the New York Tammany Society was named to honor the American Indian who made peace with the colonists, Tamanend. For many American patriots, "Saint" Tammany was an all-American substitute for Britain's patron, Saint George the dragon slayer. The fraternal order's members were known as "braves" and were governed by thirteen "sachems." At first they shunned immigrant membership, but that did not stop them from wooing the city's Catholic voters.

"Tammany gave local interest politicians a credible vehicle for posing as patriotic, nationalistic democrats, devoted to constitutional principles and Lockean idealism."[38] And when the 1800 election cycle began, New York City's most important Republicans were Tammanyites.[39]

New York's members of the Electoral College were chosen by the state legislature which, in 1799, was controlled by the Federalists. Burr's plan was to field a strong slate of assemblymen candidates to oppose Federalist incumbents in the April 1800 state election and gain control for the Republicans. If his plan succeeded, they would have the power to select New York's electors to the Electoral College committed to Thomas Jefferson.

To achieve this end, Burr put together a ticket consisting of important figures in New York State politics. The ticket included luminaries such as George Clinton, General Horatio Gates, and Judge Brockholst Livingston.[40] The Federalists were caught off guard and managed to nominate in opposition a slate of local nobodies.

For the first time in American history, Burr organized a political machine that held campaign rallies, hung candidate posters, and distributed political brochures. Burr and the New York Republicans reached out to common folks and made an issue of Federalist prejudice and opposition to naturalization. The Federalists were offended by the use of what they considered political propaganda. It was beneath their dignity to resort to what they called "Forensic Degladiation – parades, barbecues, posters, handbills."[41] They were appalled that Tammany held meetings in Martling's Tavern – the "pig pen" as they called it.

The key to the election, in Burr's judgment, was the thirteen assembly races in New York City. M. R. Werner, in his history of Tammany, describes how the society played an important role in influencing the decision of the city's electorate:

> During the Presidential election of 1800, when Thomas Jefferson became President of the United States and Aaron Burr Vice President, Tammany Hall's activities were almost exactly the same as those which we shall see were so characteristic of the organization during every period of its career. Men who intended to vote the opposition ticket were brought into the Wigwam, entertained

and persuaded, and, if there was doubt of their conviction, escorted to the polls by committees, who were appointed to see that they remained true to their promises.[42]

Republicans triumphed at the polls, managing to win all thirteen of New York City's races, and these victories assured them a majority in the state assembly. Although history was later to label Burr a rogue, in 1800 he proved himself a brilliant political organizer who effectively mobilized the voters. "If we carry this election," wrote Matthew Davies to Albert Gallatin, "it may be ascribed principally to Col. Burr's management and perseverance."[43]

The Jeffersonian concept of democracy triumphed in New York thanks in part to the small but united inner-city Catholic swing vote. Immigrant mechanics, coopers, sailmakers, tallow chandlers, and soap boilers who "were distrustful of Hamilton's schemes and his Federalist elitism" went Republican.[44] And as a result of these Republican victories, they now chose the twelve electors who would cast the vote for president in November.

The Republican juggernaut also hit the state of Maryland where members of the Electoral College were selected by the voters, not the legislature. Fearing that the people might support Jefferson, the Federalists attempted to pass legislation that would empower the General Assembly to choose electors. Leading the charge was Charles Carroll, who "approved of this step, foreseeing revolution, anarchy and military despotism if the anti-federalists emerged victorious."[45] But backlash against what many considered a crass political tactic led the legislature to refuse to change the law.

Gleeful over the victory, one Republican referred to Carroll as "that hoary-headed aristocrat" and asked "is he, old in iniquity as he is, to be the chief director of the people on the Manor? Citizens of Frederick County set Charles Carroll at defiance!"[46]

In fact, as historian Robert Kelly put it, America's largest commercial cities (New York, Boston, Philadelphia, and Baltimore) "had swung strongly Republican by 1800 through the impact of immigration from a broad and a rising working class consciousness."[47]

The election of 1796 between Adams and Jefferson had been very close, 71 electoral votes to 68. New York's 12 votes went to Adams that year, and Maryland's vote had split 7 for Adams and 4 for Jefferson. When the Electoral College met in 1800, the election was expected to be close once again, and it was. Thanks to the Catholic swing votes, New York now cast its electoral votes for Jefferson while many Maryland Catholics ignored the pleas of patriarch Carroll and cast half their votes for the victorious Republicans. These electoral shifts made the difference and Thomas Jefferson captured the presidency with 73 votes to now former President Adams's 65.

Chapter 3

The Catholic Voter in the Age of Jefferson and Jackson

In 1800, the American people witnessed for the first time a defeated incumbent president peacefully transferring his office to a victorious opponent. Elected on a platform that was diametrically opposed to that of Federalist John Adams, Democratic-Republican Thomas Jefferson described his vision of the limited role of the state in his March, 1801 inaugural: ". . . a wise and frugal Government, which shall restrain men from injuring one another, shall leave them otherwise free to regulate their own pursuits of industry and improvement, and shall not take from the mouth of labor the bread it has earned. This is the sum of good government. . . ."

This theory was to guide the government for the twenty-four years that the "Virginia Dynasty" held the executive branch. Jefferson and his successors fought for limited federal government, strict interpretation of the Constitution, strong states' rights, majority rule that respected the rights of minorities, limited government debt, free trade, and free enterprise. The less government interfered, Jefferson argued, the easier it would be for people to pursue their own well being. As he so famously put it: "That government is best which governs least." Opposing an elite that would control land and wealth, Jefferson preferred a country of small freeholders. He believed the success of the republic depended upon all men possessing the right to acquire land, to receive an education, and to freely practice one's religion. "Jefferson's natural aristocracy of wisdom and virtue, serving the good of the whole society drawn from and elected by an economically independent, educated and politically experienced citizenry, provided a balanced, moderate conception of democratic leadership and representation."[1]

Jeffersonian Democratic-Republicans were committed to the proposition that "all men are created equal," and they had an abiding faith in the ability and integrity of the American common man – of farmers and laborers. And for Thomas Jefferson and his followers, religious freedom and toleration were paramount. He believed that "the genuine doctrine of one God is reviving," and he hoped "that there is not a young man living in the United States who will not die [a true Christian]."[2]

In Jefferson's opinion, tolerance and free discussion among the various

Christian sects in America would improve social harmony when men realized they held many common beliefs. As he said in his first inaugural: "[America] was enlightened by a benign religion, professed, indeed and practiced in various forms, yet all of them including honesty, truth, temperance, gratitude, and the love of man, acknowledging and adoring an overruling Providence."

And Jefferson acted on this belief. To restrain the dominant Anglican Church in Virginia, in 1779 Jefferson offered to the Commonwealth's Assembly a bill for establishing religious freedom. The legislation stated:

> Almighty God hath created the mind free . . . all attempts to influence it by temporal punishments, or burthens, or by civil incapacitations, tend only to beget habits of hypocrisy and meanness, and are a departure from the plan of the holy author of our religion. . . . [T]he impious presumption of legislature and ruler, civil as well as ecclesiastical . . . [to] have assumed domination over the faith of others . . . tends also to corrupt the principle of that very religion it is meant to encourage.[3]

Although the Act was bottled up for years due to intense opposition, Jefferson persevered, and it became law in 1786.

James Madison, who succeeded Jefferson as president in 1809, also championed religious tolerance. As early as 1785 he wrote *Memorial and Remonstrance against Religious Assessments* in which he expressed his opposition to Patrick Henry's proposed tax to support select Christian churches. In the statement, Madison declared:

> . . . the Religion . . . of every man must be left to the conviction and conscience of every man; and it is the right of every man to exercise it as these may dictate. This right is in its nature an unalienable right. It is unalienable, because the opinions of men, depending only on the evidence presented to their minds, cannot follow the dictates of other men: It is unalienable also, because that is here a right toward men, is a duty towards the Creator. It is the duty of every man to render to the Creator such homage, and such only, as he believes to be acceptable to him.[4]

The Jeffersonians championed Madison's conclusion in the *Memorial* that "in matters of religion, no man's right is abridged by the institutions of civil society and that religion is wholly-exempt from its cognizance."[5]

In the "Age of Jefferson," America's Roman Catholics were mostly able to live and work in peace and harmony. To demonstrate his support for immigrant Catholics, Jefferson repealed the Alien Act, fixed the naturalization requirement at five years, and let the Sedition Act expire. Nativist outbursts subsided, thanks in part to Jefferson's leadership and also to a significant decrease in European immigration. For many of Europe's downtrodden, the Napoleonic wars provided plenty of job opportunities in the armed services and various war industries, hence immigration to America slowed to a trickle.

During this period, growth in America's Catholic population was a result of the 1803 Louisiana Purchase, although the Church's presence in that territory was weak. "Schism and insubordination were rampart, outsiders intruded themselves into the government of the Church and spirituality was at a low ebb."[6]

Despite the diminishing influx of immigrant Catholics, Church organization continued to develop. Baltimore became an archdiocese in 1808, and New York, Boston, Philadelphia, and Bardstown, Kentucky, were granted diocesan status. The formerly French Diocese of New Orleans now reported to the archbishop of Baltimore instead of the archbishop of Quebec.

America's Catholic population, which had stood at 35,000 in 1790, was estimated to be 195,000 by 1820. Less than half of this increase was the result of immigration.

As more Catholics were born in America or became naturalized citizens, their voting numbers grew, although in 1804 they did not have the swing-vote impact they had in 1800, even though ten of the seventeen states now chose the members of the Electoral College by direct popular vote. This was due to Jefferson's popularity. Knowing the election of 1804 was a lost cause, the weakened Federalists did not bother to hold a convention to select their presidential candidate. The president went on to decisively beat the Federalist sacrificial lamb, Charles Pickney, and Jefferson even carried the Federalist strongholds of Massachusetts, New Hampshire, and Vermont. Jefferson carried every state that had the direct popular vote, and his Electoral College totals were 162 versus 14 for Pickney.

Four years later, when President Jefferson anointed Secretary of State James Madison as his successor, the Federalists decided to put up a fight. The devastating effects of the Embargo Act of 1807 on New England's economy gave Federalists hope that they had a chance to unseat the Democratic-Republicans.

Jefferson had promoted the Embargo Act, believing the Europeans would change their belligerent attitudes toward American neutrality if they were denied essential raw materials. One unintended consequence was the policy's dramatic – and negative – impact on regional economies. East Coast exporters suffered immensely, with exports declining 75 percent and imports declining 50 percent. Philadelphia, Baltimore, and the middle states, on the other hand, prospered due to the boom in domestic manufacturing.

In 1808 once again the Federalists nominated Charles Pickney as their standard bearer, and the entire Federalist campaign was based on the embargo issue. New England partisans bellowed: "Why is the embargo like sickness? Because it weakens us. Why is it like hydrophobia? Because it makes us dread the water."[7] The *Albany Register* went so far as to claim that Jefferson and Madison were naturalized French citizens."[8] Federalists insinuated that Madison was Napoleon's slave.

Outside of New England, the Federalist strategy backfired, and they were soundly rejected – 122 electoral votes to 47 votes. The party was in shambles, and the aging Yankee leadership was bitter over its waning influence on national affairs. But America's entry in the War of 1812, which the Federalists opposed, gave them hope of electoral victories – and to help their cause they decided to employ tactics that would revive anti-Catholic sentiments.

Throughout the Napoleonic wars, Great Britain had ignored U.S. neutrality. American cargos were confiscated on the high seas and U.S. merchant seamen were pressed into service in the British Navy. The "War Hawk" 12th Congress, dominated by Westerners and led by Henry Clay, resented years of British abuse, most particularly their financing of Tecumseh's Shawnee Indians, which led to the murder of U.S. settlers. Succumbing to pressure, President Madison asked for a declaration of war against Great Britain on June 1, 1812. Seventeen days later, in a very close vote – 79 to 49 in the House and 19 to 13 in the Senate – the Congress approved the request. The bulk of the opposition came from New England Yankees.

Andrew Jackson, who raised a volunteer army to fight the British, summed up the attitude of the War Hawks when he gave this reply to a conscript who asked why America was at war:

> We are going to fight for the reestablishment of our national character, misunderstood and vilified at home and abroad; for the protection of our maritime citizens, impressed on board British ships of war and compelled to fight the battles of our enemies against ourselves; to vindicate our right to a free trade, and open a market for the production of our soil, now perishing on our hands because the *mistress of the ocean* has forbid us to carry them to any foreign nation; in fine to seek some indemnity for past injuries, some security against future aggressions, by the conquest of all the British dominions upon the continent of North America."[9]

The war, which was to drag on until early 1815, had the support of American Catholics. Many French and Irish ethnics, who hated the British, viewed the war as an act of revenge. They stood by their wartime president and voted overwhelming to re-elect Madison in November 1812.

Since Adams's defeat in 1800, the Federalists had been brooding about their electoral failures, and in 1812 they perceived an opportunity to strike back. They hated the national government's commercial restrictions, opposed the westward expansion, and believed the war was a Democratic-Republican excuse to punish New Englanders.

Running on a bitter anti-war platform, the Federalists made inroads in New England and New York local elections. Feeling his oats, Massachusetts's Governor Calef Stron sent messages to the Halifax military commander, hinting the New England states might make a separate peace with Great Britain. Unaware that peace accords had already been reached in Paris, the secessionist-minded Federalists gathered on December 15, 1814, in Hartford, and for three weeks pondered revisions to the U.S. Constitution that would limit southern power, eliminate embargoes, and limit admission of new states to the Union.

The delegates to the Hartford Convention, still resentful that Catholics had swung the election of 1800 to Jefferson, developed a strategy to curtail the growing influence of Catholics in northern cities. They made it clear they opposed "the easy admission of naturalized foreigners to places of trust, honor or profit."[10] They wanted to reinstate and expand the anti-Catholic "Alien Act" of 1798 and raise the residency requirement for naturalization from five to fourteen years. It would not be overstatement to suggest that the Federalists revealed an undisguised bigotry in their objection "to the participation in the government, [of] aliens who were no part to the compact."[11] In other words, only the Protestant heirs of the signers of the Mayflower Compact were trust-worthy Americans. The platform, if implemented, would have forbidden nat-uralized citizens from sitting in either the U.S. Senate or the House of Representatives; in fact would have barred them from holding any federal civil office.

With Andrew Jackson's January 1815 victory at New Orleans and the public announcement that peace was at hand, the secessionist part of the Federalist platform was quickly discarded. Nevertheless, the Hartford Convention had revealed a simmering anti-Catholicism that would eventually come to a boil. While the issue remained dormant during the Madison and Monroe administrations, nativist activities began to surface when the great European Immigration commenced in the mid 1820s. The resulting changes in the political demographics of the nation were to bring out a dark side of many Protestant Americans.

*   *   *   *   *

After the 1815 Congress of Vienna determined the boundaries of post-Napoleonic Europe, emigration to the New World began to rise. Religious or political persecution and poverty and starvation were the primary reasons tens of thousands of immigrants braved the perilous voyage to a new life in America.

In Ireland, religious intolerance, high tenant-farmer rents, the potato blight of 1821, and the subsequent famine of 1845–1847 caused a great diaspora. In the 1820s, 50,000 Irish had entered the United States; 207,000 in the 1830s; and 780,000 during the decade following the famine. Eighty percent of these Irish immigrants were Catholics.

Between 1820 and 1830, 143,000 people from eighteen nations arrived in U.S. ports. Church records show that 54,000 were Catholic. Regardless of the immigrant's origins, however, the long road to America was generally treacherous. Most were of peasant origin, and came from societies in which family and clan ties were paramount. They instinctively practiced the basic concept of Catholic social thought – subsidiarity, which maintains that "human life proceeds most intelligently and creatively where decisions are made at the local level closest to concrete reality."[12]

According to historian Oscar Handlin in his landmark study *The Uprooted*, these peasant families, which were the basic economic unit in villages throughout Europe, accepted or rejected all proposals – whether for business or marriage – based on the effect they would have on the entire clan. As a rule, village life provided all a person's needs, and decades might pass without one person traveling beyond the borders of his village.

The political, economic, and social upheavals in the first half of the nineteenth century brought this way of life to an end for millions of people. The city with its ghettos, so despised by Thomas Jefferson, began to dominate the European landscape.

> The seeds of ultimate change were not native to this stable society. They were implanted from without. For centuries the size of the population, the amount of available land, the quality of productive surplus, and the pressure of family stability, achieved together a steady balance that preserved the village way of life. Only slowly and in a few places were there signs of unsteadiness in the seventeenth century; then more distinctly and in more places in the eighteenth. After 1800, everywhere, the elements of the old equilibrium disintegrated. The old social structure tottered; gathering momentum from its own fall, it was unable to right itself, and under the impact of successive shocks collapsed. Then the peasants could no longer hang on; when even to stay meant to change, they had to leave.[13]

In the nineteenth century, the clans began to disintegrate, and brother turned against brother with the victor gaining control of the family plot of land. The defeated concluded that their only hope was to leave for the New World where land was abundant and man was free to determine his destiny.

By the end of the nineteenth century, 35 million had flowed from every hamlet in Europe to America.

The journey was never an easy one. Men and women left behind what mattered most to them – family. For the first time in their lives they were alone, carrying the barest of possessions. To preserve their meager capital they would travel on foot and live off the land during the long treacherous walk to the port of exit. If they were lucky enough to make it to the shipping piers, they would be forced to haggle with shipmasters over the price of passage. Often they would surrender all they had to get a spot in steerage.

Upon seeing the condition of the rickety sea crafts, many realized they might not survive the forty-day trip. These "floating coffins" were filthy and rat-infested. There was bad ventilation, brutal living conditions, subsistent rations of bad food and foul water. Dysentery was a common illness.

When they finally reached an American port city, most survivors disembarked exhausted, hungry, and destitute. During their first days in the new land, many found it hard to adapt to the unfamiliar and hostile cultural environment. Many were forced to beg for sustenance. It turned out that the streets were not paved with gold but covered with filth.

Few immigrants possessed the skills necessary to thrive in urban life, and most, if they were lucky, settled for a single day's work at a time or for piece work that entailed hard labor in harsh conditions. They became drifters and began to hang out in gangs, Gang leaders served as "general contractors," negotiating for work if it could be found or planning criminal activities if there were no jobs.

Some of the more fortunate Catholic settlers secured work as laborers on the Erie Canal project. Many settled in Utica, Rochester, and other towns and villages that flourished along the canal route. There were also scores of Catholic Germans who traveled the Cumberland Road and settled in Cincinnati and St. Louis. Later they would settle at rail junctions in Cleveland, Pittsburgh, and Chicago. Germans, who for the most part possessed farming skills, left the inner cities in search of western farmland. They settled in what became known as the German triangle, the points being Milwaukee in the north, Cincinnati in the southeast, and St. Louis in the southwest. By occupying sparsely populated regions of the growing nation, unlike the inner-city Irish, the German-Catholics escaped much of the bigotry of the nativist movement. "Our German settlers" conceded an Illinois newspaper editor in 1855, "are valuable acquisitions to the state and are doing good service in opening up its waste places to the hand of cultivation . . . . It is seldom, indeed, that we hear of one being in the poor house or under the care of a pauper committee."[14] Of course some German immigrants settled in each of these major cities, often founding breweries, some in continuous operation ever since.

Most of the Irish settled in ethnic-ghettos, and turned to their church, seeking faith, hope and charity. For the most part, the Irish congregated in inner cities due to lack of money, their natural clannish inclinations, and the Church's desire to keep them together to preserve their Catholicism. The Catholic population increased by 63 percent during the 1820s, totaling 318,000 by 1830. To meet their needs, the American church expanded to eleven dioceses.

European political unrest during the 1830s caused a rapid increase in immigration from non-English speaking countries. It is estimated that 45,000 French royalists, unhappy with the crowning of the "Citizen-King" Louis Philippe, migrated to America. Poland's submission to Russian rule prompted many revolutionaries there to leave their country. There were also numbers of politically persecuted refugees from Saxony, Hesse-Cassel, Frankfurt, the Papal States, and Italian Modena.[15] Between 1830 and 1840, more than 600,000 political, religious, and economic exiles had entered U.S. ports, half of them Catholic. The Catholic influx included 144,000 Irish, 34,000 French, and 39,000 Germans, with the rest coming from a dozen other European countries. By 1840 the total Catholic population in the U.S. was approximately 663,000.

The Catholic population as a percent of the total U.S. population was rapidly growing:

	U.S. Population	Catholic Population	% of Catholics
1790	3,172,000	35,000	1.0%
1820	7,866,000	195,000	2.4
1830	10,537,000	318,000	3.0
1840	14,195,800	663,000	4.6

The influx of Continental Catholics had a great deal to do with the revolutionary atmosphere in Europe, which reached its height in 1848. Radical socialists wreaked havoc throughout Europe. Their crusade to implement the "scientific" formulae they believed would create a perfect society was the precursor of later totalitarianism. They were intent on destroying the politics, manners, morals, economics, and literature of the Old Order. Their relativistic interweaving of morals and physics is described by Paul Johnson in *Modern Times* as "the principal formative influences on the course of twentieth century history. It formed a knife . . . to help cut society adrift from its traditional moorings in the faith and morals of Judeo-Christian culture."

The political upheaval in Europe and the famine in Ireland hastened Catholic immigration. During the 1840s, some 700,000 refugees came to America, including 530,000 Irish and 110,000 Germans, and by 1850 the U.S. population stood at 19.5 million of which 1.6 million were Catholic – 8.4% of the total population.

These rapid changes in America's demographics did not go unnoticed by political leaders. Some took the opportunity to befriend, aid, and guide the new immigrants. Others were alarmed and believed that this "barbaric invasion" would destroy the American way of life.

Even though the immigrants provided cheap labor for manufacturing plants in New York, Philadelphia, Boston, and Baltimore, there was a growing hatred and distrust of the Catholic urban poor. The Protestant "New Measures" revival, which rejected deism, lax religious practices, and propagated a rigid fundamentalism, also looked unkindly on the Catholic population, as in the case of the American Bible Society's clash with the Catholic Church. When Church hierarchy informed the Society that it was not empowered or competent to tell Catholics what version of the Bible to read, many Protestants interpreted this as an attack on the word of God. Preachers complained from the pulpit that "Jesuits threatened to drive God's word from the land."[16]

Some Protestant newspapers were founded with the express purpose of attacking Catholics and Catholicism. These included the Boston *Recorder* (1816), New York's *Observer* (1823), and the nationalist Baptist paper *Christian Watchman* (1819). By 1827 there were more than thirty such papers.

The 1829 Baltimore Provincial Council, which represented Catholic bishops in America, condemned the tone of these newspapers:

> Not only do they assail us and our institutions in a style of vituperation and offense, misrepresent our tenets, vilify our practices, repeat the hundred-times-refuted calumnies of the days of angry and bitter contention in other lands, but they have even denounced you and us as enemies to the liberties of the republic, and have openly proclaimed the fancied necessity of obstructing our progress, and of using their best efforts to extirpate our religion.[17]

Throughout the late 1820s and early 1830s, anti-popery sermons increased and debates between Protestant and Catholic leaders took place in most major cities. At first the discussions and debates concerned theological differences; but before long the Protestants used the debates as a platform to denounce the Church of Rome as an immoral cesspool.

*   *   *   *   *

These religious and cultural clashes had political implications. As an increasing number of immigrant Catholics became naturalized citizens and voters, national, state, and local politicians realized that the Catholic voter could have a major impact on the election process, especially in the thirteen states that by 1820 chose presidential electors by direct popular vote.

As the Jeffersonian Age was drawing to a close in 1824, the existing political parties were showing their age. After the embarrassing Hartford Convention, the Federalist Party had functionally ceased to exist. What remained were small pockets of diehard Yankees in the New England region. The Jefferson Democratic-Republicans had also begun to splinter. For most of their history, the northern and southern factions of the party had been united by their common hatred of the Federalists. But with the demise of the Federalists, the sectional interests that divided them became more pronounced, and the party structure began to disintegrate.

The presidential election of 1824 not only ended the one-party rule of the Jeffersonians, it also planted the seeds for the growth of new political parties that would represent emerging sectional interests.

Andrew Jackson, an opponent of political and economic elitism, was the leading member of a new generation of leaders who hoped to occupy the executive mansion. For immigrants, pioneers, laborers, and the new entrepreneurs – for all common men – Jackson, general, frontiersman, farmer, and statesman, had become a hero and a symbol of hope.

The Jacksonian movement was built on the cultural values of the emerging common man. These values included honor, self-reliance, equality, and individualism. As Walter Russell Mead points out in his essay, *The Jacksonian Tradition*:

> Jacksonians believed that the political and moral instincts of the American people are sound and can be trusted and that the simpler and more direct the process of government is, the better will be the results. . . . Jacksonians believe that the government should do everything in its power to promote the well-being – political, moral, economic – of the folk community.[18]

The emerging Democratic Party, led by General Jackson, opposed the National Bank, supported states rights and the strict interpretation of the U.S. Constitution, and took a laissez-faire attitude about the growth of new business enterprises. Those who opposed the National-Republican Party's new "American System," which championed the National Bank, high tariffs, and advocated federal programs to build canals, roads, and other national improvements, flocked to the Jackson camp.

Martin Van Buren of New York, who was primarily responsible for creating the structure of the new Democratic Party, best articulated their philosophical tenets: "The orthodox Democracy of New York State regarded the broader American System with aversion, if not horror. They cordially disliked the debts, monopolies, corruption, favoritism, and centralized control, which they alleged would follow from its operation."[19]

Many Catholics were attracted to the principles of Andrew Jackson, and as early as 1824, Democrats welcomed them into the fold. There was a bond between the Jacksonians and the immigrant Catholic who sought the freedom to use his hands and his ingenuity to build a prosperous life. After his extensive review of American society, Alexis de Tocqueville appeared to agree. In *Democracy in America* he reported.

> Among the different Christian doctrines, Catholicism appears to me, on the contrary, one of the most favorable to equality of conditions. Among Catholics, religious society is composed of only two elements: the priest and the people. The priest alone is raised above the faithful: everything is equal below him. . . . But once the priests are turned away or turn themselves away from government as they do in the United States, there are no men more disposed by their beliefs than Catholics to carry the idea of equality of conditions into the political world . . .
>
> Most Catholics are poor, and they need all citizens to govern in order to come to government themselves. Catholics are in the minority, and they need all rights to be respected to be assured of the free exercise of theirs. These two causes drive them even without their knowing it toward political doctrines that they would perhaps adopt with less eagerness if they were wealthy and predominant.

In the election of 1824, historians agree that the Catholic vote shifted toward Andrew Jackson's new Democratic Party.

John Quincy Adams, the 1824 candidate of the National-Republican Party, was known as a stubborn, self-righteous nationalist, and he also had a dark side when it came to the Church of Rome. He feared that the growing Irish Catholic presence in urban America might have a "pernicious influence" on political elections.[20] In a speech he delivered in Baltimore, Adams described the Catholic Church as a "portentous system of despotism and superstition." Historian George Lipsky reports in his biography of Adams that ". . . he particularly despised Roman Catholicism's domination in those countries where the 'sceptered tyrant' could give protection to the theology of the 'canonized fanatic.' . . ."[21]

On election day, although Jackson carried a plurality in the eighteen of twenty-four states that permitted direct popular vote, he failed to carry a majority of the Electoral College. He received 99 votes, to Adams's 84, Crawford's 41, and Clay's 37. Constitutionally, this threw the election into the House of Representatives, and the stalemate was broken when Henry Clay threw his votes to Adams. When he heard rumors that Clay had secured the office of Secretary of State for his support of Adams, a livid Jackson condemned the deal and swore revenge.

But after the election data were analyzed, the Jacksonians saw hope in the midst of defeat. In states where there was universal male suffrage (Pennsylvania, New Jersey, and Maryland), the Democrats won easily, thanks in large measure to the Catholic vote. They looked forward hopefully to 1828.

But as Jackson was plotting his comeback, the specter of anti-Catholicism appeared again in the form of a shocking case of murder and corruption, and in a political movement that at first seemed a reason for hope among Catholics but quickly became a cause of worry.

In August 1826, William Morgan of Batavia, New York, was abducted by a group of Freemasons and carted off to Niagara. Morgan, an ex-Mason, had threatened to expose the secret rituals of this anti-Catholic organization. For violating the society's secrecy oath, Morgan's captors drowned him in the Niagara River.

A shocked community demanded an investigation, but the Order of Freemasons used their influence to sweep the incident under the rug. When called upon to intervene in early 1827, even New York's governor and state legislature refused to act.

Citizen groups and newspaper editorials bellowed that there was a vast conspiracy in play to subvert the law. Believing that "the Masonic fraternity . . . outraged humanity and violated all law,"[22] anti-Mason groups organized as a political party and nominated candidates to take on what they perceived to be the Masonic-controlled state legislature. Their platform was succinct – they opposed the two major parties for failing to respond to their demands:

> The violated laws of the country and the unavenged blood of a murdered citizen were not questions of sufficient importance to withdraw them from the pursuit of political honors. . . . The people were left to oppose Freemasonry without the aid of the laws and unsupported by the countenance of leading men. Indeed, so cautious were the prominent politicians, that none of them could be induced to identify their efforts and commit their fortunes to the hands of men devoted to the cause of liberty.[23]

The call to arms spread beyond the borders of New York. Anti-Masonic editorials and the *Anti-Masonic Review* were circulated in Vermont, Connecticut, Pennsylvania, Massachusetts, and Ohio. The literature characterized Masons as elitist monsters who fancied themselves above the law. Activists also organized the Anti-Masonic Party to protect the common man from secret organizations committed to destroying individual liberties and establishing aristocratic privileges for their membership.

This populist appeal attracted the agrarian downtrodden who needed a scapegoat for their plight, but because most Masonic Lodges were located in urban areas, the anti-Masonic movement expanded to include some poor city dwellers as well. In any case, Anti-Masonry became a political and religious crusade to free rural America from urban domination.

But as Baptists, Methodists, Presbyterians, and Congregationalists joined the cause, the Anti-Masons fixed their attacks on another group that to them was a growing threat – members of the Church of Rome. This was ironic, given that Freemasonry was strongly opposed by the Catholic Church. But in the reasoning of the Anti-Masons, Freemason equaled urban and urban equaled Catholic. "Anti-Masons compared Masonic rituals and hierarchy to Roman Catholicism, which evangelical Protestants considered anathema. 'Popery and Freemasonry [are] schemes equally inconsistent with Republicanism' declared a Pennsylvania newspaper."[24]

Although the Anti-Masons proclaimed they were for democracy, they called on rights to be limited, not expanded. Catholics and immigrants, in their judgment, were by their very nature anti-American and had to be prevented from holding office or from becoming citizens.

The explosion of this political movement on the national scene threatened to have a serious impact on the presidential election of 1828. With the disintegration of the political parties from the Jeffersonian era, the Anti-Masons saw an opportunity to exploit their issues and to punish the emerging Jacksonian coalition for pandering to Catholic immigrants.

After four years in office, the aristocratic Adams was an unpopular president. Although he was a brilliant administrator and a superior foreign policy analyst, he lacked political horse-trading skills and did not suffer fools gladly. He stood firmly for high tariffs, federally financed internal improvements, and the National Bank. His inflexibility annoyed the public in every region of the country.

While Adams was alienating people, Jackson labored on cementing a new coalition of northern immigrants, western settlers, and southern Jeffersonian state-rights advocates. To appeal to this coalition of common folks, Jackson ran on a simple platform:

> We believe, then, in the principle of *democratic republicanism*, in its strongest and purest sense. We have an abiding confidence in the virtue, intelligence, and full capacity for self-government of the great mass of our people – our industrious, honest, manly, intelligent millions of freemen.[25]

The upcoming campaign had the makings of an exciting one because the candidates had well-defined opposing visions of the role of the national government. Also twenty-two of the twenty-four states would choose their electors by direct popular vote. It was also an ugly campaign with both sides guilty of gross slander and misrepresentation. Yet, as Democrats and National-Republicans were slinging mud, they realized that the greatest unknown in the election would be the impact of the Anti-Masons.

President Adams, attempting to hold on to New York's electoral votes and offset Martin Van Buren's political machine, cast his lot with the Anti-Masons. He denounced secret societies, and he even agreed to reveal the inner workings of Phi Beta Kappa.

In New York, Van Buren had established the "Albany Regency" – an informal governing council consisting of grass roots political power brokers from around the state. This council handled all political matters and divided up patronage to deserving members, particularly Catholic members of the growing Democratic Party. With universal suffrage, Van Buren Democrats cultivated New York City's Irish, French, and German immigrants and provided them with services and favors. They even placed respected members of these ethnic communities "upon their local tickets, remembering others with disposition of the humbler posts in departmental offices and in labor contracts for the City."[26]

At heart a Jeffersonian, Van Buren fought hard to destroy the remaining influence of Federalists in New York. "He belonged to the states' rights school, was strict in his interpretation of the Constitution and most important, was dedicated to the maintenance of Party harmony at all costs."[27]

To cement a winning Democratic coalition and further counteract the Anti-Masons, the popular Van Buren endorsed Jackson and agreed to run for governor.

Reading the political handwriting on the wall, even the former New York governor, U.S. senator, and mayor of New York City, DeWitt Clinton, "of the venerable Presbyterian dynasty in New York who had flirted for some years with former Federalists, was now an all-out Jackson man." In part to help salvage his waning political career, he too came to the defense of Catholic voters and helped to organize them. His actions on behalf of Catholics were to be remembered, particularly by the Irish, for decades to come. At one testimonial dinner Clinton received this praise.

> While a Senator of the United States you stood foremost in preparing and carrying into law the existing mode of naturalization . . . When many of us fled from despotism, and sought refuge in this emancipated land, the spirit of intolerance pursued us across the Atlantic and spared no effort to embitter our existence, and prolong our sorrows; . . . you rebuked with effect that churlish and savage jealousy, from which professed republicans are not always

> exempt. . . . Even here, a qualification oath was required from
> members of the Legislature, which could not be consistently taken
> by members of the Catholic faith! On this as on every other occa-
> sion, reason and justice found you their able and successful advo-
> cate.[28]

Admiring the organizational skills of Van Buren and Clinton, Democrats throughout the nation attempted to copy the New York party structure he created. To the faithful they cried:

> To the Polls! The faithful sentinel must not sleep – Let no one
> stay home – Let every man go to the polls – Let not a vote be lost
> – Let each freeman do his duty; and all will triumph in the success
> of Jackson, Calhoun and Liberty.[29]

For the Anti-Masons, stopping the evil Jackson was their raison d'être. To meet this end they put aside their pride and populist rhetoric and collaborated with the National-Republicans and the remaining New England Federalists.

The great irony of the election of 1828 was that two groups that distrusted each other, Masons and Catholics, found they had no alternative but to rally around the candidacy of Andrew Jackson. And this coalition managed to carry the day – Jackson won 56 percent of the votes cast and received 68 percent of the Electoral College. While Adams's electoral support was limited to New England, Jackson received majority support in the other sectors of the country. Old Jeffersonians delivered the South; Western settlers delivered Missouri, Tennessee and Kentucky; urban Catholics delivered popular majorities in New York and Pennsylvania. The nation's leading Jackson historian, Robert Remini, concluded that "Adams's defeat was fashioned in large measure by his failure to attract votes from among the German, Irish and Scotch-Irish population."[30] His loss in New York by only 5,000 votes was due to the overwhelming support Jackson received from Irish and German Catholics. The election of 1828 changed the balance of political power in America – the upper classes no longer controlled the mechanics of government and the new merchant class, in which middle-class Catholics participated, was preparing to take over.

*   *   *   *   *

With the National-Republican Party in total disarray and the Democratic Party in the infant stages of developing a network in every state, the Anti-Masons thought they could fill a void and become a national party. They promoted themselves as "the organization of the people against a secret society – of Republicans against grand kings."[31]

To prove they were to be reckoned with, the Anti-Masons convened their first national convention on September 11, 1830. Attending were ninety-six delegates representing ten states with New York's delegation controlling the proceedings. Unable to agree on a candidate to run for president in 1832, they decided to adjourn for one year.

During the next twelve months, plenty of political jockeying took place within Anti-Masonic circles. And one political wiz who kept an eye on their doings was the developer of the "American System" of national internal improvements – Henry Clay. Biting at the bit to take on his arch-political enemy, Andrew Jackson, Clay hoped to unify all factions opposed to the philosophy of the Democratic Party.

To endear himself to the Anti-Masons, Clay offered to help them in New York local elections if they would endorse his team of presidential electors. But in 1831 the National Anti-Masonic leadership rejected the Clay deal, preferring to run their own candidate. After former president John Quincy Adams declined their nomination, the Anti-Mason convention turned to former U.S. Attorney General William Wirt of Virginia. To contend with this candidate who could cut into his national support, Henry Clay directed his National-Republican operatives to make, whenever possible, local deals with Anti-Masons. In Ohio, Pennsylvania, and New York, the two parties agreed to support the same gubernatorial candidates. New York's Anti-Masons and National-Republicans filed a joint slate of presidential electors. In Pennsylvania, Clay's forces threw their support behind Anti-Mason electors, while in Ohio the Anti-Masons endorsed the Clay slate.

Labeled the "Siamese Twin Party," the cynical cooperation between Clay and the Anti-Masons backfired – Jackson's coalition carried the nation in 1832 with an even greater electoral majority, 219 votes, or 76 percent of the total. In Pennsylvania and New York, states where Anti-Masons were considered most powerful, Jackson triumphed. These two victories were attributed once again, to the huge turnout of Irish and German Catholics for the president. In fact, the 1832 Anti-Mason campaign served as the catalyst that cemented the immigrant Catholics' political affinity for the Democratic Party.

* * * * *

As the flow of immigration increased from a trickle in the 1820s to a flood in the 1840s, Yankee apprehensiveness began to increase dramatically. And what began as an underground anti-Catholic movement led by back-alley, low-life bigots flared into a full-fledged anti-Catholic crusade that came close to leaving major northeast cities in shambles.

A staple of the nativist movement was the publication by underground presses of spurious books attacking Catholics. Titles included *Female Convents: Secrets of Nunneries Disclosed* and *Jesuits Juggling: Forty Popish Frauds Detected and Disclosed*; Mary George's *An Answer to Six Months in a Convent: Exposing its Falsehoods and Manifold Absurdities*; Maria Monk's *Awful Disclosure of the Hotel Dieu Nunnery*; and Maria Monk's *Further Disclosures*. Although Monk's first book was discredited, it managed to sell 300,000 copies. These books accused Catholic clerics and nuns of being sexual degenerates. "The impression created by these writers was that convents and monasteries were dens of vice and iniquity in which nuns and monks wallowed in a slough of ignorance and corruption."[32] One sympathetic observer concluded, "The abuse of the Catholics is a regular trade, and the compilation of anti-Catholic books has become a part of the regular industry of the country as much as the making of nutmegs, or the construction of clocks."[33]

Incited by the Congregationalist Church's General Association proclamation of 1829 that pastors must save "the country from the degrading influence of popery,"[34] numerous Catholic homes were torched in the Boston area. Isolated acts of violence against Catholics continued throughout the early 1830s.

The anti-Catholic literature and rhetoric incited one particularly gruesome mob incident in August 1835. When an overworked and exhausted teacher abruptly left the Ursuline Convent School and then, a short time later, received permission from the bishop of Boston to return to work, rumors rapidly spread that the teacher had been forced back into the convent against her will. Angry Protestant members of the community took to the streets with the intent to destroy the convent.

On August 11, crowds gathered outside the grounds carrying banners and screaming "Down with the Cross." Over fifty men broke into and ransacked both the convent and the school's dormitory. The mob also violated the graveyard and dug up coffins. After clearing the children from the dormitory, the buildings were torched. Hundreds of onlookers, including members of the fire brigade, cheered as the structures burned.

Fearing Irish-Catholic reprisals, thousands of Protestants "policed" the streets of Boston – but they were really searching for trouble. A shack was torched that housed thirty-five Irish laborers.

After the community settled down, a trial of some of the Protestant rioters was convened. It must have seemed to most Catholics that the trial was a kangaroo court, especially when the Massachusetts attorney general, who led the prosecution, was prohibited by a judge's ruling from asking prospective jurors if they hated Catholics. "The trial lasted for ten days, the testimony . . . was 'point blank and sufficient to have convicted twenty men,' but it soon became apparent that the state had no intention of securing a conviction."[35]

When the accused were declared not guilty, thunderous applause broke out in the courtroom.[36]

Incidents of anti-Catholic mob rule were reported from all parts of the region. Guards had to be posted outside the doors of Catholic churches throughout New England. The attacks caused such extensive damage that insurance companies canceled policies on Catholic real estate.

On the first anniversary of the Ursuline Convent arson, there were parades throughout Charlestown and images of the mother superior were burned in effigy.

During this period, several anti-Catholic societies were founded, among them the Society for the Diffusion of Light on the Subject of Romanism and the Society to Promote the Principles of the Protestant Reformation. Their intent was to disseminate "No-Popery" propaganda and to encourage members to adopt radical nativist attitudes.

Followers were asked to believe that immigrants were plotting with the Roman Catholic Church to destroy the United States. They were informed that the pope and European royalty, by way of Catholic New Orleans, were going to seize control of the Mississippi Valley. The claim was made that Catholic pioneers migrating west were plotting to unite with a papal army and launch an insurrection. One nativist organization declared: "We regard the Pope as an imposter; and the Mother Church as the mother of abominations. We don't believe in the close-shaven, white-cravated, black-coated priesthood, who profess to 'mortify the flesh' by eschewing matrimony and violating nature. We don't believe in the mummeries of prayers in unknown tongues; nor in the impious assumption of the power to forgive sins – to send the soul of a murderer to heaven, or to curse the soul of a good man down to the other place. We don't believe in Nunneries, where beauty that was made to bloom and beam on the world is immured and immolated, not to say prostituted."[37]

Pamphlets warned Protestants in the Mississippi Valley that Rome wanted to dominate the region and "build up a system of ignorance, priest craft and superstition, such as now casts a blight over some of the fairest portions of Europe."[38]

In New York, Samuel F. B. Morse, inventor of the telegraph, wrote an anti-Catholic series – in twelve parts – for the *New York Observer*. Morse asserted his belief in "a foreign conspiracy against the liberties of the United States." He accused Austria of collaborating with the Catholic Church in urging immigrants to destroy American freedom and impose a Catholic tyranny. He urged Protestants of all sects to oppose the election or appointment of Catholics to public office, and he advocated more restrictive immigration and laws to weaken Catholic schools. His essays, which were published in pamphlet form and distributed across the nation, contained this warning:

Americans, you are marked for their prey, not by foreign bayonets, but by *weapons surer of effecting the conquest of liberty* than all the munitions of physical combat in the military or naval store-houses of Europe. Will you not awake to the apprehension of the reality and extent of your danger? Will you be longer deceived by the pensioned Jesuits, who having surrounded your press, are now using it all over the country to stifle the cries of danger, and lull your fears by attributing your alarm to a false case? Up! Up! I beseech you. Awake! To your posts! Let the tocsin sound from Maine to Louisiana. Fly to protect the vulnerable places of your Constitution and Laws. Place your guards; you will need them, and quickly too. – And first, shut your gates."[39]

Believing the truth of Morse's accusations, some nativists urged Congress in 1838 to investigate the alleged Catholic conspiracy in order to determine if: "a plan in operation, powerful and dangerous . . . for the subversion of our civil and religious liberties, to be effected by the emigration of Roman Catholics from Europe, and by their admission to the right of suffrage with us in our political institutions."[40]

It was further alleged that a Catholic conspiracy was under way to take control of schools that received government funding. Nativist propagandists hoped mainstream Protestants would be attracted to their cause by the specter of the corruption of American youth. This seemed likely to some when the Catholic bishops expressed their objection to the use of the King James Bible in public school classrooms. The stage was set for a clash between the Protestant leaders and the Catholic hierarchy.

The stated goal of the New York City Public School Society was to "inculcate the sublime truths of religion and morality contained in the Holy Scripture."[41] The city's Common Council, which received appropriated state funds, delegated authority to the society for both spending and the implemen-tation of educational policies.

As a result, both the King James Bible and Protestant textbooks that degraded Catholics were utilized in New York's classrooms. History texts described the Catholic Church as a corrupt organization. "The presence of these books in a public school system receiving support from the state cer-tainly gave Catholics the right to demand more just treatment."[42]

New York's Whig governor, William Seward, acceded to Catholic requests and voiced support for "the establishment of schools in which . . . [students] may be instructed by teachers speaking the same language with themselves and professing the same faith."[43] Pleased with the governor's position, Catholics began opening their own schools and requested funding from the state. The Public School Society objected, however, and the Com-mon Council succumbed to pressure and refused to appropriate state money to Catholic schools.

The newly appointed bishop of New York, John Hughes, decided to issue a direct challenge to the Common Council. Bishop Hughes was known to be outspoken, and he was also vigorous and tireless. He let it be known that Catholic children had a fundamental right not to be proselytized in public schools, and he petitioned the Common Council to appropriate a fair share of funds for the operation of parochial schools. "We are unwilling," he declared, "to pay taxes for the purpose of destroying our religion in the minds of our children."[44]

The Protestants did not look kindly upon the requests. Tempers flared in the pulpit and in the press. One minister told his congregation, "I do say that if the fearful dilemma were forced upon me, of becoming an infidel or a Roman Catholic, according to the entire system of popery, with all its idolatry, superstition and violent opposition to the Holy Bible, I would rather be an infidel than a papist."[45]

Putting pressure on the Common Council, one newspaper declared that the government ought not to give funds "to train their children to worship a ghostly monarchy of vicars, bishops, archbishops, cardinals and popes. They demand of us to take away our children's funds and bestow them on the subjects of Rome, the creatures of a foreign hierarchy."[46]

Although the Common Council rejected Hughes's request, he refused to give up and asked the state legislature to intervene. Governor Seward sided with the Catholics and wrote to the Public School Society, "I seek the education of those whom I have brought before you . . . not to perpetuate any prejudices or distinctions which deprive them of instruction, but in disregard of all distinctions and prejudices. I solicit their education less from sympathy, than because the welfare of the state demands it and cannot dispense with it."[47]

With opinions split, and with New York City local elections looming that would decide the fate of fifteen state legislators, Albany decided to bide its time on the issue.

Angered by the legislative impasse, Bishop Hughes called a town-hall meeting of Catholic voters four days before the election. To punish the Democrats for sidestepping the issue, Hughes unveiled an independent slate of Catholic candidates. Hughes was fully aware that this move would probably cost the Democrats the election – but it would prove that the immigrants' vote was decisive and could not be taken for granted.

On Election Day, the Whigs carried the day by a 2,200 vote margin – the exact amount the Catholic ticket received. "Hughes had demonstrated beyond reasonable doubt that the Democrats could not afford to cast off their Catholic supporters if they wanted success."[48]

To make amends with New York City's Catholics, the Democrats passed and Governor Seward signed the Maclay Bill that abolished the Public School Society's role in education and established a secular board of elected education commissioners who would supervise the schools and dispense funds in their respective wards.

Under the headline, "Triumph of the Roman Catholics," the *New York Observer* lamented that "the dark hour is at hand. . . . People must only trust in God to be saved from the beast." Bishop Hughes's house was stoned, and armed guards were required to protect Catholic churches.

While nativist candidates won the majority of school board seats in the June 1843 elections, Catholics did manage to carry seats in their heavily populated neighborhoods. And the Catholic representatives had enough sway to establish policies that ended classroom reading of Protestant bibles to Catholic children.

These victories did, however, cause "No-Popery" sentiment to grow. Hughes was frequently described in the press as a "crafty priest" and a "dictator." "A new group of propaganda writers, both in the press and through books and pamphlets, agreed that the sole reason Papists sought to control state educational funds was to propagate their doctrines of error and win converts from among Protestants."[49] Newspapers called for the punishment of Governor Seward for his approval of the Maclay Bill, and in the 1843 election he was booted out of office.

Anti-Catholic groups began to unite throughout the nation. At its 1843 National General Assembly, the Presbyterian Church passed this resolution:

> Resolved, That it is the deliberate and decided judgment of this General Assembly, that the Roman Catholic church has essentially apostatized from the religion of our Lord and Savior Jesus Christ; and therefore cannot be recognized as a Christian Church.
>
> Resolved, That it be recommended to all in our communion to endeavor by the diffusion of light by the pulpit, the press and all other Christian means, to resist the extension of Romanism, and lead its subjects to the knowledge of the truth, as it is taught in the word of God.
>
> Resolved, That it is utterly inconsistent with the strongest obligations of Christian parents to place their children for education in Roman Catholic Seminaries.[50]

To many Catholics, it may have seemed as though they had never been so unwelcome in the United States. Some must have speculated that things were so bad that they surely could not get worse.

They could not have been more wrong.

Chapter 4
The Catholic Voter Versus the Nativist Voter

Violence was on the rise – New York, Boston, Philadelphia, Baltimore, Detroit, Cincinnati, and St. Louis all experienced disorder. Philadelphia was a tinder box because the Catholic population was on the verge of outnumbering the Protestants. In 1808, there were 10,000 Catholics out of a total population of 47,000. By 1832, there were 100,000 Catholics of Irish and German descent out of a total population of 258,000.

In 1843 the legislature of the Commonwealth of Pennsylvania, fearing both the growing Catholic presence in the state and a consequent increase in anti-Catholic activities, passed a resolution that prevented any religious sect from gaining control of the public schools. The final section of the law read:

> Resolved, That this Board cannot but consider the introduction or use of any religious exercises, books, or lessons into the Public Schools, which have not been adopted by the Board, as contrary to the law; and the use of any such religious exercises, books, or lessons, is hereby directed to be discontinued.[1]

On paper, religious liberty in the schools was guaranteed – and religious indoctrination banned – but the law did not stop some militantly anti-Catholic teachers from pursuing their own agenda.

After a Catholic teacher was wantonly fired, the bishop of Philadelphia, Patrick Kenrick, wrote to the Public School Board of Comptrollers demanding fair play. He requested that the 5,000 Catholic children in the school system be permitted to read a Catholic version of the Bible and that anti-Catholic text books be removed from the classrooms. Kenrick forced the hand of the board, and this resolution was passed:

> Resolved, that no children be required to attend or unite in the reading of the Bible in the Public Schools, whose parents are conscientiously opposed thereto:

> Resolved, that those children whose parents conscientiously prefer and desire any particular version of the Bible, without note or comment, be furnished with same.[2]

But if this was reason for Catholics to celebrate, the resolution also outraged some in the Protestant community. With what they took to be community support, more than a few Protestant teachers simply ignored the board's order, and the poor treatment of Catholic children actually grew worse. Bishop Kenrick's insistence that the "Liberty of Conscience" resolution be enforced was ignored. "Legitimate authorities would not protect the religious liberty of Catholic children nor the religious rights of their parents."[3]

Protestant sentiment was rapidly approaching hysteria. The American Protestant Association, whose Constitution called Catholicism "subversive of civil and religious liberty," was appalled by Kenrick's statements and stirred up a backlash. One commentator wrote, "The interference of foreign prelates and of a foreign ecclesiastical power should perish at our threshold. Let a grave be sunk then, over which even the great papal hierarch himself cannot stop."[4] At an Independence Square rally on March 11, 1844, the audience was urged to pledge the following:

> That the present crisis demands that without distinction of party, sect, or profession, every man who loves his country, his Bible, and his God, is bound by all lawful and honorable means to resist every attempt to banish the Bible from our public institutions.[5]

Tensions grew and on May 3, assemblies turned into mobs and took to the streets. Three days later a nativist group, the American Republicans, fired shots at an Irish firehouse and one nativist was killed.

Crowds gathered throughout the city by torchlight, and violence broke out. While some, including Bishop Kenrick, were trying to cool tempers, *The Native American* newspaper threw fuel on the blaze with this May 7 editorial:

> Heretofore we have been among those who have entered out solemn protest against any observations that would bear the slightest semblance of making the Native cause a religious one, or charging upon our adopted fellow-citizens any other feeling than that of a mistaken opinion as to our views and their own rights. We hold back no longer. We are now free to declare that *no terms whatever* are to be held with these people.
>
> Another St. Bartholomew's day is begun on the streets of Philadelphia. The bloody hand of the Pope has stretched itself forth to our destruction. We now call on our fellow-citizens, who regard free institutions, whether they be native or adopted, to arm. Our liberties are now to be fought for; – let us not be slack in our preparations.

Urged on by such rabble-rousing editorials, nativist mobs attacked Irish neighborhoods. An unenthusiastic militia failed to hold back the crowd, and St. Michael's Church was torched on the third day of the riots.

While pleading for peace from the steps of St. Augustine's Church, Bishop Kenrick was pushed aside by an angry mob who burnt to the ground the Church and an adjoining monastery with its 5,000 book library. "The crowd gave a big cheer when the cross on top of the steeple fell to the ground."[6] Even some peace-loving Quakers sided with the nativists. They announced, "the Papists deserve all this and much more. . . . It were well if every Popish church in the world were leveled to the ground."[7]

By May 8 sixteen had died, and scores of Catholic homes had been destroyed. News of this destruction spread rapidly and, in New York, the American Republicans urged a national crusade:

> They have commenced the war of blood. Thank God, they are not yet strong enough to overcome us with brute force. There is yet time to stay the bloody hand of tyranny. A revolution has begun. "Blood will have Blood." It cannot sink into the earth and be forgotten. The gory vision will rise like the ghost of the murdered Banquo, and call for revenge.[8]

Hearing that nativist mobs were roaming New York's streets hoping to replicate the actions of their Philadelphia comrades, Bishop John Hughes publicly condemned the violence in Philadelphia. He told one Catholic group:

> Convents have been burned down, and no compensation offered to their scattered inmates; Catholic churches have been burned down, while whole neighborhoods have been, under the eye of public officers, reduced to ashes. People have been burned to death in their own dwellings; or if they attempted to escape, have been shot down by the deadly messenger of the unerring rifle. Crosses have been pulled down from the summits of God's sanctuary. Priests have been tarred and feathered. Ladies have been insulted for no crime except that of having devoted themselves to the service of their divine Master in a religious state, in the hope of conferring aid or consolation on their fellow-beings. . . . These things were the work of what is called mobs; but we confess our disappointment at not having witnessed a prompt and healthy, true American sentiment in the heart of the community at large in rebuke of such proceedings, and so far as reparation was possible, in making it to the injured parties whom they had failed to protect.[9]

Believing that Philadelphia Catholics should have defended Church property, he warned New York's City nativist mayor, James Harper: "If a single Catholic Church were burned in New York, the City would become a second Moscow."[10] The thought of New York City looking like the Moscow Napoleon left in ashes in 1812 had the desired effect: nativist forces backed down.
America's cities did calm down, and through the remainder of the decade, there were only occasional isolated incidences of anti-Catholic violence. The American Republican Party was discredited, and nativism collapsed as a political movement. But nativist sentiment did not completely disappear, and various groups, some open and some secret, continued to organize throughout the nation, hoping for an opportunity to strike. In 1849 alone, more than 2-million pages of nativist propaganda were distributed.[11]

* * * * *

In the spring of 1834, a group of men gathered to form what was to become the political home of Henry Clay, Daniel Webster, and Abraham Lincoln – the Whig Party. Committed to ending the Jacksonian era, the Whigs attempted to meld the loyalties of National Republicans, advocates of the "American System," opponents of states' rights, and the Anti-Masonic movement as well. In the party's 1836 national debut, the Whigs ran electoral slates in every state but could not agree on a single presidential candidate. As a result, electors committed to William Henry Harrison were filed in fifteen states, for Hugh L. White in nine southern states, and for Daniel Webster in Massachusetts. While this fragmented alliance could not stop the election of Jackson's chosen successor, Martin Van Buren, America now had in place two political parties that would debate the great issues confronting the nation in the pre-Civil War period.

By 1840, the Whig Party had unified around Harrison, the hero of the 1811 victory over Tecumseh at the battle of Tippecanoe. The "Panic of 1837" had wrecked the economy, and the Whigs believed they had a chance to unseat President Van Buren. They promoted their candidate as another Andrew Jackson and copied the Democratic Party's grass-roots operation.

Van Buren, who had written the blueprint for party organization back in New York, continued to pay close attention to the needs of local ward healers, but he knew that his party was divided over the nation's economic mess, and he also knew that the old religious coalition was crumbling.

While Catholics stayed within the Democratic fold, Presbyterians, Baptists, and Congregationalists aligned themselves with the Whigs.[12] Nativist Protestants circulated the rumor that some priests were getting favors for their flocks in exchange for delivering Democratic votes. However he may have felt about it in his heart, Harrison went along with the nativist sentiment, because he had been stung by their venom. In 1835, after he had made a visit to Mount St. Mary's, a Catholic girls school, a petition condemning him was sent to Congress.[13]

Inner-city Whigs also sided with the nativist elements, while rural voters aligned with the Whigs because of the party's economic platform. The Whigs promoted themselves as "the party of law, of order, of improvement, of benef-icence, of hope and of humanity,"[14] and they portrayed the Democrats as wild-eyed Irish drunkards and reprobates. The Whig Party that took on Van Buren was an amalgamation of groups that opposed Jacksonian democracy and immigrants in America's inner cities.

For the first time in America's history both parties organized "get out the vote" operations in every state. Convention delegates came from every walk of life, not simply from aristocratic cliques.

Harrison was the first candidate to stump for votes. Ironically, the Whig nominee described himself as just another common folk while he portrayed his Jacksonian Democratic opponent as an aristocratic dandy.

The efforts succeeded with a record-breaking 80.2 percent turnout of eli-gible voters. In New York, for instance, 91.9 percent of the voters marked a ballot. William Henry Harrison succeeded in bringing the Age of Jackson to a close by receiving 52.9 percent of the vote versus Van Buren's 46.8 percent. The total votes cast were 2.4 million, a 900,000 increase over the 1836 total of 1.5 million. Harrison managed to carry nineteen states representing 234 electoral votes. Van Buren, who received 400,000 more votes than he had tal-lied in 1836, wound up with only 60 electoral votes from seven states.

The Whigs carried New York and Pennsylvania by narrow margins. In New York the margin of victory was only 12,000 votes out of 438,000 cast and in Pennsylvania the margin was even closer. Out of 280,000 votes cast, Harrison beat Van Buren in the Keystone State by 1,000 votes.

The race was tight in these two states because the Catholic vote came out in droves for Van Buren. In the Catholic-dominated New York boroughs of Manhattan and Queens, Van Buren won by wide margins. In Pennsylvania, Van Buren carried heavily Catholic-populated Philadelphia and the German-Catholic agricultural counties. New York's Whig governor, William Seward, who was friendly with Catholic leaders, conceded that in 1840 "the Irishmen ... voted against us generally, and far more generally than heretofore."[15]

On Inauguration Day, March 4, 1841, the triumphant Whigs gathered in Washington to bid farewell to the Jacksonians – but their joy was short-lived. Standing in the rain, the sixty-eight-year-old President Harrison read a nine-ty-minute inaugural address – the longest in U.S. history – caught pneumonia and died on April 14. Succeeded by "his accidency," John Tyler, a southerner chosen to balance the ticket – was not much of a Whig. Tyler was "a strict constructionist, an ardent champion of states' rights and a defender of the South's domestic institutions."[16]

Frustrated by the Whig's inability to implement the "American System" program, Henry Clay convinced his party in 1844 to dump Tyler and to nominate himself.

The Democrats, split over the annexation of Texas issue, refused to renominate former President Van Buren who was hesitant on the issue. Instead, they turned to Tennessee Governor and former Speaker of the U.S. House of Representatives, James Polk.

Sensing that the nation was evenly split on the issues of the day, the sly Clay tried to appeal to rapidly growing Catholic votes without upsetting his Protestant base. This was a difficult task for Clay, because the nativist movement was once again on the rise. In New York City, for instance, the newly formed nativist splinter party, the American Republicans, had made serious inroads in the local elections of 1843. They received 8,600 votes versus 14,000 for the Whigs and 14,410 for the Democrats. In the spring of 1844, the American Republicans triumphed at the polls and with 25,570 votes elected James Harper the city's mayor. The Whigs came in third place receiving 5,297 votes versus 20,538 for the Democrats. The nativists also scored 184 victories in Philadelphia County municipal elections.

When the American Republican Party petitioned Clay to support the languishing congressional bill to restructure the naturalization laws, the Great Compromiser attempted to straddle the issue. On the one hand, he conceded that the American Republican Party was right on naturalization "if conducted with discretion and prudence," but on the other hand he questioned "whether it be expedient to throw any new issues into the Presidential Canvass."[17] Clay wanted the support of the nativists but he did not want to make a direct plea to them. And to further complicate his strategy, the Whig Party nominated New Jersey anti-Catholic, Theodore Frelinghuysen, to be Clay's running mate. This former chancellor of New York University and Senator from New Jersey was to play the role of defender of the Whig platform that endorsed "discriminating for the protection of the domestic labor of the Country."

James Polk's Democrats pursued a strategy to keep the nativist issue alive. They knew the election would be close and that the states with large Catholic populations, New York and Pennsylvania especially, could decide the election. Their platform encouraged unrestricted immigration and endorsed cultural pluralism. They clung to "the liberal principles embodied by Jefferson and the Declaration of Independence, welcomed the oppressed of every nation and opposed repressive 'Americanization' laws."[18]

Sensing the election moving against his party, Daniel Webster publicly called for the Whigs to adopt "an efficient reformation of the naturalization laws"[19] and urged his party to align themselves with the nativists. He proposed that the Whigs support local nativist candidates in exchange for the American Republican Party's endorsement of the national ticket. Not all the Whigs went along with this approach. At a June 12, 1834,Whig gathering in Springfield, Illinois, a young lawyer named Abraham Lincoln broke with his party and proposed this resolution:

> Resolved, That the guarantee of the rights of conscience, as found in our Constitution, is most sacred and inviolable, and one that belongs no less to the Catholic, than to the Protestant; and that all attempts to abridge or interfere with these rights, either of Catholic or Protestant, directly or indirectly, have our decided disapprobation, and shall ever have our most effective opposition.[20]

In Pennsylvania, for instance, Whig newspapers openly attacked Democratic gubernatorial candidate, Henry Muhlenberg, as a pro-Catholic. The Democrat was condemned for participating in a Catholic Church groundbreaking ceremony and for supporting the Church's position on education funding. Democratic papers retaliated by condemning Whigs as bigots who believed "there can be no peace until the Catholics are exterminated from this country."[21]

In New York, the pleas of leading Whigs Horace Greeley and William Seward to avoid alliances with the nativists fell on deaf ears. But local political operatives made deals to form common slates of Whig and American Republican Party candidates. Believing his nativist strategy was making headway with the electorate, a confident Henry Clay told supporters in late October that: "Judging from the strong assurances which are given me . . . the Whigs will carry all four great states of New York, Pennsylvania, Virginia and Ohio [giving me] a larger electoral vote than was given to General Harrison in 1840."[22]

As expected, the election was very close. Out of 2.6 million votes cast, Polk won by a plurality of only 27,000. Clay's boasting fell flat – the only one of the big four states he carried was Ohio. The Electoral College broke down as follows: Polk's 170 versus Clay's 105. Four years earlier, Harrison had carried nineteen states for a total of 234 electoral votes.

In New York and Pennsylvania, where nativist activities had incited riots, Clay lost by the narrowest of margins.

	Polk	Clay	Polk	Clay
New York	237,588	232,482	50.5%	49.5%
Pennsylvania	167,535	161,203	50.9	49.1

In New York counties where there was a significant Catholic population, Polk had slim majorities:

	Polk	**Clay**
N.Y. County (Manhattan)	28,296	26,385
Queens County	2,751	2,547
Oneida	7,717	6,982
Onondaga	6,878	6,495

The results were similar in Pennsylvania's Catholic counties:

	Polk	**Clay**
Bucks	5,251	4,862
Lehigh	2,811	2,553
Montgomery	5,596	4,491

Philadelphia, the state's largest voting county, and the site of America's first major riots, was carried by Clay but not by enough to put the state in his electoral column.

	Polk	**Clay**
Philadelphia	18,851	23,289

Historian Lee Benson concluded that 95 percent of the Irish and 80 percent of the Germans voted Democratic in 1844. The Irish in New York, that state's largest immigrant group, voted 95 percent Democratic. The *Albany Evening Journal* claimed that 98 out of every 100 Irish supported Polk, and it was now clear that the old Federalist-Whig counties of upstate New York were feeling the political impact of the Catholic immigrants who had settled in their domains. The Town of Bombay in Whig Franklin County dominated by Irish farmers voted Democratic. In the Town of Java in Wyoming County, Polk received nearly 60 percent of the vote thanks to the newly settled Irish. German Catholics in Croghan in Lewis County voted more than 80 percent Democratic. French Canadians also sided with the Democrats, especially in Clinton County, where nearly three-quarters went Democratic, and in Chautauqua, where the Democrats received 72 percent. Viewing the election results, the Albany Whig newspaper concluded: "Catholic Irish voted Democratic in New York State, whether they lived in urban or rural communities, whether they were day laborers or free-hold farmers – in short, their voting represented an ethno-cultural or religious group, not a place or class, phenomenon."[23]

The election of 1844 proved that in many Northern states, particularly in

New York, the Catholic vote was becoming a major political factor and this growing power was causing ethnic tensions. The Anglo-American, Scotch, and Welsh looked upon these Catholic immigrants as "ignorant, immoral, drunken, violent, unable to delay sensual gratification for the achievement of future goals, given to crimes with sharp instruments and blessed only with a certain dumb willingness to engage in physical labor, musical talents, and a comical temper – attributes commonly applied by white Americans to Afro-Americans."[24] For their part, the Irish and German Catholics, a parochial people by nature, came to loathe the elitism and nationalism of the Yankee Whigs. "Germans loved their beer and their convivial Sundays and were offended by the aggressively Yankee tone of the public schools – which in truth were often established for the sole purpose of Anglicizing their children."[25] Irish immigrants felt the same.

Many of the Whigs who had approved of the alliance with nativists became bitter and brooding, and attacked the Democrats for courting the Catholic vote. "We deplore the want of true American patriotism," wrote one Whig, "which our opponents have exhibited throughout this contest in their appeals to foreigners and religious sects."[26] Many Whigs blamed their losses on "the spurious and illegal foreign vote."[27]

Practical Whigs, who analyzed the results, were forced to admit, however, that the nativist strategies backfired and cost them states Harrison had carried four years earlier. One Pennsylvanian asked, "Can we blame adopted citizens, under such circumstances, for leaving us?" Others conceded that the choice of vice-presidential candidate Frelinghuysen was a major error. A New York Whig complained that "Mr. F.'s nomination made the Catholic opposition intense."[28] Former Treasury Secretary Thomas Ewing, echoed this sentiment: "I felt during the whole canvass that we were suffering greatly by the connection of Mr. Frelinghuysen with our ticket. We . . . could not obviate the objections to Frelinghuysen on the part of most Catholics."[29] A future president, Millard Fillmore of New York, in a letter to Henry Clay, gave this analysis:

> [T]he abolitionists and *foreign* Catholics have defeated us in [New York]. . . . Our opponents, by pointing to Mr. Frelinghuysen, drove the *foreign* Catholics from us and defeated us. (emphasis added)

Reflecting on his loss, even Henry Clay conceded, "If there had been no native party or if all of its members had been truer to their principles; or if the recent foreigners had not all been united against us; or if the *foreign* Catholics had not been arrayed on the other side . . . we should have triumphed."[30]

Learning from his mistakes, Clay worked the comeback trail. He spent the next four years portraying himself as a friend of the immigrants while avoiding any criticism of his party for making arrangements with the American Republicans. In an 1847 address in the city of New Orleans, Clay flaunted his newly found humanitarian side by calling on the national government to provide relief to famine-stricken Ireland. During the Mexican War, he tried to appeal to Catholics by describing the plight of Mexicans as similar to the "poor, gallant, generous and oppressed Ireland."[31] His approach didn't work. Appalled by Clay's duplicity and his willingness to say anything to achieve the presidency, the Whigs rejected Clay in 1848 and turned to General Zachary Taylor, about whom more below.

After four years in the executive mansion, President Polk decided one term was enough. He could look with satisfaction on the American victory in the 1846–1848 war with Mexico – and the acquisition of 500,000 square miles of territory in the southwest that came with it – but he also knew he had alienated large segments of the population with his tariff increase. There were also two issues on the front burner that he preferred his successor to handle: the expansion of slavery and the nativist movement. Catholics and nativists were clashing on city streets, and bitter Van Buren supporters, resentful of their hero's rejection from four years earlier, were hatching a scheme to run an anti-slave splinter candidate for president.

On the fourth ballot at their 1848 convention, the Democrats nominated Senator Lewis Cass of Michigan for president and William O. Butler of Kentucky for vice president. They were optimistic of their chances for victory because General Taylor had never before sought office and was perceived as lacking political savvy. When asked where he stood on the nativist issue, the general managed to offend both sides with the comment that he was "a Whig but not an ultra Whig."

What saved the 1848 election for the Whigs, however, was a split in the Democratic Party. Former President Martin Van Buren accepted the nomination of the newly-formed Free Soil Party and Charles Francis Adams (son of John Quincy Adams) ran as his running mate. Organized in Buffalo, New York, on August 8, 1848, the Free Soil Party ran on a platform of "no more slave states and no more slave territory." Their battle cry was "free soil, free speech, free labor and free men."

Although on Election Day Van Buren and Adams received no electoral votes, they did receive 291,363 popular votes, or just under 18 percent of the total. In New York, Van Buren's home state, Free Soil won 41 percent of the total and outpolled the Democrats, and the Free Soil Party's totals provided the margin of defeat for Cass and Fillmore in Connecticut, Maine, Massachusetts, and Vermont. Catholics voters did stay with the Democrats, but the split with Free Soil diminished their impact. But the importance of the Catholic voter would increase dramatically in the next decade when anti-Catholic fervor reached its heights.

* * * * *

By mid-century, the membership of the Catholic Church in the United States was growing at a rapid pace and extended to all corners of the nation. In 1850 there were thirty-two dioceses with six of them archiepiscopal sees. Structurally, the Church doubled in size during the 1840s. Catholic membership reflected a combination of natural growth and mass European immigration, particularly from Ireland and Germany.

	U.S. Population	U.S. Catholic Population	% of Population
1840	14,195,000	663,000	4.6%
1850	19,553,000	1,606,000	8.2%
1860	26,922,000	3,103,000	11.52%

This growth had a dramatic impact on America's political demographics. In most presidential and local elections, the ever-increasing Catholic vote mattered. Democrats (and on occasions, the Whigs) not only sought their votes but sought out Catholic leaders to run for local offices in urban centers. Catholic councilmen, aldermen, and state legislators were elected and promoted laws that would enhance the quality of life for their constituents.

This Catholic political activism and Catholic electoral successes only increased nativist suspicion. And the 1845 severance of diplomatic relations and subsequent war with Mexico were grist for the nativist conspiracy mills.

After the breakdown of relations, the Mexican government sent troops north of the Rio Grande that engaged the soldiers of General Zachary Taylor. When word of the incident reached the executive mansion, President Polk demanded and received from the Congress a declaration of war.

The American armed forces experienced rapid success in the war. In May 1846, General Taylor defeated the Mexicans and occupied the City of Monterey. The Army's senior general, Winfield Scott, who took command of the Mexico City expedition in November 1846, captured Vera Cruz by March 1847 and Pueblo by May 15. American forces, under Scott, triumphantly entered Mexico City on September 11 and forced General Santa Ana to sue for peace.

While America was victorious on the battlefield, domestic propagandists were ignoring the news and instead were using the war to agitate anti-Catholic sentiment among some Protestants.

Nativists were appalled by a war with a Catholic nation, and many were convinced it was a Vatican plot. They feared that the spoils of war – acquisition of New Mexico and California – would flood the Nation with hundreds of thousands of dark-skinned Catholics.

Throughout the war rumors circulated that U.S. Catholic troops were deserting to defend the Mexican cause. This was false, but the lie spread within the ranks of the advancing Army. Catholic troops were ordered, on occasion, to attend Protestant services that included anti-Roman sermons. When President Polk appointed two Catholic chaplains to meet the spiritual needs of Catholic troops, there were outbursts against this decision throughout the nation. One paper denounced the move as a "flagrant outrage upon the Constitution."

But the conqueror of Mexico City had his own presidential ambitions, and he tried to keep peace between Protestant and Catholic troops. A "high-Anglican" Episcopalian, Scott had his daughters educated at Catholic convents. Throughout the war, he made sure that Catholic churches were not destroyed, and he even attended a victory Mass. Scott's courtesies prompted one Whig to complain, "our military saphead, Roman Catholic Scott, compelled the American Armies to prostate themselves in the mud whenever a crucifix or an idolatrous doll baby passed along . . . ."[32]

But that became a minority sentiment, and the Whig Party's success with General Taylor in 1848 led to the selection of Winfield Scott as their standard bearer in 1852, because they believed the war hero would appeal to Catholics. Besides, there continued to be schisms within Democratic ranks, and the Whigs thought the time was ripe to make significant inroads in urban areas densely populated with Catholic immigrants.

Irish Catholics were especially alienated when some Democrats joined an 1851–1852 New England coalition to prohibit the sale of alcohol. They were offended that their party accepted the widespread Protestant belief that the Irish were wicked because they were slaves to the "creature" – whiskey. Cracks in Catholic support of Democrats widened when the party in Massachusetts placed a temperance candidate on its gubernatorial ticket.

There were other incidents of Democratic disloyalty: When the entire statewide ticket in Pennsylvania was swept into office except the Irish-Catholic candidate, many Catholics concluded there had been a fix. Tensions were so high that the Whigs were convinced the Irish would swing their way in the next election.

While the Whigs were crowning General Scott, the Democrats, after much bickering, turned to Franklin Pierce of New Hampshire. Described as a "citizen-soldier," he had served in the New Hampshire legislature, U.S. Congress, and the U.S. Senate. In the Mexican War, he served with distinction as a brigadier general under Commander-in-Chief Winfield Scott. "The Democrats nomination of Pierce clinched the Whig's decision to seek Catholic and immigrant voters, for Pierce seemed particularly vulnerable to the charge of anti-Catholic bigotry."[33]

Because New Hampshire refused to repeal its constitutional provision that excluded Catholics from holding office, Whigs asserted that Pierce had to be anti-Catholic because he didn't push for change.

Charles O'Connor, a prominent New York Catholic did, however, come to Pierce's defense. He explained that in New Hampshire, a constitutional change required two-thirds support of the legislature – a super majority the Democrats did not control. Also, evidence was provided that proved Pierce attended a town meeting in Concord, New Hampshire, for "Friends of Democratic Equality and Religious Tolerance." The meeting came out against the ban on Catholics officeholders.

To counter the charges against Pierce, the Democrats unearthed dirty laundry in Scott's political closet. They released pro-nativist letters authored by Scott in the 1840s. In the most damaging letter he insisted that immigrant men, after naturalization, should be ordered to serve two years in the U.S. Army before being permitted to vote.[34] To counter these charges, Scott came up with an appeal that he hoped would sway Catholics in his audiences. In numerous Northeastern cities, he would say:

> I recognize before me persons of different parties, of different creeds, and of different countries. . . . I am proud to address native and adopted as American citizens. . . . I am proud to belong to the same country with you all. I detect in those cheers, gentlemen, a brogue I am always happy to hear. I have been in many tight places in my life, but I have never been deceived or betrayed by that brogue (cheers). I have always been sustained by the natives of the glorious Emerald Isle. . . . We had a goodly number of Irish soldiers who fought bravely in the Mexican War, and as I said, they never disappointed me – always brave and faithful.[35]

Scott apparently learned nothing from Henry Clay's 1844 attempt to play both sides of the fence on the Catholic vs. nativist issue. And just like Clay before him, the strategy backfired. "By early September, reports that virtually all Irishmen and Germans would go for Pierce far outnumbered predictions of significant Whig inroads into the immigrant vote."[36] Whigs sympathetic to the nativist movement wanted to punish Scott. Knowing that overt support for Pierce might drive Catholics into the Scott camp to siphon votes, they put up Daniel Webster as a third candidate in New York, New Jersey, and Pennsylvania. These Whig dissidents also supported the "Free Soil" candidate, John P. Hale.

When the results were tabulated, Scott was badly defeated. He carried only four states, and his vote total was 44 percent. "Some Whigs . . . recognized that alienating Protestants by wooing Catholics was a disastrous, and perhaps irredeemable, mistake."[37] Pierce carried his home state of New

Hampshire and all the states targeted by the Whig's Catholic strategy: Maine, Illinois, Michigan, Missouri, New Jersey, New York, Ohio, and Pennsylvania. All the major cities with large blocks of Catholic voters – Baltimore, Chicago, New York – went for Pierce. "The presidential election [of 1852] placed Franklin Pierce, a Democrat, in office and both Whig and nativists agreed that the foreign-born vote was largely responsible . . ."[38]

Election totals revealed that the Democrats carried 1,110 counties, 350 for the first time. Whigs carried the smallest number of counties in their history, 434. Counties that encompassed Catholic-dominated inner cities were easily carried by the Democrats.

The disastrous results shattered the Whig Party. Angry and bitter nativists began to look for a new home to harbor their hatred of Catholics, and New York's Charles Allen, founder of the Order of the Star Spangled Banner, sensed the time had come to turn his crusade into a national political movement.

In 1852, Allen successfully united nativist groups and societies throughout the nation. A national council was established to guide the blossoming state and local councils. This conglomerate of secret fraternal organizations formed the American Party in 1854 and were called by the general public, "Know-Nothings."

In the early 1850s, New York nativist Charles Allen founded a secret society of Protestants pledged to stop immigration. He called it the Order of the State Star Spangled Banner. The *sine qua non* for membership was affiliation with a Protestant sect. His Order, which had secret member handshakes and code words, joined with other fraternal organizations to form the American Party in 1854. If members were asked by outsiders about their society, they were ordered to give this simple answer, "I know nothing" – hence they were called by outsiders the "Know-Nothing" Party.

The Know-Nothings began to build political councils throughout America. In a nutshell, their platform called for stronger immigration laws and prohibition of Catholics from holding public office. Their activities were to seriously impact the body politic and contribute to the destruction of the Whigs.

The Know-Nothings promoted a philosophy of hate directed toward Catholic immigrants. Fearing their potential political and economic influence, the Know-Nothings hoped to curb future growth by extending naturalization laws to a twenty-one-year residency and by prohibiting Catholics from holding public office.

The new party's initial memberships consisted primarily of lower-class Protestants, who believed their woes were caused by immigrant Catholics. Some blamed Catholics for flooding the labor pool and driving down wages, and others believed Catholic voting power would destroy America. When the

Papal States fell in 1849, and the pope retreated behind the walls of the Vatican, many Know-Nothings convinced themselves the pope was planning to move to the Mississippi Valley and establish a new kingdom there. Still others believed that the Democratic Party had become the instrument by which Catholics would grab power and control America's governing institutions. Archbishop John Hughes added to this frenzy when he publicly admitted the Church's aim to convert America:

> There is no secret about this. The object we hope to accomplish in time, is to convert all Pagan nations, and all Protestant nations, even England with her proud Parliament and imperial sovereign. There is no secrecy in all this. It is the commission of God to his church, and not a human project. . . . Protestantism pretends to have discovered a great secret. Protestantism startles our eastern borders occasionally on the intention of the Pope with regard to the Valley of the Mississippi, and dreams that it has made a wonderful discovery. Not at all. Everybody should know it. Everybody should know that we have for our mission to convert the world – including the inhabitants of the United States, – the people of the cities, and the people of the country, the officers of the navy and the marines, commanders of the army, the Legislatures, the Senate, the Cabinet, the President, and all![39]

When President Pierce appointed Catholic James Campbell of Pennsylvania as the new postmaster general, the Know-Nothings concluded this action confirmed their conspiracy theories: the president wasn't just paying off political debts, he was setting the stage for a Catholic coup d'état.

Even though Know-Nothings had a diverse membership – northern abolitionists, southern slave owners, Whig "American System" supporters, states'-rights advocates, free traders, and high-tariff supporters – one issue kept them united: anti-Catholicism.

In 1854, American Party candidates defeated Democrats and the remnants of the Whig Party in local elections throughout the northeast and border states. Their greatest triumph was in Massachusetts where they elected a governor and 377 out of 378 state legislative seats.

By the fall of 1855, the Know-Nothings could boast political control of Delaware, Rhode Island, Connecticut, Kentucky, New York, Maryland, California, Pennsylvania, Virginia, Georgia, and Mississippi.[40] Seven governors, eight U.S. senators, and 104 congressmen were elected on anti-Catholic platforms. The nativists were swing votes in other states, and they effectively put the Whig Party out of business.

With the states they controlled totaling 44 percent of the Electoral

College, the Know-Nothings convinced themselves that by 1856 the executive mansion would be within their grasp. Boston's Catholic newspaper, *The Pilot*, conceded that American Party control of the national government was inevitable.

Recognizing the growing power of the Know-Nothings, displaced Whig Horace Greeley, a leading abolitionist and founder of the *New York Tribune*, sheepishly conceded that while disagreeing with their aims, he understood their frustrations:

> We have seen Irish bands of two or three hundred armed with heavy clubs, traversing the streets on election day and clearly provoking a fight. We have seen men taken to courts to be naturalized and put through like a sheep washing, when they did not know what they swore and when they were in no condition to take on the responsibilities of citizenship . . . [41]

Even Roman Catholic James Gordon Bennett, the New York editor, blamed Catholics for the growing strength of the Know-Nothing Party:

> . . . The Honorable William H. Seward, seeking to raise himself to power . . . seduced Archbishop Hughes from his pulpit and his altar and persuaded him to address an Irish meeting at Carroll Hall, surrounded by grog-shop politicians. This drew the line between Irishmen and Americans.
>
> . . . From the day the Irish were thus organized as a separate race in America, voting on principles of their own and having apparently no principles or feelings in common with the American masses – a native reaction was inevitable.[42]

John Hughes rejected this view and told the *New York Daily Times* that the Know-Nothings would fail: "It is not a pyramid resting on broad foundations – it is merely an inverted sugar loaf. It is too narrow at the base to support its top heaviness; and even if it were not, the political heats which it is exposed to bear will melt it down, so that, though it may last for years, still in the history of the nation it will be remembered only as the disappearance of a snow shower which fell toward the end of April."[43]

And the archbishop's comments were not off the mark: When the 34th Congress convened in 1855, the demands of the Know-Nothings fell on deaf ears because they did not control a majority. Their bill to extend naturalization laws from five to twenty-one years languished in congressional committees.

But even in states where they had majority control of local legislatures, they failed to implement their agenda. This was most evident in Massachusetts. Like other states that had Know-Nothing majorities, Massachusetts's 1855 class of freshmen legislators consisted primarily of une-ducated people. They had no clue how to run a government, draft legislation, direct it through the maze of committee hearings, or to manage the bills on the floor of legislature. Even when Know-Nothings succeeded in appointing a "Nunnery Committee" to investigate the charges that convents were bordellos, they looked like buffoons when Church hierarchy pointed out there were no convents in Massachusetts. The Commonwealth of Massachusetts, as well as every state in which there were Know-Nothing majorities, failed to pass any nativist legislation.

> The complete failure of the Know-Nothing party both in Congress and in the state legislatures made its inherent weaknesses clear. Horace Greeley had been correct when he wrote in 1854 that the party "would seem as devoid of the elements of permanence as an anti-Cholera or anti-Potato-rot party would be." Know-Nothingism had nothing permanent to offer. Its principles were inimical to those on which the American nation had been found-ed; its demands were of a sort that could never be realized in a country constituted as was the United States. Thus the country's success contributed to its failure, for its leaders, once in power, were helpless, and the people, realizing this, began to desert the organization as rapidly as they had joined.[44]

This became strikingly clear in the presidential election of 1856.

While the Know-Nothings were incompetent in organizing legislatures, they did excel at marshaling lawless gangs that threatened Catholic voters at election time. Police forces were not large enough to fend off American Party gangs like the Black Snakes, Tigers, Rough Skins, Gladiators, and Rip Raps. To curtail their threat, the Democrats encountered them with their own Irish-dominated gangs.

Baltimore, New Orleans, St. Louis, Louisville, and numerous other cities reported violent clashes at the polls that often ended with dead bodies on the streets. The City of Baltimore, which endured the most violence, mounted a cannon at one polling place. On August 5, 1855, editorials in the *Louisville Journal* incited a riot that killed twenty and injured several hundred.

These riots, legislative incompetence, bombastic and hateful anti-Catholic rhetoric, and secrecy rules began to take its toll on the movement. As fair-minded individuals dropped their rose-colored glasses, another issue began to overtake in importance even the imagined threats of papal plots – slavery.

* * * * *

When President Polk petitioned the Congress for $2 million to negotiate a peace and acquire land from the defeated Mexico, a congressman from Pennsylvania, David Wilmot, amended the appropriation to forbid slavery in any new territories. While the Wilmot Proviso, as it was called, was eventually defeated, it caused quite a stir in the country.

Reacting to this controversy, the aging Henry Clay managed his last great piece of legislation, the Compromise of 1850. To preserve the union, he crafted, with the help of Stephen Douglas of Illinois, resolutions that admitted California as a free state; created territorial government without deciding the slavery issue for New Mexico; settled Texas boundaries disputes; mandated federal commissioners to return runaway slaves to owners; and terminated slave trade in the District of Columbia. For many, the question of slavery was settled forever, hence it was not an issue in the 1852 election. But the tranquility was short-lived; the slavery issue resurrected when Kansas and Nebraska petitioned to join the Union.

In 1854, Senator Stephen Douglas of Illinois authored the Kansas-Nebraska Act which permitted "popular sovereignty" to decide if slavery should be permitted in the new states. It was passed with the expectation of Kansas being pro-slave and Nebraska anti-slave. Disgusted with this approach, a new party was created based on the principles articulated in the Wilmot Proviso – the Republican Party. This anti-slavery party combined members of the defunct Whig and Free Soil parties.

As the election of 1856 rolled around, most Democratic bigwigs concluded that President Pierce was not re-electable. His signature on the Kansas-Nebraska Act infuriated northern and southern Democrats, although for opposite reasons. To replace the president, the Democrats turned to former Secretary of State James Buchanan of Pennsylvania. For many Democrats, the sixty-five-year-old Buchanan was the perfect candidate because throughout his career, he managed to avoid taking sides on the controversial issues of the day – particularly the sectional issues.

> Buchanan's greatest assets to his party as a candidate in 1856 were his lifelong aversion to sectional politics; the fact that he had fortuitously escaped association with the four great crises of his era – the Compromise of 1820, nullification, the Compromise of 1850, and the Kansas-Nebraska Bill – which had weakened all the major participants; his political experience; and the unassailability of his personal life. Buchanan had been in England as United States minister from 1853 until a month before his nomination and thus had escaped the mud bath which had spattered every prominent participant in the Kansas struggle. He came before the pub-

lic in the role of the wise trustworthy and experienced old captain,
the kind of man to whom the ship of state could safely be entrust-
ed in a storm.[45]

They also took on the Know-Nothings by opposing "adverse political and
religious tests which have been secretly organized by a party claiming to be
exclusively American." "No party," the platform declared, "can be justly
deemed national, constitutional or in accordance with American principle
which bases its exclusive organization upon religious opinions and accidental
birth place. And hence a political crusade in the nineteenth century and in the
United States . . . against Catholics and foreign born is neither justified by the
past history of the country nor in unison with the spirit of toleration and
enlightened freedom which particularly distinguishes the American system of
popular government." To further please their Catholic constituents, in their
platform they repudiated the Know-Nothing ideology by condemning any
"attempt to enforce civil and religious disabilities against the rights of acquiring and enjoying citizenship in our own land."[46]

The fledging Republican Party walked a tightrope. They wanted to avoid
looking like a sectional organization yet they did not want to be perceived as
a nativist party either. If they failed they knew thousands would flee to either
the Democrats or the Know-Nothings. One man who did not fear repudiating
the bigoted nativists was Abraham Lincoln. In an 1855 letter to an old friend,
Joshua Speed, he clearly explained his position:

> I am not a Know-Nothing. This is certain. How could I be? How
> can any one who abhors the oppression of negroes, be in favor of
> degrading classes of white people? Our progress in degeneracy
> appears to me to be pretty rapid. As a nation, we began by declar-
> ing that *"all men are created equal."* We now practically read it
> "all men are created equal, *except negroes."* When the Know-
> Nothings get control, it will read "all men are created equal,
> except negroes, *and foreigners, and catholics."* When it comes to
> this I should prefer emigrating to some country where they make
> no preference of loving liberty – to Russia, for instance, where
> despotism can be taken pure, and without the base alloy of
> hypocrisy. . . .[47]

To cover all the bases, the Republicans nominated the "Great Pathfinder"
– John C. Frémont. This renowned naturalist and explorer had led over a
dozen expeditions between 1838 and 1854 that had mapped huge portions of
the west, including the Rocky Mountains. He fought to maintain California as
a territory and made a fortune during the Gold Rush. Since the forty-two-year-

old Frémont had no legislative record on the controversial issues, he was expected to be a safe standard bearer. After declaring that he was against nativism and the extension of slavery, he managed to get through the remainder of the campaign without making another statement on the issues. Frémont was a charismatic campaigner. He portrayed himself a representative of a "Young America," a candidate who would open new opportunities for the upcoming generation.

At their June 1855 convention, the Know-Nothings made the fatal error of endorsing a pro-slavery position to appease their southern supporters. Since the anti-Catholic issue did not rouse southern passions (there were very few Catholics residing in the region), American Party leaders thought their slavery stand would cement the loyalty of voters below the Mason-Dixon Line. This approach offended many abolitionists, and it came back to haunt them at their convention.

The candidate they believed could keep the various elements of their party united was former President Millard Fillmore of New York. Fillmore, a former Whig, succeeded to the presidency after Zachary Taylor's death and signed into law the Fugitive Slave Act. He was still brooding over being dumped by his old party in 1852, and so he agreed to run.

> Fillmore was an unfortunate choice. His record as president had been unimpressive and most northerners looked upon him as an avowed advocate of the slavocracy. Nor could he win the votes of sincere nativists. He had joined a Know-Nothing lodge in 1855, hoping to reap political reward by membership in the party, but his past utterances indicated no enmity either for Catholics or foreigners. By a strange freak of fate he was in Europe and had just sought and obtained an audience with the Pope when news of his nomination reached him, a fact that turned many Know-Nothings against him. Actually nativism was almost forgotten by Fillmore during his campaign. He mentioned the danger of unrestricted foreign immigration in a few speeches, but most of his campaign was devoted solely to means for preserving the union.[48]

The campaign of 1856 was a free-for-all. To keep disenchanted Know-Nothing voters from siding with the Republicans, Democratic Party operatives circulated rumors that Frémont was a drunkard, slave holder, thief, foreign born, and a secret Catholic. Scurrilous pamphlets titled *Frémont's Romanism Established*, *Colonel Frémont's Religious History*; *Authentic Account*, *Popist or Protestant: Which?*, *The Romish Intrigue* were distributed. One pamphlet's author even accused Frémont of being a Jesuit.

Although he was not a Catholic, he had to do some intense politicking to distance himself from the charge. The political waters were muddied when, at one point in the campaign, he admitted that he had been in a Catholic Church "possibly twelve or fifteen times – not more – and never except from motives of curiosity."[49]

Sensing that blocks of voters were being influenced by this controversy, a pro-Frémont New York newspaper published these comments:

> Col. Frémont's religious sentiments have been canvassed with far more bitterness and ferocity than his political opinions . . . he is pronounced a liar . . . and the blackguardism is caught up and echoed by every Know-Nothing organ and orator in the country. The virulence and malignity of party politics seems to have let loose the vilest passions of the worst men in the whole community – and the whole atmosphere is polluted by their exhalatives.
>
> We are not in the least degree fearful of their effect upon the public mind. If they have any result other than to bring contempt upon their authors and render the man they aim to injure still dearer to the public heart, we shall have sadly mistaken the character of the American people.[50]

Meanwhile, the Democrats utilized every trick to confuse voters by playing every side of the issues to fuse a winning coalition. They appealed to pro-slavery voters in the South by playing on their fears. In the North, they captured the Catholic vote by stressing the wedge issues that separated them from Republicans and Know-Nothings.

The northern Know-Nothings who attempted to drown the slavery issue by shouting anti-Catholic epithets, received little help from their candidate. On the stump, Fillmore sounded more like an old Whig than a Know-Nothing. He preached the cause of Union. ". . . When I left the Presidential chair," he told an audience, "the nation was prosperous and contented. . . . But where are we now? Alas threatened at home with Civil War." He predicted dire consequences if a sectional Republican was elected: "Our Southern brethren [would never] submit to be governed by a [Republican]. . . . Therefore you must see that if this sectional party succeeds, it leads inevitably to the destruction of this beautiful fabric reared by our forbearers."[51]

Fillmore avoided making any scurrilous remarks about Catholics. In fact, in Newburgh, New York, he stated, "As an American, I have no hostility to foreigners. . . . Having witnessed their deplorable conditions in the old country, God forbid I should add to their suffering by refusing them an asylum in this land."[52]

Adding to Know-Nothings' woes, the Roman Catholic bishop of Fillmore's hometown of Buffalo, New York, had kind words for him. The bishop reminded his flock that the "esteemed" Fillmore donated the bell to St. Joseph's Cathedral and sent his daughters to Buffalo Academy for Young Ladies that was run by the Sisters of the Sacred Heart. The bishop actually recorded in his diary that he wouldn't be shocked if Fillmore became a Catholic.

The Democrats spent the remainder of the campaign sowing chaos in the hope the Know-Nothings would siphon off enough votes to sink the Republicans. And this divisive strategy did pay off. Buchanan collected enough votes from the South, Far West, and Pennsylvania to forge an electoral victory of 174 votes. Pennsylvanian Catholics, whose voting power pushed the Keystone State's twenty-four electoral votes into Buchanan's column, made victory possible.

Frémont's 114 electoral votes came from the anti-slave northeast. He managed to capture Connecticut, Maine, Massachusetts, New Hampshire, Vermont, and the big prize – New York. Even with its large Democratic Catholic block and significant American Party presence, the anti-slave crowd was able to slip through with a plurality 46 percent of the vote.

The hapless Fillmore performed poorly. Nationally, Fillmore received only 21 percent of the vote, and he managed to carry only Maryland's eight electoral votes. The American Party, which only a year earlier swept all of Massachusetts, was particularly humiliated by its pathetic 11 percent showing in that state.

James Buchanan was elected president by a plurality of 45 percent. His electoral victory was a fragile coalition of which Catholics were an essential component. The anti-Catholic rhetoric of the Know-Nothings and the Catholic smears against Frémont gave the Democrats their last shot at the White House for a generation. Historian Michael Holt agrees that this strategy worked: "To keep northern Know-Nothings out of Frémont's column [the Democrats] fanned the false rumor that Frémont was Catholic, a charge that more than anything else prevented him from winning the Presidency."[53]

The Know-Nothings' dismal showing at the polls, and the shifting national focus toward the issue of slavery and states' rights, drove anti-Catholic prejudice underground at least for a while.

Chapter 5

The Catholic Voter in the Age of Lincoln

During the ante-bellum period, the Roman Catholic Church in America maintained a middle position on the question of slavery that neither condemned nor endorsed the practice. Members of the Church hierarchy articulated their support of Pope Gregory XVI's dated apostolic letter *In Supremo Apostolatus*, which condemned the slave trade but concluded that although slavery was a social evil, it was not necessarily a moral evil. For the pope, slavery "was not contrary either to the divine or the natural law. In other words, slavery was not incompatible with a moral life or an impediment to salvation. Actually, the Church considered the master more likely to sin through the abuse of his power, and so, strong emphasis was placed on a master's obligation to treat his slaves with justice and charity. Slaveholders were also encouraged to free their bondmen whenever circumstances would permit them to improve their lives."[1]

In a textbook he authored for U.S. seminarians, Archbishop Patrick Kenrick of Baltimore argued that slavery was not necessarily a violation of natural law and neither affirmed nor denied that it was a social evil. As president of the Ninth Provincial Council, he issued an 1858 pastoral letter which contained this language:

> Our clergy have wisely abstained from all interference with the judgment of the faithful, which should be free on all questions of polity and social order, within the limits of the doctrine and law of Christ. The peaceful and conservative character of our principles . . . has been tested and made manifest in the great political struggles that have agitated the country on the subject of domestic slavery. . . . Among us there has been no agitation on the subject.[2]

Since the Church's primary concern was the salvation of souls, many bishops were reluctant to make policy pronouncements on divisive political issues. And this approach encouraged extremists on both sides of the slavery issue to accuse the Church of straddling.

Abolitionist suspicions about the Church escalated when the Supreme Court, led by Catholic Chief Justice Roger B. Taney, handed down the Dred Scott Decision in March 1857, which determined that a slave was not a U.S. citizen and, therefore, didn't have standing in court; that the federal government, having no sovereignty over territories, could not prohibit slavery therein; and that a slave's residence in a free state did not make the slave a free man. Taney was accused of believing that "a Negro had no rights which a white man had to respect."[3]

The abolitionists chose to ignore Taney's abhorrence of slavery, which was clearly stated in an earlier decision: "A hard necessity indeed compels us to endure the evil of slavery for a time. It was imposed upon us by another nation while we were yet in a state of colonial vassalage. It cannot be easily or suddenly removed, yet while it continues it is a blot on our national character; and every lover of real freedom confidently hopes that it will be effectually, though it must be gradually, wiped away, and earnestly looks for the means by which this necessary object may be best attained."[4]

Another reason why abolitionists (many of whom were former Know-Nothings) were suspicious of Catholics was their allegiance to the pro-slavery Democratic Party. Out of party loyalty, many inner-city Catholics turned a deaf ear to slavery. Others feared that a free black man would compete with the Catholics for northern unskilled jobs. These attitudes prompted many American Irish Catholics to ignore the appeals of the great Irish patriot, Daniel O'Connell, and the 60,000 in Ireland who signed his petition urging support of the anti-slavery cause.

By early 1860, it was evident that President Buchanan, a weak man with a prissy disposition, was dominated by southern advisors. Bad economic times and the violent conflicts in territories concerning slavery brought the president's popularity to all-time lows. The Democrats looked to dump him, and Republicans nursed hopes of victory.

When the Republicans met in Chicago for their nominating convention, they faced the fact that they had serious problems with Catholic voting blocs. They were aware that their party membership included many former Whigs, Free-Soilers, and nativists who hated Catholics. Republican bigwigs also knew that party zealots during the past four years had made countless pronouncements promoting policies that had further alienated the Catholic population. In 1859, for instance, the Republican-controlled Massachusetts legislature called for a state constitutional amendment to extend by two years the waiting time for newly naturalized citizens to vote. It was a move that infuriated Catholics. Attempts by Republican-controlled state legislatures to copy the 1831 Maine law that forbade liquor sales or public consumption on Sundays, offended German and Irish Catholics.

Realizing that these issues might later haunt his own candidacy, Abraham Lincoln came out forcefully against the Massachusetts voting law in the spring of 1860: "I am against its adoption, not only in Illinois, but in every other place in which I have the right to oppose it. . . . It is well known that I deplore the oppressed condition of the blacks, and it would, therefore, be very inconsistent for me to look with approval upon any measure that infringes upon the inalienable rights of white men, whether or not they are born in another land or speak a different language from our own."[5]

Another tactical error was a pronouncement by *The New York Tribune*'s Republican Editor, Horace Greeley, that he could support John Bell, Edward Bates, or John Botts for president in 1860. Each of these men was a former Know-Nothing who had supported Millard Fillmore in 1856, and Catholics were indignant that they were being considered seriously for the presidency.

To make up for these blunders, the Republicans decided to pursue a strategy they hoped would neutralize Catholics. In their platform they included a provision opposing changes in federal and state naturalization and voting laws. Recognizing the importance of the German-Catholic vote, particularly in Illinois and Pennsylvania, they hired a political consultant, Carl Schurz, to drum up German votes. The selection of compromise candidate, Abraham Lincoln, also worked into their strategy to attract or neutralize Catholic voters.

Lincoln had the advantage of being *out* of public office most of his career while William Seward, Salmon P. Chase, Edward Bates, and other contenders had extensive public records that either offended immigrants or Know-Nothings. Lincoln's stand on slavery straddled the middle ground – he hated slavery but did not call for its immediate elimination. Lincoln was also supportive of the Homestead Act and high-tariff proposals that appealed to foreign voters. While Republicans were unifying behind their nominee, the Democrats were splitting at the seams. Compromises on slavery issues that kept the northern and southern elements together during the 1840s and 1850s no longer worked.

The leading candidate, Stephen Douglas of Illinois, broke with Buchanan and called for ballot-box approval of slavery in new states and territories. His belief that this even-handed approach would appeal to all sections of the party was a serious miscalculation. Southern convention delegates did not want to surrender to popular choice; they wanted the federal government to exercise its authority to expand slavery.

When it became evident that the nomination of Douglas was a certainty, southern delegates from eight states bolted the convention in Charleston. Fearing violence, the convention was recessed and then re-convened in Baltimore to officially nominate Douglas. The dissident southern delegates held their own convention in Richmond and nominated pro-slavery John C. Breckinridge of Kentucky as their presidential candidate. Adding to this electoral confusion, old-time radical Whigs and bitter Know-Nothings founded the Constitutional-Union Party and nominated John Bell of Tennessee for president.

As the race for president commenced, it became evident that there would be two very different campaigns to determine the executive mansion's next occupant: in the North, Lincoln vs. Douglas, and in the South, Bell vs. Breckinridge. Since it was likely that the man elected president would win only by a plurality, every vote mattered. Hence, the Republicans hotly pursued their German strategy while Douglas Democrats, knowing their only chance for victory was to outpoll Lincoln in the North, made every effort to keep Catholics, particularly the Irish, in their camp.

> The Irishman's hero in national politics was Senator Stephen A. Douglas of Illinois, the "Little Giant." He was a pugnacious, combative politician driven by dreams of greatness and of the White House. A Jacksonian Democrat, he attacked banks, tariffs and paper money. The cause to which he gave himself most passionately, however, was the expansion of the frontier of settlement into the immense territories beyond the bend of the Missouri. As early as 1844, Douglas had introduced a bill that would have opened the Nebraska region to settlement by providing a territorial government. He called for the building of a railroad to the Pacific and persistently advocated homesteading bills to make the public domain free to settlers.[6]

Stephen Douglas did not condemn slavery but did condemn racial equality: "We do not believe in the equality of the Negro, socially or politically, with the white man."[7] The Catholics, who feared black migration to the North, agreed with Douglas that the future of slavery should be left to the people of a given state to decide.

The fledging northern labor movement and its Catholic members viewed the abolitionists as fanatics dead set on destroying the Union. They asked "why abolitionists were not interested in the industrial exploitation of workingmen in the North. They insisted that their situation was, if anything, worse than that of slaves."[8] Congressman Michael Walsh of New York became a hero to his constituents when he told the House of Representatives: "The only difference between the Negro slave in the South and the wage slave of the North is that one has a master without asking for him, and the other has to beg for the privilege of being a slave."[9]

When the results came in, Lincoln easily carried the Electoral College with 180 votes, but his popular vote totaled only 39 percent:

	Lincoln	Rep. Douglas	Dem. Breckinridge	Dem. Bell Const.-Union
Popular Votes	1,866,452	1,376,957	849,781	588,879
Electoral Votes	180	12	72	39

Since Lincoln's name was not permitted to appear on the ballot in ten southern states, he had to forge his victory in the North and Midwest. Historian William Dodd claimed in 1917 that if one in twenty votes had shifted to Douglas in the North, Lincoln would have lost. He believed that "the election of Lincoln and, as it turned out, the fate of the Union, were thus determined not by native Americans but by voters who knew least of American history and institutions."[10] Opinions like Dodd's forced the question, did the Catholics elect Lincoln?

The Republicans did wage an aggressive campaign to swing German voters their way. Their hired consultants hit the hustings and campaigned heavily in German communities in Pennsylvania, Illinois, Wisconsin, and Missouri. In Pennsylvania, for instance, the Republicans created a Naturalization Committee which "was happy to aid in seeking prompt naturalization of Republican voters of foreign birth."[11]

But it appears that these efforts did not move German Catholics into the Republican column. The hired gun, Carl Schurz, was labeled by Catholic Germans as a "Red Republican infidel" and a "German Jacobin." These Catholics did not accept the political posturing of former temperance advocates, abolitionists, Whigs, and Know-Nothings suddenly masquerading as Republican friends, sympathetic to their plight – and they cast their votes accordingly.

A key battleground for Republican strategists was Lincoln's home state of Illinois, which he carried by a small majority:

	Lincoln	Douglas	Breckinridge	Bell
Popular Votes	172,161	160,215	2,404	4,913
Percentage	50.7	47.1	.59	1.47

To carry this state, Republicans made a concerted effort to woo German farmers. And their campaign appears to have succeeded only with Lutheran free-soil Germans. The message of Carl Schurz and his operatives fell on deaf Catholic ears as the chart on page 79 demonstrates:

The two German-Catholic communities, New Trier in Cook County and Benner in St. Clair County, stayed overwhelmingly with the Democratic Party. Cook County, which includes Chicago, reeked of anti-Catholicism, particularly in the editorial pages of the *Chicago Tribune*, which added to Catholic misgivings of Republican sincerity.

The German vote may have been decisive for Lincoln, who carried Illinois with 172,000 votes versus Douglas's 160,000 votes – but it was not German Catholics who put him over the top. Political scientist Paul Kleppner, in an article, "Lincoln and the Immigrant Vote: A Case of Religious Polarization," concluded:

The reorganization of these Know-Nothing elements into a new political organization meant that the Republican party assumed a negative reference group characteristic *vis-à-vis* Catholic voters. The cumulative effect of the negative reference group reaction was to encourage a continuation of the polarization of German-American voting behavior into Catholic-Democratic and Protestant-Republican subdivisions.[12]

Democratic Party Percentages of Total Votes Cast
Selected German-Populated Precincts of Illinois,
Biennial Elections, 1850–60[13]

Precinct, county	1850	1852	1854	1856	1858	1860
Addison, Du Page	91.7	47.8	5.6	32.7	35.8	30.8
New Trier, Cook (Catholic)	82.6	97.5	21.1	63.7	70.8	64.7
Bremen, Cook	83.9	83.7	0.0	1.1	14.4	15.4
Belleville, St. Clair	–	77.8	45.8	34.4	42.4	38.6
Mascoutah	–	68.0	13.9	18.2	33.1	28.0
Benner, St. Clair (Catholic)	–	94.0	19.8	71.3	53.7	65.3
Centreville, St. Clair	–	93.0	64.5	75.7	38.7	35.8

Pulitzer-Prize-winning historian, James McPherson, writing in *Battle Cry of Freedom*, agrees: "Republicans made a special effort headed by Carl Schurz to reduce the normal Democratic majority among German-Americans. They achieved some success among German Protestants – enough, perhaps, to make a difference in the close states of Illinois and Indiana – though the lingering perceptions of Republican dalliance with nativism and temperance kept the Catholic vote overwhelmingly Democratic."[14]

In Irish-Catholic communities the results were similar. These inner-city Catholics who endured greater mistreatment than rural Germans, remained loyal to the party that had reached out and given them a helping hand when they arrived in American ports. "They were mostly members of the Democratic Party who did not want to go against their political allies in the South and above all, did not want to align themselves with their persecutors in the North."[15]

As nationalists who had been dominated by a foreign power – England – the Irish understood the importance of remaining united. Disunion in their judgment only destroys the foundation of a nation.

They remained true to the Democratic party and opposed to movements which threatened the unity of either the party or the nation. While a prominent Irish-American like John Mitchel could go over to the extreme pro-slavery position, the majority took no positive stand on slavery as such. They favored making such concessions to the South as were needed to preserve the Union, but the main emphasis was on the preservation of the Union rather than on the defense of the institution of slavery.[16]

In the hotly contested battle for New York, the Republicans also made a major effort to sway the immigrant Catholic vote. In September 1860, they distributed a campaign brochure containing excerpts of Pope Gregory's opposition to the slave trade. The Democrats countered by publicizing a railroad magnate's plan to buy slaves and employ them instead of Irish laborers to lay rail.

New York's leading ethnic newspaper, the *Irish American*, endorsed Douglas and reminded the Irish of their duties as naturalized citizens:

> When [Irish-Americans are advised] to abdicate the most glorious characteristic of their attachment to their adopted home, and become sectional upholders of geographical distinctions, [the advisor] forgets that the naturalization by which they were raised to the dignity of citizenship is not local, but national in its nature; that it derives no force from individual states, and demands no allegiance save such as subserves the interests of all. The adopted citizen cannot without incurring the guilt of deliberate perjury, take his stand without the Constitution and recognize one section of the country to the prejudice of its whole. For him there is no North, no South, no East, no West, beyond what is necessary for the direction of the internal economy of each.[17]

The election results in this key state which contained more Irish than Dublin proved that Catholics stuck with the Democrats:

New York State 1860 Election Results

	Lincoln	Douglas	Breckinridge	Bell
Popular Vote	362,646	312,510	0	0
Percentage	53.7%	46.3%	0	0

While Lincoln may have narrowly carried the state, the results in the Catholic-dominated areas were dramatically different:

New York County

	Lincoln	Douglas
Popular Vote	41,913	62,482
Percentage	39.0%	60.1%

Kings County (Brooklyn)

	Lincoln	Douglas
Popular Vote	15,883	20,599
Percentage	43.5%	56.4%

Queens County

	Lincoln	Douglas
Popular Vote	3,749	4,391
Percentage	46.1%	53.9%

Westchester County

	Lincoln	Douglas
Popular Vote	6,771	8,126
Percentage	45.4%	54.5%

* * * * *

Although Lincoln had made it clear throughout the 1860 campaign that he would happily tolerate the continued existence of slavery as the price to maintain peace and unity, this position did not satisfy the South. South Carolina voted to secede from the Union in December 1860, and by the time Lincoln was sworn in as president on March 4, 1861, six more states had followed South Carolina's lead. These words in Lincoln's inaugural fell on deaf ears: "I have no purpose, directly or indirectly, to interfere with the institution of slavery in the States where it exists. I believe I have no lawful right to do so, and I have no inclination to do so. . . . In your hands, my dissatisfied fellow countrymen, and not in mine, is the momentous issue of civil war. The government will not assail you."

And as Lincoln was calling for volunteers to bear arms to humble the rebellious states, many northern Catholics, while deciding what to do, were able to assess the issues better than most.

While Lincoln and his fellow Republicans condemned secession as illegal and the Union more important than states rights, the Catholics remembered that the Republican's political forbears, the northern Federalists, had called for secession at the Hartford Convention in reaction to the naturalization laws that gave immigrant Catholics the right to vote. They also knew that the North hid behind "states' rights" to evade the Dred Scott decision and to ignore the Fugitive Slave Law. Catholics were able to judge objectively the grandstanding on both sides because they were not slave owners nor were they the proprietors of northern manufacturing plants who viewed slavery as an unfair labor advantage. Understanding the political contradictions and hypocrisy, most Irish Catholics in the North agreed to fight essentially for one reason – to preserve the union at all costs. On the other hand, German-Catholics in Pennsylvania and the Midwest agreed to fight because they staunchly opposed slavery and its extension into new territories.

Finally, all Catholics realized that the war gave them the opportunity to show their appreciation, loyalty, and solidarity to their adopted nation. From scores of northern pulpits, priests called on the faithful to don a blue uniform because, "The Union must and shall be preserved."[18]

As brother turned against brother, the Church tried to stay above the fray. The hierarchy encouraged priests to act as chaplains and nuns to work as nurses in order to minister to the needs of all the faithful. At times, however, northern and southern church leaders had to face their differences and disagreements were inevitable. Archbishop Hughes of New York lectured one southern bishop:

> . . . the flag on the cathedral [St. Patrick's in New York] was erected with my permission and approval. It was at the same time an act of expediency going before a necessity likely to be urged upon me by the dictation of enthusiasm in this city. I preferred that no such necessity of dictation should overtake us, because, if it had, the press would have sounded the report that Catholics were disloyal, and no act of ours afterward would successfully vindicate us from the imputation. On the whole, however, I think, my dear Bishop, that the Catholics of the North have behaved themselves with great prudence, moderation, and a dignity which had, for the moment at least, inspired, among the high and the low, great respect for them as a religious body in the Union. I regret that I cannot say as much for the Catholics and for some of the clergy in the South. In their periodicals in New Orleans, and in Charleston, they have justified the attitude taken by the South on principles of Catholic theology, which I think was an unnecessary, inexpedient, and, for that matter, a doubtful if not a dangerous position, at the commencement of so unnatural and so lamentable a struggle.[19]

Nevertheless, on St. Patrick's Day, 1861, when bishops across the nation spoke out on the war, Archbishop Hughes expressed the Church's position best when he told the New York's faithful that "there is but one rule for a Catholic wherever he is, and that is, to do his duty there as a citizen."[20] The bishop of Buffalo, John Timon, forcefully declared from his pulpit: "Our Country, it is our duty not to question, but to obey. So much the more holy will be the war, as it is not one of passion, but of duty."[21]

When the Conscription Law of 1863 was signed by Lincoln, many Catholics feared that its draft quotas would treat them unfairly. They also believed that the loophole, which permitted draftees to buy legally substitutes for $300, was de facto discrimination against poor Catholics. Rich Anglo-Saxons could buy their way out of the service by enticing poor men (Catholics or Protestants for that matter) to take the $300. In fact, one future president, Grover Cleveland, and the fathers of two future presidents, James (father of Franklin) and Theodore Roosevelt, Sr., took advantage of the Conscription Law's escape clause. In New York, the Irish resented that Negroes were exempt from the draft, and they further were convinced that quotas were fixed to penalize Democratic Catholic voting precincts and to destroy the memberships of the fledging craft unions. The *New York Daily News* contended that, "it was the intention to draft the Democrats so that the Republicans should be able to control the election." As the following chart demonstrates, this charge was probably true:

Statement of Population, Draft Numbers, Voters, Etc.[22]
(Predominantly Protestant Districts)

Congressional District	Population	Draft	Vote of 1862
29th	114,556	1767	20,097
17th	111,526	1838	17,882
23rd	116,980	2088	22,535
28th	129,365	2015	21,026
15th	132,232	2260	23,165
27th	135,488	2416	25,601
30th	141,971	2539	21,385

New York and Brooklyn Districts[23]
(Predominantly Catholic Districts)

District	Population	Draft	Vote of 1862
3rd	132,242	2697	16,421
2nd	151,951	4146	15,967
6th	117,148	4538	12,777
8th	175,998	4892	15,195
4th	131,854	5881	12,363

These numbers reveal that in the heavily Catholic Congressional districts in Manhattan and Brooklyn, a disproportionately higher number were drafted compared to the Protestant-dominated upstate congressional districts.

Irish Catholics were not alone in their opposition to conscription. In Minnesota and Wisconsin, German-Catholics objected to being drafted into an Army that lacked Catholic chaplains to meet their spiritual needs.[24] Angered by the draft and the fact that war aims were changing from preservation of the Union to the abolition of slavery; many Catholics joined the "Copperheads," the northern Democrats' peace movement. Catholic Copperheads believed that their people were being sent to die on battlefields so New England Protestant manufacturers could reap greater profits off a prolonged war. They also subscribed to the position that the war could be quickly over if slavery was permitted to continue in the South.

The bishops realized the draft plus the new war aims could inflame northeastern cities. Archbishop Hughes warned Secretary of War Simon Cameron: "The Catholics, so far as I know, whether of native or foreign birth, are willing to fight to the death for the support of the Constitution, the government and the laws of the country. But if it should be understood that, with or without knowing it, they are to fight for the abolition of slavery, then, indeed they will turn away in disgust from the discharge of what would otherwise be a patriotic duty."[25]

When draftees were being yanked off the streets and put in uniform, tempers flared and mobs took to the streets to protest. Outbreaks were reported in New England, Pennsylvania, Ohio, New Jersey, Illinois, and Wisconsin. "Two marshals were attacked in Boston, hardware stores were robbed of knives and guns, and several persons were killed. . . . In Rutland, Vermont, Irish quarry workers drove off enrolling officers with clubs and stones. In Pottsville, Pennsylvania, armed Irish miners resisted the Draft. . . . In Ozaukee County, Wisconsin, Germans had threatened to lynch several Republicans . . . and there were disturbances in parts of Indiana and in the Irish mining section around Dubuque, Iowa."[26]

In an intemperate Independence Day speech, New York's Democratic governor, Horatio Seymour, told his constituents, "Remember that the bloody and treasonable, and revolutionary doctrine of public necessity can be proclaimed by a mob as well as a government." *New York Tribune* editor Horace Greeley compounded the inflammatory rhetoric in a July 9, 1863, editorial addressed to Archbishop Hughes in which he complained that "your people had helped create the war by their adhesion to the Democratic Party, in the election of Polk in 1844, by supporting the Mexican War, and by the refusal of priests to preach abolition of Negro slaves." "Your people," he scolded, "for years have been and today are foremost in the degradation and abuse of this persecuted race."[27]

This rhetoric plus the commencement of the draft bred trouble and on July 13, 1863, all hell broke loose in the City of New York. After lots were drawn at the Ninth Congressional District Draft Office, a mob of foreign laborers attacked the building. This incident sparked riots that would engulf the city for the next few days. Residences, draft offices, hotels, saloons and restaurants were gutted. Important and rich uptown Republicans and free blacks were attacked.

Horace Greeley, watching his city burn, now turned to the archbishop he had recently attacked to quell the riots. The dying Hughes spoke out but reminded Greeley he was culpable:

> In spite of Mr. Greeley's assault upon the Irish, in the present disturbed condition of the city, I will appeal not only to them, but to all persons who love God and revere the holy Catholic religion which they profess, to respect also the laws of man and the peace of society, to retire to their homes with as little delay as possible, and disconnect themselves from the seemingly deliberate intention to disturb the peace and social rights of the citizens of New York. If they are Catholics, I ask, for God's sake – for the sake of their holy religion – for my own sake, if they have any respect for the Episcopal authority – to dissolve their bad association with reckless men, who have little regard either for divine or human laws.[28]

By July 15, military brigades arrived from Gettysburg and began to clash with the rioters. That evening, Archbishop Hughes had flyers posted all over the city that read:

To the Men of New York who are now called in many of the papers Rioters:

> Men! I am not able, owing to rheumatism in my limbs, to visit you, but that is not a reason why you should not pay me a visit, in your whole strength. Come then, to-morrow, Friday, at two o'clock to my residence, northwest corner of Madison Avenue and 36th Street. I shall have a speech prepared for you. There is abundant space for the meeting around my house. I can address you from the corner of the balcony. If I should be unable to stand during its delivery you will permit me to address you sitting. My voice is much stronger than my limbs. I take upon myself the responsibility of assuring you that in paying me this visit, or in returning from it, you shall not be disturbed by any exhibition of municipality or military presence. You who are Catholics or as many of you as are have a right to visit your Bishop without molestation.

> †John Hughes
> Archbishop of New York[29]

Five thousand people gathered outside the Archbishop's residence. Too weak to stand, the ailing Hughes addressed them sitting in a chair. He reminded his flock, ". . . a man has a right to defend his shanty, if it be no more, or his house, or his church at the risk of his life; but the cause must be always just; it must be defensive, not aggressive. . . ." After cheers and a final benediction, he told the crowd to go home and they answered in unison, "We will."[30] Hughes's appeal worked. The riots simmered down, but the damage was done. Millions in property was destroyed and 105 were dead – 84 killed by police or soldiers and 11 blacks and 10 police killed by the rioters.[31]

In the aftermath, to avoid future violence the Protestant leader of Tammany Hall, Boss William Marcy Tweed, created a fund to pay the $300 exemption fee for "hardship cases." The influential Protestant magazine *Harper's* had a calming influence when it repudiated the harsh rhetoric of the likes of Horace Greeley:

> It happens that, in this city, in our working classes, the Irish element largely predominates over all the others, and if the populace act as a populace, the Irish are naturally prominent therein. It happens, also, that from the limited opportunities which the Irish enjoy for education in their own country, they are more easily misled by knaves, and made the tools of politicians when they come here than are the Germans, or men of other races. The impulsiveness of the Celt, likewise, prompts him to be foremost in every outburst, whether for a good or an evil purpose.
>
> But it must be remembered in palliation of the disgrace which, as Archbishop Hughes says, the riots of last week have heaped upon the Irish name, that in many wards of the city, the Irish were during the late riot staunch friends of law and order; that Irishmen helped to rescue the colored orphans in the asylum from the hands of the rioters; that a large proportion of the police, who behaved throughout the riot with the most exemplary gallantry, are Irishmen; that the Roman Catholic priesthood to a man used their influence on the side of the law; and that perhaps the most scathing rebuke administered to the riot was written by an Irishman – James T. Brady. It is important that this riot should teach us something more useful than a revival of Know-Nothing prejudices.[32]

*   *   *   *   *

When the presidential election of 1864 rolled around, the hardened, bitter inner-city Catholics still represented a significant proportion of the "Copperheads," and they looked to their party to give them a candidate who would bring the war to a rapid close.

Congressman Samuel Cox of Ohio and Democratic-banker-powerbroker August Belmont of New York persuaded the party to nominate General George McClellan. The thirty-seven-year-old "Little Napoleon" was perceived as a dynamic loyal Democrat whose military background would diminish their party's "Copperhead" reputation. Even though McClellan was fired by Lincoln as Commander of Army of the Potomac in November 1862, he was still nationally popular.

To make the case for McClellan, Belmont reminded his party of their "devotion to the Union and the Constitution" while condemning "four years of misrule [which] had well-nigh brought the Republic to the verge of ruin."[33] While the party passed a peace plank that called for a halt in the war before negotiations, candidate McClellan publicly reversed the order calling for "Union first then peace."[34]

Many Irish Catholics, with their experience of British tyranny, and many German-Catholics, who had witnessed the terror of the Revolution of 1848, viewed Lincoln as a dictator. The prominent Catholic congressman, Edward Ryan of Wisconsin, reminded his people that "blind submission to the Administration of the Government is not devotion to the Country or the Constitution. The administration is not the government."[35]

But with the war going well, the Democratic strategy failed to stop the Republicans. In November 1864, Lincoln was elected to a second term with 52.7 percent of the vote, 3,012,833 versus McClellan's 2,703,249. He carried the Electoral College 214 to 80. Republicans won all twelve gubernatorial races and picked up forty-two seats in the house and three in the senate.

But it was the Catholics, staying within the Democratic ranks, that made the race close in the two states that sent the most troops into the ranks of the Union armed forces – New York and Pennsylvania. While Lincoln carried both states, his margins were slim. Pennsylvania was carried by only 31,000 votes (52% of the total vote) while the margin of victory in New York was a mere 6,740 votes out of 730,712 cast.

Counties with large Catholic populations voted overwhelmingly for McClellan and were responsible for the closeness of the race:

New York County

	Lincoln	McClellan
Popular Vote	36,681	73,709
Percentage	33%	67%

Kings County (Brooklyn)

	Lincoln	McClellan
Popular Vote	20,838	25,726
Percentage	43%	57%

Queens County

	Lincoln	McClellan
Popular Vote	4,284	5,400
Percentage	44%	56%

Westchester County

	Lincoln	McClellan
Popular Vote	7,607	9,355
Percentage	45%	55%

Richmond County

	Lincoln	McClellan
Popular Vote	1,564	2,874
Percentage	35%	65%

Albany County

	Lincoln	McClellan
Popular Vote	10,206	12,935
Percentage	44%	66%

Rockland County

	Lincoln	McClellan
Popular Vote	1,445	2,287
Percentage	39%	61%

*   *   *   *   *

While there were strong political differences between Catholics and Protestants about the reasons for fighting, no one could ever deny that Catholics made a major contribution to the war effort and showed great valor on the battlefield.

When the war began, there were 2.2 million Catholics in the United States, with 1.6 million of them Irish. The U.S. Sanitary Commission reported that 144,221 Irish served in the Union armed forces. The breakdown: 51,206 from New York, 17,418 from Pennsylvania, 12,041 from Illinois, 10,007 from Massachusetts, 8,129 from Ohio, 3,621 from Wisconsin, and 4,362 from Missouri.[36] Approximately 40,000 German-Catholics served as did 5,000 Polish immigrants. With only a few thousand Italians in America, "the proportion of Italian officers and enlisted men who served during the Civil War was perhaps the highest of any ethnic group in America."[37] Numerous Catholics earned prominent ranks of the armed services that included over fifty generals and a half dozen admirals.[38]

For the North, prominent Catholics included General William D. Rose-crans, Generals Hugh and Charles Ewing, and General Phillip Sheridan.[39] General Grant referred to Sheridan as a man who had no superior as a general, either living or dead and perhaps not an equal. [40]

In the South, at least 40,000 Irish served in the Confederate Army. Catholic officers who distinguished themselves in battle included General Pierre Beauregard, General James Longstreet, General William Hardee, and Admiral Rafael Semmes.[41]

Catholics also wrote numerous lyrics that were popular in Army camps. They included: Dixie by Daniel Decatur Emmett, Bonnie Blue Flag by Harry McCarthy, and Maryland, My Maryland by James Ryder Randall.[42]

By the end of the Civil War, the Roman Catholic Church s prestige was greatly enhanced. The Church remained unified; her soldiers fought bravely, and Americans witnessed uncountable acts of Catholic charity. The Daughters of Charity, the Sisters of Mercy, and other religious orders, in helping the wounded and distraught, made a great impression on the public. Catholic and non-Catholic comrades, living, marching and fighting together, put to rest many old prejudices.

Mrs. Jefferson Davis, while destitute in the post-war era, praised the charity and kindness of Catholics:

> No institution of my own church offered to teach my poor children. One day three Sisters of Charity came to see me and brought me five gold dollars, all the money they had. They almost forced me to take the money, but I did not. They then offered to take my children to their school in the neighbourhood of Savannah, where the air was cool and they could be comfortably cared for during the summer months.[43]

As for the dominant ethnic group among Catholics that participated in the war, the Irish historian, Florence Gibson, insightfully summed up their role:

> The Irish-American conduct in the Civil War presents a picture of decided contrasts. On the one hand, the fighting men and their families who supported them had written a proud chapter of sacrifice and patriotic loyalty to their new nation. On the other hand, the mob who had let themselves be led by the politicians into the draft riots had brought down on the heads of their fellow-nationals extensive criticism and unpopularity in the city. The bulk of the Irish population had an unshakeable loyalty to the Union and while they might follow politicians in a carping policy against the administration, they remained true to the United States throughout the war.[44]

Chapter 6
The Catholic Voter in the Gilded Age:
The Golden Years

As the Civil War ended, Catholics could note with some pride that their position in American society had improved significantly. Unlike some Protestant denominations that had split over the war, the Church was largely unaffected by sectionalism, since most of its members resided in Union states.

Recognizing the importance of Catholic manpower and acknowledging the influence the clergy had on men in uniform, representatives of the national government began to consult key members of the episcopate on a regular basis. Before Archbishop Hughes died in 1864 President Lincoln had called upon him to handle delicate missions, on one occasion sending him to France as an unofficial State Department emissary. In return, Lincoln had urged the Vatican to bestow upon Hughes the cardinal's red hat.

In October 1866, the American hierarchy held a plenary council in the nation's first episcopal see, Baltimore, in an effort to demonstrate Church unity. Seven archbishops, thirty-seven bishops, and two abbots led the opening procession. President Andrew Johnson and the mayor of Washington attended the closing session – a clear tribute to the growing importance of the Catholic presence in America,

During the early days of Reconstruction, Catholics could detect a slight change in the Anglo-Saxon establishment's attitude. These victorious northerners displayed an air of confidence that caused many of them to shed their fear of Catholic Europe. Also, many former nativists – now a mere faction of the radical Republicans – were busy pursuing new agendas. For one thing, in the war's aftermath they were less concerned about persecuting Catholics and more interested in punishing the South.

Catholics began to witness a new attitude toward immigration among some Protestants. The new states of the Northwest, for instance, actively encouraged European immigration as a means of populating and developing their vast open lands. Laborers were in great demand for post-war reconstruction, particularly the building of the nation's railroads. For many open-minded Protestants, "*E pluribus unum*" expressed "the essence of America's cosmopolitan faith – a conviction that this new land would bring unity out of diversity as a matter of course."[1] They subscribed to the belief that "Know-Nothingism . . . tramples down the doctrine of human brotherhood. It judges men by the accidents of their condition, instead of striving to find a common lot for all, with a common access to the blessings of life."[2]

Politically, the Republicans had firm control of the national government in the post-war era. By 1867, the party controlled two-thirds of the House of Representatives and most of the statehouses. And as Republicans appeared to prosper, the Democrats seemed to be in shambles.

The Democratic Party now consisted of two semi-autonomous groups – the northern wing of the party, dominated by inner-city Catholics, and the southern wing, dominated by former Confederates. Often the only dialogue between these two groups came during their quadrennial national conventions. The increasingly Catholic character of the Democratic Party in the North revived the fears of some nativists. In July of 1867, *The Nation* declared that Catholic politics was "drilled, organized, massed, and can be thrown with resistless weight upon a given point. Time after time it has been used to defeat Republican candidates and causes; to baffle attempts at municipal reform; to sustain municipal corruption; and to carry the measures of a sham Democracy against the intelligence and moral sense of the community."

Although more than a few Republicans at the time were convinced they had an almost divine calling to rule the nation, voting patterns in the post-civil-war era reveal that their hold on the government was tenuous at best. For the twenty-four years after the Civil War, Republicans may have dominated the executive mansion but their margins of victory were often very narrow:

Presidential Votes of Party

	Republicans %	Democrats %
1868	52.66	47.34
1872	55.63	43.83
1876	47.95	50.97
1880	48.27	48.25
1884	48.25	48.50
1888	47.82	48.62
1892	42.96	46.05

Congress changed hands frequently during this era, and is a better barometer than the presidency for measuring local political sentiments. The Republicans controlled the Senate for eighteen years between 1868 and 1893 while the Democrats had a majority in the House of Representatives for twelve. For most of the post-war period, voting patterns reveal that the nation was, as political scientist Paul Kleppner has concluded, engaged in the "politics of stalemate."[3] And as this chapter will demonstrate, the Catholic vote was decisive – particularly in the close presidential elections during this period.

Because it possessed the largest block of electoral votes – thirty five, or 19 percent of the total, needed for victory – New York was a key political battle ground. And with Catholics becoming a significant portion of New York's inner-city voting totals, their political allegiance mattered to every presidential contender. But the Catholic vote was also significant in other parts of the country. As many ethnic Catholics moved to the Midwest and settled on farms or in inner cities such as Detroit, Chicago, and Milwaukee, their influence at the polls contributed to the shifting balance of power. Kleppner has concluded that "by 1890, Catholics were the largest single bloc within the electorate in Michigan and Wisconsin."[4] And their presence made these previously bedrock Republican states more competitive in every election cycle.

Percentage of the Electorate in Urban Areas[5]

	1870	1890
Michigan	16.6	22.3
Ohio	21.4	30.4
Wisconsin	13.7	19.2

Religious Groups as an Estimated Percentage of the Electorate

	Michigan		Ohio		Wisconsin	
	1870	1890	1870	1890	1870	1890
Baptist	10.0	5.0	10.0	5.0	5.0	5.0
Congregat'list	10.0	15.0	10.0	5.0	5.0	5.0
Lutheran	5.0	15.0	10.0	25.0	15.0	30.0
Methodist	25.0	15.0	20.0	15.0	10.0	5.0
Presbyterian	5.0	5.0	10.0	5.0	5.0	5.0
Catholic	10.0	20.0	15.0	25.0	20.0	35.0

Unfortunately, as these political changes unfolded, making elections more contentious and competitive, they also gave rise to renewed episodes of anti-Catholicism.

*   *   *   *   *

After much bickering at their 1868 convention, a divided Democratic Party turned on the twenty-second ballot to New York's former Governor, Horatio Seymour, as a compromise candidate. He ran on a platform that pledged to restore former Confederate states to their pre-war status and condemned radical-Republican moves to strip the nation's chief-executive powers.

Although Seymour was a bland candidate who aroused little enthusiasm, Catholics liked him because he spoke out on the inequities of the Civil War draft. Reacting to Seymour's pro-Catholic attitude, Thomas Nast vilified him in *Harper's Weekly* in cartoons such as *"The Lost Cause*, showing a former Confederate and a New York Irishman searching with a light; *Out, damned spot*, showing Seymour as Lady Macbeth, attempting to eliminate the spot on his record caused by the New York draft riots of 1863; and a double cartoon, *Matched*, picturing Seymour and the draft rioters in comparison with Grant at Vicksburg, both in July 1863."[6]

That same Ulysses S. Grant was nominated without opposition at the Republican convention in Chicago. His party added these planks to their platform hoping to attract the votes of Catholic immigrants:

- The doctrine of Great Britain and other European powers, that because a man is once a subject, he is always so, must be resisted, at every hazard, by the United States, as a relic of the feudal times, not authorized by the law of nations, and at war with our national honor and independence. Naturalized citizens are entitled to be protected in all their rights of citizenship, as though they were native-born; and no citizen of the United States, native or naturalized, must be liable to arrest and imprisonment by any foreign power, for acts done or words spoken in this country; and, if so arrested and imprisoned, it is the duty of the Government to interfere in his behalf.
- Foreign immigration, which in the past, has added so much to the wealth, development of resources, and increase of power to this nation . . . should be fostered and encouraged by a liberal and just policy.

- The asylum of the oppressed of all nations – should be fostered and encouraged by a liberal and just policy.

- This Convention declares its sympathy with all the oppressed people which are struggling for their rights.[7]

While his supporters were certain of victory, the candidate had to endure campaign epithets, such as "Grant the Butcher" and "Grant the Drunkard," as well as false claims that his vice-presidential candidate, Schuyler Colfax, was a former nativist congressman. And there were occasional anti-Catholic outbursts. In the Republican *Chicago Post*, for example, the following appeared on September 8, 1868, describing the paper's perception of a typical Irish-Catholic Democratic voter:

Teddy O'Flaherty votes. He has not been in the country six months.

> . . . He has hair on his teeth. He never knew an hour in civilized
> society. . . . He is a born savage – as brutal a ruffian as an untamed
> Indian. . . . Breaking heads for opinion's sake is his practice. The
> born criminal and pauper of the civilized world . . . a wrong, abused
> and pitiful spectacle of a man . . . pushed straight to hell by the
> abomination against common sense called the Catholic religion . . .

But General Grant did receive the overwhelming support of the soldiers
he had led, and this was enough to give him a large Electoral College victory:
214 votes to Seymour's 80. However, upon closer examination, voting patterns
in 1868 had to make Republicans queasy. Grant received only 52.7 percent of
the popular vote – not exactly a landslide for the general who had driven Lee
from Richmond to Appomattox.

Grant's victory was narrow in spite of the fact that three Southern states
– Virginia, Mississippi and Florida – were not permitted to vote. Also, Deep
South states like South Carolina and North Carolina were carried by Grant
because many former Confederates were denied the franchise. "Although
Grant won 991 counties to Seymour's 711, 359 counties remained unheard
from, primarily in the unreconstructed states of Mississippi, Texas and
Virginia. . . . GOP majorities in Indiana, New Hampshire, North Carolina, and
Pennsylvania were distinctly less than comfortable; in Alabama, Arkansas and
Connecticut, they were quite narrow; and in Nevada and California, Grant's
edge was almost infinitesimal."[8]

Seymour narrowly carried New York: 429,883 votes to 419,883. The fact
that a Democrat carried the Empire State for the first time since 1852 can be
attributed to Catholic loyalty. In New York City the former governor received
69 percent of the vote (156,000 vs. Grant's 108,000) with similar margins in
Brooklyn and Queens counties. These heavily Catholic areas made the difference for Seymour.

In modest recognition of the political power of Catholics, the Grant
Administration steered some patronage their way. General Patrick Jones, an
Irish Catholic, was named Postmaster of New York City, and Catholics were
appointed to lower-rank federal jobs in the post office and customs house.

While Republican political pros who analyzed the numbers knew the
importance of endearing themselves to Catholics, they were foiled by numerous congressional Republicans committed to a rigid ideology. Many of these
radicals who were trying to remold the South "argued that the North, too,
needed reconstruction. New York, Boston, Chicago, San Francisco, and other
cities possessed large, heavily Catholic immigrant populations, and striking
gains by the Democratic Party in local elections after the war suggested an
untutored, or, worse, manipulated electorate. One prominent minister
explained in 1868 that 'the Jesuit is master of the Great Metropolis.' And

Harper's Weekly argued, 'The dependence of the Democratic party at this moment is upon the Ku-Klux feeling both in the Northern and Southern States, and upon the Roman Catholic vote.'"[9] Governor Oliver Morton of Indiana referred to the Democratic Party as "a common sewer and loathsome receptacle, into which is emptied every element of treason North and South, and every element of inhumanity and barbarism which has dishonored the age."[10]

> In the first decade after the war, leading Republican politicians, ministers, and editors – including Grant, Garfield, and Hayes, George William Curtis and Eugene Lawrence at *Harper's Weekly*, E.L. Godkin of the *Nation*, Joseph Medill of the *Chicago Tribune*, and the editors of the *New York Times* – all emphasized the Catholic threat. They worried that an authoritarian church continued to stand against liberal reform, that an international church threatened national unity, and that Catholicism might slow scientific and intellectual progress.[11]

One Catholic issue that came to the forefront and was to ignite political flames for the remainder of the century was education. Concerned that the public schools were hopelessly Protestant-dominated, the Church hierarchy dedicated itself to building a parochial school system. While the bishops at the first and second plenary councils (1852 and 1866), "entreated" and "urged" parishes to build schools to educate Catholic children, by the 1870s, bishops pushed the faithful even harder to expand the education network.[12] In one pastoral letter the faithful were lectured that "the public school system is controlled absolutely by Protestants, conducted on Protestant principles and made an instrument for debauching the faith of Catholic children . . . ."[13] In 1884, the third plenary council "'decreed' that a parochial school would be erected within each parish within two years. It also 'decreed' that all Catholic parents send their children to such schools."[14]

With the building of Catholic schools, orphanages, and hospitals increasing at a rapid rate, the Church aggressively sought government aid to help finance these projects. The rationale for the aid was simple: since Protestantism was preached in state-financed public schools, Catholics were entitled equal support to propagate their religious tenets in their schools. They also argued that since parish schools relieved the government of financial and operational burdens, they were entitled to financial assistance. If help was denied, they further argued, Catholics in effect paid double – public school taxes and Catholic School tuition.

Catholics were urged to support candidates for office who were sympathetic to their school positions, while Protestants, fearing Catholic schools would prevent proper immigrant assimilation into the American cultural mainstream, championed opposition to school aid. Another important reason for Protestant opposition was the belief that flourishing Catholic schools would give the Church too much power over their flocks, leading Catholic political and cultural clout to equal or surpass Protestant hegemony.

In New York, for instance, Tammany Hall boss William Tweed, a Protestant, made sure that Protestant, Catholic, and Jewish charitable and educational institutions received government aid. Since Catholics had the greatest number of schools, orphanages, and reformatories, they received the largest share of state and city aid. Protestants resented this situation and *The Nation's* editorial page reacted by proclaiming, "the Catholic Church is the established Church of [New York]."[15]

In 1869, New York's Union League Club took the lead in organizing opposition to Tammany's aid to parochial schools. The issue came to a head in 1872 when the Democratic candidate for governor, a Catholic named Francis Kernan, was denounced by Republican newspaper editors for his support of state aid. In *Harper's Weekly* Thomas Nast published a derogatory caricature of a papal proclamation that read "Vote for Kernan, he is a Roman Catholic and will obey the orders of the Church."[16]

The school aid issue caused Kernan to run behind the rest of the Democratic ticket and to lose the election. It was estimated that 60,000 Democratic Protestants deserted Kernan to vote for his Republican opponent.

The demand for state aid to parochial schools was spreading throughout the nation. In New Haven, Westbury, and New Britain, Connecticut, the election of Catholic Democrats to various school boards resulted in financial aid to parochial schools. Throughout the Northeast, Catholics strove to implement what became known as the Poughkeepsie Plan. Under this approach, local municipalities built and maintained a school and then leased it to a Catholic parish. The school board appointed qualified nuns or Catholic laymen as teachers. Religious instruction took place in the facility after normal school hours. In effect, the Catholic Church was hired by the government to run a public school whose student body was exclusively Catholic.

The Poughkeepsie Plan was successfully adopted in many communities in New York and Connecticut, and variations were instituted in other areas. In the Midwest, for instance, heavily populated German-Catholic regions pushed for the adoption of the plan. They had some limited success, but in Missouri and Ohio legislative efforts failed due to the opposition of rural Protestants. In Cincinnati, Cleveland, St. Louis, Chicago, Jersey City, Detroit, Indianapolis, Kansas City, St. Cloud, and other urban areas where Catholics had numerical clout, they pushed their school agenda and often experienced some form of success.

There were other victories as well. In Ohio, Catholics pursued the issue of the King James Bible being read in public schools all the way to the state's highest court. In 1873, the Ohio Supreme Court "ruled that the Bible was a sectarian book and should henceforth be banned from public schools."[17] Another Ohio court victory that year was the exemption of Catholic Church property from taxation.

> At the same time, in Wisconsin and Ohio, Catholics sought and obtained legislation allowing their priests to minister to inmates in public institutions. Also in 1874 the Catholic hierarchy in Ohio mobilized public sentiment against the new state constitution and its clause prohibiting any religious organization from having control over state school funds. In 1878 in Michigan, Catholics were successful in defeating the Emerson Bill, which would have outlawed the use of ecclesiastical sanctions within the Church. These types of battles persisted into the 1880's, as Catholics successfully opposed legislation in Ohio to provide free text books in public schools, and in 1881 and 1887 defeated attempts in the Michigan Legislature to prevent bishops from owning all of the church property within their dioceses.[18]

These regional ballot-box and court victories increased the enmity of some Protestants, who feared Catholic domination of their cities, towns, and villages. As a result, Anti-Catholic groups, once again, began to emerge.

Ministers formed the Evangelical Alliance which called on Protestants to end "infidelity, popery and other forms of superstition, error and profaneness."[19] The founder of the order of the American Union, former Know-Nothing James Barker of New York, directed his organization to halt "the repeated efforts of the emissaries of Rome to corrupt our elections, destroy the public school system and place the Holy Bible beyond the reach of our youth in the public schools."[20]

These nativist groups, which by 1876 claimed 500,000 members in twenty-nine states, directed their followers to vote only for native born and to fight "the formation of Roman Catholic political organizations in America and their interference in the political affairs of the nation."[21]

They also called for the passage of state and federal constitutional amendments that would forbid any public financial aid to church schools. In the 1870s, numerous states adopted variations of their amendment including: Missouri, Illinois, Pennsylvania, New Jersey, Nebraska, Texas, Colorado, and Minnesota. Catholic opposition defeated similar amendments in Rhode Island, New York, and Connecticut.

These state battles also crept up onto the national stage and impacted presidential elections.

* * * * *

Ulysses S. Grant was a reluctant candidate for president in 1868. He had proved to himself and the nation that he was an able warrior, but he knew that every non-military endeavor he had pursued throughout his life had ended in failure. As general-in-chief of U.S. Armed Forces, he outranked any soldier in America's history with the lone exception of George Washington. The job also had life tenure, and this meant much to a man who had endured periods of extreme poverty. Nevertheless, he succumbed to the pressure to run from Republicans who believed that Grant, waving the "Bloody Shirt" of war, would rally veterans to polling booths and give them a victory.

Throughout his first term, Grant generally sided with the more conservative factions of his party, particularly in domestic matters. Republican reformers grew disgusted with President Grant because his administration had not heeded their calls for civil service reform, free trade, and a conciliatory southern policy. These reformers, who believed "Grantism" represented corruption, inefficiency, and nepotism, broke from the party and formed a group known as "Liberal Republicans." This splinter group's leaders included Carl Schurz, B. Gratz Brown, Charles Sumner, Lyman Trumbull, Charles Francis Adams, and New York newspaper editor Horace Greeley.

Sensing that this rift in the Republican Party could work to the Democrat's advantage, August Belmont of New York, the Democrats' national chairman, looked to broker a deal with the dissident Republicans. He sold the group on the concept of a "fusion" candidate for president who would appeal both to regular Democrats and to members of reform movements throughout the nation. The fusion of these groups, Belmont believed, would assemble enough electoral votes to topple the Grant administration. A pact was sealed with the Liberal Republicans whereby Belmont agreed to endorse their candidates for president and vice president.

When the Liberals met on May 1, 1872, at Cincinnati's Exposition Hall, Belmont expected the newly formed party to nominate Boston brahmin, Charles Francis Adams. This son and grandson of U.S. presidents, Belmont believed, would add the touch of class necessary for the scheme to succeed at the polls. But the plan backfired: after much bickering, the Liberals nominated the least attractive candidate, none other than Horace Greeley. But the unhappy Belmont kept his part of the bargain and engineered the Democratic Party to endorse the ticket of Greeley and Gatz Brown.

For most his life, Horace Greeley was a Whig and a Republican who had denigrated Democrats, particularly if they were Catholic. He expressed his anti-pluralistic view in 1860 when he proclaimed: "He who votes in our election as an Irishman or a German, has no moral right to vote at all." For decades the erratic, impulsive, and emotional Greeley attacked Democrats as "slave holders," "slave whippers," "traitors," and "Copperheads."[22] In addition, Greeley had "proved a poor executive with little business talent, a poor judge of men and money, both gullible and giddy. Many considered him fit neither to lead a party nor govern a nation."[23]

Catholics, particularly in New York, were appalled that Greeley represented their party. "Straight Democrats" broke ranks with their party and nominated the first Roman Catholic to run for president, Charles O'Connor of New York. Dissident Catholics, labor members, and state-rights groups, turned to this former U.S. attorney and 1848 gubernatorial candidate, hoping to punish their party.

This discord guaranteed Grant's re-election, and his results were dramatically better than in 1868.

	Grant	Greeley	O'Connor
Popular Vote	3,597,132	2,834,125	39,489
Percentage	55.6%	43.8%	0.60%
Electoral Vote	244	47	0

Grant received the highest majority of any election from 1836 to 1892.

Angry Democrats had punished their party. Even Chairman Belmont voted for the failed candidacy of his old friend Charles O'Connor rather than support the odious Greeley. And Catholics showed their disgust with Greeley by either staying home or holding their noses and voting for Grant. In fact, the New England, Middle Atlantic, East, North, Central and Pacific states recorded a decline in voter turnout.

Presidential Vote
Heavily Populated Catholic Counties

	1868		1872	
	Democrat	**Republican**	**Democrat**	**Republican**
New York City	108,316	47,748	77,814	54,676
Brooklyn, NY	39,838	27,711	38,108	33,368
Queens, NY	6,388	4,973	5,655	6,082
Baltimore, MD	21,702	9,103	24,694	19,527
Oakland Co., MI	4,442	4,738	3,326	4,490
Wash'ton Co. WI	3,073	1,213	2,727	947
Anglaize Co., OH	2,756	1,266	2,535	1,180
Vinton Cty., OH	1,554	1,499	1,340	1,314

This change in voting habits even cost the Democrats the home state of their standard bearer, New York. The only part of the country where Democrats actually improved their vote totals was in the South. Large numbers of ex-Confederates who could now vote showed their contempt for corrupt Reconstruction policies by sticking with the party of Andrew Jackson.

The second Grant Administration was rocked by the financial depression known as the "Panic of 1873" and by numerous other scandals. Both his former vice president, Schuyler Colfax, and his present vice president, Henry Wilson, were tarred by a railroad scandal. Various Cabinet members were also accused of corrupt dealings. While Grant himself was known to be an honest man, the scandals began to take its toll on his administration, which began looking for opportunities to change the political discussion. And one issue he pursued to accomplish that end was the Catholic school debate.

Grant, in his pre-Civil War civilian days, had flirted with the Know-Nothing movement. Brought up as an Ohio Methodist, he had a jaded eye when it came to Catholics. During the war, for instance, he let it be known that he did not trust Catholic bishops, because they were critical of their flock being slaughtered in battle due to Grant's attrition strategy.[24] Grant must have noticed that the specter of anti-Catholicism had also appeared in the presidential campaign of 1872. The Republican-slanted *Harper's Weekly* went after Catholics: "The unpatriotic conduct of the Romanish population in our chief cities during the late rebellion is well known. They formed a constant menace and terror to the loyal citizens; they thronged the peace meetings, they strove to divide the Union; and when the war was over, they placed in office their corrupt leaders and plundered the impoverished community."[25] In 1872, the magazine opposed the election of Democrat Francis Kernan as New York's governor because he was a Catholic who supported aid to parochial schools. Harper's even attacked, on February 3, 1872, a recently enacted New York State law that permitted the Church to incorporate Catholic property in the name of the ordinary of the Diocese:

> The danger of this unprecedented law, this gross departure from the principles of equality and freedom, is increased by the fact that the Romish priesthood have formed themselves into a distinct political party. Not content with humane toleration accorded them among us, they labor to control the elections, and rule by the disunion of their opponents. Of all the religious sects they alone enter into the strife of parties as a united and well-organized body. They make no secret of their purpose. They propose to destroy the common schools, and to gain such an influence in the State as shall best serve to advance the interests of their Church. If they obey the papal syllabus they must labor to make their religion the religion of the State, to the exclusion of all others.[26]

Catholic Historian Thomas T. McAvoy, accurately pointed out that "the editors of *Harper's Weekly* pretended that they were defending American institutions against a degrading influence. They were at the same time defending the Republican opponents of the Irish Catholic candidates."[27]

President Grant was no fool. He understood that religion injected into politics could "stir the pot." In one speech he remarked "there are three great political parties: the Republican, the Democratic, and the Methodist Church."[28] He knew that sectors of the country were influenced by dominant religious sects, just as his Methodist Church had exerted influence in his home state of Ohio.

In an October 29, 1875, speech before a group of Veterans in Des Moines, Iowa, he warned those gathered (including General William Tecumseh Sherman) that money should never "be appropriated for the support of any sectarian school." Aid to parochial schools, he argued, would wreck public schools, "the promoter of that intelligence which is to preserve us as a nation." He also stoked the flames of anti-Catholicism with this remark: "If we are to have another contest in the near future of our national existence, I predict that the dividing line will not be the Mason and Dixon's, but between patriotism and intelligence on the one side and superstition, ambition and ignorance on the other."[29]

In 1875, Grant called on the Congress to adopt a constitutional amendment directing each state to establish free public schools for all children. "As Grant saw it, the schools should be entirely secular: The teaching of religion would be banned and public aid to sectarian schools would be forbidden."[30] He also asked Congress to send him legislation that would permit the government to tax church property.[31] Grant believed that this legislation would prevent tyranny "whether directed by the demagogue or by priestcraft."[32] And one Democratic senator "wryly commented that the Republican matadors were looking for another beast to slay now that Jeff Davis and the 'bloody shirt' were losing their popular appeal. 'The Pope, the old Pope of Rome, is to be the great bull that we are all to attack.'"[33]

Responding to Grant's appeal, Congressman James G. Blaine of Maine, introduced a federal constitutional amendment that would stop the use of any public property, revenues, or loans to support any school or institute of any kind under the control of a religious organization. The bill passed the House, but Democrats killed it in the Senate.

As the 1876 presidential race approached, Grant whispered to key politicos that despite scandals and the indictment of 238 persons connected with government corruption, he was interested in running for a third time. Methodist Bishop Gilbert Haven, an anti-Catholic, tried to drum up support for another term for Methodist Grant. The bishop publicly declared in Boston that the president was "the only man who could conquer their enemies." The *Boston Herald* editorial board, reacting to the comments, warned their readers that Grant should not be re-nominated on a "no-popery platform."

The Republicans turned to another Ohioan at their convention, two-term Governor Rutherford B. Hayes. The Harvard-educated lawyer had attained the rank of major-general during the Civil War and was elected to Congress where he had embraced the reconstruction program of the Radical Republicans.

Like Grant, there was also a dark side to Hayes, another Methodist, when it came to Roman Catholics. When Ohio Republicans had to choose a candidate for governor in 1875, they rejected Judge Alphonso Taft because he supported, in his hometown of Cincinnati, a school board decision to ban classroom reading of the Bible in public schools. Viewing his stand as pro-Catholic, convention delegates nominated Hayes, who publicly condemned the decision.

As he campaigned for governor, Hayes accused Democrats of colluding with Catholics to destroy the Ohio public-school system. Immigration historian John Higham described Hayes as working "fiercely to smear Democrats as subservient to Catholic designs."[34] In a letter Hayes warned Republicans not to "let the Catholic question drop out of sight." He also complained that "the sectarian [Catholic] wing of the Democratic Party rules the party today in the great commercial metropolis of the nation. It holds the balance of power in many of the large cities of the country. Without its votes, the Democratic Party would lose every large city and county in Ohio, and every Northern State."[35]

When the Republicans gathered in Cincinnati in June 1876 for their convention, they broke the deadlocked presidential balloting on the seventh ballot by nominating Hayes as a compromise candidate. And in their platform they included this plank that opposed funding to Catholic Schools:

> The public school system of the several states is the bulwark of the American republic; and, with a view to its security and permanence, we recommend an amendment to the constitution of the United States, forbidding the application of any public funds or property for the benefit of any school or institution under sectarian control.[36]

When the Democrats gathered at their convention site in St. Louis, they smelled victory. The Republicans, who had controlled the executive branch for sixteen years, had a record to defend that included failed Reconstruction and economic policies and extensive corruption in numerous executive departments. Two years earlier, the Democrats had begun their comeback by gaining control of the House of Representatives and picking up governorships in New York, New Jersey, Missouri, and Massachusetts.

Samuel Tilden's sweeping 1874 gubernatorial victory in New York put him on the top of every political wag's list of presidential hopefuls, and by the time the convention gavel came down, most assumed he would be crowned. Trying to avoid the charge that they were papal puppets, the Democrats, with nominee Tilden's blessing, adopted a resolution supporting the public school system.

The Catholic issue was very much alive in the fall campaign. Pamphlets were distributed throughout the nation accusing Church leaders of ordering their flock to vote for Tilden. One pamphlet stated that life as we know it in the United States would be destroyed "if the ultramontane element of the Church, through the success of the Democracy, should obtain control of our National Affairs."[37]

Hayes didn't pull any punches during the campaign. At one gathering, he said that if the Bible being read in public schools "[doesn't] suit other people, let them remain east of the Ohio or go West. . . . I don't propose to have them undermine the foundations and pull the house down around our ears without at least a protest."[38]

When the Democratic-controlled House of Representatives passed a watered down version of the Blaine Amendment that made the law unenforceable (and seemed thus to open the door for public funding of parochial schools), Hayes condemned it calling it the "Jesuitical Clause." The Republican-controlled Senate followed Hayes's advice and advanced tough legislation that denied tax dollars to any religious institution for any reason. Senate Democrats complaining that the Hayes's version was "nearly an accusation of disloyalty" managed to bottle up the bill.

> When Rutherford Hayes spoke of the Catholic question and referred to their threat to the public school system, he was not conjuring up an imaginary foe. He was attempting to impart political salience to deeply rooted, albeit frequently latent, religious animosities. He was appealing to matters which concerned people immediately and directly. Voters could perceive the relationship between the Democratic Party and the Catholic Church, and the relationship between that church and their religious values, much more clearly than they could see a relationship between their economic status and the tariff policy, and the tariff and party positions. The religious relationships were clear precisely because they were in accord with the voter's perception of his world. The Republican strategy was not a cynically concocted scheme divorced from social reality. It was successful because it was rooted in that reality. The number of Catholics in the electorate *was* increasing rapidly in the 1870's and 1880's. Their political power *was* growing more rapidly than that of other groups.   Catholic

voters *did* identify strongly with the Democratic Party. That party *was* responsive to the demands of its Catholic supporters. And, most importantly, the attitude of the Catholic hierarchy had shifted from defense to offense.[39]

Catholics did not sit idly by during the campaign. The Boston Catholic paper *The Pilot* accused Hayes of being "supported by every anti-foreign, Know Nothing clique that disgraces the country." Catholics also exposed a letter that Hayes wrote to the Republican National Committee that stated his "opposition to Catholic interference with political affairs and especially with schools."[40] While the Catholic school controversy was not the only issue in the campaign, it did have an impact on what was to be one of the closest elections in American history.

When the votes were counted, Governor Tilden was ahead by 250,000 votes and the Republican *New York Tribune* on November 8 declared him the winner. Thanks to the overwhelming support of the Catholic vote, Tilden carried, by a razor-thin margin, states that no Democrat had carried in decades. In addition to sweeping the South, Tilden carried Connecticut, Delaware, Missouri, New Jersey, and New York. And he narrowly lost Illinois, Ohio, and Pennsylvania. In each of these cases, the Catholic vote made the races extremely close.

In numerous urban centers dominated by Catholics, their vote for the Democrats increased over the 1872 totals:

	Democrats 1872	Democrats 1876
New York City	58.3%	65.4%
Hartford, CT	50.0	52.0
New Haven, CT	49.8	53.2
Hudson Cty., NJ	52.6	60.7
Union Cty., NJ	48.8	53.7
Cook County, IL	37.6	50.7
Philadelphia, PA	25.0	44.0

The Catholic vote in these states helped Tilden carry or come close to carrying tightly contested swing states:

	Tilden	Hayes
New York	521,949	489,207
Connecticut	61,934	59,034
New Jersey	115,962	103,517
Illinois	258,601	278,232
Pennsylvania	366,204	384,184

Thanks to Catholic turnout in various Ohio cities, Tilden almost carried Hayes's home state:

Ohio

Tilden	323,182	49.0%
Hayes	330,698	50.2
Greenback Candidate	3,057	0.46
Prohibitionist Candidate	1,636	0.24

To keep control of the executive mansion, desperate Republicans challenged the results in three states: Florida, Louisiana, and South Carolina. A Republican-appointed electoral commission took four months to recount the numbers in their favor and to cut a deal with southern Democrats to go along with the new totals.

With the Republican promise to end Reconstruction, recall the military, and to send millions in federal grants to rebuild their infrastructure, southern Democrats sold northerner Tilden down the river, despite the fact that he was a fiscally conservative, Jeffersonian states'-rights advocate.

At 4 A.M. March 2, 1877, after eighteen hours of haggling, it was announced in the Congress that Rutherford B. Hayes was elected president by a margin of one electoral vote – 185 to 184.

One unfortunate result of the disputed election of 1876 was the discrediting of the Poughkeepsie Plan. The seed was successfully planted in the minds of many that state support of Catholic education threatened the future of the nation's public-school systems. This widely accepted perception permitted nativists to pursue an anti-Catholic agenda that was victorious not only in congressional and state elections but in local school-board elections as well.

As the 1880 election rolled around, President Hayes announced that he would keep his 1877 pledge to serve only one term. Senior Republicans were not unhappy with his decision. They were constantly bickering with the man who was referred to by many as President "Rutherfraud" B. Hayes.

Hayes's preferred choice to succeed him was Treasury Secretary John Sherman of Ohio. But Sherman was shunned because he was viewed as being pro-Catholic. Opponents complained he was guilty of appointing too many Catholics to positions in the Treasury Department.[41]

Instead Republicans settled for another compromise candidate, James Garfield of Ohio. Garfield had served nine terms in Congress and was appointed by his state legislature as U.S. senator on January 6, 1880. He was nominated on the thirty-fifth ballot. He agreed to run on a platform that opposed aid to parochial schools and endorsed a constitutional amendment to enforce the position.

Meanwhile, the Democrats turned to a Yankee war hero, General Winfield Scott Hancock, of Pennsylvania. Party pros believed he could peel off enough northern states to secure a narrow victory.

The campaign was low key since neither candidate possessed any real charisma. Also, with the economy in good shape, there were no burning issues that excited the electorate.

James Garfield, like the other Republican Ohio presidential candidates who had preceded him, distrusted the Catholic voter. In correspondence to one supporter, he warned that if their party was to lose it would be due to "the combined power of rebellion, Catholicism and whiskey . . . a trinity very hard to conquer."[42] And this was not a newly inspired position: Several years earlier while campaigning for Rutherford Hayes's Ohio gubernatorial race, Garfield told his candidate: "It is evident that the Catholic Church is moving along the whole line of its front against modern civilization and our fight in Ohio is only a small portion of the battlefield."[43]

Reacting to Garfield's candidacy, General Sherman's Catholic wife, Ellen Ewing Sherman, wrote to the *Catholic Herald*, warning that as president, Garfield "would do all he could to injure our Holy Catholic Church."[44]

> Two weeks later the *New York Truth*, New York's penny newspaper, commented on Mrs. Sherman's letter. It stated that no more fatal blow could be given to General Hancock than to have it supposed that he would aid the Catholic Church as against all others. The *New York Truth* felt that no better campaign document could have been circulated for Garfield than a statement that he was the champion of Protestantism and the inveterate enemy of Catholics. A secret fear existed among Protestants and Freethinkers of the gradual encroachment of the Catholic Church in America.[45]

Garfield also had a long public history concerning the education of America's children. As early as 1875 he made it clear that the attack upon our common schools came from the ecclesiastical leaders of the Catholic Church.[46]

> [Garfield] interpreted the opposition to the public school system as another way of attacking "the safety of our republican institutions. . . . " Garfield defended most vigorously the common schools. To him their purpose was to educate people, for only through an intelligent citizenry could liberty and freedom be maintained; they were a bulwark of democracy. On the other hand, he observed the Catholic clergy in America attempting to carry out the encyclical letter of Pope Pius IX, issued on December 8,

1864, among which Garfield contended were the following pro-scriptions and condemnations: "The liberty of the press; the liber-ty of conscience and worship; the separation of the church from the State; and the secular education of youth." Hence, the attack on the public schools, concluded Garfield, was equal to an attack on its democratic institutions and principles, and was the logical result of the doctrines of Roman Catholicism.[47]

To energize their Protestant base, Republicans circulated rumors that Hancock was a Catholic. Edwin Cowles, editor of *The Cleveland Leaders*, published in his paper this outlandish picture of how the church would man-age the executive mansion if Hancock were sworn in as President:

A Roman Chapel would be fitted up in it [the White House] with the superstitious paraphernalia of Roman worship. The White House would become the headquarters of priests, nuns, monks and so on. The Pope of Rome would be influential in that house through Mrs. Hancock who would be the Romish power behind the throne! The tradition of the American people inherited from their Protestant Revolutionary forefathers is opposed to an intol-erant Church, which favors the suppression of religious freedom, from having control of the White House. Mrs. Hancock is a big-oted Romish, from all we can learn, and like Mrs. Sherman will make everything politically and financially, subject to the interests of the Romish Church.[48]

The election results proved once again that America's voters were evenly divided. Garfield carried the popular vote – 4,453,211 vs. Hancock's 4,445,842; a plurality of 7,368 votes. While Garfield carried many of the states where Catholics mattered, the pluralities were very slim:

	Republican	Democrat	Plurality
Connecticut	67,071	64,415	2,655
New York	555,544	534,511	21,033
Pennsylvania	444,704	407,428	37,276

The public-school debate, however, did have an effect on the populace. The fear and hatred promoted by national and local Republicans caused many to believe that the Roman Catholic Church was employing a strategy to cap-ture enough tax dollars to conquer and control America's educational system. This fear led, in the 1880s, to the creation of the United Order of Deputies and the American League – anti-Catholic organizations that were the forerunners of the American Protective Association, which would become the largest and most influential. The membership of these groups and the bigoted beliefs they promoted were to have an impact on the presidential race of 1884.

Six months after he was sworn in as president, James Garfield was assassinated by the frustrated job-seeking Charles Guiteau. His successor was Chester Arthur, a man who had never before held elective office and had been named vice president only because he was the chief lieutenant to boss Roscoe Conkling of New York. Prior to his election as vice president, he was head of the patronage-laden customs house of New York.

While Arthur managed to survive his three and a half years in the executive mansion without scandal, he knew there was little support for his renomination. Realizing he couldn't stop the James Blaine juggernaut, he announced his intention to retire.

While there was still a large sub-set of anti-Catholic Republicans (this was evident by the opposition to General William Tecumseh Sherman for president because he had a Catholic wife and a son who had become a priest), there were members of the GOP who had a different perspective. There were those who realized that the closeness of recent presidential races, the growing numbers of Catholic voters in northern and midwestern cities, and the Democratic hold on the South might end the GOP electoral lock on the presidency. It was these like-minded Republicans who turned to Blaine as their nominee, believing he could win by siphoning some portion of the Catholic vote.

Blaine was an interesting choice. Born to a Presbyterian father and a Roman Catholic mother, Blaine claimed he was brought up as a Presbyterian while his siblings were baptized Catholics. Throughout his career, many Catholics looked fondly upon Blaine because of the opposition he received from diehard Protestants who questioned his religious loyalties. The *Irish World* and the *Irish Nation* newspapers actually endorsed him for president in 1884. There were rumors circulated by Catholic supporters that Blaine would resolve the issue of Ireland's freedom in the first months of his administration.

There was another reason why the Blaine camp was optimistic – they could pick up numerous Catholic votes; the Democratic nominee, Governor Grover Cleveland of New York, was not a favorite son of the Catholic political establishment.

When New York City's Protestant boss, William Tweed, was sent off to prison for stealing millions from the municipal treasury, the machine was taken over for the first time by a Roman Catholic – Big John Kelly. At the 1882 New York Democratic Convention, in order to stop a power play by the Brooklyn machine, Kelly agreed to support Buffalo Mayor Grover Cleveland for governor.

While Big John did not expect to call every shot in the Cleveland Administration, he did expect the governor to be grateful and to consider some of his requests. But Cleveland turned his back on Tammany Hall and embraced a reform agenda. Reporting on Democratic disunity, *The New York Times* stated: "The cry has gone up that Mr. Cleveland is against the Irish, therefore, the Irish of his state are against him."[49]

Lack of patronage was not the only reason Democrat pols were angry with their governor. Catholics were annoyed that he refused to help push the state legislature to pass the "Freedom of Worship" bill. This law was important to the Democrats because, if enacted, all levels of state government would be mandated to treat all religions equally. Cleveland was also labeled a "Presbyterian Bigot" because he vetoed legislation that would have permitted state aid to the Catholic Protectory, an orphanage system. And his greatest offense: in the name of Civil Service Reform he rejected state job applications of Irish Democrats.

Attempting to stop Cleveland's presidential nomination, Tammany Hall circulated rumors that his friends and advisors were anti-Catholic and that he opposed home-rule for Ireland. They also spread the false charge that in a convention seconding speech for Cleveland, General E. S. Bragg of Wisconsin had stated "the Irish may go and be damned."

Although Tammany's efforts failed, the bad blood that existed after the convention gave Republicans hope that they could make inroads in Catholic communities. They suddenly established Irish Republican associations and hired Irish pols to lecture their fellow Hibernians who for too long had been taken for granted by the Democratic Party. These hired guns portrayed Catholics as dupes who were used by Democrats. Still other Catholics bellowed that a Cleveland administration promoted a free-trade policy that would result in cheap British merchandise flooding U.S. markets and eliminating Catholic manufacturing jobs.

Democrats tried to keep Catholics on the party's reservation by reminding them that Blaine introduced the Amendment to stop aid to Catholic schools. They also circulated the false rumor that he was a prominent member of the Know-Nothings in the 1850s.

Blaine did, however, have a few Catholic cards to play. In Catholic settings he emphasized that his mother and siblings were Catholic and that he had a cousin who was a Mother Superior in a Roman convent. He reminded his audiences that he was belligerent toward the British and had sided with the Irish during the Land League struggle. Blaine would ask Catholic audiences how they could be loyal to the Democratic Party that supported free trade with their ancient enemy, the British. "The solution," Blaine argued, "was to vote Republican and guarantee an end to American subservience to John Bull."

The campaign was hard fought, and there was much mud slinging. But the Blaine supporters believed they had an edge. The sachems at Tammany

Hall were still sitting on their hands, and indications were they were successfully chipping away segments of the Catholic vote. Their candidate stormed
the nation and loved campaigning while Cleveland ran an unaggressive front-
porch campaign from Albany. Republicans also taunted Cleveland for father-
ing an illegitimate child with the chant: "Ma, Ma, where's my Pa?" Both sides
knew the election was going to be close and that New York could decide the
outcome. Hence, New York City's half million Irish Catholics became the key
to the outcome of the 1884 presidential election. And Blaine's people felt they
were making excellent inroads in the Irish community until events overtook
their campaign on "Black Wednesday," October 29, 1884.

Before making a final campaign swing in New York City's Irish neighborhoods, Blaine attended a morning rally of Protestant clergymen at the Fifth
Avenue Hotel. The welcoming speech was delivered by a Presbyterian minister, Rev. Samuel D. Burchard, who stated: "We are Republicans and don't propose to leave our Party and identify ourselves with the party whose
antecedents have been *Rum, Romanism and Rebellion.*"

At first, Blaine did not pay much attention to the comment, but after sitting through a number of speeches, he turned to the event organizer James
King and said, "That 'Rum, Romanism and Rebellion' remark is exceedingly
unfortunate."[50]

But it was too late to curb the damage. Notes of the meeting were already
on their way to Democratic Headquarters whose printers churned out, by the
next day, pamphlets exploiting the anti-Catholic statement. Tens of thousands
of the pamphlets were distributed after parish masses throughout the
Northeast.

Upon reading the notes, Colonel John Tracey of the Democratic Party's
New York news bureau gleefully declared, "If anything will elect Cleveland,
these words will do it."[51]

James King tried to get Burchard to issue this retraction to the press:

> In addressing Mr. Blaine on October 29, I used the phrase rum,
> Romanism and rebellion in characterizing some of our political
> opponents. I would desire simply to say that perhaps the remark
> was inopportune and under the circumstances it would have been
> more politic not to have made it. But I also desire to say that while
> the utterance might have been in timeliness inexpedient, it embod-
> ied historical and painful truth and as an individual citizen I
> assume the responsibility for its accuracy."[52]

Unfortunately, for the Blaine campaign, Burchard declined to sign this apology.

Although Blaine condemned the remark as "an unfortunate expression
of another man" and "a disrespectful allusion to that ancient faith in which

my revered mother lived and died" – he could not overcome the impact of the "Rum, Romanism and Rebellion" comment had on the Catholic community in the eleventh hour of the campaign. Catholic clerics denounced "Blaine's renunciation of his Catholic religion."[53] From the pulpit one priest bellowed: "Few Catholics will vote for the old Know Nothing who to this day is but too willing to avail himself of Know Nothing prejudice, and what makes it worse, not from anything like honest passion or prejudice, but from cold-blooded self-interest."[54] Even Boss Kelly and his Tammany Hall henchmen read the handwriting on the wall and went to work for Cleveland in the Catholic wards.

As the election results slowly trickled in, it was evident that in spite of the Burchard disaster, Blaine did pick up numerous Catholic votes and that he surpassed Garfield's 1880 numbers in numerous Catholic neighborhoods.

> In spite of Burchard, Blaine polled a bigger Irish vote in New York City, Chicago, and Boston than any Republican presidential candidate before him. Thus, in Brooklyn, Cleveland actually got fewer votes than Hancock had in four of the twenty-five wards: the top three Irish wards, and one that ranked seventh. Six of the seven most heavily Irish wards ranked among the seven in which Cleveland's percentage of the vote declined the most. By contrast, Blaine improved on Garfield's share of the vote in only five wards, all but one of them among the top five Irish wards. In Troy, the pattern was even more distinct: Cleveland's percentage decline from Hancock's was worst in four of the five most Irish wards. This did not mean that the Irish joined the Republicans as a whole; in both cities, the most Irish wards were also the most Democratic ones, as usual. But the party's margin had been slimmed considerably, and of course every vote lost was one less to offset the usual Republican majorities upstate.[55]

The morning of Wednesday, November 5, 1884, Americans woke to learn that their nation was evenly divided with 181 electoral votes for Cleveland and 182 for Blaine. The election of the next president came down to the closely contested race in New York, where it took another three days to tabulate the results.

When the count was official, Cleveland carried the Empire State by the razor-thin margin of 1,149 votes. Even with voter erosion, enough Catholics stood with Cleveland to save the day. Nationally, Cleveland was elected to the Oval Office with 4,874,986 votes to Blaine's 4,851,981.

In the election of 1884, Catholics were the most sought-after bloc of voters. And while Blaine did surpass Garfield's totals in Catholic areas, one faux pas cost him just enough votes in the Roman Catholic communities to lose a national election.

1880–1884 Comparison
Voter Results in Heavily Catholic Neighborhoods

	1880 Garfield	1884 Blaine
New York State	534,511	563,154
New York City	81,730	90,095
Brooklyn	31,751	53,516
Queens	6,971	8,151
Erie	20,300	24,149

	1880 Garfield	1884 Blaine
Illinois	318,036	337,469
Cook County	54,816	69,251

If any lesson was learned by the major political parties in 1884, it was they could not ignore or offend the Catholic voter.

Chapter 7

The Catholic Voter in the Gilded Age:
The Silver Years

The national political stalemate continued for four more years. The key issue in presidential politics became tariffs, an issue that boosted Catholic emotions, especially in the form of the Bayard-Chamberlain Treaty.

Tariff levels were a hot issue because so many Catholic laborers believed free trade would cost them their jobs. The Bayard-Chamberlain Tariff Treaty that President Grover Cleveland sent to the Senate angered Irish-Catholics because it recommended a Canadian fishing rights settlement between the U.S. and that traditional enemy of the Irish, Great Britain.

Keeping an eye on the Irish-Catholic vote, the Republicans organized opposition against the treaty. Arguing that the agreement was an embarrassing sellout to Great Britain, the GOP was able to drum up thirty nay votes – enough to defeat the treaty and embarrass the president. The English-hating Irish applauded the Republican maneuver. "There seems to be no doubt," wrote historian Florence Gibson, "that the rejection of the treaty was a bid for the Irish vote."[1]

Not to be outdone, President Cleveland urged Congress to punish our northern neighbors for violating our fishing rights just two days after the senate defeat of the Bayard-Chamberlain Treaty. He asked that the executive branch be given the power to halt the movement of goods (particularly fish) over the border. This bold – albeit impractical – move trumped the Republicans and received the cheers and approval of the Irish. The *Irish American* wrote: "Promises of future help in the contest against Erin's hereditary foe avail nothing against the effective action of the immediate present. The Democracy regains once more the cohorts that marched under the party's banners through sunshine and defeat in the past, and the President is the idol of the hour."[2]

During the campaign of 1888, Catholics took a serious interest in the tariff issue. After the president asked Congress in 1887 to help promote overseas trade by slashing tariffs, the Republicans saw an opportunity to wreak political havoc. Portraying the GOP as the traditional defender of high tariffs, party operatives reminded Irish-Catholics that Cleveland's stand would help create jobs in England at the expense of American jobs.

Even after Republicans at their political convention rejected James Blaine, the favorite of many Catholics, in favor of another Ohio citizen, Benjamin Harrison, a former Civil War general, U.S. senator, and grandson of the first Whig president, they thought they could still attract Catholic votes.

To achieve this goal, they included in their platform opposition to Cleveland's low-tariff policies and endorsed home rule for Ireland. Irish Catholics were particularly sensitive to this issue since the Balfour government had defeated the home-rule bill and were enacting coercive policies in Ireland.

The mixed reaction of most northeastern Catholics was expressed in this *Irish World* editorial: "The result of the Chicago Convention, although a disappointment to the ardent admirers of Blaine and especially to the Irish, is not unacceptable to the Republicans generally. The nominees are worthy gentlemen and the platform has the true ring in it. Nevertheless, the Republican Party, in my judgment, will find the road to Washington a hard one to travel the coming Fall."[3]

During the campaign, Republicans resurrected the charge that Cleveland was anti-Catholic. They published an affidavit by an alleged school friend of Cleveland's who charged that the president had stated in 1881 that he would never appear on the same political ticket with an Irish Catholic.[4]

The Democrats, having learned a lesson from backlash to the 1887 treaty, paid close attention to their Irish-Catholic constituency. They reminded Catholics that it was Democrats who protected them from the evil designs of the nativists. They reminded them that the Cleveland Administration broke all records when it came to awarding patronage to Catholics. They also made much of a reported 1876 statement made by Harrison (which was later proven to be false): "If it were not for [the Irish] we would not need half our penitentiaries, which are almost full of them. They are only good to shovel dirt and grade railroads, for which they receive more than they are worth, as they are no acquisition to the American people."[5]

One election stunt by a Pomona, California, orange grower, George Osgoodby, put British-Irish enmity on the political front burner. Posing as an immigrant Englishman using the alias "Charles Murchison," Osgoodby sent a letter to the British minister in Washington asking for confidential advice about the coming elections. He asked Sir Lionel Sackville-West if Cleveland was really pro-British. Murchison wrote that he and other Brits were uncertain as to Cleveland's sincerity based on the president's recent moves against trade with Canada:

> Sir: The gravity of the political situation here and the duties of those voters who are of English birth but still consider England

the mother land constitute the apology I hereby offer for intruding for information . . .

I am one of these unfortunates with a right to vote for President in November. I am unable to understand for whom I shall cast my ballot, when but one month ago I was sure Mr. Cleveland was the man. IF CLEVELAND WAS PURSUING A NEW POLICY TOWARD CANADA, TEMPORARILY ONLY AND FOR THE SAKE OF OBTAINING POPULARITY AND CONTINUATION OF HIS OFFICE FOUR YEARS MORE, BUT INTENDS TO CEASE HIS POLICY WHEN HIS RE-ELECTION IS SECURED IN NOVEMBER AND AGAIN FAVOR ENGLAND'S INTEREST. THEN I SHOULD HAVE NO FURTHER DOUBTS, BUT GO FORWARD AND VOTE FOR HIM. . . .

As you are at the fountain head of knowledge on the question, and KNOW WHETHER MR. CLEVELAND'S PRESENT POLICY IS TEMPORARY ONLY, AND WHETHER HE WILL, AS SOON AS HE SECURES ANOTHER TERM OF FOUR YEARS IN THE PRESIDENCY, SUSPEND IT FOR ONE OF FRIENDSHIP AND FREE TRADE, I apply to you privately and confidentially for information, which shall in turn be treated as entirely secret. Such information would put me at rest myself, and if favorable to Mr. Cleveland enable me, on my own responsibility, to assure many of our countrymen that THEY WOULD DO ENGLAND A SERVICE BY VOTING FOR CLEVELAND AND AGAINST THE REPUBLICAN SYSTEM OF TARIFF. As I before observed, we know not what to do, but look for more light on a mysterious subject, which the sooner it comes will better serve true Englishmen in casting their votes.[6]

Falling into the Republican trap, the Ambassador's reply revealed his political bias:

Sir: I am in receipt of your letter of the 4th inst., and beg to say that I fully appreciate the difficulty in which you find yourself in casting your vote. You are probably aware that any political party which openly favored the mother country at the present moment would lose popularity, and that the party in power is fully aware of this fact. The party, however, is, I believe, still desirous of maintaining friendly relations with Great Britain, and is still as desirous of settling all questions with Canada, which have been unfortunately reopened since the retraction of the treaty by the Republican majority in the Senate, and by the President's message, to which you allude. All allowances must, therefore, be made for the political situation as regards the Presidential election thus created. It is, however, impossible to predict the course which President Cleveland may pursue in the matter of retaliation, should he be elected, but there is every reason to believe that, while upholding the position he has taken, he will manifest a spirit of conciliation in dealing with the question involved in his message. . . .[7]

When the letter became public on October 23, all hell broke loose. A great rally, sponsored by the Republicans at New York's Madison Square Garden, included many Irish-Catholic leaders, who condemned Cleveland. James Blaine exploited the situation and electrified the predominantly Catholic audience with his denouncement of the British-Cleveland disgrace. Former Treasury Secretary John Sherman attacked Cleveland as pro-British and demanded that he be sacked.

There is no doubt that Irish-Americans, many of whom were at best lukewarm in their support of President Cleveland, were being influenced by the incident. On October 30, this telegram was sent from the Democratic National Committee in New York to Washington: "Washington telegrams in to-day's papers are most disappointing about the Sackville matter. Does the President know that the Irish vote is slipping out of our hands because of diplomatic shilly-shallying? . . . Something ought to be done to-day."[8]

Knowing he was in a bind, Cleveland took the politically expedient route and actually asked a friendly country to recall its minister. While the British procrastinated over the request, the U.S. secretary of state made the next move by sending Sackville-West his passports. In the world of striped-pants diplomats, this was the subtle approach to telling a foreign minister to go packing.

Booting out Sackville-West did stop the erosion of Catholic support and may have even brought back some into the Democratic fold. But to avoid another explosive situation, the announcement of the engagement of Secretary of War William Endicott's daughter to British Member of Parliament (and future Colonial Minister) Joseph Chamberlain was kept under wraps until after Election Day.[9]

Not unlike 1884, both sides sensed a close election. Possessing the largest bloc of electoral votes, New York was viewed as the key swing state. And once again the Catholics held the balance of power that would decide who would occupy the executive mansion.

Throughout the State of New York, particularly in Cleveland's home base of Buffalo, manufacturers were unhappy with the president's tariff reforms.

Managers spread the word to employees that low tariffs and free trade would cost domestic jobs. Upstate managers were so angry at Cleveland that they were handing out Harrison buttons at company picnics. Meanwhile, downstate manufacturers were financing anti-Cleveland protectionist pamphlets that were being distributed on street corners in Catholic laborer neighborhoods.[10]

Local elections also affected Cleveland's chances to carry his home state. Governor David Hill, who was up for reelection, was the target of reformers because of his alignment with shady New York City officials. The "Mugwump" reformers put Cleveland on the spot by leaning on him to support their cause publicly to rid the state of Hill. When Cleveland tried to stay above the battle, Irish Catholic Democratic Party regulars were livid that the president refused to campaign publicly for their designated candidates, especially Hill. When reminded that he belonged to the same party as Hill, Cleveland said: "I don't care a damn if [Hill] is – each tub must stand on its own bottom."[11] This remark further infuriated party loyalists.

Adding to Cleveland's woes was Democratic disharmony in New York City's local elections. When incumbent Democratic mayor, Abrams Hewitt, decided to seek another term of office, Tammany bosses put up their own candidate, Hugh Grant, against the quirky, reform-minded incumbent. Controlling the city's patronage with Grant was more important to local Democrats than the reelection of a president who had already alienated large segments of his own party.

There were other New York problems facing Cleveland's campaign. In Jamestown, Buffalo, and Troy, for instance, Republicans organized Civil War veterans who were unhappy with Cleveland's pension vetoes. The press in Cleveland's home turf in Erie and Monroe Counties called on farmers and manufacturers to support Harrison – "the Champion of the successful American Protective System."

When the results were tallied, the election was once again very close:

Presidential Vote

	1884		1888	
Democratic	4,874,986	48.5%	5,540,329	48.7%
Republican	4,851,981	48.2	5,439853	47.8
Minor	175,370	1.7	249,506	2.2
Minor	150,369	1.5	146,935	1.3

While Cleveland carried a plurality of the popular vote (100,476 margin) over Harrison, the Electoral College broke the other way: 233-Harrison, 168-Cleveland.

The Democrats held onto the South, but the GOP's protectionist rhetoric in key states paid off. Indiana, which Cleveland had carried in 1884, switched hands by the narrow margin of 2,348 votes out of 524,374 cast. And the big enchilada, Cleveland's home state of New York, once again decided the election. This time the state went Republican by 13,002 votes with 648,759 for Harrison versus Cleveland's 635,757.

New York's Democratic Party was in disarray. Charges of vote trading with the GOP – Democrats voting for Harrison in exchange for Republicans supporting Tammany's mayoral candidate – hurt Cleveland's totals. But it was the desertion of some New York Catholics over the British controversy, plus the loss of upstate voters over tariffs, that cost Cleveland the presidency. In fact, Catholics and tariff supporters in the president's home base of Erie County, New York, voted against him. "In the final analysis," concluded presidential historian Robert Wesser, "the President had not taken care of matters at home and he lost his bid for re-election by failing in the Empire State."[12]

*   *   *   *   *

The presidential races of 1884 and 1888 had proved how important Catholics were as a voting block. Anti-Catholics feared this growing power and reacted by attacking both major parties for courting papists. Cleveland had been accused of having a direct phone wire to the chancellery office of Baltimore's Cardinal Gibbons so he could receive his marching orders. Bigots also circulated the falsehood that Cleveland had appointed Catholic bosses to positions in the federal bureaucracy so they could shake down employees for donations to the Sisters of Charity. His successor was also accused of making numerous Catholic appointments to shore up their support.

As president, Benjamin Harrison managed to alienate large segments of the population, including Catholics. Signing the 1890 McKinley Tariff led many to believe the president was responsible for increasing the cost of living. The president's liberalized federal pension policy, which increased the number of participants from 670,000 to 970,000, caused many to think government was getting extravagant with the taxpayers' money. And this perception persisted because under Harrison's watch, federal budget expenditures exceeded $1 billion for the first time. Also, Republican bosses, such as Matthew Quay of Pennsylvania, Thomas Platt of New York, and Thomas Reed of Maine, were unhappy with the president's self-righteous attitude. He refused to play ball with the bosses, particularly when it came to patronage.

Harrison was also hurt in the Catholic community by his policies with regard to the Bureau of Indian Affairs. Early in Harrison's term, Father J. A. Stephan, director of the Bureau of Catholic Indian Missions, publicly disapproved of the president's "anti-Catholic" appointments to the U.S. Indian Affairs Commission. One appointee to the commission, Baptist Rev. Thomas Morgan, was publicly known for his favorite sermon, "Rome Opposed to

American Institutions." Another Harrison appointee, as superintendent of Indian schools, the Methodist Rev. Daniel Dorchester, authored a book titled *Romanism versus the Public Schools*, in which he had concluded that Catholicism was education's greatest demon.

When these men came out against federal financing of Indian schools because the largest percentage of Indian mission schools were Catholic, Stephan urged a group of Catholic archbishops to ask the president to reconsider the appointment of Rev. Morgan and several of the commission's policy decisions. But, according to Morgan, the president informed the Catholic clerics that "the reasons you state for the withdrawal of the name of the Indian Commissioner are chiefly the reason that prompted me to send his name."[13]

When pressure by the Catholic hierarchy to deny Senate confirmation failed, Commissioner Morgan announced that he would not "hold any official communication whatsoever with the insolent and infamous Bureau of Catholic Indian Missions," which he accused of "disreputable lobbying." Father Stephan reacted by pledging to organize opposition to Republicans in general and President Harrison in particular.

The GOP suffered serious political setbacks under President Harrison. Increased Catholic opposition only added to their political woes. In the 1890 off-year elections, the Republicans suffered the greatest losses in their forty-year history. They lost 78 congressional seats, which gave the Democrats 235 seats versus the GOP's 88 seats. Even the champion of tariffs, William McKinley, lost his congressional seat.

Sensing political weakness, former President Grover Cleveland decided to seek a rematch against Harrison. Even though Cleveland was not all that popular with the party rank and file, his conservative fiscal views – free trade and opposition to free silver – coincided with the prevailing philosophical stands of the Democratic power brokers.

> Southerners embraced Democratic *laissez faire,* not simply for reasons of tradition. Energetic governments might intervene to protect minority voters in southern elections. Elsewhere, people weary of Reconstruction commitments, resentful of taxation, and suspicious of centralization gravitated toward Democratic ranks. In an era when religious affiliation helped mold political views, Roman Catholics, German Lutherans, and other non-moralistic groups welcomed Democratic opposition to prohibition, Sabbatarian legislation, and similar attempts to use government to control individual standards of behavior. From immigrants to entrepreneurs there were many in the late nineteenth century who approved the Democratic "master-wisdom of governing little and leaving as much as possible to localities and to individuals."[14]

Father Stephan's activities also helped to bring Catholics back on to the Cleveland bandwagon. In July 1892, Stephan released a report describing the anti-Catholic Indian policies of the Harrison Administration, and sent the report to every priest in America. The report, which portrayed President Harrison as "not much less bigoted" than Commissioner Morgan and dedicated to destroying the Catholic parochial school system, was also distributed to over 100,000 homes. Father Stephan also traveled the nation lecturing on the shabby treatment Catholic Indians and their schools received from the Harrison Administration. He told the Catholic faithful "to take off their coats and defeat Harrison."[15]

For many Catholics the school issue was paramount. The Illinois bishops circulated a pastoral letter that was read from every pulpit right before the election. "It is not right" the bishops declared, "that we Catholics should have to contribute to the support of both public and parochial schools."

Other issues led Catholics back to the Democratic Party. For Catholic laborers these issues included excessive tariffs used to finance government extravagance and the 1892 steel-laborers' "Homestead" strike against Andrew Carnegie's company, which ended in violence prompted by hired detectives.

The *Irish American* summed up the views of most inner-city Catholics on the Homestead strike:

> But, on the eve of a national election, when the system of political economy that breeds such results is to be the chief issue, the lesson that is taught by the shameful details of the Homestead riot must surely work out the remedy to be expected at the polls. The whole breed of protected monopolists, fostered by Republican legislation, must be made to feel that the day of Federal taxation for the benefit of private greed has gone forever, and that the Democratic doctrine of tariff for revenue only is the one under which true prosperity can be enjoyed by the whole country.

Widely distributed anti-Catholic propaganda also made it easier for Catholics to return to the Democratic fold. The American Patriotic League distributed pamphlets that stated: "The Catholic hierarchy seeks to promote its interests by covertly advocating the election of Grover Cleveland. . . . Every Patriot should vote against such tactics." Handouts in Ohio stated that the election of 1892 was "Catholic versus Republicans."[16]

Organized anti-Catholics in Michigan (many of whom were Masons) took control of the Republican machines in Detroit, Grand Rapids, Saginaw, Bay City, Lansing, and Jackson, and spread their bigoted beliefs.

In Detroit, for instance, Catholics were appalled by the passage of the Coffin Resolution that decreed that a person wishing to take the teacher's certification examination had to receive his entire education in the public schools. Parochial school graduates could not apply. The uproar of Catholic voters was so loud that the Republican-controlled board modified the resolution – Catholic graduates were permitted to take the exam *but* now public-school graduates were exempt from the test and automatically received their teaching certificates.

Issues like these energized the Catholic voters, and they contributed to Cleveland's victory over President Harrison. It was the first and only time a previously defeated president was returned to office. Cleveland received 46 percent of the vote with 277 electoral votes to Harrison's 42.9 percent and 145 electoral votes. For the third time, Cleveland received more votes than his Republican opponent.

Democrats carried Illinois and Wisconsin for the first time since 1856. Harrison won in his home state by only 570 votes out of 850,000 cast. Democrats kept control of the House of Representatives and gained a majority in the Senate.

In the key swing state, New York, Catholics returning to the fold helped Cleveland carry the state 694,868 vs. 609,330. The inner-city Catholic areas were responsible for putting Cleveland over the top:

	1888		**1892**	
	Cleveland	**Harrison**	**Cleveland**	**Harrison**
New York City	162,735	106,922	175,267	98,967
Brooklyn	82,507	70,052	100,160	70,505
Queens	12,683	11,017	15,195	11,704
Staten Island	5,764	4,100	6,122	4,091
Westchester	14,948	13,799	16,088	13,436

Most analysts agreed the increasing strength of the Catholic voter in cities throughout the nation made an important contribution to Cleveland's victory. "A large share of the labor vote and increased strength in the cities gave added significance to [the Democrats'] achievement. Gaining strikingly among immigrant, Catholic and labor voters, they carried New York, Chicago, San Francisco, Milwaukee, Harrison's own Indianapolis, and other cities. Disgruntled Republicans complained that 'the slums of Chicago, Brooklyn and New York' had decided the election, but the complaint measured envy as much as anything else. The Democrats had won votes virtually everywhere."[17]

* * * * *

In the fall of 1892 Democrats were jubilant – they not only defeated an incumbent president but took control of both branches of the Congress. Their joy, however, was short-lived.

Within weeks after he moved back into the executive mansion, Grover Cleveland realized that the economy, which had been very weak in 1892, had now slid into a depression. The Reading and Philadelphia railroads announced they were broke in February 1893. The collapse in May of the National Cordage Company set off a panic in the overleveraged stock market. Over 600 banks in the South and West failed; fourteen thousand businesses closed and unemployment hit 20 percent. The nation was suffering from industrial stagflation and collapsing farm prices. Thousands of farms foreclosed, and two and a half million people were looking for jobs.

As the depression deepened, desperate people turned to the streets. There were violent strikes and "Coxey's Army," a "living petition" of unemployed demanding federal work programs, marched on Washington. In the president's home city of Buffalo, a thousand disgruntled laborers fought the city's police. When the president sent federal troops to quell the Pullman strike, mobs reacted by rioting for two days. There was fear in many quarters that "mobocracy" would rule the country. "Indeed many Americans expressed serious doubts about the nation's social stability and the viability of its democratic institutions."[18] Henry Adams speculated that the United States was "on the edge of a new and last great centralization, or of a first great movement of disintegration."[19]

Formulas to solve the economic woes centered on the monetary issue. Captains of industry and finance believed the depression was caused by silver inflation while the downtrodden believed it was due to a shortage of "cheap" money. Desperate farmers in the South and West demanded "free silver" to end price deflation.

President Cleveland did not agree with the growing sentiment within his party on the silver issue. In his judgment the Silver Purchase Act of 1890, which permitted paper money to be backed by cheap silver, had caused both the inflation and the depression. The Act had to be repealed.

Cleveland refused to yield on this issue, and a grudging Congress finally complied with his wishes on October 30, 1893. But to get his way, Cleveland had to depend on Republicans for support. Western and southern congressional Democrats, who viewed the president as a big-business and Wall Street lackey, deserted him on this issue. Twenty-two of the forty-four Democratic Senators and seventy-eight House Democrats voted against repeal.

In his second inaugural, Cleveland stated, "While the people should patriotically support their government, its functions do not include the support of the people." In the depression, the president stood by these words and promoted his fundamental belief that the panacea for the national economic malaise was sound money.

The president's position was viewed by members of his own party – farmers and urban unemployed – as cold and distant. And this discomfort was registered at the polls in November 1894. Democratic losses were staggering. In the House of Representatives the Democrats went from 218 seats to 105. A 50 percent decline. In the Senate, Democrats lost five seats and control of that body. These great losses were primarily in the urban Northeast and the agrarian Midwest. When the new Congress convened in January 1895, the only Democratic congressman from the New England region was John "Honey Fitz" Fitzgerald – grandfather of a future president, John F. Kennedy.

While Republicans benefited the most from the economic despair and gained control of the Congress, there were other forces brewing in the nation that would not bode well for either of the established major parties.

In the South and West, despondent people, disgusted by depressed farm prices and lack of credit and markets for their produce, turned to the growing political populist movement known as the "People's Party."

The promoters of the populist movement were dedicated to undermining the "money powers" and championing the cause of the "common man." In a statement of principles, they declared:

> There are but two sides in the conflict that is being waged in the country today. On the one side are the allied hosts of monopolies, the money power, great trusts and railroad corporations, who seek the enactment of laws to benefit them and impoverish the people. On the other side are the farmers, laborers, merchants and all others who produce wealth and bear the burdens of taxation. The one represents the wealthy and powerful classes who want the control of the Government to plunder the people. The other represents the people, contending for equality before the law, and the rights of man. Between these two there is no middle ground.[20]

These populists had a sacred mission to uphold Jeffersonian agrarian principles and to oppose Hamiltonian urban values. Historian Frederick Jackson Turner pointed out that the populist agenda was directed to "the survival of the pioneer, striving to adjust present conditions to his old ideals."[21]

Support for the movement came primarily from southern cotton farmers, wheat growers in Kansas, Nebraska, and the Dakotas and mountain-state silver miners. In 1890 populist candidates won nine Congressional and two Senate seats. The People's Party 1892 presidential candidate garnered 1 million votes and twenty-two electoral votes from Colorado, Kansas, Nebraska, North Dakota, Oregon, and Illinois. As the recession deepened, their vote totals increased. In the off year elections of 1894, their vote increased 42 percent. They elected 6 U.S. senators, 7 congressmen, and 465 state legislators.

A young Democrat who grasped the growing populist sentiment was William Jennings Bryan of Nebraska. This dynamic orator, who possessed the rural and missionary qualities of a tent-preaching revivalist, was determined to lead the people he loved – farmers and westerners. His evangelical message, according to historian Richard Hofstadter, created a great awakening in large segments of the nation. "Bryan's hold on the West," Hofstadter wrote, "lay in the fact that he was himself the average man of a large part of that country; he did not merely resemble that average man, he was that average man."[22]

An emotional man, he freely admitted he knew little of economics, but he had an inspired belief that the presidential campaign of 1896 was to be "a struggle between those who wanted money cheap and those who wanted it dear."[23]

Bryan was attractive to westerners because his philosophy was deeply rooted in the Jeffersonian principles of individualism and his belief that all social problems were moral problems.

> I assert that the people of the United States . . . have sufficient patriotism and sufficient intelligence to sit in judgment on every question which has arisen or which will arise, no matter how long our government will endure. The great political questions are in their final analysis great moral questions, and it requires no extended experience in the handling of money to enable a man to tell right from wrong.[24]

He also believed in the old Jacksonian tradition of "equal rights to all and special privilege to none."[25]

But there was another side to Bryan. He was brought up in a household that "believed in the supremacy of the Anglo-Saxon race."[26] With urban issues beginning to overshadow rural ones, he looked to eastern urban America "as the enemy's country."[27] During a congressional campaign, he told his constituents that he was "tired of hearing about laws made for the benefit of men who work in shops."[28] Bryan took a shot at immigration when he declared he was opposed to "dumping of the criminal classes upon our shore."[29] For Bryan and many of his followers, "the city was symbolized as the home of loan sharks, dandies, fops and aristocrats with European ideas who despised farmers as hayseeds."[30]

Bryan's fundamentalist-revivalist oratory and agrarian radicalism upset many urban immigrants. According to political analyst Samuel Lubell, "The traits which made Bryan seem like the voice of pious morality to his Prohibitionist, rural, Protestant following – the liberal use of Biblical phrases, the resonant Chautauqua tones, the heaven-stomping energy – made him sound like the voice of bigotry to the urban masses."[31]

When the 1896 Democratic convention convened in Chicago, a panicking party disavowed many of the policies of their incumbent president and adopted numerous planks of the populist platform. Bryan made it perfectly clear where he stood with these words: "I want to suggest to my Democratic friends that the party owes no great debt of gratitude to its President."

Forces supporting cheap money took control of the convention. The platform endorsed "free and unlimited coinage of both silver and gold at the ration of sixteen to one."

When Bryan, then thirty-six years old and a Nebraska delegate, took to the podium on July 8, 1896, his oratory electrified the audience and precipitated a stampede to nominate him for president. These closing words brought down the house:

> Having behind us the producing masses of this nation and the world, supported by the commercial interests, the laboring interests, and the toilers everywhere, we will answer their demand for a gold standard by saying to them: You shall not press down upon the brow of labor this crown of thorns, you shall not crucify mankind upon a cross of gold.

Although some members of the People's Party were angry that the Democrats had stolen their thunder, their leaders were practical enough to know that they would only split the Free Silver vote if they ran independent presidential electors. So, on September 14, 1896, People's Party chairman, William V. Allen, informed Bryan that he was unanimously nominated as their standard bearer:

> In your nomination our party has risen above mere partisan surroundings, adopting a high plane of patriotism, believing that a division of forces would result in the election of William McKinley, the foremost advocate of a deeply burdensome and unnatural taxation and the criminal policy of the single gold standard, resulting ultimately, if not in some manner checked, in the complete destruction and disintegration of our form of government.
>
> Your elevation to the Chief Magistracy of the Nation would be regarded as a vindication of the right of the people to govern, and we entertain no doubt that you will prove a worthy successor of the immortal Jefferson and Lincoln, and that your public life, like theirs, will illustrate the purity and loftiness of American statesmanship. . . .[32]

Watching from the wings were Republicans, who were carefully analyzing the power shift in the Democratic Party. Mark Hanna, the multimillionaire Cleveland industrialist, who many considered the first modern-day political consultant, developed the GOP plan to exploit these divisions to help elect his friend, Governor William McKinley of Ohio.

William McKinley was different from other Civil War veterans who competed for the office of president. McKinley began his military career not as an officer, but as a private who rose to the rank of major. This small-town Ohioan learned to appreciate the values and thinking of the common soldier when serving in the Twenty-Third Ohio Volunteer Infantry.

Having lived and fought with men of every station and religion, he returned to civilian life and devoted his civic and political career to uniting, not polarizing, his community.

> His devout Methodism did not lead him to concern himself with dogma or denominational differences. The loving kindness of God was McKinley's religion, and the source of his inner serenity. . . . He made many friends among Canton's large Roman Catholic population of German and Irish extraction. In a day of sharp sectarianism, McKinley was devoid of bigotry possessing as a grace of his nature the tolerance that is unconscious of its own virtue.[33]

Elected Stark County's district attorney in 1869, the affable McKinley was serving in Congress by 1877. He got along in Washington power circles, and he had the advantage of being on a first-name basis with three fellow Ohioans – Presidents Hayes, Garfield, and Harrison.

In the late 1880s, the United States government was incurring large surpluses. Believing that this money would be wasted on pork projects, McKinley, as chairman of the House Ways and Means Committee, proposed a restructuring of tariff rates (the government's primary revenue stream before the creation of the personal income tax) to bring down revenues and to protect American interests. His plan reduced the tax on many projects but also increased the tariff rate on specific commodities that harmed domestic production. To discourage wheat imports, tariffs were increased. On the other hand, to increase international sugar supplies, duties were lowered.

This "McKinley Tariff," as it became known, was viciously attacked by reformers as a sop to special interests. This smear, plus the public's perception of the Republican-controlled Congress as free spenders who broke the "Billion Dollar" budget barrier, caused a Democratic landslide in the 1890 election, and McKinley himself was one of the seventy-eight Republicans who went down in defeat.

This loss did not, however, end his career. He was nominated for governor of Ohio in 1892 and was elected not once but twice. He succeeded at the polls because he was different from many other Republicans; he sought to bring laboring people, many of whom were Catholics, under the GOP tent.

The son of a furnace laborer, McKinley always had an affection for men who worked by the sweat of their brows. In 1876, he enhanced his reputation as a friend of labor when he defended thirty-three Stark County coal miners jailed for rioting during a strike. Thirty-two of the accused were found innocent. Later, as governor, he instituted a state labor arbitration system and proposed laws that permitted streetcar employees to join unions. McKinley's interest in these issues "reflected his career as a labor lawyer, his understanding of labor's growing strength and changing status and his sympathy with the workingman's problems."[34] Mark Hanna best summed up McKinley's credo: "The one absorbing purpose in William McKinley's political career was to keep closely in touch with the people."[35]

Nominated for president by a united Republican party, McKinley campaigned on three basic themes: Free silver would cause runaway inflation and would endanger workingmen's wages and savings; judicious tariffs would end the depressed markets, help create jobs, and improve the economy; and the class warfare espoused by Bryan delegates would be deleterious for the country – McKinley called for a unified nationalism led by a unified political party:

> My countrymen, the most un-American of all appeals observable in this campaign in the one which seeks to array labor against capital, employer against employed. It is most unpatriotic and is fraught with the greatest peril to all concerned. We are all political equals here – equal in privilege and opportunity, dependent upon each other, and the prosperity of the one is the prosperity of the other.[36]

Running on the slogans "Advance agent of prosperity" and "A full dinner pail," Republicans sought to peel away portions of the labor vote, particularly in predominantly Catholic Northeast urban centers. GOP campaign manager, Mark Hanna, grasped that Bryan's rhetoric, evangelical piety and his constant harping on silver ("The fight for silver is a cause as holy as the cause of Humanity") did not sit well with many Catholics.

McKinley's positive attitude toward Catholic laborers disgusted with the country's leading anti-Catholic organization, the American Protective Association (APA), and this benefited his campaign. In April 1896, the APA's national board publicly announced that they were troubled that McKinley was overly favorable to Catholics. In their judgment, he had appointed too many Roman Catholics to Ohio's state government. They promoted the rumor that McKinley was under the thumb of the Columbus, Ohio, ordinary, Bishop John Watterson, and that his campaign manager, Mark Hanna, was secretly a Catholic.

> One of the major developments of the campaign was the announcement by Archbishop Ireland of the St. Paul diocese that

he supported McKinley in opposition to the "socialistic" proposals of the Democrats. In the years following the campaign rumors
persisted that the Republicans in certain areas had given campaign
money to the Catholic Church. The McKinley-Hanna organization
was aware of the strategic importance of Catholic voters in the
nation's urban centers and particularly of the Catholic voters in the
growing Midwestern cities. The APA attack on McKinley initiated an orientation on the part of these voters toward McKinley and
the Republican Party.[37]

APA tactics also backfired at the GOP's platform hearings. They successfully browbeat committee members into adopting a resolution opposing
any federal funding for sectarian institutions. Hearing of this move,
Archbishop Ireland sent a telegram to a Montana Republican national committeeman, Thomas Carter, a Catholic, who said: "The Republican Party
should not lower itself to recognize [this] directly or indirectly." Persuaded by
the archbishop's message, the committee reversed its vote and threw out the
APA plank. This was indeed a strong message to the Catholic community.

The 1896 campaign for president was one of the most expensive and hard
fought in America's history. The rhetoric was tough and colorful. Bryan was
accused of being a Popocrat, anarchist, communist, serpent, and slobbering
demagogue. In a speech urging the election of McKinley, young Teddy
Roosevelt shouted, "Messrs. Bryan, Altgeld, Tillman, Debs, Coxey and the
rest have not the power to rival the deeds of Marat, Barrère, and Robespierre,
but they are strikingly like the leaders of the Terror of France in mental and
moral attitude." A Catholic priest in New York "denounced Bryan from his
pulpit as a 'demagogue whose patriotism is all his jaw-bone.'"[38]

McKinley was called a "plunderer," "shylock," "tool of Wall Street,"
"plutocrat" and "robber." The APA distributed thousands of brochures calling
McKinley a Catholic, that his father was buried in a Catholic cemetery, two
of his children lived in a convent, and that his executive secretary was a
Jesuit.[39]

By the end of the campaign it appeared that Mark Hanna's strategy was
working: Voters, particularly in the Northeast and Midwest perceived Bryan
as "the leader of a ragtag band of radicals that would upset the foundations of
the Republic."[40] McKinley, on the other hand, was being perceived as a reasonable person who would rescue the common man from the Democratic
depression. And the results proved the success of the strategy. McKinley won
with 7,102,246 votes (51 percent) to Bryan's 6,492,559 (46 percent).
McKinley carried 23 states with 271 electoral votes to Bryan's 22 states and
176.

More people cast votes for the Republican and Democratic candidates than in any previous election. The tally topped the 1892 total by 2 million votes. McKinley was the first presidential candidate to get a majority of the votes since 1872. Bryan's strength was primarily in the South and west of the Mississippi. And there were very close state races for each candidate.

Closely Contested States Carried by McKinley

	Bryan	McKinley	Margin
Oregon	46,662	48,779	2,117
Kentucky	217,890	218,171	281
Indiana	305,573	323,754	18,181
North Dakota	20,686	26,335	5,649
West Virginia	92,927	104,414	11,487

Closely Contested States Carried By Bryan

	Bryan	McKinley	Margin
North Carolina	174,488	155,222	19,266
Tennessee	166,268	148,773	17,495
Virginia	154,985	135,388	19,597
Nebraska	115,999	103,064	12,935
South Dakota	41,225	41,042	183
Wyoming	10,941	10,072	869

The most dramatic voting shifts took place in the Northeast. McKinley received over two-thirds of the New England vote, and he carried the Mid-Atlantic states by large majorities.

McKinley managed to carry the industrial voters handily – both management and labor. "Bryan's failure to capture the urban vote was a telling blow, and his inability to tie the workers' interests to the farmers carried his crusade down to defeat through economic and geographic sectionalism."[41]

And the most significant contribution to Bryan's failure was the movement of large segments of the Catholic voting population toward the GOP. Bryan's style and rhetoric offended many Catholics. They viewed him as an evangelical Protestant agrarian opposed to urban industrialization. They believed that their traditional party had deserted them.

It is estimated that 40 percent to 45 percent of the Catholic vote was cast for William McKinley,[42] which explains why McKinley carried America's ten largest cities. In New York, a closely contested swing state during the post-Civil War era, McKinley not only carried the heavily Protestant upstate region but New York City as well. This combination resulted in a decisive victory for the GOP.

	1892		1896	
	Cleveland	**Harrison**	**Bryan**	**McKinley**
NY State	654,868	609,330	551,369	819,838
NY City	175,267	98,967	135,624	156,359
Brooklyn	100,168	70,505	17,882	109,133
Westchester	16,088	13,436	11,752	19,337

There were other Republican inroads. In the Midwest, German Catholics, who generally opposed prohibitionist-leaning Republicans, switched to McKinley. Political analyst Kevin Phillips, pointed out that "McKinley learned from Ohio how important the German vote was, and in 1896, his national campaign had a German division, which wooed both Catholics and Lutherans."[43] The German-American newspaper, the *Illinois Staats–Zeitung* confirms this view:

> The German voters decided the [1896] election in Ohio, Indiana, Michigan, Illinois, Wisconsin, Iowa, Nebraska and Minnesota. . . . They have many complaints against the Republican party, which . . . sought to combat the influence of Germans in every way, and annoyed them continually with Prohibition laws, Sunday closing laws and school laws. The Germans consequently turned their backs on the Republicans, with the result that Cleveland was twice elected, and if the Democrats had not inscribed repudiation, bankruptcy and dishonor on their colors as a result of the union with the Populists, the Germans would have supported them this time also. . . .[44]

As the following charts demonstrate, the Catholic vote in key midwestern states (populated primarily by Germans) did shift to the Republicans:

Presidential Vote
Wisconsin – Predominantly Catholic Counties

	1892		1896	
County	**Democrat**	**Republican**	**Democrat**	**Republican**
Outagamie	4,515	2,733	4,096	5,433
Grant	3,685	4,217	3,683	5,315
Kenosha	1,928	1,628	1,732	2,827
Ozaukee	2,094	652	1,947	1,535
Pipin	539	865	436	1,301
St. Croix	2,220	2,467	2,475	3,462
Washington	2,624	1,700	2,404	2,877
Portage	2,570	2,291	2,890	3,537

Presidential Vote
Ohio – Predominantly Catholic Counties

County	1892		1896	
	Democrat	Republican	Democrat	Republican
Auglaize	3,774	2,113	4,939	2,900
Jackson	2,622	3,223	3,786	4,439
Perry	3,430	3,359	4,112	3,989
Vinton	1,743	1,710	1,821	2,035
Stark	10,227	9,231	11,339	12,111

Presidential Vote
Michigan – Predominantly Catholic Counties

County	1892		1896	
	Democrat	Republican	Democrat	Republican
Clinton	6,470	2,756	3,467	3,480
Houghton	7,324	2,607	1,996	6,141
Keweenaw	612	202	45	411
Monroe	7,021	3,769	4,208	4,053
Presque Isle	834	471	371	763
Washtenaw	10,448	5,568	5,348	5,671

In 1896 the Republican Party established a new political coalition that would give the GOP control over the national government for twenty-eight of the next thirty-six years. "McKinley," Kevin Phillips concluded, "quietly masterminded three epochal shifts in American politics: a domestic sea change in which a Protestant establishment welcomed churchgoing immigrants and embraced labor, creating a long lived coalition; economic initiative that favored the global gold standard while shielding local industries and high industrial wages behind a protective tariff; and an international realignment that allied the United States with Britain and entangled the country in its first Asian wars."[45]

Numerous Catholics, while remaining loyal to their local Democratic candidates, deserted the national ticket because they found McKinley more attuned to their values than the Bible-thumping, tambourine-playing Bryan. This break caused New York City's former Democratic mayor, Abram Hewitt, to conclude, "The Democratic Party is dead as we know it."[46] And for the next thirty-six years, the Democrats would be split culturally and economically: Agrarian-Nativist-Protestant versus Urban-Immigrant-Catholic.

Chapter 8

The Rise of the Urban Catholic Voter

In the last decades of the nineteenth century and the early years of the twentieth, Catholic immigrants flooded the nation. So great was the influx – some 9 million in all – that the Catholic Church became the largest denomination in America.

There was, however, a marked difference in the origins of this "new" immigrant population. Unlike earlier waves that consisted primarily of Irish and Germans, many of those arriving in the new wave were born in eastern and southern Europe. Political upheaval in these regions prompted hundreds of thousands to look to America as the land of hope. The creation of the dual Austro-Hungarian monarchy, the peasant subdivision of farmland, racial animosities and jealousness caused a mass exodus from the Balkans. The unification of Italy, the battle over papal property and the incompetence of the newly centralized government caused peasants to flee their homeland.

Emperor Napoleon's defeat in the Franco-Prussian war and Bismarck's anti-Catholic German *Kulturkampf* drove the faithful from these countries to "seek a newer world." In Ireland, when pro-Catholic reform battles over the land-tenure system and home rule prompted by nationalist uprising of the Home Rule Party, the Land League, and the Irish National League failed, a second diaspora commenced.

Growth of Select Catholic Immigrants[1]

	1871–1880	1881–1890	1891–1900	1901–1910	1911–1920
Austria-Hungary	46,230	134,000	232,000	553,000	239,000
France	4,000	15,000	4,000	26,000	18,000
Germany	175,000	400,000	105,000	36,500	10,000
Italy	27,000	130,000	390,000	802,000	275,000
Poland	4,000	78,000	190,000	608,400	250,000
Ireland	180,000	300,000	40,000	10,000	70,000

Growth of U.S. Catholic Population[2]

Catholic Population	1870	4,504,000
Total Catholic Growth	1871–1880	1,755,000
Total Catholic Population	1880	6,259,000
% of U.S. Population		14.4%
Catholic Population	1880	6,259,000
Total Catholic Growth	1881–1890	2,650,000
Total Catholic Population	1890	8,909,000
% of U.S. Population		16.1%
Catholic Population	1890	8,909,000
Total Catholic Growth	1891–1900	3,132,000
Total Catholic Population	1900	12,041,000
% of U.S. Population		18.0%
Catholic Population	1900	12,041,000
Total Catholic Growth	1901–1910	4,322,000
Total Catholic Population	1910	16,363,000
% of U.S. Population		20%
Catholic Population	1910	16,363,000
Total Catholic Growth	1911–1920	3,465,000
Total Catholic Population	1920	19,828,000
% of U.S. Population		20.9%

As Poles and Czechs settled in Chicago and Detroit, Italians in New York and Boston, Hungarians and Slovaks in Pittsburgh and Cleveland, Ukrainians in Pennsylvania, they centered themselves socially and politically in family, parish, and neighborhood, consequently reflecting the basic principle of Catholic social thought – subsidiarity.

This approach to dealing with the vagaries of life was first articulated by Aristotle, who believed that the "man of the city" by his very nature is endowed with an appetite and inclination for social life. People enjoy the company of others with whom they want to share their joys and sorrows and naturally come together socially, educationally, politically, and economically in communities. Aristotle pointed out that "the first thing to arise is the family . . . the association established by nature for the supply of men's everyday wants. . . . But when several families are united and the association aims at something more than supply of daily needs, the first society to be formed is the village . . . when several villages are united in a single complete community, large enough to be needy or quite self-sufficing; the state comes into existence. . . . Hence it is evident that the state is a creation of nature, and that man is by nature a political animal."[3]

Catholic Population of Select Cities with a
Total Population Over 100,000 People in 1916[4]

	Membership 1916	Parishes 1916
Albany	39,769	16
Boston	294,914	63
Cambridge	28,206	8
Chicago	1,150,000	202
Cincinnati	101,931	60
Columbus	31,948	19
Dayton	26,923	17
Denver	28,772	22
Indianapolis	31,601	17
Louisville	53,474	41
Minneapolis	51,776	27
Nashville	5,845	7
New Orleans	147,696	40
New York	1,545,562	326
Portland, Ore.	20,113	16
Providence	111,525	25
St. Paul	63,321	28
Scranton	54,443	24
Washington	51,421	27
Total	3,839,240	985

People depend on one another: first upon their parents and then upon friends, neighbors, teachers, employers, etc. Individuals and families naturally broaden their associations to meet their mutual needs in *subsidiarity*, the principle which affirms that decisions are most appropriately made by the local agencies closest to relevant daily realities, and by the next highest agencies only when decisions and actions are beyond the capacities of those at lower levels.

In his encyclical *Quadragesimo Anno* (1931), Pope Pius XI defined subsidiarity as "the fundamental principle of social philosophy, fixed and unchangeable, that one should not withdraw from individuals and commit to the community what they can accomplish by their own enterprise and industry."[5]

According to sociologist Andrew Greeley, subsidiarity means "no bigger than necessary" and by structuring life according to this principle, "one can protect, promote and defend the freedom, the dignity, the authenticity of the individual human person."[6]

In their search for protection in hostile cities, immigrants depended on their families for support. For the immigrant, the family was sacred. It represented the basis of their religious tradition and offered stability against the established social orders of hatred toward immigrants. Marriage was looked upon as a sacramental and everlasting bond. Marriage and family instilled in immigrants the character to achieve moral excellence in their daily activities.

The family unit turned to the parish – for it was the parish that introduced them to a unified body of believers who could help and comfort them both spiritually and materially. The parish "erected a series of structural fences to keep the ethnic individual closely articulated to the community."[7]

Immigrants happily gave their hard-earned nickels and dimes to local pastors to build magnificent parish churches whose architectural style reflected the places of worship in the old country. These grand structures that stood out in tenement-filled ghettos also reflected the gratitude they felt toward an all-loving God whom they believed had permitted them to escape to the shores of America.

Due to this tremendous growth in non-English-speaking Catholic immigrants, local bishops implemented policies that permitted the establishment of national-ethnic parishes as opposed to the traditional policy of territorial parishes. Polish, Slovak, Italian, and German parishes sprouted up throughout America's inner cities. This type of church brought together people of similar language and ethnic cultures. Parishioners were loyal to their local churches, and they identified and introduced themselves to others by simply announcing the names of their parishes.

These parishes provided vital services for immigrants trying to find their way in the new land. The parish organized social activities for its flock through the Holy Name Society, Women's Sodality, and Communion breakfasts. The pastor got kids off the streets and out of gangs by organizing sports played in the parish yard and dances held in the church hall. Parish activities helped build self-confidence in people – immigrants were treated as special persons with God-given abilities and not as victims. "The Church taught the immigrants to work hard, to obey the law, to respect their leaders and to concentrate on private, familial relationships."[8]

The parish school also provided an essential service for immigrant children. The teaching nuns, brothers, and priests taught discipline – both moral and physical. They taught benevolence, forgiveness, and atonement through the Catechism and by marching students to weekly confession. Parish schools instilled a moral compass in hundreds of thousands of first generation children.

These parishes took on traits that reflected the customs and culture of each ethnic group. For the Irish, the parish was the center of life, and church attendance and obedience to church rules mattered enormously. For Italians, parish life meant loyalty to religious symbols and observance of feast days. Czechs, on the other hand, used the local church as the headquarters for social-service associations. But these parishes also provided "spiritual unity amidst the ethnic diversity."[9] They helped their congregations "maintain spiritual identity in a strange environment."[10]

Nationality Parishes in the United States[11]

Ethnic Groups	1900	1920
Poles	144	404
Italians	52	257
Germans	336	280
Slovaks	12	107
French Canadians	86	93
Lithuanians	17	95
Magyars	6	51
Mexicans	–	13
Maronites	3	22
Czechs	29	34
Croatians	1	19
Melkites	–	13
Slovenians	10	31
Portuguese	5	16
Romanians	–	9
Spanish	–	9
Belgian	4	5
English	11	6
Dutch	1	1
Maltese	–	1
Tyrolese	–	1
Albanian	–	1
Chaldean	–	1
Scandinavian	1	1
	737	1,470

Richard Cardinal Cushing, Archbishop of Boston from 1958 to 1970, best summed up the role of the parish in America: "The Catholic parish, with its pastor and priests, its altar and confessionals, its pulpit and its schools, its good works, its sinners, its saints – the Catholic parish so constituted is a microcosm, it is the whole church in miniature, and through the parish, Christ does for a limited group what He founded the universal church to do for the whole world."[12]

In urban centers throughout late-nineteenth-century America, the Catholic parish was becoming the key social institution in neighborhoods.

Sociologist Andrew Greeley has observed that "the neighborhood as it is known in the northeast and north central parts of the United States, is the result of the immigrant's experience."[13] And the neighborhoods reflected the growing impact of the immigrant on political and economic affairs.

For many, attempting to eke out a living in the inner cities meant enduring awful living conditions in dilapidated, overcrowded tenements that had poor lighting, poor ventilation, and unsanitary plumbing. These same people also endured unhealthy working conditions in plants and sweatshops. But thanks to the spiritual comfort they received from the Catholic parish, immigrants were able to survive.

Because of their instinctive practice of subsidiarity, the Catholic inhabitants of neighborhoods were primarily attached to and protective of their neighborhood, of a turf that was often nothing more than a stretch of sidewalk or a tenement stoop.

Because neighbors were friends or relatives who shared the same faith, they were always available to help each other. Mothers policed the neighborhoods keeping a watch over neighbors' children as well as their own. As a result, families were safe and did not need to lock their apartment doors.

For millions of Catholics who came to America, the neighborhood served as a social harbor where one was accepted for who one was. In New York's "Little Italy" for instance, relations were so tight that a given block would be inhabited by immigrants from the same town or village. These people struggled to secure a piece of land they could call their own. As Michael Novak pointed out, to achieve moderate success in America, the ethnics took the route of "loyalty, hard work, family, discipline and gradual self-development."

Poles and Czechs founded building-and-loan associations to pool their money to aid one another in becoming homeowners. "The small lot, comfortable home, and secure neighborhood became the New World equivalent of that Old World farm and peasant village. In their social values, the immigrants were traditional and conservative, preoccupied with the need to preserve what they had almost lost in the Old World."[14]

Neighborhoods promoted loyalty. In the meeting places – candy stores, pubs, pool halls – people would stand up for one another. "It is easy to see in this mutuality of obligation," writes Greeley, "a continuation in the urban environment of the old peasant loyalties of village and clan."[15]

As the Catholic immigrant population increased in significant portions of urban centers, Catholic leaders began to organize them and promote their interests in the political arena. As described earlier in this work, as early as 1800, organized Catholic communities had an impact on the outcome of close political races. But, throughout the first half of the nineteenth century, this emerging voting block was managed by Protestant political leaders, such as

Aaron Burr and William Tweed. In the post-Civil War era, however, Catholics began to realize they didn't have to settle for a few crumbs of the political spoils. They soon realized that they could organize their neighborhoods themselves, become a powerful voice in the running of their cities, and grab a bigger share of the political swag.

The Irish in the Cities, 1870[16]

	Irish-Born as Percentage of Total Population	Foreign-Born as Percentage of Total Population	Total Population	Rank (by Total Population)
Boston	22.7	35.1	250,526	7
Jersey City	21.5	38.6	82,546	17
New York	21.4	44.5	942,292	1
Albany	19.1	32.0	69,422	20
New Haven	18.9	28.2	50,840	25
Brooklyn	18.7	36.5	396,099	3
Providence	17.5	24.9	68,904	21
San Francisco	17.3	49.3	149,473	10
Pittsburgh	15.2	32.3	86,076	16
Philadelphia	14.3	27.2	674,022	2
Chicago	13.4	48.4	298,977	5
Newark	11.9	34.2	105,059	13
Cleveland	10.7	41.8	92,829	15
St. Louis	10.4	36.1	310,864	4
Rochester	9.7	34.0	62,386	22
Buffalo	9.6	39.3	117,714	11
Detroit	8.8	44.5	79,577	18
Cincinnati	8.6	36.8	216,239	8
New Orleans	7.7	25.3	191,418	9
Louisville	7.6	25.5	100,755	14
Allegheny	7.6	28.8	53,180	23
Washington, DC	6.4	12.6	109,199	12
Baltimore	5.7	21.1	267,354	6
Milwaukee	5.3	47.3	71,440	19
Richmond	2.4	7.4	51,038	24

Note: This table includes the twenty-five cities with a population greater than 50,000 in 1870.

For about eighty years after the Civil War, Democratic Catholic political machines ruled most of urban America. The late Daniel Patrick Moynihan, scholar and politician, wrote that the Irish had a genius for organization. The Irish, who were the largest ethnic bloc, drafted the blueprints for most of the

big-city political machines, and – being Roman Catholic – they were spontaneous advocates of subsidiarity. They built from the bottom up: neighborhoods were organized block by block, through parishes, clubhouses, saloons,
pool halls, and candy stores. This was the system that provided and dispensed
patronage, contracts and franchises to the faithful.

Realizing that with the exception of menial jobs many employment
opportunities were closed to immigrants and their offspring ("Irish need not
apply" signs were common during this era), Catholic pols concluded that government jobs would provide upward mobility for their people.

Since the Irish were the first large ethnic group to reside in America's
major cities, it was natural that they dominated the staffing of the police force,
the fire department, and public works. And as other ethnic groups began to
flood inner cities, the Irish were smart and flexible enough to adjust to the
changing demographics. Because the Irish spoke the language and understood
the bureaucrats and municipal law, they promoted themselves as the friend of
the new immigrants and encouraged them to turn to the political clubs when
in need of help. The leaders of the political clubhouses were skilled in doing
informal good for public welfare. The clubhouse provided access for patronage and favor seekers, as well as political kibitzers. They also sponsored
dances, bazaars, athletic events, picnics, and parades to entertain the poor and
to get kids off the streets and out of alleyways. In his memoir, *Up to Now*,
Alfred E. Smith fondly recalled that in his youth the local political bosses, particularly "Big Tim" Sullivan of the Bowery, sponsored holiday parades, out-
ings, and contests.

It was clubhouse leaders who organized the block captains who helped
with day-to-day problems from garbage removal to road, park, sewage, and
bathhouse maintenance. It was the block captain who brought turkey to the
poor at Thanksgiving and Christmas and represented the clubhouse at weddings, baptisms, and funerals.

Ward leader George Washington Plunkitt, writing in 1905, expressed the
job of the successful block captain:

> There's only one way to hold a district: you must study human
> nature and act accordin'. . . . To learn real human nature you have
> to go among the people, see them and be seen. I know every man,
> woman, and child in the Fifteenth District, except them that's been
> born this summer – and I know some of them, too. I know what
> they like and what they don't like, what they are strong at and what
> they are weak in, and I reach them by approachin' at the right side.
>
> For instance, here's how I gather in the young men. . . .
> There's the feller that likes rowin' on the river, the young feller
> that makes a name as a waltzer on his block, the young feller that's

handy with his dukes – I rope them all in by givin' them opportunities to show themselves off. I don't trouble them with political arguments. I just study human nature and act accordin'.

But you may say this game won't work with the high-toned fellers, the fellers that go through college and then join the Citizens' Union. Of course it wouldn't work. I have a special treatment for them. I ain't like the patent medicine man that gives the same medicine for all diseases. The Citizens' Union kind of a young man! I love him! He's the daintiest morsel of the lot, and he don't often escape me . . .

Among other things I watch the City Record to see when there's Civil Service examinations for good things, then I take my young Cits in hand, tell him all about the good thing and get him worked up till he goes and takes an examination . . .

What tells in holdin' your grip on your district is to go right down among the poor families and help them in the different ways they need help . . . It's philanthropy, but it's politics, too – mighty good politics.[17]

By controlling and wisely dispensing these various benefits, the Irish pols held on to their power and by 1890 their political machines controlled many of America's major cities:

Catholic Leaders of Major Cities in Late 19th Century

Municipality	Boss-Leader
New York City	John Kelly and Richard Croker
Brooklyn	Hugh McLaughlin
Chicago	Mike McDonald
Boston	Pat Maguire
San Francisco	Christopher Buckley
Buffalo	William Sheehan
Jersey City	"Little Bob" Davis

Boston serves as an excellent example of the rise of Catholic political hegemony: the first Irish-Catholic mayor was elected in 1886. By 1899, Catholics held a majority of the city council. A second Catholic mayor, Patrick Collins, was elected in 1901, and he was succeeded by Catholics John "Honey Fitz" Fitzgerald (grandfather of the future American president, John F. Kennedy) and James Michael Curley.

The alliance between Catholic pols and the fledging labor movement was natural. Working together, the politicians and the union leaders tried to improve working conditions for the poor, by seeking to alleviate low pay and long hours. The Irish skill in organizing labor, however, did not always mean peaceful negotiations with management.

One of the earliest labor confrontations, led by Irish Catholics, was in the coal fields of Pennsylvania. The "Molly Maguires," a secret society of coal miners, handled labor disputes by terrorizing mining bosses from 1865 until 1875. After being infiltrated by undercover Pinkerton detectives hired by the Reading Railroad, twenty Irish miners were convicted and hanged. Appalled by their violence, Frederick Wood, bishop of Philadelphia, condemned this secret organization and their actions in a pastoral letter. Although the bishop's opposition to the Molly Maguires did not mean that the Church opposed Catholic labor organizations and their attempts to negotiate basic rights for laborers.

In 1884, for instance, when the Vatican sided with Canadian bishops and forbade Catholic membership in the Knights of Labor (because it was a secret society with rituals), many American bishops, sympathetic to the labor movement, ignored the edict and chose to believe the edict applied only to our northern neighbor.

When Canadian Archbishop Taschereau insisted that Rome's order applied not only in Canada but to all Catholics, America's leading prelate, James Cardinal Gibbons of Baltimore, traveled to Rome to defend the Knights' mission to improve labor conditions. Through Gibbons's efforts, the Vatican relented and agreed that Catholics could join the Knights of Labor so long as its platform did not advocate socialist or communist tenets.

By the late 1880s, when Samuel Gompers's American Federation of Labor began organizing workers, many Catholics moved quickly into A.F. of L. leadership positions. Other unions formed to represent coal miners, steelworkers, manufacturing, craft, and various trades had heavy Catholic membership. And, for the most part, the Catholic hierarchy blessed these new unions for attempting to improve the lot of the faithful. In his book, *Our Christian Heritage*, Cardinal Gibbons "supported the right of workers to organize unions, condemned child labor and attacked monopolies."[18]

The 1891 publication of Pope Leo XIII's encyclical letter, *Rerum Novarum*, was a great victory for Cardinal Gibbons and the bishops who defended organized labor's agenda.

In the document, the pope restated the Church's fundamental social teaching about the primacy of the family in social organization: that institutions created by society have an obligation to protect the sanctity of the family. The pope rejected the ideological tenets of socialism and its concept of class conflict because they could destroy the inherent dignity of the human person and his family. According to Leo, the state must exercise a positive role in protecting not only the rights of property owners but those of workers as well. In calling for regulations to humanize the workplace, the encyclical insisted that the state should "save unfortunate working people from the cruelty of men of greed." Leo reasoned that there are human limits to the amount of work one can do, hence "daily labor . . . should be regulated as not to be protracted over longer hours than strength admits." He also addressed the plight of Pennsylvania coal miners: "Those who work in mines and quarries and extract coal, stone and metals from the bowels of the earth should have shorter hours in proportion as their labor is more severe and trying to health."

The pontiff also addressed the issue of child labor: "Great care should be taken not to place [children] in workshops and factories until their bodies and minds are sufficiently developed."

Leo acknowledged the right of laborers to form unions and concluded that such associations can serve the common good. Unions, he explained, have intrinsic value and can offer "the means of affording not only many advantages to the workmen . . . [and] should become more numerous and more efficient." And on the subject of strikes, he wrote: "When working people recourse to a strike, it is frequently because the hours of labor are too long, or the work too hard, or because they consider their wages insufficient."

To prevent strikes and labor-management conflicts, Leo called on governments to enact laws that would "forestall and prevent such troubles from arising; they should lend their influence and authority to the removal in good time of the causes which lead to conflict between employers and employees."

Since the Church, Catholic political machines, and Catholic labor unions were perceived as champions of the common man, many Protestants became alarmed. Sensing that the power of well-organized immigrant Catholics might threaten their way of life and position in American society, some Protestant leaders encouraged three approaches designed to create political backlash: the creation among lower classes of nativist societies; the support among middle and upper classes of political "reform movements" to evict Catholic bosses; and the promulgation among intellectuals of pseudo-scientific eugenic theories and programs, the intent of which was to stop the immigration of "undesirable" eastern and southern Europeans.

*   *   *   *   *

The American Protective Association (APA), a secret anti-Catholic society, was founded in 1887 by Henry Bowers in Clinton, Iowa. Similar to the Know-Nothings, the APA instituted secret handshakes and rituals. They welcomed the remnants of pre-Civil War anti-Catholic movements as well a new generation of extremists – all united under one umbrella to fight the "papist horde". Inductees had to take this oath:

> I hereby denounce Roman Catholicism. I hereby denounce the Pope now sitting in Rome or elsewhere. I denounce all his priests and emissaries all over the world, and the diabolical intrigues of the Roman Catholic Church. I will not knowingly vote for,

recommend for nor appoint, nor assist in electing nor appointing a Roman Catholic nor any one sympathizing with Roman Catholicism to any political position whatever, and in all my public and political actions will be governed by the principles of this order.[19]

The APA permitted some foreigners to join so long as they believed in God and hated Catholics. In their Declaration of Principles they declared that "no Roman should be allowed any position in our public schools . . . the institutions of our country are in danger from the machinations of the Church of Rome . . . only by the removal of Roman Catholics from offices of public trust can justice be right and true . . . and that by the concerted continued efforts of the lovers of American liberty only can such results be consummated and continued."[20]

Many Protestants flocked to the APA because they feared the "new" Catholic immigrants entering American harbors. Poles, Slovaks, and Italians were viewed as filthy, depraved socialists, radicals, and anarchists who were committed to destroying U.S. institutions. One writer sympathetic to this position wrote an editorial in 1886 that contained these phrases:

These people are not Americans, but the very scum and offal of Europe. . . . an invasion of venomous reptiles.

. . . long-haired, wild-eyed, bad-smelling, atheistic, reckless foreign wretches, who never did an honest hour's work in their lives . . . crush such snakes . . . before they have time to bite . . .

. . . a danger that threatens the destruction of our national edifice by the erosion of its moral foundations.

. . . Europe's human and inhuman rubbish.[21]

Protestant fears increased when they read on the front pages of their newspapers accounts of the May 4, 1886, "Haymarket Riot" in Chicago: After several workmen striking for an eight-hour work day were shot by the police, August Spies, editor of the anarchist German-American newspaper *Arbeiter-Zeitung* organized a rally at Chicago's Haymarket. Although the meeting was peaceful, 180 police ordered the crowd to disperse. One participant – never identified – reacted by throwing a bomb that killed seven policemen and wounded sixty others. According to immigration historian, John Higham, the ensuing riot "was to go down as the most important single incident in late nineteenth century nativism."[22] Fear and panic spread throughout the nation – many thought the "reds" had hatched a revolution.

Events like the "Haymarket Riot" played into the hands of APA organizers, and membership rolls skyrocketed. The APA also pursued railroad workers to join their ranks by promising to remove all Catholic railroad employees within one year. The APA also organized Protestant laborers in manufacturing plants to demand that Catholics be dismissed. By 1892, these tactics had helped APA ranks to swell to 2.5 million.

In order to publicly enter the political fray, the APA dropped secrecy oaths and secret handshakes. Candidates were fielded for various local offices and in the spring of 1892, APA members won elections in Nebraska, Iowa, Illinois, and Ohio. The APA regaled those who would listen with tales of Jesuitical plots to overtake the government. They circulated phony documents that claimed Catholics intended to exterminate Protestants. To thwart the coming Catholic reign of terror, APA candidates promised to get every employed Catholic fired. To achieve this end, they called on their followers to boycott merchants and companies who employed Catholics.

Anti-Catholic speaking bureaus, leaflets, and newspapers were financed by the APA in Cleveland, Chicago, Minnesota, St. Louis, and Denver. APA members also gained control of existing Protestant publications in Boston, New York, Philadelphia, Detroit, and San Francisco. The low point came in October 1892, when the APA provided its publications with the text of an encyclical, supposedly written by Pope Leo himself. The counterfeit document read in part:

> We proclaim the people of the United States to have forfeited all right to rule said republic, and also all domination, dignity, and privileges appertaining to it. We likewise declare that all subjects of every rank and condition in the United States, and every individual who has taken any oath of loyalty to the United States in any way whatever, may be absolved from said oath, as also from all duty, fidelity, or obedience, on or about Sept. 5, 1893, when the Roman Catholic Congress shall convene at Chicago, Ill., as we shall exonerate them from all engagements; and on or about the feast of Ignatius Loyola, in the year of our Lord 1893, it will be the duty of the faithful to exterminate all heretics found within the jurisdiction of the United States.[23]

Additional fears of possible armed conflicts were aroused when Catholics celebrated the 400th anniversary of the landing of Christopher Columbus. Catholic school children, Catholic societies, and papal knights in full regalia marched in parades throughout the nation commemorating the man who was thought to be the first white European – a Catholic – to reach the New World. Rumors were spread by APA chapters that those marching (including the children) were prepared to take up arms hidden in church basements and to forcibly take control of local governments.

None of this stopped either the Republicans or the Democrats from aggressively seeking Catholic votes in the election of 1892, which led the APA to complain that the entire body politic was corrupt. And by 1896, the nativists believed that they had enough clout to reform the political system strictly along lines dictated by their principles.

While numerous local Republicans had accepted support of the APA in the elections of 1892 and 1894, the party's national leaders were increasingly skeptical about future dealings with the organization. As mentioned earlier, Governor William McKinley of Ohio had good relations with Catholic and labor voters and was willing to endure APA disapproval when he appointed Catholics to government positions. Political analyst Seymour Martin Lipset has pointed out that the Republican Party's "surprisingly large depression-based victory, particularly in the East, in the congressional election of 1894, suggested that too close a link with the APA might mean the loss of a possible opportunity to make inroads among the rapidly growing immigrant population of the large cities. . . . Consequently . . . McKinley . . . and his advisers rejected the APA as an ally."[24]

Local Republicans subsequently followed the lead of their national leaders and repudiated APA support. This move plus the focus of the campaign on the economics of free silver versus gold, bankers versus farmers versus industrialists, pushed issues based on religion onto the back burner.

Because the APA had no role in producing the landslide victory of William McKinley, its membership declined rapidly, and by 1900 it was a mere shell of its former self. "Statistical analysis of the 1896 Presidential returns," Lipset concludes, "indicates no significant relation between APA strength and Presidential vote. . . . Political rejection by the Party of Protestantism with which it identified, seems to have contributed to its rapid decline thereafter."[25]

* * * * *

As the anti-Catholic APA movement of unskilled laborers was falling apart, the educated upper classes were pursuing their own brand of religious bigotry under the guise of political reform.

During America's "Gilded Age," the urban upper crust began a crusade to take back their municipalities from Catholic pols and to reform what the elite believed to be their corrupt ways. In private men's clubs, they lectured one another on the inherent evil of the Irish-Catholic bosses who built urban machines by buying off ignorant immigrants with political favors in return for votes against those most suited to govern – namely themselves. As sociologist Andrew Greeley has observed, "Reform was merely an attempt on the part of native-born Protestants to take what they had lost to the Irish in a fair fight."

Voting Power of Inner City Immigrants[26]

	Percentage of Voting-Age White Immigrants Naturalized				Number of Voting-Age White Immigrants			
	1900	1910	1920	1930	1900	1910	1920	1930
NYC	55.6	38.4	42.6	54.4	539,746	828,793	1,797,882	2,147,979
Jersey Cy	61.5	43.9	50.0	64.6	27,104	37,707	70,677	66,662
Albany	70.1	58.9	61.8	65.4	7,768	8,192	16,348	16,980
Boston	53.3	46.3	46.5	52.8	81,058	103,160	221,036	216,349
Chicago	68.6	50.2	54.8	64.2	271,962	379,850	743,803	800,515
San Fran.	68.4	48.0	52.3	55.3	56,102	75,768	128,791	145,606
Phila.	51.0	41.6	49.4	66.7	127,915	167,072	361,456	349,555
Pittsbgh	54.3	41.1	53.3	70.5	55,958	70,148	111,907	104,013

In every major city Anglo-Saxon elites were contemptuous of Catholic working-class values. Their prejudices were not necessarily a function of wealth or schooling; but rather of a shallow sophistication that rejects the fundamental American belief that people can and should be relied on to govern themselves.

New York City's much-maligned Tammany Hall stood as the premier example of the political machine the reformers despised. At its best Tammany was represented by the likes of George Washington Plunkitt, who made the city work through "honest graft," and at its worst by William Tweed, who made the city work almost entirely for himself and a few cronies. Plunkitt helped thousands of immigrants assimilate into mainstream American life. Tweed, ultimately unable to govern, found his lease on city hall terminated with a jail sentence.

The reformers who claimed credit for saving the cities were, in Plunkitt's words, "short-lived morning glories."[27] The tenure of the good government patricians – known as "Goo Goos" – was always brief. For instead of rolling up their sleeves and mixing it up with the people, they appointed blue-ribbon committees to study charter reform and otherwise attempted to govern the people at arm's length. The local political machines, on the other hand, as even *The New York Times* admitted in 1923, "wore human spectacles." The Goo Goos failed because they "attempted to deal with . . . municipal government as though it were a private corporation, and they a board of directors whose only aims were efficiency and economy. [They forgot] that a city administration must have a heart as well as a head."[28]

Templeton prize winner Michael Novak contrasted the reformers with the ethnic machines this way:

> Reform government is impersonal in conception and in execution.
> Elect a reformist mayor, and you elect six new agencies. To poorer

> people, the great value of "the machine" is that it is not a machine.
> It is not at all like a reformist bureaucracy, which is patently
> mechanical, abstract, a puzzling maze of rules and laws and fine
> print. The ethnic machines – Irish, Italian, Polish, Jewish,
> Lithuanian, etc. – are not impersonal but personal. Your street light
> is out? You call the precinct captain or the alderman. The garbage
> men are banging up your cans? The telephone. You get results the
> same day. You feel significant. You *have* "participatory democra-
> cy." Participatory democracy, ethnic style, is not participation in
> making *rules*; it is participation in a network of people who
> exchange *services*.[29]

Boston's colorful Mayor, James M. Curley, held a similar view: "reform
administrations suffer from a diarrhea of promises and a constipation of performance."[30]

Catholic politicians, unlike reformers, understood that their constituency
was not driven by scientific formulas and promises of good government. Their
people were concerned with jobs, garbage removal, housing, and a hundred
other matters, large and small. The pols who organized a city's political subdivisions were, especially through their precinct captains, very much in touch
with the needs of the people.

And although reformers did have occasional electoral victories on major
cities, their tenures were usually short-lived. "Reform politics," explains
Andrew Greeley, "ultimately does not work because it is incapable of keeping
touch with the complexities of urban problems. Political organizations, on the
other hand, are more likely to work because machine politicians, bent on preserving their own jobs and being elected, are much more likely to be in touch
with the personal needs of a majority of the electorate than are the principal
ideological reformers."[31]

Frustrated by their inability to remove Catholics political control at the
ballot box, the nativists turned to Washington, D.C., and to the latest pseudo-
scientific fad, eugenics, to save them from the immigrants.

*   *   *   *   *

The belief that the evolution of the human race may be improved by programs
of breeding which foster more desirable traits than nature alone may provide
is called eugenics or *positive* eugenics. *Negative* eugenics (also known as dys-
genics or cacogenics) would "purify" the gene pool by breeding out undesirable traits or by disposing of undesirable human beings; individuals, ethnic
groups, or whole races.

The American intellectual leader of this social Darwinist movement was
Yale Social Science Professor, William Graham Sumner. This former

Episcopal priest sought to unify the Protestant ethic, the doctrines of classical economics, and Darwinian natural selection.[32]

Influenced by British philosopher, Herbert Spencer, Sumner concluded that "Democracy itself, the pet superstition of the age, is only a phase of the all compelling movement"[33] For Spencer, in society only the fittest would survive, and in his mind the fittest were Anglo-Saxons, who controlled land and lived by the Protestant work ethic. He summed up his views in this statement:

> Let it be understood that we cannot go outside of this alternative: liberty, inequality, survival of the fittest; not-liberty, equality, survival of the unfittest. The former carries society forward and favors all its best members; the latter carries society downwards and favors all its worst members.[34]

The views of Darwin, Spencer, and Sumner had a tremendous impact on America's Progressive movement. According to Temple University professor Mark Haller, the educated Americans at the turn of the twentieth century "came increasingly to identify themselves and their values with the Anglo-Saxon race . . . and its love for liberty. That same love of liberty caused the peoples of northern Europe to accept Protestantism while more servile people of southern Europe remained under the domain of Rome."[35]

To northeastern progressives, the Irish, Italian, and Eastern-European Catholic immigrants who settled in America's cities were distasteful if not repulsive. In New York, the Reverend Frank Marling of the Second Avenue Presbyterian Church declared: "The vast hordes flocking to this land strike at our national life, which we count most precious, while the ballot gives them power which they know too well how to use."[36] Margaret Sanger, one of contemporary feminism's greatest heroines, said in 1921 that eugenics is "suggested by the most diverse minds as the most adequate and thorough avenue to the solution of racial, political and social problems. The most intransigeant [sic] and daring teachers and scientists have lent their support to this great biological interpretation of the human race." Sanger, founder of Planned Parenthood, boldly championed "more children for the fit, less from the unfit, [as] the chief issue of birth control."[37]

This movement, which began in the 1890s, would take thirty years to secure a victory. Writing in the October 5, 2003, edition of the *New York Times*, eugenics expert Daniel J. Keveles asserted that "the Eugenics movement provided a biological rationale for the Immigration Act of 1924, which discriminated against immigrants from eastern and southern Europe."

But before this 1924 victory, there were numerous clashes between the Catholic voter and the social Darwinists.

*   *   *   *   *

While William McKinley was the first Republican elected president with significant Catholic support, international events in his first administration at times made relations difficult with both Church hierarchy and the Catholic faithful.

At the end of the nineteenth century, many Americans called for the end of "ecclesiastical dominion and inquisitional persecution" in Cuba.[38] From Protestant pulpits, preachers railed against the injustices inflicted on Cuban peasants by the Church and even questioned if American Catholics would be loyal if the U.S. went to war with Spain. An editorial in Notre Dame University's publication *Ave Maria* summed up the American Catholic reaction to these charges:

> We have carefully examined the documents lately issued by the Spanish Legation in Washington, and are fairly persuaded of two points: first that Cuba has no valid and irremediable grievance against the mother country; and second, that if Spain were not a Catholic country misrepresentation of her government would not be so general, and there would be less enthusiasm for Cuba in both pulpit and press.[39]

When the battleship *U.S.S. Maine* mysteriously blew up in Havana harbor on February 15, 1898, the Church tried to take a middle ground. At a Requiem Mass for the 190 Catholic sailors who died on the *Maine*, James Cardinal Gibbons emphasized in his sermon that "no sane man can believe that a chivalric nation would be guilty of such inhumanity."[40] President McKinley's close friend, Archbishop John Ireland of St. Paul, reminded the public that "nothing has yet come to light that would, in my judgment, call for a rupture between the U.S. and Spain."[41]

To prevent war, Spain petitioned the pope to name Archbishop Ireland to mediate the dispute. Even though the White House welcomed the appointment, the press and Protestant clergy did not. In New York, for instance, Methodist minister James King spoke for many Protestants when he said, "We want no overtures from our government for settlement of the burning question confronting us as a nation, based upon propositions emanating from Rome."[42]

While the Catholic hierarchy in America remained neutral during the "splendid little war" – as the Spanish-American conflict was described – this did not stop Americans from doubting the loyalty of Church members. Rumors circulated that Catholics, under orders from the pope, were preparing to revolt against the U.S. government. Editorials in Catholic papers condemned reports that Cuban priests and nuns were responsible for murdering American troops.

The bishops, fearing an anti-Catholic backlash, issued a pastoral letter in

May 1898 explaining the American Church's position on the Spanish-American War:

> Whatever may have been the individual opinions of Americans prior to the declaration of war, there can now be no two opinions as to the duty of every loyal citizen. . . . We, the members of the Catholic Church are true Americans, and as such are loyal to our country and our flag and obedient to the highest decrees and the supreme authority of the nation.[43]

Also, numerous American Catholics who volunteered to fight were Catholic. California's First Volunteers, for instance, were 75 percent Catholic, and scores of priests and nuns served as chaplains and nurses.

But Catholic-Protestant tensions further heightened when Admiral George Dewey destroyed the Spanish fleet at Manila Bay, and it appeared the U.S. would occupy the Philippines and Cuba. Some Protestants, hoping to liberate and then convert the Catholic population in these islands, subscribed to the positions expressed in the Protestant newspapers:

- "When Cuba and the Philippines are freed from the Spanish yoke, two more fields will be open for the free proclamation of the Gospel."

- "The war with Spain has an added interest, in that the success of American arms in Cuba and Manila may mean the promulgation of a purer and reformed Christianity."

- "Break the clutch which Rome has put upon these people, and give them a chance for a civilization which is something more than Christianized paganism."[44]

Catholics were angered that the war was turning into a crusade to stop the free expression of the faith.

When an armistice was signed with Spain in August 1898, Archbishop Ireland warned the White House about potential problems confronting the peace conference. He was fearful that while political freedom might be guaranteed to Cuba, Puerto Rico, and the Philippines, the religious freedom of the Church might be crushed.

Influenced by Archbishop Ireland's pleas, President McKinley changed the membership of the peace delegation to ensure that religious claims would be addressed fairly. The Catholic hierarchy was pleased that the peace treaty signed on December 10, 1898, did permit freedom of religion for the

Philippines and Puerto Rico and protected the property of "ecclesiastical civil bodies."

Unfortunately, the treaty was frowned upon by segments of the U.S. Protestant population. The *New York Post* editorial page demanded that Filipino Spanish friars be expelled.[45] The Methodist *Christian Advocate* concluded that the U.S. had "an obligation resting upon us to plan a pure form of Christianity [in the Philippines]."[46]

John Brooke, the governor general of Cuba, did not improve the situation. He violated the directive that "severance of church and state" should proceed without "violating the legal rights of the Roman Catholic Church."[47] Brooke confiscated Church property and implemented a policy that recognized only civil marriages, not Catholic Church weddings.

When former Rough Rider and governor of New York, Theodore Roosevelt, was nominated in 1900 to be McKinley's running mate, he counseled the president that the Cuban marriage policy was infuriating Catholics in eastern states and could harm their election chances. McKinley reacted by replacing Brooke with the fair-minded General Leonard Wood, who cancelled the marriage regulation. A jubilant Roosevelt congratulated Wood on "fair play shown the Catholics in Cuba."

In the presidential election of 1900, McKinley once again faced his old foe, William Jennings Bryan. And while McKinley's electoral vote margin increased by 21 votes from the 1896 race (271 versus 292 electoral votes), his popular vote remained about the same 7.1 million versus 7.2 million. He did lose some ground with Catholics due to the international situation – unlike 1896 he did not carry New York City or Boston. Nevertheless, Catholic defections were not massive. Teddy Roosevelt was convinced that the change in Cuban policies helped maintain Catholic support, but there was more to it. Inner-city Catholic bosses did not like the Bryan forces that controlled the machinery of the national Democratic Party. They were treated shabbily at the conventions, and their counsel was ignored. And many Bryan enthusiasts nurtured an anti-Catholic bias. As a result of these attitudes, most inner-city Democratic clubhouses, until 1928, had little interest in the fate of the top of their ticket. Their main concern was electing their local congressional, state, and city candidates. The party faithful were, in effect, given a pass on the presidential elections and could vote as they pleased. This policy undoubtedly helped Republicans sweep the entire Northeast in the election of 1900 and was to be very helpful to the career of the accidental president – Theodore Roosevelt.

Chapter 9

The Catholic Voter in Peace and War

When the forty-two-year-old Theodore Roosevelt ascended to the presidency after the assassination of William McKinley, the American people soon realized the new tenant in the White House was a human dynamo.

The youngest man to hold the office, TR was also one of the best-read and certainly one of the most prolific writers ever to be president. In his twenties he wrote what is still considered a classic history, *The Naval War of 1812*.

Roosevelt was a walking contradiction. Historian Richard Hofstadter aptly describes him as the "Conservative as Progressive." Roosevelt, writes Hofstadter, "convinced people that he was a reformer and businessmen that he was sound."[1] He hated the *nouveau riche* but was not a great advocate of the poor because he feared the mob. And while in his writings and policies he exhibited a bias against Catholic immigrants, this did not stop TR from befriending the Catholic hierarchy and seeking the votes of their flocks.

After being elected in 1881 to represent Manhattan's wealthy upper east-side "Silk Stocking" district in the New York legislature, Roosevelt displayed a *noblesse oblige* attitude toward governing. He subscribed to the notion that the governing class should consist of high-minded Anglo-Saxon people who applied efficient principles of municipal administration. TR believed that his reform-minded ideas would cure New York City's ills and dislodge the Irish-Catholic bosses. In Albany, he aligned himself with other Anglo-Saxon legislators who "saw nothing wrong with Thomas Nast's cartoon portrayals of the Irish as ignorant apes in *Harper's Weekly*."[2]

After his first encounter with Catholic legislators, TR reported they were "vicious, stupid looking scoundrels with apparently not a redeeming trait beyond capacity for making exceedingly ludicrous bulls."[3] He assessed the legislature's two-dozen Irish-Catholic members as a "stupid, sodden vicious lot . . . equally deficient in brains and virtue."[4]

As assemblyman, unsuccessful candidate for mayor of New York, and member of the New York City Board of Police Commissioners, Roosevelt constantly expressed his opposition to liberal immigration laws and professed his admiration for the eugenics movement.[5]

Roosevelt mourned what Harvard anthropologist Madison Grant called the "passing of the great race" and embraced Social Darwinism to rationalize his Anglo-centrism. Influenced by eugenicist Brooks Adams, Roosevelt called for the sterilization of criminals and scolded the upper classes for committing "race suicide." (He was upset that Harvard graduates were producing only one-half to two-thirds of their original number.)

As president, Roosevelt encouraged the creation of an immigration commission that would establish a case to limit the immigration of Italians and East European Slavs, Poles and Jews. The forty-two-volume report of the Dillingham Commission (named after Commission Chairman Senator William Dillingham of Vermont), which Roosevelt endorsed, was an anti-Catholic, anti-Semitic eugenics diatribe that provided the pseudo-scientific foundations for the restrictive immigration laws of 1924. The findings (which Oscar Handlin noted were "neither impartial nor scientific") rationalized the position of Grant, the intellectual leader of the American nativist movement, that new immigrants were not

> Members of the Nordic race as [were] the earlier ones. . . . The new immigration contained a large and increasing number of the weak, the broken, and the mentally crippled of all races drawn from the lowest stratum of the Mediterranean basin and the Balkans, together with hordes of the wretched, submerged populations of the Polish ghettos. Our jails, insane asylums, and almshouses are filled with this human flotsam and the whole tone of American life, social, moral, and political, has been lowered and vulgarized by them.[6]

Roosevelt biographer William Harbaugh also reports he "had little patience with the doctrine of papal infallibility and he especially resented the Roman Church's authoritarian structure. His frequent emphatic support of the free public school system and his implied criticisms of parochial education even suggested a latent anti-Catholicism."[7]

But this man of many contradictions also exhibited a practical and sympathetic side toward Catholics.

> In fact, Roosevelt carried on occasional campaigns against anti-Catholicism which suggested he had a clear awareness of the political dividends which could be earned. His campaigns against anti-Catholicism earned him much support from Catholic immigrants, just as his public attitudes toward blacks were often well received among Afro-Americans. Virtue and self-interest met in each instance to win him favor among both groups. Writing his sister Anna in the fall of 1882, he chided a friend who "shows a strong tendency to trace all evils from the absence of rain to the fight with the Arabi Pascha, to the presence of Roman Catholics in America."[8]

The Boston Catholic Newspaper, *The Pilot*, praised TR as early as 1895: "If the party which Theodore Roosevelt honors with his support were one-tenth as honorable and honest as he is, it would be the only party in America."[9]

When the APA was at the height of its influence, Roosevelt refused to endorse their activities. "When I find," he wrote, "that a secret organization, whatever may be its principle, does, as a matter of fact, discriminate against certain Americans, no matter whether good or bad, because of their creed, why I cannot approve of any such organization."[10]

As president, Roosevelt reached out to Catholic leaders – particularly America's leading prelate, James Cardinal Gibbons. Catholic historian John Tracy Ellis points out that "with the advent of Theodore Roosevelt to the Presidency, there opened a span of years for Cardinal Gibbons during which he was probably on more intimate terms with the occupant of the White House than any other time of his life."[11]

Roosevelt consulted Gibbons on military-chaplain appointments and other policy matters. The president knew that if he was to be the first non-elected president to successfully seek an additional full term in office, he had to at least neutralize the Catholic vote.

In the Philippines, TR made changes in the structure of the American-Philippine government and removed blatant anti-Catholic administrators. He appointed respectful officials and permitted American Catholics to teach in Filipino public schools. The Boston *Pilot*, approving of his actions, headlined their report "President Roosevelt's Justice to Catholics."[12] Pleased with the progress in the Philippines, Cardinal Gibbons wrote to the president, "I am happy to say that the suspicions and criticisms manifested toward the government by some religious journals in this country are gradually diminishing in proportion as new light is thrown on the situation in the Philippines."[13]

TR's popularity increased in Catholic circles when Protestants attacked his policies. One such petition to Congress sponsored by the United American Mechanics, demanded that ". . . to maintain none but patriotic Protestant Americans in the control of our Public School system in the Philippines which, like our Public Schools to the United States, are daily being assailed by the Jesuits and Roman Catholic Church."[14]

Catholics during this period began to organize outside the Democratic machines. Bishop James McFaul of Trenton was the prime mover in creating the American Federation of Catholic Societies. This umbrella group, which represented 2 million Catholics, strove to promote unified Catholic opinion on important issues.

At their August 1900 convention in Chicago, Bishop Messmer warned the attendees that "It is a great mistake to suppose that politics have nothing to do with religion."[15] Bishop McFaul picked up on this theme when he told the crowd:

> If this organization had been ready for action at the outbreak of hostilities between Spain and America, the religious difficulties incident to the occupation of our new possessions might have received the immediate attention which would have allayed, if not prevented, the unfortunate friction now so deeply deplored. . . . Why should the administration have been led to believe that Catholics are satisfied with what had been done to the Philippines when the very contrary was the fact.[16]

In the election of 1904, a split Democratic Party turned to New York's Chief Judge of the Court of Appeals Alton B. Parker. With Catholic bosses more concerned with salvaging their local candidates, they ignored the national ticket, which they expected would lose badly.

This attitude played into Roosevelt's hand, and significant portions of the Catholic press helped him. The *San Francisco Monitor*, for instance, wrote:

> It becomes more evident every day as this campaign progresses, that it is essential that a Republican House of Representatives should be elected this Fall. . . . We may mention that the Boston *Pilot*, the *Irish World*, and other representative Catholic papers, have heartily endorsed Mr. Roosevelt's nomination and are earnestly advocating his election.[17]

Archbishop Ireland also told Roosevelt that "among Catholics you have far more supporters than you could well believe."[18]

It was true. Theodore Roosevelt was elected to a term in his own right, receiving 56.4 percent of the vote. He received the highest Republican majority since U.S. Grant's 55.6 percent in 1872. Democrat Parker received 37 percent of the vote and carried only the twelve southern states. While Roosevelt did lose the heavily Catholic populated cities of New York, Boston, and Jersey City, he ran well ahead of the Republican congressional vote, which means that many Catholic voters split the ticket. This was most evident in New York City:

New York City 1904 Results

	Democrats %	Republicans %
Presidential Vote	51.3	48.6
Congressional Vote	57.0	43.0

Roosevelt was delighted with the election results and expressed these sentiments in a letter to the Irish-American humorist, Finley Peter Dunne:

> One of the things I am most pleased with in the recent election is that while I got, I think, a greater proportion of the Americans of Irish birth or parentage and of the Catholic religion than any previous republican candidate, I got this proportion purely because they know I felt in sympathy with them and in touch with them.[19]

The friendly relations between TR and the Catholic hierarchy continued throughout his second term and were easily transferred to the president's chosen successor, William Howard Taft. It was Taft who, as governor-general of the Philippines, tactfully carried out Roosevelt's fair play for Catholics policy. One Catholic journal viewed Taft's Philippine tenure as "one of extraordinary difficulty and it is fair to say that he seems to have fulfilled it as satisfactorily as any other citizen could have done . . . all these stamp the statesmanship of [Taft] as large-minded, straightforwardness and in harmony with the best traditions of the Country."[20]

Catholic impressions of Taft further improved when he was sent by TR to head a three-man mission to the Vatican. The mission relieved numerous church-state tensions and was viewed by the *Catholic World* as additional "evidence of the sane methods now being adopted toward the Church."[21] While the U.S. government and the Vatican did not see eye-to-eye on every issue, nevertheless, historian Frank Reuter concluded that "the relationship between the U.S. government and the Roman Catholic Church vastly improved as a result of the Taft mission."[22]

In 1908, many Democratic Catholics were disappointed when their party nominated William Jennings Bryan for president a third time. The northeast bosses, particularly in New York, were fed up with the Western fundamentalist wing of the party that Bryan represented, and chose once again to sit on their hands during the fall campaign.

Taft, the Republican nominee, did catch some flack during the campaign from Protestants and Catholics due to his membership in the Unitarian Church. Since the Unitarians denied the divinity of Christ, many believed any member of this sect was not fit to be president. Back in Taft's home state of Ohio, a Protestant minister close to a branch of the Taft family, denounced the candidate and announced he intended to vote for Bryan.

Taft was also accused of being too friendly with Catholics. To this charge, he replied, "I deny utterly that I have ever cultivated the Catholic Church for political purposes, I believe the Catholic Church to be one of the bulwarks against socialism and anarchy in this country, and I welcome its presence here, but I decide every question that comes up on its merits as I understand them. . . . But it is useless to persuade a man with the anti-Catholic virus to look with patience at any treatment of the Catholic Church that does not involve hostility."[23]

In spite of the Unitarian controversy, Republicans reached out to Catholic voters, reminding them of Taft's special relationship with the Vatican. And to protect their neighborhood candidates, numerous machine-controlled cities – New York in particular – saw sample ballots circulated by the political leadership that showed a mark next to Taft's name and then marks for the Democrats on the rest of the ticket. Newspapers in New York City accused Democratic boss Charles Murphy of cutting a deal with a Republican state committeeman, Herbert Parsons, whereby Democrats would support Taft in exchange for Republicans voting against reform candidates.[24]

The results add some credence to these claims: Democratic support for Bryan in New York City in 1908 was 48 percent, versus 53 percent for Parker in 1904. Additional evidence is that the combined Democratic vote in New York City for congressional candidates, 51 percent, was higher than the percentage garnered by the top of the ticket. Bryan's own supporters also explained his defeat by pointing to the desertion of Catholic voters. Bryan biographer Louis Koenig reported that many angry Democrats "cited the exceptionally heavy vote for Taft in large Eastern cities and contended that instructions to vote for Taft were read widely in Catholic churches the Sunday before the election."[25] Angry supporters wrote Bryan asserting that he was defeated by "Rum, Romanism and Capitalism;" "Catholicism, Commercialism and Coercion;" or "Wall Street Gold and Jesuitical conspiracy."[26]

*   *   *   *   *

By 1912, a bitter ideological and personal split developed between President Taft and former President Roosevelt. This rift caused TR to run for president against Taft as the candidate of the newly formed Progressive "Bull Moose" Party.

This squabbling within Republican circles gave the Democrats their first real shot at capturing the White House since 1892. And at their national convention in Baltimore, the deadlocked delegates, after a series of maneuvers by inner-city Irish-Catholic bosses, nominated Governor Woodrow Wilson of New Jersey.

Born in 1856, Woodrow Wilson was the son of a Presbyterian minister. He grew up in the southern towns of Staunton, Virginia; Augusta, Georgia; Columbia, South Carolina; and Wilmington, North Carolina; and went on to earn a degree in law from the University of Virginia and a doctorate in American History from Johns Hopkins University. In 1891, he joined the faculty of Princeton University and was chosen as its president in 1902.

As Princeton's CEO, the strictly Presbyterian Wilson did not suffer fools gladly. When his master plan for Princeton's graduate school was defeated, the self-righteous Wilson displayed a mean-spirited temper, attacked his opponents mercilessly, and accused trustees and administrators of traitorous acts. Reacting to Wilson's tantrum, Princeton trustee and former president Grover Cleveland called him "a dishonorable [man] who was careless about facts and had a volatile, vindictive temper."[27]

To escape Princeton, Wilson permitted wealthy New Jersey conservative Democrats to arrange his nomination for governor in 1910. Hoping to take away the control of New Jersey from Bryan partisans, Wilson's supporters convinced Catholic political boss Jim Smith of Jersey City that Wilson's candidacy was their only hope to achieve that end. Smith swung the convention to Wilson and provided the full power of his machine to help elect him that November.

As soon as he was sworn in as governor, the pious Wilson turned on Boss Smith. Throughout his two years of service, Wilson constantly railed against political machines and refused to admit it was the Catholic bosses who were responsible for his election. The shocked Smith reacted much like Cleveland had at Princeton and complained that Wilson's actions were "striking evidence of his aptitude in the art of foul play."[28]

Wilson displayed these same traits at the 1912 Democratic Convention that nominated him for president. He denied that the Catholic bosses Tom Taggart of Indiana and Roger Sullivan of Illinois had provided the necessary momentum to nominate him at the deadlocked convention. Progressive Era historian George Mowry points out that Wilson's nomination was "achieved by a traditional bundle of bargains and compromises that defied ideology."[29] Even though these bosses made a series of deals with Wilson managers William McCombs and William McAdoo, Wilson preferred to give the sole credit to William Jennings Bryan.

When dealing with Catholics, Wilson had a mixed record. At Princeton, he appointed the first Catholic to the faculty, and in the campaign of 1912 he tried to appeal to the Catholic vote by frequently repeating this comment:

> The only reason why government did not suffer dry rot in the Middle Ages . . . was that so many of the men who were efficient instruments of government were drawn from the Church – from that great body which was then the only Church, that body which we now distinguish from other religious bodies as the Roman Catholic Church. . . . [It] was then, as it is now, a great democracy.[30]

But back in 1901, Professor Wilson had objected to the ethnic origins of the new wave of Catholic immigrants that were coming through the gates of

Ellis Island. He wrote that there was "an alteration in stock which students of affairs marked with an uneasiness."[31] The European sturdy stocks, according to Wilson, were being replaced by "men of the lowest class from the south of Italy and men of the meaner sort out of Hungary and Poland, men out of the ranks where there was neither skill nor energy nor any initiative of quick intelligence; and they came in numbers which increased from year to year, as if the countries of the south of Europe were disburdening themselves of the more sordid and hapless elements of their population, the men whose standard of life and work were such as American workmen had never dreamed of hitherto."[32]

To further illustrate his position on the "new" immigrant, Wilson described Poles and Hungarians as filthy illiterates and concluded "the Chinese were more to be desired as workmen, if not as citizens, than most of the coarse crew that come crowding in every year at the eastern ports."[33]

During the 1912 presidential campaign, Wilson bit the hand that fed him by publicly condemning the Irish Catholic bosses. At a September 12 address before the New York Democratic Party committee in Syracuse, Wilson "intimated bluntly that the New York Democrats should rid themselves of the incubus of [Charles] Murphy."[34] Wilson was seemingly unaware of the role that Tammany leader Charles Francis Murphy had played in breaking the deadlock at the Democratic Convention that led to his nomination. Agreeing that Murphy was a significant player in implementing a "masterly strategy," the *New York Telegram* conceded, "Mr. Murphy is a bigger factor here today than any Tammany Hall leader has ever been in a National Convention."[35]

Several weeks later, Wilson again condemned Murphy and told his political advisors, "I will put my foot down and put it downward against boss control of the New York State situation."[36]

Wilson's ethnic comments and Anglo-centrism haunted him during the campaign. His views expressed in his work *Congressional Government*, which glorified America as a country whose political and social traditions were strictly British, did not go over well in Irish-Catholic communities. His attitudes toward "hyphenated" Americans offended other Catholic ethnics and led Archbishop John Ireland to state plainly that Wilson was anti-Catholic. George Reedy, who was press secretary under Lyndon Johnson, explained Wilson's attitudes:

> The most important of the Wilson personality failures, however, was his lack of understanding of the ethnic groups who made up so much of the American scene. To him, Irish-Americans, Polish-Americans, Italian-Americans, German-Americans, and Swedish-Americans were "hyphenates." The thought never seemed to have crossed his mind that his own admiration for British institutions could easily have earned him the hyphenated tag "Anglo-

American." He was basically a WASP reformer, who detested the
city machines as much for their lack of style as for their venality.
He did not understand that they were filling a need – providing
much-needed services for people at the bottom of the social ladder.[37]

The American Association of Foreign Language newspapers, whose
membership represented 20 million readers, struck a blow at Wilson when
their newspapers published this comment: "No man who has an iron heart like
Woodrow Wilson, and who slanders his fellowmen, because they are poor and
many of them without friends when they come to this country seeking honest
work and wishing to become good citizens, is fit to be President of the United
States."[38]

These charges appeared to have an effect. A poll of 2,300 Catholic priests
in the Catholic strongholds of New York, Boston, Hartford, Cleveland,
Indianapolis, St. Louis, Louisville, Chicago, Milwaukee, and Detroit, revealed
that 90 percent of the Italian and 70 percent of Polish priests intended to vote
for Bull Moose candidate Theodore Roosevelt.

In a counter effort, the Wilson campaign commissioned the prominent
Catholic professor James Monaghan, who had the chair of economics and history at Notre Dame, to pen a brochure titled *Is Woodrow Wilson a Bigot?* to
prove that the candidate was "kindly disposed towards Catholics." When a
false charge surfaced from evangelicals that Wilson had accepted a membership in the Knights of Columbus, he tried to silence both sides with this reply:
"I am a normal man, following my own natural cause of thought, playing no
favorites, and trying to treat every creed and class with impartiality and
respect."[39]

When the results came in, Woodrow Wilson was elected with a plurality:

Wilson (D)	6,293,019	41.85%
Roosevelt (Progressive)	4,119,507	27.39
Taft (R)	3,484,956	23.18
Debs (Socialist)	901,873	5.99
Chafin (Prohibitionist)	207,828	1.65

With his numbers lower than Bryan's past totals, it appeared that Wilson
was not popular with either wing of his party. If it were not for the Republican
split, Wilson would have gone down in flames.

An analysis of vote totals can lead one to conclude that the Irish-Catholic
bosses vilified by Wilson sat out the presidential election. It appears that
once again the bosses gave their ward leaders a pass when it came to turning

out the faithful for the top of the ticket, but on the other hand, insisted that they vote the rest of the ticket straight Democratic. This was most evident in Charles Murphy's New York. In the 1912 presidential election, Woodrow Wilson received only 46 percent of the vote (Bryan garnered 48 percent in 1908, and the 1904 standard bearer, Alton Parker, got 53 percent) and, the congressional delegation ran ahead of his total receiving 49 percent of total votes cast.

States and Cities with Strong Catholic Democratic Presence
1912 Wilson Results

State	Wilson %
New York	41
Massachusetts	35
Illinois	35
New Jersey	41
Pennsylvania	32

City	Wilson %
New York City	46
Boston (Suffolk County)	47
Jersey City (Hudson Co.)	43
Chicago (Cook County)	30

Wilson's White House and cabinet appointments reflected the Democratic Party's Electoral College strength – southern and western. And the longtime leader of that coalition, William Jennings Bryan, was rewarded with the top cabinet post, Secretary of State. To placate Catholics, he appointed Jersey City Irish pol, Joseph Tumulty, as his assistant.

Joe Tumulty worshiped at the altar of Woodrow Wilson. In New Jersey, he had loyally served Governor Wilson and guided him through the state's political minefields. He was the front man defending Wilson to the Catholic community when the governor broke his word and tried to destroy boss Jim Smith. And Tumulty sacrificed any political future for himself in New Jersey by sticking with Wilson through thick and thin.

But loyalty and sacrifice meant little to Wilson. He was known to treat Tumulty poorly, and he happily listened to the complaints voiced by those envious of his Irish secretary. Colonel House, the *eminence grise* during most of the Wilson years, complained that Tumulty was socially unfit to speak for the president and too parochial besides. "He cannot see beyond Hudson County [New Jersey]," House whined to the president.[40] Tumulty was also accused of withholding information from the president, and rumors spread throughout Washington that his main agenda was to establish the Catholic Church as the official church of the United States. One of Wilson's correspondents accused Tumulty of being a "monstrous and fiendish political plunder head and enemy of mankind."[41] And Wilson stoked the flames by frequently threatening to fire Tumulty. Southern Democrats also tried to end Tumulty's career by spreading rumors that he was a secret agent of the Vatican. At one point, Wilson succumbed to these pressures and offered Tumulty to a federal "collectorship" back in New Jersey – but the stubborn Tumulty refused to budge, and Wilson did not have the courage to fire him outright.

Throughout his presidency, Wilson had rocky relations with Roman Catholics – bishops and common people alike. When Wilson recognized the Mexican government of President Venustiano Carranza, many Catholics were livid. The hierarchy forcefully complained that the U.S. should not support a government that publicly restricted the practice of Catholicism. The Jesuit magazine *America* condemned Wilson and described Carranza "as a villain, destroyer, liar and murderer."[42] Catholic historian Theodore Maynard reported that Wilson was also rude to members of the hierarchy:

> It was a distinct shock to the eighty-three-year-old Cardinal [Gibbons] when he called upon the President to be dismissed in a few minutes without even being asked to sit down. When [Archbishop] Ireland, who had heard of this, was about to call at the White House he said, "Well, he won't treat *me* in that way" – but he got just the same treatment. Upon this, Archbishop Bonzano, the Apostolic Delegate, let it be known that he would not call at all upon Wilson, and consented to do so only after the presidential secretary, Joseph Tumulty, a Catholic, had promised that he would be received with fitting dignity. But he, too, was not asked to sit down, much to his indignation.[43]

After war broke out in Europe in 1914, Wilson's neutrality was under constant assault by Irish and German Americans. Wilson's policies, they claimed, reflected his pro-British outlook.

The Wilson Administration's silence after the British crushed Ireland's 1916 Easter Rebellion infuriated Irish-Catholic Americans. When the rebel "Easter Martyrs" were executed by the British, many Irish in the U.S. supported the German war cause, particularly after the Kaiser recognized Ireland's right to independence.

Wilson's popularity with Irish Catholic leaders further declined when it became public that the administration had turned over to Britain captured documents that sealed the fate of Irish gun runner Roger Casement.

Captured by the British on a German boat that contained contraband arms, Casement was tried and sentenced to death. The *Gaelic-American*, a newspaper owned by Irish American leader Judge Daniel Cohalan of New York, "repeatedly accused Wilson of being the evil genius behind this tragedy."[44]

Wilson further alienated Irish and German Americans when, in a series of national speeches, he criticized "hyphenates" (i.e., Catholic immigrants) and claimed they were "pouring poison into the veins of national life."[45]

In one speech, Wilson "praised the Revolutionary War hero John Barry as an Irishman whose 'heart crossed the Atlantic with him.' He described other Americans, with little doubt as to his meaning, as needing hyphens in their names because only part of them has come over."[46]

By early 1916, Democratic pols were nervous that Wilson's comments and "Pro-British" diplomatic policies would upset delegates attending their upcoming Baltimore convention and destroy their chance at retaining the White House for another term. So, to avoid a calamity and to defuse Irish and German anger, it was agreed that in no uncertain terms the Democratic Platform Committee would support American neutrality.

The platform summoned "all men of whatever origin or creed who would count themselves Americans, to join in making clear to all the world the unity and consequent power of America. This is an issue of patriotism. To taint it with partisanship would be to defile it. In this day of test, America must show itself not a nation of partisans but a nation of patriots." [47]

All, however, did not go smoothly at the Democratic Convention. Ohio Governor James Cox told Wilson's managers that the Catholic press in Ohio, Illinois, and Wisconsin was pounding the president as an anti-Catholic. Wilson supporter Rev. Edward Flannery of New York reported that in his home state as well as in New Jersey, Connecticut, and Massachusetts, Irish Catholics were livid over Wilson's foreign policy. The ever-loyal Tumulty had to deny claims that the president offended various cardinals, archbishops, and the papal legate.[48] The *Catholic News Bulletin* publicly supported Republican presidential nominee Charles Evans Hughes, and the *Irish World* described Wilson as the Anti-Christ.[49]

Although numerous political leaders within the Irish and German Catholic communities vehemently opposed the president's reelection, some of their tactics backfired and actually helped Wilson. When one Irish leader, Jeremiah O'Leary, sent an obnoxious telegram to the president predicting his defeat, Wilson replied publicly: "I would feel deeply mortified to have you or anybody like you vote for me. Since you have access to many disloyal Americans and I have not, I will ask you to convey this message to them."[50] O'Leary's twenty-three-page reply denying his disloyalty and listing his Civil War record as a member of New York's "Fighting Irish" 69th brigade was ignored by the White House. Joe Tumulty believed the president's reaction added life to their reelection campaign.

When the November 1916 election results were tallied, it appeared that Woodrow Wilson's neutrality theme, "too proud to fight" actually paid off. The extremely close election split at 277 electoral votes for Wilson versus 254 for Hughes.

For the first twenty-four hours after the polls closed, it appeared that Hughes would win. But when the final votes were counted in California, Wilson's 3,000-vote margin (out of 1 million cast) swung the election in his favor.

With 49.24 percent of the total popular vote, Wilson was still a minority president, but he did patch together the successful coalition that had eluded Bryan in his three races for the office: Wilson won both the solid South and the West. Wilson carried twenty-seven of the twenty-nine southern and western states, losing only Oregon and South Dakota. His total vote was almost 3 million more than in 1912, 9.1 million versus 6.3 million.

In the Northeast and Midwest, however, Wilson fared poorly. Hughes carried all the states with large urban Catholic populations: New York, Connecticut, Massachusetts, Pennsylvania, Illinois, Michigan, Indiana, and New Jersey. Minnesota and Wisconsin, states with large German-Catholic populations, also went for Hughes.

But while many Irish Catholic leaders who viewed Wilson as pro-British strongly opposed him, it appears the rank and file in urban wards bought Wilson's rhetoric on neutrality at any price. As the following chart reveals, Wilson's 1916 support in densely Catholic-populated Northeast and Midwest cities significantly improved:

Wilson Vote Percentages
Catholic Populated Cities

	1912	1916
New York City	46%	52%
Suffolk Co. (Boston)	47	59
Cook County (Chicago)	30	46
Philadelphia	26	31

While many Catholics did stick with Wilson in 1916, the president would quickly learn that their support was shallow.

*   *   *   *   *

Wilson, elected in 1916 on a peace platform and on a slogan, "He kept us out of war," took the nation into war six months into his second term.

Tired of German violations of American neutrality, Wilson appeared before the Congress on April 2, 1917, and delivered a war message. Four days later, the president signed legislation that approved a declaration of war against Germany and its allies.

To avoid any misconceptions of its stand on the war, the U.S. Catholic bishops published this statement:

> Moved to the very depth of our hearts by the stirring appeal of the President of the United States and by the action of our national congress, we accept wholeheartedly and unreservedly the decree of that legislative authority proclaiming this country to be in a state of war. . . . We stand ready . . . to cooperate in every way possible . . . to the end that the great and holy cause of liberty may triumph.[51]

America's senior and most beloved prelate, James Cardinal Gibbons, also spoke out forcefully on the obligation of American Catholics: "The primary duty of a citizen is loyalty to country. . . . It is exhibited by an absolute and unreserved obedience to his country's call."[52]

The Church took an active role in ministering to Catholic troops, and it created the National Catholic War Council (NCWC), which raised millions from parishes to help meet the costs of providing spiritual services. In addition, the Supreme Knight of Columbus, James Flaherty, received approval to establish a Catholic "YMCA." The Knights set up over 250 overseas and 350 domestic facilities that provided recreational, spiritual, and social aid to Catholic soldiers. The Church also created the military ordinate to supervise the 1,500 chaplains that served in the war. Patrick Hayes, auxiliary bishop of New York (and future cardinal archbishop), was named the first ordinary.

Over 1.1 million Catholics put aside ethnic animosities and allegiances and joined the armed forces. While the Catholic population in 1917 represented about 15 percent of the nation, over 20 percent of the total troops that served during the war were members of the Church.

Scores of Catholic troops served with distinction. Colonel William "Wild Bill" Donovan, who led the famed "Fighting Irish" 69th Regiment from New York, was awarded the Medal of Honor. (Donovan would later start the Office of Strategic Services, or OSS, the precursor of the CIA.)

While Wilson's call to make the world "Safe for Democracy" inspired Catholic Americans to help win the war, it was Wilson's compromises to win the peace that caused a major rift between the Catholic voter and the Democratic Party.

When President Wilson left for Europe in 1919 to establish what he believed would be a new world order at the Versailles Conference, many Irish, German, Italian, and Eastern European Catholics were concerned about the treatment their former homelands would receive from the victorious allies.

Many Catholics wanted to believe Wilson when he said that the peace would be based on fourteen points, including: "Open covenants of peace openly arrived at . . . , removal of trade barriers, freedom of seas, equality of trade, reduction of armaments" and most important "that peoples and provinces are not to be bartered about from sovereignty to sovereignty so if they were pawns in a game . . . [instead] every territorial settlement . . . must be made in the interest and for the benefit of the populations concerned, and not as part of any adjustment or compromise of claims amongst rival states . . . "

The hopes and dreams of Catholic Americans, however, were soon dashed. To save his precious League of Nations, Wilson abandoned his mighty rhetoric and ideals at the 1919 Versailles Peace Conference and managed to alienate almost every Catholic ethnic in America by surrendering to the demands of the crafty, vengeful leaders of the victorious allies.

Although he had arrived in Europe to the cheers of millions, Wilson quickly proved his ineptness at the negotiating table, particularly against experienced statesman such as Lloyd George of England and George Clemenceau of France. His "touch of visionary . . . combined with unreal academic habits of mind and a sensitive, humorless vanity"[53] did not mix well with other Versailles conferees. And before long, the cheering stopped – particularly among Irish-, Italian-, and German-American Catholics, who now believed that in the peace treaty Wilson had sacrificed the interests of their former homelands in order to win approval of his League of Nations.

The first cracks in Wilson's political coalition appeared when Irish-American leader Judge Daniel Cohalan of New York dared to ask publicly in 1919, "What about Ireland?" Angered that Cohalan questioned his integrity, Wilson refused to meet with Cohalan. When Joe Tumulty warned the president that the snub would create serious tensions, Wilson told his aide, "That's just what I want to do, Tumulty."[54]

And that's exactly what happened: When the Irish press learned of the snub, they turned Cohalan into a national martyr. Nervous congressmen reacted by passing a house resolution, by a vote of 216–45, urging the Versailles Peace Conference to "consider the claims of Ireland to the right of self-determination."[55]

In April 1919, three members of the American Committee for Irish Independence met with Wilson and requested that he seek British permission to permit the shadow president of Ireland, Eamon de Valera, to address the Versailles Conference. De Valera sought to urge the delegates to support Ireland's independence.

Lloyd George not only refused the request but persuaded France and Italy to permit vetoes at the conference they could employ to stop the appeals of small countries like Ireland.

Tensions increased when Wilson broke the news to the Irish-American leaders. One exasperated member reminded Wilson that the Allies' job was "to help a small nation realize one of Wilson's ideals, self-determination. Had Wilson forgotten that article of the Fourteen Points?"[56]

In a sudden epiphany, an exhausted Wilson confessed that his principles had not prevailed and that he was failing: "You have touched on the great metaphysical tragedy today. . . . My words have raised hopes in the hearts of millions of people. . . . There were a lot of things I hoped for but did not get."[57]

Italian-Americans also turned on Wilson when Prime Minister Vittorio Emanuele Orlando complained that the president was denying Italy its just rewards. Wilson created a major uproar when, against the advice of his staff, he publicly explained in Europe his rejection of the Italian demand to occupy the port city of Fuime near the Yugoslavian border.

Back home, Italian-American newspapers denounced Wilson. Resolutions were actually passed in the legislatures of New York, Massachusetts, and Illinois supporting Prime Minister Orlando's position. Reacting to the controversy, an angry Wilson told his secretary, "They will never get Fuime while I have anything to do with it."

Many Eastern European Catholics were offended because the newly drawn lines of Poland, Czechoslovakia, Rumania, and Yugoslavia established national borders without consideration of ethnicity. Many of the countries that emerged from the former Austro-Hungarian Empire threw together ethnic groups which had despised one another for centuries. Finally, German-Americans were angered because the peace treaty was not based on the Fourteen Points as Wilson had promised. They were angry that tens of thousands of Germans were starving because France insisted on a trade blockade which prevented Herbert Hoover, head of the American Relief Administration, from getting food to Germany. The German-Americans were also displeased that Article 231 of the Treaty of Versailles contained the German "war-guilt clause" and that Germans were forced to pay $33 billion in reparations to cover civilian damages and Allied war pensions.

Many American Catholics were angry that Wilson had abandoned his quest for "self determination" to get his League. They were angry that he sat by while France and England cut up the world to suit their imperialistic needs. He permitted 1.1 million square miles of land and 17 million people to be turned over to the French and British.

> At one point in these negotiations, Wilson, almost talking to himself, said, "I am obliged to remain faithful to my Fourteen Points, but without inflexibility." The words convey an image of a man desperately refusing to face the truth about what he was doing – what his precious covenant, for which he had permitted hundreds

of thousands of German civilians to starve, was becoming. Behind his back, Clemenceau laughed at the president. "I never saw a man talk more like Jesus Christ and act more like Lloyd George," the French premier remarked. Lloyd George also expressed bemused bafflement. "He believed in mankind but distrusted all men," the Welsh Wizard remarked.[58]

As Wilson sailed back to America expecting to enter New York harbor triumphantly with the Treaty of Versailles, he was unaware that a war-weary nation was in the throes of a political backlash.

In Massachusetts, the legislature overwhelmingly condemned "the so-called Covenant of the League of Nations claim to commit this republic to recognize the title of England to own and rule Ireland."[59]

Judge Cohalan, Jeremiah O'Leary, and other Irish leaders snubbed by Wilson turned against the president and denounced him in Irish communities. "Friends of Ireland" rallies were held throughout the nation demanding that Wilson be impeached. A young Italian politician and veteran aviator, Fiorello LaGuardia, turned on the League and urged Italians to vote Republican to prove Wilson was "discredited at home."[60]

Although Wilson readily compromised his vision in Europe, he refused to even discuss the concerns of the Republican majority in the U.S. Senate, led by Henry Cabot Lodge of Massachusetts. Lodge was willing to approve a treaty that included the League but was frustrated that the president had refused to consider Lodge's own "Fourteen Reservations," which included an insistence that the U.S. not participate in any League of Nation acts of war without prior approval of a joint resolution of Congress.

Believing the Senate would succumb to public pressure, Wilson decided to go over their heads to speak directly to the people and to rally them to his side. Wilson's national tour, which began on September 3, 1919, and covered 8,000 miles in 22 days, did not go exactly as planned. In California, Irish-Catholic U.S. Senator James D. Phelan warned Wilson that "the Irish are in a fair way to leave the Democratic Party."[61] In Pueblo, Colorado, Wilson offended numerous ethnic-Americans who questioned the treaty, by claiming that the only people who opposed him were "the forces of hyphenated-Americans."[62]

The campaign for the League came to an abrupt halt on September 25 when Wilson collapsed. He suffered a serious stroke that paralyzed his left side.

He was back in the White House by October 2, but the true extent of his illness was never made public. The cover-up was maintained for the next year and half by his wife, Edith, who made many executive decisions in Wilson's name.

The ailing Wilson, who refused to negotiate with Senator Lodge, was informed on November 19, 1919, that the Treaty of Versailles had been denied Senate approval.

Another issue that infuriated Catholics throughout the nation during Wilson's second term was Prohibition.

> Prohibition was the product of the age-old conflict of country against city, of the God-fearing, solid, dry Yankee farmer against the corrupt urban rich and the immigrants with their foreign religions and customs, and their imported beer and rum. Prohibition represented the last attempt of rural America to stem the tide of history that was transforming the country from an agricultural into an industrial nation. It stood for tradition and the old American way of life.[63]

Since the end of the Civil War, the Temperance Movement, particularly in the South and West, was rapidly growing. Thirty states by 1900 had local-option laws that permitted municipalities to stop the sale of liquor in their jurisdictions. When Oklahoma entered the Union in 1912, its constitution made the state thoroughly "dry." It was so extreme that Catholic priests were not permitted to use altar wine during Mass.

By 1917, the political process had made Congress overwhelmingly dry in its sensibility. In December, Congress approved an amendment to the Constitution prohibiting the "manufacture, sale or transportation of intoxicating beverages," which was then submitted to the states.

While awaiting state ratification of the amendment, Congress and President Wilson approved wartime food-control measures that restricted the manufacture of liquor. To further the dry cause, Congress passed a rider to an appropriation bill of July 1, 1919, that would have stopped distilled spirits or wine from being sold.

Joe Tumulty urged Wilson to veto the appropriation bill, fearing that millions of urban Catholic voters would abandon the Democratic Party. Tumulty, who described the Congress's actions as "mob legislation pure and simple," was ignored, and Wilson signed the measure into law. One year later, the Eighteenth Amendment took effect, and over Wilson's veto the Volstead Act, which provided federal enforcement of Prohibition, became law on October 28, 1919.

In 1920, a deadlocked Democratic Convention turned on the 44th ballot to Ohio governor James M. Cox. In a visit to the White House, Cox told President Wilson: "We are going to be a million percent with you and your Administration and that means the League of Nations."[64]

Meanwhile, at the deadlocked Republican Convention delegates embraced on the 10th ballot another Ohioan, U.S. Senator Warren G. Harding. Viewing a nation torn by union unrest, a post-war recession, and soaring inflation, the dark-horse candidate told the nation that "America's present need is not heroics but healing, not nostrums but normalcy."

While Cox stormed the nation campaigning and Harding ran from his front porch, Catholic forces angered by Wilson's attitude and policies worked to punish the Democratic Party.

Inner-city bosses sick of Wilson's self-righteousness wanted to exorcise the party of his influence. New York's Tammany boss, Charles Murphy, wrote off the 1920 race as doomed and was already thinking about 1924 and his favorite son, Governor Alfred E. Smith.

Missouri Democratic politician Frank Walsh, chairman of the Commission for Irish Independence, stumped the nation urging Irish-Catholics to reject the party of Woodrow Wilson. George Viereck, leader of the German-American Conference, wrote Walsh: "We have decided there must not be another Democratic president for a generation."[65] Democratic New York Supreme Court Judge Daniel Cohalan, now known as the "peerless leader of 20 million of the Irish Race in America," actually went to the Republican National Convention and urged delegates to oppose the League and to support Irish independence.[66]

Irish Democrats trying to save their own skins deserted their party's standard bearer in droves. In Massachusetts, Cox was asked to make only a whistle stop visit. A speech by Cox on the League of Nations in Worcester caused the city to vote heavily Republican.[67] A week before the election, 50,000 Irish Americans assembled at New York's Polo Grounds to hear Wilson's anti-Ireland policies denounced. In the *Gaelic American*, John Devoy wrote, "Cox wears Wilson's collar on the League of Nations."[68]

Italian-Americans also turned out against Wilson and his League. Their newspapers denounced the president, and the Federation of Italian Societies in America instructed their members to forget party allegiance in 1920 and to vote for Harding. Democratic vice-presidential candidate Franklin Delano Roosevelt further stirred the ire of Italians when he said they were only "fifty-fifty citizens."

On November 2, 1920, the Democratic Party suffered the greatest national defeat in its history:

1920 National Results

Harding (Rep)	16,133,314	60.30%
Cox (Dem)	9,140,884	34.17
Debs (Soc)	913,664	3.42

Cox carried only eleven states of the old South for a total of 127 electoral votes. Harding carried the rest of the nation, including the former Confederate state of Tennessee for a total of 464 electoral votes. States with large Catholic populations voted decisively for the Republican presidential candidate:

	Harding	**Cox**
New York	64.6%	27.0%
Massachusetts	68.6	27.8
Connecticut	62.7	33.0
New Jersey	67.7	28.4
Pennsylvania	65.8	27.2
Illinois	67.8	25.5
Michigan	72.8	22.3
Wisconsin	71.1	16.2
Minnesota	70.6	19.4

Most humiliating for the Democratic nominees was the beating they suffered in the Catholic-dominated inner cities:

**Democratic Presidential
Results in Major Catholic Cities**

	1900	1904	1908	1912	1916	**1920**
New York City	57%	53%	48%	46%	52%	**30%**
Boston (Suffolk Co.)	54	54	48	47	65	**38**
Jersey City (Hudson County)	54	51	48	53	48	**38**
Chicago (Cook Co.)	47	39	39	30	46	**23**

The results in New York City (particularly since a New Yorker – F.D. Roosevelt – was on the ticket) were particularly embarrassing. This bastion of Catholic Democrats, which had once swung national elections for Jefferson, Jackson, and Cleveland, had repudiated the Democratic Party. Cox-Roosevelt lost the city by over 400,000 votes. The 30 percent they received in the city was the lowest share any Democratic presidential candidate ever received – before or since. In New York and other major urban centers, Irish, Italian, German, and Eastern European Catholics simply abandoned the Democratic Party. One Democratic analyst called it right when he wrote, "The bitterness toward Wilson is evident everywhere and deeply rooted. He hasn't a friend."[69]

Chicago Catholic Ethnic Democratic Vote – 1920

	Czechs	Poles	Italians	Germans
President	40%	35%	31%	14%
Senator	59	49	39	37
Governor	51	42	35	30

Grover Cleveland once predicted that: "Woodrow Wilson would go far in politics but when he finished, there would be very little left of the Democratic Party."[70] The 1920 election results proved Cleveland a seer. But Woodrow Wilson – incapable of admitting any faults – reacted to the elections of 1920 by pointing his finger at American voters and declaring: "They have disgraced us in the eyes of the World."[71]

Chapter 10
The Campaign of 1928

The city of bright lights, champagne, and silk hats – that was New York in the 1920s. Walking down Broadway for the first time in 1921, British journalist G.K. Chesterton considered the colorful neon display and proclaimed: "What a glorious garden of wonders this would be to anyone who was lucky enough to be unable to read."

During the Roaring Twenties, New York's Tammany Hall reigned supreme thanks to its gifted leader, Grand Sachem Charles Francis Murphy.

Murphy, who ran New York City politics for a generation, was instinctively conservative and a pragmatist who understood the needs and cultures of the city's diverse immigrant neighborhoods, and his machine was built on meeting those needs. For instance, after the March 25, 1911, tenement fire that killed 146 young women in the Triangle Shirtwaist factory, Murphy's support for Al Smith's safety-code legislation was "based more on political demands than socialist theory."[1]

Unlike most bosses of his time, Murphy craved respect more than riches; and to enhance his image, he sponsored and promoted men of quality like Al Smith and Robert Wagner. The members of his tightly knit organization revered the low key "Mr." Murphy. *The New York Times* commented: "A caller on Mr. Murphy at Tammany Hall rarely talked to him more than two minutes. With immobile features, Mr. Murphy would listen to him attentively without moving a muscle. A nod of assent or of negation would usually be all that the seeker for favor would receive." He was certainly tight lipped – at one political gathering a reporter noticed that Murphy wasn't singing "The Star Spangled Banner." When he mentioned this to one of the pols in attendance, the reporter was told that perhaps "Mr. Murphy didn't want to commit himself."[2]

But if he wasn't as avid in his taste for wealth as some earlier bosses had been, Murphy also wasn't opposed to political patronage nor, in order to support the clubhouse, was he against leaning on appointees for pieces of their salaries. His philosophy was simple: "When I can do it without violating the law, it is perfectly right to give our contracts to organization men. If I can I will."[3] And Boss Murphy did maintain control and rarely was there a charge of corruption.

But Murphy's greatest asset was his ability to recognize and advance men with talent and principles. "Charles Murphy's Tammany Hall," Robert Wagner, Sr. said in 1937, "was the cradle of modern liberalism in America."

It was the "Charles Murphy Institute" that permitted men like Wagner, Al Smith, Edward Flynn, and James Farley to become major players in the political process. Murphy explained it this way:

> Formerly, it was difficult for young men of talent and ambition to get into public life. They were discouraged at every step by those already in who wished to keep the influence within as narrow bounds as possible. I encouraged the selection of young men for public office, particularly for legislative positions, encouraged them to develop their talent, to keep free from demoralizing influences, to speak their minds, do what was right and develop character and a reputation which would do credit to themselves and reflect favorably upon the organization and my leadership. These young men went out into public life and made good. . . . They gave you a different viewpoint of what Tammany Hall is and its aims and aspirations.[4]

The reign of Boss Murphy begat Al Smith, and it was Smith who, as governor of New York, managed to implement a state agenda that embodied the principle of subsidiarity.

Al Smith was born in the shadow of the Brooklyn Bridge on December 30, 1873. Upon the death of his father, a manual laborer, thirteen-year-old Al dropped out of the Lower East Side's St. James Parish grammar school to take on various menial jobs to help support his penniless family.

For Smith, like so many of his time, the Catholic parish served as the spiritual, social, and educational center of life. The nuns and priests instilled in him love of God, family, neighborhood, and country, as well as a belief in the dignity of work.

After spending long hours rolling fish barrels at the Fulton Fish Market (in later years he would boast that his alma mater was F.F.M.), Smith would spend his leisure time participating in parish plays and oratory contests. And it was at these activities that he caught the eye of a Tammany Hall district leader named Tom Foley.

Hired by the clubhouse as a county process server, Al Smith advanced to become municipal court clerk, state representative, speaker of the Assembly, Manhattan sheriff, president of New York City's Board of Alderman and, in 1918, election to the first of four terms as governor.

Smith was certainly one of the most colorful politicians during the

Roaring Twenties. He was easily spotted on the streets of New York in his brown derby hats, striped suits, and with an ever-present cigar. On the "rad-dio," his gravelly voiced New York accent was unmistakable. But he was also widely recognized for his firm grip on human and public affairs and for his integrity and independence.

From his suite at the Hotel Biltmore in 1925, Governor Al Smith gazed upon a booming city. He was proud of the achievements of his three terms as the state's chief executive, and he expected little opposition to a fourth term in 1926. So his ambitions now went beyond New York; his goal now became fixed on Washington, D.C. – and the presidency.

Smith assumed that the 1928 election would probably be his only shot at the White House, and he was not going to let anything or anyone stand in his way. In his judgment, the time had come for the cities to promote one of their own to lead the national government, and who better epitomized the rise of urban leadership than the Manhattan-born governor of New York?

The importance of the cities were confirmed by the 1920 census figures, which showed that for the first time ever a majority of Americans lived in cities. Between 1910 and 1920 New York's population had jumped 23 percent, Chicago 25 percent, Detroit 57 percent, and Los Angeles 115 percent. In the first twenty-five years of the century, 70 percent of the nation's population growth had occurred in urban areas. The outlook of many Americans was shifting, and it was headed right in Al Smith's direction. Most of Democratic politicians were no longer interested in either the tariff or in William Jennings Bryan's silver crusade; they were now concerned with public welfare, sanita-tion, school bonds, and zoning laws – every one an urban issue.

Alfred E. Smith had built his career by appealing to New York's diverse political constituencies. Although he was a loyal son of Tammany Hall, the sponsor of his many races for office, he was also respected by the "Goo-Goos," the good-government patricians who were impressed with his stream-lining of state government and his support of social-minded reform legisla-tion.

It was Master Builder Robert Moses, Belle Moskowitz, and Frances Perkins who worked with Smith and "astounded their friends even before his nomination for governor by arguing not only that Smith was not a typical Tammany politician but . . . was in fact the best hope that existed for the actu-al enactments into law of the social welfare measures for which they have fought so long with so little real success."[5]

Indeed, Smith earned the affection of the good-government types and the machine pols because he got things done. Unlike most progressives, he was not embarrassed to deal with politicians and to bargain for programs that enhanced the quality of life of the ethnic residents in his beloved neighbor-hoods. His record was remarkable: hospitals were built that helped crippled children, the deaf and the blind, tuberculosis patients, and disabled veterans. He built a state health laboratory, asylums for the mentally ill, and the state teachers' college. He constructed a network of parks and beaches from Long Island to Niagara Falls, and he oversaw construction of 5,000 miles of roads. Social legislation was enacted that: eliminated sweat shops, regulated child and female labor, established the forty-eight-hour work week, created workmen's compensation, developed housing projects, regulated milk prices, and consolidated school districts.

To himself and his New York supporters, Smith was ready for 1600 Pennsylvania Avenue. The question was whether or not the national party was ready for him. His heartbreaking experience at the 1924 Democratic National Convention convinced Smith that before the 1928 prize could be his, there was much hard political work to be done.

Jim Farley once stated that "a political convention blows in and out like a ninety mile gale." In June of 1924 an ill wind blew the prejudices of the fragmented Democratic Party into the City of New York. The Democratic National Convention, held at the Madison Square Garden, was attended by scores of Klansmen and Prohibitionists as well as more sensible, rank-and-file delegates.

The convention's highlight came when polio-stricken Franklin D. Roosevelt, struggling on his crutches, rose to the podium before a stunned and silenced audience that marveled at his courage. The Hudson Valley patrician, fully aware of the rigidity and bigotry of many of the delegates, boldly placed in nomination the name of a graduate of the Lower East Side's Fulton Fish Market. He spoke with caution and admiration:

> You, equally who come from the great cities of the East and the plains and hills of the West, from the slopes of the Pacific and the homes and fields of the Southland, I ask you in all sincerely, in the balloting on the platform tomorrow, to keep first in your hearts and minds the words of Abraham Lincoln – "with malice towards none, with charity to all."

Roosevelt closed with these stunning words:

> He has a power to strike error and wrongdoing that makes his adversaries quail before him.. . . He has a personality that carries to everyone here not only the sincerity but the righteousness of what he says. He is the "Happy Warrior" of the political battlefield . . . Alfred E. Smith.

One onlooker recalled that a band struck up "The Sidewalks of New York," and "the crowd just went crazy. Oh, it was stupendous, really stupendous! "But there were those who marched to the words of another tune:

> United we stick
> Divided we're stuck
> The better we stick
> The better we Klux!

The Grand Goblins and Exalted Cyclopses cared little for the words of Lincoln. They proclaimed "America for Americans" and believed that African-Americans, Catholics, and Jews were so many knives pointed at the heart of America.

* * * * *

More than three decades after the end of Reconstruction, the Klan, which had flourished during the years just after the Civil War, underwent a revival. In 1915 it was revamped in the image of the old Know-Nothings, and by the early twenties could boast a nationwide membership of 4 million. Its newspaper, *The Fiery Cross*, had a circulation of 400,000 – larger than a few major urban dailies – and it viciously attacked blacks, Jews, and Catholics.

This was the recommended policy toward the Jews:

> The Jew patronizes only the Jew unless it is impossible to do so. Therefore, we Klansmen, the only real Americans, must, by the same methods, protect ourselves, and practice by actual application the teachings of klannishness. With this policy faithfully adhered to, it will not be long before the Jew will be forced out of business by our practice of his own business methods, for when the time comes when klansmen trade only with klansmen then the days of the Jew's success in business will be numbered and the Invisible Empire can drive them from the shore of our own America.[6]

The activities of the Klan were not confined to the back woods of the Deep South. Chapters appeared in many northern and midwestern cities. In New York's second largest city, Buffalo, the Klan's activities in 1922 had caused significant religious and racial tensions. An imperial official, who visited the city in 1922, threatened to help elect their kind of mayor and told the media:

> Klansmen don't doubt the loyalty, integrity and bravery of Catholics, Jews, negroes [*sic*] and foreign born persons. We realize that

these classes proved themselves good and brave Americans during the recent war and we are not against them. Catholics bar themselves [from the Klan] by their allegiance to the Pope; the Jews because they do not believe in the birth of Christ and negroes [*sic*] because of their color. We want only Caucasians, who, so far as their allegiance is concerned, have it all confined within the boundaries of the United States. That does not mean that we are opposed to them. We are organized to maintain American principles and are opposed only to lawlessness and lack of Americanism.[7]

Reacting to the Buffalo hostilities, Governor Smith and Senate Majority Leader James J. Walker did not endear themselves to the Klan when they engineered passage of a bill "which called for the yearly filing by unincorporated associations, a list of members, by-laws and oaths."[8] Although menaced by angry Klan members, New York's highest tribunal, the Court of Appeals, upheld the constitutionality of the law.

While their terrorist methods – lynchings, bombings, and arson – eventually discredited the Klan and led by 1929 to its rapid decline, in 1924 it was at the height of its power and forced itself upon the Democratic convention.

Al Smith knew bigotry; he had felt the back of the hand of the New York Republicans who were repulsed by the waves of Irish, Italian, and Eastern Europeans who invaded New York. He was familiar with the words of the Rev. Frank Harling of the Second Avenue Presbyterian Church: "The vast hordes flocking to this land strike at our national life, which we count most precious, while the ballot gives them power which they know too well how to use." In New York, Smith fought the likes of Henry Stimson, Charles Evan Hughes, and others who embraced the notions of Social Darwinism to rationalize their Anglocentrism. This bigotry wrapped under the scientific jargon of the eugenic social engineers, however, was mild compared to the Democratic delegates that hit New York in 1924.

To this crowd Al Smith was the captive of Tammany Hall, and Tammany was a brothel whose allegiance was pledged to the "Whore of Babylon" – the Pope of Rome. One delegate who prided himself on his Klan membership stated: "We want the country ruled by the sort of people who settled it. This is our Country!" The leading presidential candidate, William G. McAdoo, slandered New Yorkers with his declaration that their city was "reactionary, mercenary, sinister and sordid."

It was this atmosphere that caused the 1924 Democratic Convention to drag on for 103 ballots and to reject Klan condemnation by a vote of 543 to 542. To break the deadlock the convention turned to corporate lawyer John W.

Davis – who was "not a Catholic or a machine politician nor a believing Protestant or an enthusiastic prohibitionist."[9] He wasn't much of anything, and the results proved it – he got 28.8 percent of the vote.

Total Size of Klan membership in Large American Cities[10]
1915–1944

Akron	18,000	Minneapolis-St. Paul	18,000
Albany-Schenectady-Troy	11,000	New Haven	2,000
Allentown-Bethlehem	2,000	New York-Yonkers New Rochelle	16,000
Atlanta	20,000	Newark-Elizabeth, NJ	5,000
Baltimore	5,000	Philadelphia-Camden	35,000
Boston-Somerville-Cambridge	3,500	Pittsburgh-Carnegie	17,000
Bridgeport	1,500	Providence, R.I.-Mass	3,000
Buffalo	7,000	Reading, Penn	1,500
Chicago	50,000	Rochester	1,500
Cincinnati-Covington	15,500	St. Louis-E. St. Louis	5,000
Cleveland	2,500	Scranton	2,500
Columbus	16,000	Springfield, Ill.	2,500
Dayton	15,000	Springfield-Holyoke, Mass.	2,000
Detroit	35,000	Springfield, Ohio	3,000
Fort Wayne	3,000	Syracuse	1,500
Grand Rapids	2,000	Toledo	1,500
Hartford	2,000	Trenton	2,000
Indianapolis	38,000	Utica-Rome, N.Y.	1,500
Jersey City-Bayonne	4,000	Wilmington, Del.-N.J	3,500
Milwaukee	6,000	Worcester	2,500

Yes, the Democratic candidate for president in 1924 received the lowest vote in the party's history. Even when the Democrats were split three ways in 1860, the official candidate Stephen A. Douglas managed to fare better, receiving 29.46 percent of the vote.

In 1924, millions of inner-city Catholics and Jews, insulted by Klan activities at their convention, deserted their party. While some went for Republican Calvin Coolidge, most cast their vote for Progressive candidate Robert M. LaFollette.

1924 Presidential Election Returns

Calvin Coolidge Rep.	John W. Davis Dem.	Robert LaFollette Prog.
15,717,553	8,386,169	4,814,050
54.06%	28.84%	16.56%

An analyst at *The New York Times* observed: "The prevailing opinion of political experts was that the great body of Democratic voters in the cities, mostly workers, had deserted their party's presidential candidate to vote for the Wisconsin Senator [LaFollette]."[11] Inner-city Catholics, once again, deserted the top of the Democratic ticket, but for the most part, returned to their party to support the remaining candidates.

1924 Chicago Democratic Vote
Select Catholic Ethnics

	Czechs	Poles	Italians	Germans
President	40%	35%	31%	14%
Senator	59	49	39	37
Governor	51	42	35	30

Catholic ticket splitting was high in New York City because Al Smith's name appeared on the ballot.

1924 New York City Democratic Vote

Davis for President	399,000	34%
Smith for Governor	936,000	70
Congressional Total	704,000	48

Smith proved his electability in a state where registered Republicans outnumbered Democrats 1,773,051 to 1,284,407 by winning easily and running statewide 700,000 votes ahead of Davis.

Total 1924 Vote Cast in New York State for Democrats

Davis for President	950,796
Smith for Governor	1,627,111
N.Y.S. Assembly Total	1,328,779

Smith's vote in fifty-seven counties (out of sixty-three) exceeded Democratic enrollments.

The election of 1924 left the Democratic Party in shambles. Many urban

Democrats were angry that the aging Bryan wing of the Democratic Party had embarrassed them again. And for them, their urban hero, Al Smith, was the man to lead their party out of the desert and on to victory.

* * * * *

By late 1927, most Democratic pros conceded that the 1928 presidential nomination was Smith's for the taking. His easy 1926 re-election to a fourth term as governor, plus the fact that the national party was financially broke, held minority status in the U.S. Senate, the House of Representatives and governorships, made Smith appear invincible.

1926 New York Gubernatorial Race Results

Alfred E. Smith (D)	1,523,813
Ogden L. Mills (R)	1,276,137
Democratic Enrollment	1,344,574
Republican Enrollment	1,483,780

Smith's votes exceeded Democratic enrollment in fifty-three counties.

But just because Smith's 1928 nomination seemed to be in the bag, it did not mean everyone – including many Democrats – was pleased. Supporters of Governor Smith were accused of forming an "alien Catholic conspiracy to overthrow Protestant, Anglo-Saxon majority under which the country has achieved its independence and its greatness."[12]

The gauntlet was first thrown publicly by New York corporate lawyer and Episcopalian Charles C. Marshall in an April 1927 *Atlantic Monthly* article "An Open Letter to the Honorable Alfred E. Smith."

In the essay, Marshall quoted reams of ancient papal encyclicals and bulls which included pronouncements on the Church's temporal and spiritual authority over its members. Marshall asked Smith to explain to Americans how these doctrines would affect his public-policy decisions. He also asked how a Smith presidency would handle Catholic parochial schools, non-church marriages, and foreign-policy conflicts with Catholic nations. Marshall concluded his article with this query:

> Citizens who waver in your support would ask whether, as a Roman Catholic, you accept as authoritative the teaching of the Roman Catholic Church that in case of contradiction, making it impossible for the jurisdiction of that Church and the jurisdiction of the State to agree, the jurisdiction of the Church shall prevail; whether, as statesman, you accept the teaching of the Supreme Court of the United States that, in matters of religious practices

which in the opinion of the States are inconsistent with its peace
and safety, the jurisdiction of the State shall prevail; and, if you
accept both teachings, how you will reconcile them.[13]

Smith's first reaction was to ignore the article. He told his staff, "I've
been a devout Catholic all my life and I never heard of these bulls and encyclicals and books."[14] But Smith's senior adviser, Belle Moskowitz, successfully
argued that the Marshall article could not go unchallenged. And to help him
draft a reply, Smith turned to Judge Joseph Proskauer and World War I hero,
Father Francis P. Duffy.

In the May 1927 issue of the *Atlantic Monthly*, Smith took on his critic in
an essay titled "Catholic and Patriot: Governor Smith Replies." Smith refuted
Marshall's charge that there existed "a conflict between his religious loyalty to
the Catholic faith and his Patriotic loyalty":

> What is this conflict about which you talk? It may exist in some
> lands which do not guarantee religious freedom. But in the wildest
> dreams of your imagination you cannot conjure up a possible con-
> flict between religious principle and political duty in the United
> States, except on the unthinkable hypothesis that some law were to
> be passed which violated the common morality of all God-fearing
> men. And if you can conjure up such a conflict, how would a
> Protestant resolve it? Obviously by the dictates of his conscience.
> That is exactly what a Catholic would do. There is no ecclesiasti-
> cal tribunal which would have the slightest claim upon the obedi-
> ence of Catholic communicants in the resolution of such a con-
> flict.[15]

As to choosing between a conflicting political and religious duty, Smith
said: "I have taken an oath of office nineteen times. Each time I swore to
defend and maintain the Constitution of the United States. . . . I have never
known any conflict between my official duties and my religious beliefs."[16]

And Smith summed up his credo as an American Catholic politician with
these sentiments:

> My personal attitude, wholly consistent with that of my church, is
> that I believe in peace on earth, good will to men, and that no
> country has the right to interfere in the internal affairs of any other
> country. I recognize the right of no church to ask armed interven-
> tion . . . merely for the defense of the rights of a church. . . . I
> believe in the worship of God according to the faith and practice
> of the Roman Catholic Church. I recognize no power in . . . my
> Church to interfere with the operations of the Constitution of the

United States for the enforcement of the law of the land. I believe
in absolute freedom of conscience and equality of all churches, all
sects, all beliefs before the law. . . . I believe in the absolute separation of Church and State. . . . I believe that no tribunal of any
church has any power to make any decree of any force in the law
of the land, other than to establish the status of its own communi-
cants within its own church. I believe in the support of the public
school as one of the cornerstones of American liberty . . . in the
right of every parent to choose whether his child shall be educated in the public school or in a religious school supported by those
of his own faith. . . . And I believe in the common brotherhood of
man under the common fatherhood of God.

In this spirit I join with fellow Americans in a fervent prayer
that never again will any public servant be challenged because of
his faith . . .[17]

While the essay was well received in many political circles, Smith was
premature in concluding the reply would "end all whisperings and innuendo."

At the 1928 Democratic convention in Houston, Franklin Roosevelt nominated the Happy Warrior for the second time. Smith received over two-thirds
of the delegate vote on the first ballot and selected "dry" U.S. Senator Joseph
Robinson of Arkansas as his running mate.

The Convention, however, was not completely harmonious: While the
Democratic platform contained a "dry" plank, Smith made it clear he was
"wet" and would support modifications of the Volstead Act.

The campaign of 1928 which matched Smith against Herbert Hoover was
one of the most vicious in American history. Because he was Catholic with
tenement origins, Smith had to endure virulent attacks across America from
people of every walk of life.

In the South and West, Smith was portrayed as the first citizen of
America's leading brothel – the City of New York. "New York was to millions
of Americans the home of sin. It was where Catholicism, Tammany and liquor
coalesced in the person of Al Smith. Smith was an acknowledged drinker,
ring-kisser (he had kissed the ring of Cardinal Bonrano, the papal legate . . .
in New York during Smith's governorship) and a proud and loyal son of
Tammany."[18]

In September when Smith made his first rail tour into America's farm
heartland – Nebraska and Kansas – he witnessed publicly for the first time
bigoted reactions to his candidacy. Flaming crosses along the rail tracks greeted the governor. Klan- and Protestant-sponsored flyers were distributed at
whistle-stops describing Smith and his family as bootleggers and harlots.

The editor of the Emporia, Kansas, *Gazette*, the renowned William Allen

White revealed his anti-Catholicism when he described Smith as the leader of the saloon and gambling interests. Mabel Walker Willebrant, a Coolidge Justice Department assistant attorney general, told the delegates at an Ohio Methodist Convention to urge their 600,000 state members to war against the Catholic Al Smith.

Nauseated by the fiery crosses, the vicious pamphlets, and the specter of western and southern Democrats deserting his candidacy, Smith decided, against the advice of staff, to take the whispering campaign head on in a September 28 speech in Oklahoma City before an auditorium crowd of 30,000.

Smith boldly lectured the group on intolerance:

> I have been told that politically it might be expedient for me to remain silent upon this subject, but as far as I am concerned no political expediency will keep me from speaking out. . . . I attack those who seek to undermine [our institutions] not only because I am a good Christian, but because I am a good American and a product of American institutions. Everything I am, and everything I hope to be, I owe to those institutions.
>
> The world knows no greater mockery than the use of the blazing cross, the cross upon which Christ died – as a symbol to instill in the hearts of men a hatred for their brethren, while Christ preached and died for the love and brotherhood of man.[19]

While Smith showed great courage in exposing the bigotry issue, the speech fell on deaf ears. The next day in the same auditorium, 30,000 cheered the popular evangelist Dr. John Straton, who preached on "Al Smith and the forces of Hell."

During this period, dissident Georgia Democrats formed an anti-Smith Democratic Party whose platform contained this plank: "We stand for complete separation of Church and State as a cornerstone of American liberty and denounce the efforts of Governor Smith to amend the Constitution of his state so as to allow the appropriation of public money to denominational institutions, a thing dangerous to religious liberty."[20]

Bigoted reactions were not limited to the South and West; mainline northern and midwestern Christian organizations and newspapers also denounced Smith. The August 1928 issue of New York's *Methodist Christian Advocate*, tried on the one hand to deny much opposition to Smith, yet on the other hand conceded any opposition was justified:

> The fact that Smith is a Catholic is rarely mentioned – and then not in whispers but in a frankly expressed doubt as to the wisdom of entrusting the chief magistry, with all its delicate international

relations, to a man whose religion, which should be a matter concerning only himself and his God, unfortunately cannot be wholly isolated from the arrogant political theory of the Roman Church.[21]

The *American Lutheran*, a New York monthly, titled their September editorial, "The Reformation Festival This Year," which condemned the temporal power of the Catholic Church and concluded:

> The mere mention of a Roman Catholic as President of the United States has aroused Lutherans all over the country. Today Rome has reached one of its long-sought goals. It well behooves us to emphasize before our people those cardinal principles which came forth as fruit of the Reformation, on which our government is founded and which have made Lutheranism possible. . . . Rome has not changed and it is her boast that she never changes. To our mind a sound presentation of the subject Lutheranism and Americanism, at this year's Reformation festival will be very timely. "Eternal vigilance is the price of liberty."[22]

The lead editorial in Cincinnati's *Christian Leader* which declared that no Catholic "man of sin" was fit to head the government, concluded by reminding the readers that:

> A Roman Catholic assassinated President Lincoln.
> A Roman Catholic assassinated President Garfield.
> A Roman Catholic assassinated President McKinley.[23]

The *American Standard* headlined one story: "Rome Suggests That Pope May Move Here."

Protestant religious leaders denounced Smith's candidacy from pulpits across the nation. A survey of 8,500 Southern Methodist preachers revealed that only 4 supported Al Smith.[24] The moderator of the Presbyterian Church declared: "The plain duty of every churchman is to work and pray for the election of Herbert Hoover."[25]

In addition to these mainline attacks, millions of warped, vicious anti-Smith/anti-Catholic pamphlets, flyers, and newspapers were written, printed, and distributed by the Klan and other crack-pot anti-Catholic organizations across America. Over one hundred anti-Catholic newspapers were pumping out 5 million copies each week.

Smearing the character of Smith and his family was also a popular tactic. In pamphlets and sermons, Smith was often described as a drunkard. Rumors were spread he was loaded when he delivered the speech accepting the Democratic nomination. During campaign stops, word spread that he was bombed before he got up to speak.[26]

In *What Price Tolerance?* – a 350-page book published in 1928 by the All American Book Lecture and Research Bureau of Hewlett, Long Island, New York – author Paul Winter included a photograph of New York's Cardinal Hayes and Governor Smith together at some solemn event with this caption:

> Picture published in a Roman Catholic newspaper, showing Cardinal Hayes and Governor Alfred E. Smith, with a priest supporting the Governor from behind.

The inference was that Smith was drunk and had to be held up. In fact, the priest was innocently walking behind Smith on crowded church steps.

John Roach Straton of New York City's Calvary Baptist Church declared that Smith represented "card playing, cocktail drinking, poodle dogs, divorces, novels, stuffy rooms, dancing, evolution, Clarence Darrow, overeating, nude art, prize fighting, actors, greyhound racing, and modernism."[27]

The popular fundamentalist preacher, the self-proclaimed "Ambassador of God" Billy Sunday, referred in his sermons to Smith's male supporters as "the damnable whiskey politicians, the bootleggers, crooks, pimps and businessmen who deal with them" and his female supporters as "street walkers."[28]

Governor Smith was most distraught when the bigots, descending to new lows, went after his wife, Kate. *The Christian Century* reported that "the Katie issue had become the most wide-spread whispering campaign of all." Mrs. Smith was accused of having inadequate social training. A frequently asked question was "Can you imagine Mrs. Smith in the White House?"[29]

While Herbert Hoover stayed on the sidelines and tried to seem above religious controversy, there were nonetheless many accusations of Republican dollars financing anti-Democratic activities.

A U.S. Senate investigation after the campaign confirmed Republican foul play, as for instance in this description of activities in Oklahoma:

> The Republican Headquarters was the parlor affair, the real place of activity was across the street in the so-called Hoover-Democrat Headquarters, and every item of expense paid by the Republican Headquarters, numerous paid speakers, big and little, constantly speaking all over the state with the most horrid stories of what the Pope would do to the people of this country. The Republican State Headquarters financed, managed and directed this activity.[30]

The "Great Commoner of the Urban Masses" fought valiantly to the end, but he could not turn back the tide of religious prejudice. And on Tuesday, November 6, 1928, Smith lost to Hoover 40.77 percent of the vote versus 58.20 percent. Hoover carried the Electoral College 444 to 87.

While Smith was hurt, angry, and depressed by his rejection at the polls, a careful analysis of the results proved that all was not bleak in his unsuccessful quest for the presidency. Al Smith's 15,000,185 votes significantly exceeded those received by every previous Democratic presidential nominee. In fact, he doubled the average of the votes received by late nineteenth and early twentieth century Democratic candidates.

Votes Received by Democratic Presidential Candidates
1884–1928

1884	Grover Cleveland	4,874,621
1888	Grover Cleveland	5,534,488
1892	Grover Cleveland	5,551,883
1896	William J. Bryan	6,511,495
1900	William J. Bryan	6,358,345
1904	Alton Parker	5,082,898
1908	William J. Bryan	6,406,801
1912	Woodrow Wilson	6,293,152
1916	Woodrow Wilson	8,546,789
1920	James Cox	9,140,884
1924	John Davis	8,386,169
1928	Alfred E. Smith	15,000,185

The turnout of eligible voters in 1928 was 67.5 percent, or 10.9 percent more than 1924. This surge was due to the great awakening of Catholic voters who cast 80 percent of their votes for Smith. For the first time in the post-Civil War era, inner-city Catholic political leaders and their ward constituents were enthusiastically mobilized to support the top of their ticket, and the results in northern and midwestern cities proves it. Smith carried America's twelve largest cities by a plurality of 38,000. The 1920 and 1924 Democratic presidential candidates lost those cities by 1,636,000 and 1,252,000 votes, respectively.[31] Smith, and therefore the Democratic Party, carried for the first time 122 northern Republican counties.

Smith 1928 Results in 13 Largest U.S. Cities

Baltimore	48%	Milwaukee	53%
Boston	67	Newark	41
Chicago	47	New York	62
Cleveland	46	Philadelphia	40
Detroit	37	Pittsburgh	47
Los Angeles	29	St. Louis	52
	San Francisco	50	

Counties a Democratic presidential candidate carried for the first time included Albany, Clinton, and Franklin in New York; Chittenden in Vermont; and Berkshire and Bristol in Massachusetts.

Smith's candidacy brought out "new" Catholic immigrant voters (Poles, Italians, and Czechs) in record numbers. In Massachusetts, New Jersey, and New York, up to 40 percent more women – mostly Catholics – registered over the 1927 registration totals, and these women voted for Smith.[32] Boston's turnout was 93 percent, double that of the previous election. "Smith," wrote analyst Samuel Lubell, "stirred a new sense of political consciousness among workers of immigrant and Catholic origin."[33]

Rhode Island and Massachusetts, although they had Catholic majorities, had always voted Republican until 1928, but now Smith carried both states.

Smith also made inroads with Illinois, Montana, and Nebraska farm voters. Disgusted with Coolidge policies and continued depressed produce prices, many farmers turned to Al Smith:

	Davis 1924		Smith 1928	
Illinois	576,975	23.4%	1,312,235	42.2%
Montana	33,867	19.4	78,638	40.5
Nebraska	137,299	29.6	197,950	36.2

The most significant fact was that the inner-city voters started a new shift in the balance of political power in the United States. In his extraordinary 1952 work, *The Future of American Politics*, Lubell reviewed the 1928 results and concluded, "the Republican hold on the cities was broken not by [Franklin] Roosevelt, but by Alfred E. Smith. . . . Before there was a Roosevelt Revolution there was an Al Smith Revolution."[34] Republican analyst Kevin Phillips agrees: "Even before the Great Depression, Smith sparked a revolt of the urban ethnic groups which foreshadowed the makeup of the New Deal coalition."[35]

Chicago Ethnic Voting for President[36]

	Wilson 1912	Wilson 1916	Cox 1920	Davis 1924	Smith 1928
Polish	30%	68%	39%	35%	**71%**
German	26	44	18	14	**58**
Italian	39	68	31	31	**63**
Jewish	34	67	15	19	**60**

The Italian Vote in Boston, 1916–28; Support for Political Parties in Sanitary Districts in Boston Having an Italian Population of Approximately 75 Percent[37]

Year	Democratic	Republican	Third Party
1916	67%	33%	–
1920	43	50	7% (Socialist)
1924	45	35	20 (Progressive)
1928	**95**	**5**	–

Democratic Presidential Results[38]
City of Pittsburgh, 1924 and 1928

Ward	Davis 1924	Smith 1928
1	10.0%	77.3%
2	6.5	74.9
3	4.4	46.1
4	10.1	51.4
5	5.5	38.4
6	4.8	57.5
7	12.4	35.3
8	14.1	52.5
9	6.8	63.0
10	8.4	56.2
11	10.8	35.5
12	8.5	56.4
13	9.4	36.8
14	11.7	35.8
15	7.1	54.1
16	7.0	71.8
17	5.6	63.8
18	6.6	46.7
19	9.0	44.8
20	8.3	44.7
21	6.8	47.5
22	8.8	44.0
23	6.1	57.1
24	5.1	60.8
25	6.9	36.0
26	7.3	35.3
27	8.7	47.6
28	10.0	32.6
City	8.4	48.0
State	19.3	33.9

Although many inroads were made by the Smith candidacy, anti-Catholic sentiment outside the major inner cities was a major factor in his defeat. The distinguished liberal Republican Senator George Norris of Nebraska bluntly told the press: "The greatest element involved in the landslide was religion. Regret it and conceal it as we may, Religion had more to do with the defeat of Governor Smith than any other one thing."[39]

"Most of [the voters] were cast against the Democratic candidate," admitted *The New York Times,* "because he was a Catholic."[40] In a questionnaire Franklin Roosevelt had sent to Democratic leaders throughout America, 55.5 percent attributed Smith's defeat to Religion, and 33 percent to Smith's "wet" position.[41] All this was confirmed in Allan J. Lichtman's monumental study, *Prejudice and the Old Politics: The Presidential Election of 1928*. Lichtman's exhaustive analysis concludes "that Al Smith's Catholicism was the salient issue, overriding all other concerns."

> Yet when all analysis was done, it remained a bleak fact that a man qualified by integrity, talent, and achievement had been denied the Presidency in a campaign marred by religious hatred, racial bigotry, and snobbery toward a self-made man. Several states in the traditionally most loyal section of his party had rejected him. Thousands, and perhaps millions of voters, who admired his public record still voted for the other candidate. It was not that he had become just another defeated candidate. It seemed rather that the country had rejected Smith as a person, his family and his social origins, his vision of America. His thirty long years of self-education, of personal growth, of honest achievement seemed to have no meaning and no value after all. It is not surprising that in the years that followed Smith did not move on to new ideas and further growth but turned back inward upon himself. The promise of Brooklyn Bridge had not been fulfilled.[42]

In spite of the defeat, it was Smith's Catholicism that was the key to ballot-box uprising in America's major cities. "What Smith really embodied," wrote Samuel Lubell, "was the revolt of the underdog urban immigrant against the top dog of 'Old American' stock. While the Democratic Party of William Jennings Bryan represented the struggling poor in the Bible Belt, the Smith's Democratic Party now represented the 'underpaid melting pot.'"[43]

Smith's campaign actually helped reconstruct a much larger and more vibrant party. And this was not missed by the upcoming generation of ambitious Democrats. William F. Haywood, a member of the Democratic National Committee, wrote in December 1928 to his friend governor-elect Franklin

Roosevelt of New York, "The Democratic Party is stronger than it has been since the Civil War." Roosevelt, already contemplating a presidential run that would unify a coalition of southern and urban Democrats, agreed.[44]

Chapter 11

The Catholic Voter in the Age of Roosevelt

Franklin Delano Roosevelt's early life did not suggest he would earn distinction as one of America's greatest presidents. He was a child of privilege who received "gentleman C's" at Harvard but dropped out of Columbia Law School. He did pass the New York bar exam but was never much of a lawyer or entrepreneur, and he was suckered into various get-rich-quick schemes. When they failed, he always turned to his domineering and wealthy mother, Sarah Delano Roosevelt, to bail him out.

But Roosevelt discovered he had a knack for politics, and in the election of 1910, running as a Democrat, he won the New York State Senate seat representing heavily Republican Dutchess County. Immediately upon being sworn in, Roosevelt joined a rebellious cabal that took on Tammany boss Charles Murphy. FDR declared publicly that "C.F. Murphy and his kind must like a noxious weed be plucked out."[1]

In 1911 FDR and his reform-minded friends in the legislature objected to the U.S. Senate nomination of one of Murphy's corporate lawyer friends, "Blue-eyed Billy" Sheehan. (Members of the U.S. Senate were chosen by state legislatures until 1914.) Roosevelt convinced eighteen insurgent Democratic legislators to skip their party's caucus in order to cripple the advancement of Sheehan's nomination. Murphy held out for ten weeks, but finally broke the deadlock and switched his support to a more acceptable Tammany member, Irish-Catholic Supreme Court Judge James O'Gorman.

Murphy was actually happier to have O'Gorman in the Senate than his first choice, but he vowed not to forget FDR's challenge to his authority. He would always remember FDR's public threat: "From the ruins of the political machines we will reconstruct something more nearly conforming to a democratic conception of government."[2]

And after the Sheehan battle, FDR found himself frozen out of the legislative process by Tammany legislators who "regarded Roosevelt as anti-Irish, anti-Catholic and ridiculed him as a top-lofty snob."[3] FDR also felt the rather heavy hand of the Catholic Church when Bishop Patrick Ludden of Syracuse denounced him as being motivated by "bigotry and the old spirit of Know Nothingism."[4] Up and coming legislative stars Al Smith, Robert Wagner, Sr., and James J. Walker refused to recognize Roosevelt's existence.

The state senate clerk expressed the general attitude when he described FDR as one of "the snobs in our party. . . . political accidents . . . fops and cads who come as near being political leaders as a green pea does a circus tent."[5] FDR's demeanor also hurt his status in Albany. His Harvard accent and his habit of standing tall and looking down at people through his pince-nez caused many Albany pols to refer to him as the "English Duke."

As a Democrat hoping to attain high public office in New York, Roosevelt knew he had to ingratiate himself with Catholic political and church leaders; hence he vehemently denied anti-Catholic accusations. Nevertheless, historians have recorded lapses that reveal Roosevelt's prejudices not only against Catholics but Jews as well.

Historian Geoffrey Ward reports that FDR's expanding political relationship with Catholics and Jews "startled both his mother and wife."[6] Roosevelt biographer Conrad Black observed: "His family had generally looked with suspicion on the Roman Catholic Church as a vast, secretive, autocratic, alien and somewhat primitive institution and many of its adherents as loyalty risks. [FDR's father] preferred to avoid hiring Irish Catholic domestics."[7]

In a 1942 White House conversation with Catholic economist Leo T. Crowley, FDR said: "Leo, you know this is a Protestant country, and the Catholics and Jews are here under sufferance. It is up to you [Crowley and Henry Morgenthau] to go along with anything that I want."[8]

On another occasion Roosevelt gave Morgenthau, his Jewish secretary of the treasury, this lecture concerning quota appointments of Catholics and Jews:

> Let me give you an example. Some years ago a third of the entering class at Harvard were Jews and the question came up as to how it should be handled. . . . I talked it over at the time with your father [Ambassador Henry Morgenthau, Sr.]. I asked him whether we should discuss it with the Board of Overseers and it was decided that we should. . . . It was decided that over a period of years the number of Jews should be reduced one or two per cent a year until it was down to 15%. . . .
>
> I treat the Catholic situation just the same. . . . I appointed three men in Nebraska – all Catholics – and they wanted me to appoint another Catholic, and I said that I wouldn't do it. . . . You can't get a disproportionate amount of any one religion.[9]

Eleanor Roosevelt revealed similar prejudices. After FDR brought home for lunch a young lawyer named Felix Frankfurter, Eleanor described him to her mother-in-law "as an interesting little man but very Jew."[10] Another time, after a function hosted by financier Bernard Baruch, Eleanor complained that: "The Jew party [was] appalling. I never wish to hear money, jewels, or labels mentioned again."[11] Eleanor's cousin, nationally syndicated columnist Joseph

Alsop, explained her distaste for Catholics, particularly prelates: "Eleanor still believed the anti-Catholic nonsense she heard during her childhood."[12]

The Sheehan battle may have given the freshman senator the opportunity to boast to his rural constituents that he had beaten the city bosses, but privately he admitted that if he was to advance his political career he had to at least have a truce with Tammany Hall. This need became most evident to FDR when he watched an angry Boss Murphy flex his political muscle and engineer the impeachment and removal of a sitting Democratic governor, William Sulzer, in 1913. Sulzer was punished for betraying Tammany Hall.

Because he led the 1912 New York presidential campaign for Woodrow Wilson, FDR was rewarded with an appointment to assistant secretary of the navy, the same position cousin Theodore Roosevelt had held in the first McKinley Administration. Murphy was happy to be rid of Roosevelt's presence in New York, but he was gone for barely a year when the ambitious FDR resurfaced on the New York scene in 1914, and the boss had his opportunity to settle the score.

Roosevelt surprised New York's political establishment when he announced in August that he would seek the Democratic U.S. Senate nomination to fill the seat of retiring Republican Elihu Root. Believing President Wilson was behind his candidacy, Roosevelt thought he had an excellent chance to win the state's first-ever direct-vote primary.

But the Roosevelt juggernaut was derailed. Boss Murphy chose as his candidate another Wilson appointee, James W. Gerard, who was ambassador to Germany. Gerard was a wealthy liberal with friendly ties to Tammany.

FDR's confidence was shattered by the choice: Murphy not only outmaneuvered him but boxed him in a corner. Because Gerard was also a member of the Wilson Administration, the president had to remain neutral. What's more, FDR couldn't attack a colleague. And with the war situation heating up in Europe, Ambassador Gerard stayed at his Berlin desk, ostensibly working for peace and remained above the political fray.

Unable to fight his opponent, FDR had no choice but to run against "bossism."

"I have only one possible opponent," Roosevelt constantly reminded voters, "an opponent who works in the dark underground passages of the crookedest political by ways, an opponent who with a few trustworthy lieutenants, has for years used the Democratic voters of this state to further his own selfish ends. I refer to Charles F. Murphy."[13]

On Primary Day, September 28, 1914, the Murphy machine flattened FDR, who lost with 76,888 votes to Gerard's 210,765. The assistant secretary of the navy received an embarrassing 26.5 percent of the vote. Roosevelt biographer Nathan Miller, points out that this devastating defeat taught FDR that in the future, "he could not openly defy Tammany and expect to carry New York State."[14]

For the next fourteen years, FDR devoted his energies to maintaining a reputation as a squeaky clean progressive while, at the same time, forging a peaceful relationship with New York's dominant ethnic group, Irish Catholics.

To achieve this end, he endorsed Al Smith's candidacy for New York's sheriff in 1915. And when Smith ran for governor in 1918, FDR campaigned vigorously for him and tried to ingratiate himself with Smith's key advisors, Robert Moses, Belle Moskowitz, and Frances Perkins.

But even while campaigning for Smith in his home town of Hyde Park, FDR revealed his snobbish side when he urged his neighbors, "farmers like you and I [sic]," to support Smith because he "had *risen* above the Tammany background from which he had sprung."[15]

After Smith was sworn in as governor in January 1919, FDR could not get Smith's political cronies to accept him as an equal, no matter how hard he tried. "It was inevitable that he should feel awkward in Smith's suite at the Biltmore [Hotel],"[16] journalist Robert Caro concluded. Oscar Handlin agreed: "[FDR] could not, without denying his own background, fail to disapprove of the kind of people Al and his friends were."[17] At one point FDR confessed to a staff member that he had a hard time relating to "city people."[18]

Smith's entourage also had a hard time relating to the "gentleman" farmer. To them he was a haughty "feather duster" and they ridiculed "his glittering, sweeping discourses" and wrote him off as a "hopelessly impractical intellectual."[19]

Al Smith summed up the attitude of city pols toward Roosevelt when he said to a friend: "Franklin just isn't the kind of man you can take into the pissroom and talk intimately with."[20]

Yet even with this uneasiness, it did not stop Smith and Roosevelt from using one another. Knowing that Roosevelt could promote his national candidacy in Harvard's Yard, in Manhattan's "Silk Stocking" district, and on Boston's Beacon Hill, Smith twice had FDR take the national stage to nominate him for president. Roosevelt in turn used Smith to introduce him to notable lay Catholics and to members of the Church hierarchy.

In 1928, to add strength to the Democratic ticket in upstate New York, Smith leaned heavily on the reluctant FDR to run to succeed him as governor. And on election night, while Al Smith was being defeated nationally, FDR squeaked passed his Republican opponent, Albert Ottinger, by 26,000 votes out of 4.2 million cast.

Upon being sworn in as New York's forty-fourth governor, however, FDR turned on Smith, fired Smith's closest advisors, treated Smith as a pariah, and began plotting his own road to the White House.

By 1932, President Herbert Hoover's handling of the Depression had convinced most Democrats that the White House was theirs for the taking. And while Roosevelt was viewed as the front runner, there were others interested in the nomination as well, including House Speaker John Nance Garner and the president of the Empire State Building Corporation, Alfred E. Smith.

If only because of all the abuse he had endured in 1928, Al Smith and many Catholic ward leaders in New York, Pennsylvania, Connecticut, Rhode Island, and Massachusetts believed he deserved another shot at the White House. A concerned FDR tried to dissuade Smith; he knew Tammany delegates would side with the ex-governor, and he feared the embarrassment of being a sitting governor incapable of delivering his own state's convention delegates to himself.

In an attempt to sidestep the Smith threat, Gov. Roosevelt made numerous attempts to befriend key members of the Catholic community. He constantly reminded important Catholics that a cousin, James Roosevelt Bayley (who was also the nephew of America's first native-born saint, Elizabeth Ann Seton), was an American Catholic archbishop. Bayley was the founder of Seton Hall University and had been secretary to Archbishop John Hughes. He was the first bishop of the Newark Diocese, and when he died in 1877 was serving as Archbishop of Baltimore.

Governor Roosevelt was also grooming his own stable of Catholic political operatives. James Farley, Bronx boss Edward Flynn, money-man Joseph P. Kennedy (father of the future president), Senator Thomas Walsh of Montana, Missouri's Tom Pendergast, and Mayor James Michael Curley of Boston were all part of the FDR camp.

At times his efforts to reach out to Catholics seemed effective: when the Fordham University president mentioned FDR as presidential timber at the 1929 commencement, the audience of 10,000 gave the governor a standing ovation. Catholic newspapers praised Roosevelt after he signed into law the 1932 Love-Hayes Bill, which forbade New York public-school administrators from asking prospective teachers about their religious beliefs.

But such overtures were insufficient to attract many Catholic political leaders away from the Happy Warrior. In New York Smith's supporters were led by Manhattan's boss John Curry, by Brooklyn's John McCooey, and by Queens's John Theofel, and across the Hudson River Jersey City's mayor, Frank "I am the Law" Hague, promised to deliver his delegates to Smith, as did key leaders in other densely Catholic populated cities and states.

During the 1932 Democratic primary season, Smith decisively beat Roosevelt in Massachusetts, receiving 73 percent of the vote, and by convention time Smith had garnered all of the delegates from Massachusetts, Connecticut, and New Jersey as well as two-thirds of New York's and close to half of Pennsylvania's. Smith entered the convention with about 200 pledged delegate votes, which were enough to stop FDR from getting the two-thirds margin required to win a first-ballot nomination.

As Roosevelt was organizing his presidential campaign, he faced a serious problem that threatened to anger both the Tammany boys and the goo-goo reformers, namely the administration of New York City's Irish-Catholic mayor, Jimmy Walker. Elected mayor in 1925, James J. "Beau" Walker personified the excesses of the Jazz Age. He charmed the citizenry with his wit and style and ran the government from speakeasies and night clubs. This lovable rogue even wrote a musical hit for his city, "Will You Love Me in December as You Do in May?"

During Walker's tenure, the Tammany Hall bosses reigned supreme and political nepotism flourished. Questioned about a particular incompetent he had appointed to the Children's Court, Walker replied, "The children will now be judged by one of their peers."

In the fall of 1931, the state legislature's Joint Legislative Committee, to investigate the affairs of the City of New York, met in Manhattan's county courthouse. The chief counsel, Judge Samuel Seabury, began to question Thomas M. Farley, Sheriff of New York County, leader of the 14th Assembly District and Tammany Hall sachem. Farley was asked to explain how in six years he had saved $400,000, while his annual salary had been only $8,000. The following exchange ensued:

Seabury: Where did you keep these moneys that you had saved?
Farley: In a safe-deposit box at home in the house.
Seabury: Whereabouts at home in the house did you keep this money that you had saved?
Farley: In the safe.
Seabury: In a safe?
Farley: Yes.
Seabury: In a little box in a safe?
Farley: A big safe.
Seabury: But a little box in a big safe?
Farley: In a big box in a big safe.
Seabury: Now, in 1930, where did the extra cash come from, Sheriff?
Farley: Well, that is –, My salary check is in there.
Seabury: No, Sheriff, your salary checks are exclusive of the cash deposits which during the year you deposited in those three banks.
Farley: Well, that came from the good box I had. [Laughter.]
Seabury: Kind of a magic box?
Farley: It was a wonderful box.
Seabury: A wonderful box. [Laughter.] What did you have to do – rub the lock with a little gold, and open it in order to find more money?
Farley: I wish I could.[21]

(This exchange was immortalized in "Little Tin Box," a hit song from the 1959 musical *Fiorello!*)

The Seabury investigation revealed corruption in the Walker administration and reform politicians looked to Governor Roosevelt to prove his good-government credentials by removing Walker and using the full weight of his office to prosecute Tammany. Fearful that any action would further offend inner-city Catholic leaders, Roosevelt tried to avoid the issue, but when former Woodrow Wilson counselor Col. Edward House strongly warned him that he was beginning to look like a captive of city bosses, FDR moved into action and in 1932 removed several Tammany appointees accused of accepting pay-offs.

So as Democrats arrived at the Chicago Democratic Convention, Tammany's hatred of Roosevelt had reached new heights. Because of this and the steadfast support for Smith, the convention deadlocked.

It was two Irish Catholics, Joe Kennedy and Jim Farley, who after the third ballot convinced publishing magnate William Randolph Hearst to persuade his candidate, John Nance "Cactus Jack" Garner of Texas, to release his delegates in favor of Roosevelt. To sweeten the pot, they authorized Hearst to offer Garner the vice-presidential nomination. This deal broke the deadlock, and FDR was nominated on the fourth ballot with the combined support of southern and western delegates. But bitter Catholic delegates from the northeast stuck with Smith to the end and refused to make FDR's nomination unanimous.

Some segments of the Catholic establishment were not pleased with the convention's outcome. They viewed FDR as the nominee of the forces that had deserted Smith in 1928. The Springfield, Massachusetts, newspaper, *The Catholic Mirror*, claimed that bigots had used a "steamroller in 1932" to nominate FDR, and Notre Dame's *Ave Maria* magazine criticized the help FDR received at the convention from anti-Catholic Democratic leader William McAdoo. And a *New York Times* editorial on June 21, 1932, expressed outrage that southern delegates would now support a "wet" northerner: "The same people who rejected a 'wet' Smith have now accepted a 'wet' Roosevelt because the latter is not a Catholic." Some Catholics were threatening to vote for socialist Norman Thomas, and Massachusetts delegates vowed not to vote for FDR, whom they labeled the "Klan" candidate.

Knowing that angry Catholic voters could cost him the election, FDR began to campaign hard among Catholic religious, financial, and political leaders. And Catholic inner-city bosses, fearful that a victorious Roosevelt would cut them off from the patronage trough, began to sing the praises of their party's new leader. FDR's advisors also spent weeks convincing Al Smith to put aside personal animosities and embrace the ticket. Their efforts paid off, and at a Boston rally of 15,000 on October 27, Smith endorsed FDR and refuted anti-Catholic charges. Smith told the crowd, "There can be no bigotry and there can be no resentment in the Catholic heart. It cannot be there."[22]

Smith's New England campaign tour had the desired effect – Catholics began to return to the Democratic fold. To further cement his relations with Catholics, Roosevelt actually quoted the 1931 encyclical *Quadragesimo Anno* (Pius XI's update of Leo XIII's *Rerum Novarum*). In a speech given in Detroit speech, FDR called the encyclical "one of the greatest documents of modern times."[23] Finally, the very popular national radio priest, Rev. Charles E. Coughlin, publicly supported FDR and urged his followers to do the same.

On election day, Roosevelt triumphed; receiving 27.8 million votes to Hoover's 15.7 million. In the nation's thirteen largest cities, FDR topped Smith's 1928 vote.

Smith 1928 Results versus FDR 1932 Results in 13 Largest U.S. Cities

	1928	1932
Baltimore	48%	61%
Boston	67	67
Chicago	47	55
Cleveland	46	50
Detroit	37	57
Los Angeles	29	57
Milwaukee	53	65
Newark	41	45
New York	62	70
Philadelphia	40	42
Pittsburgh	47	52
St. Louis	52	63
San Francisco	50	64

In the Northeast, carrying the Catholic vote was key to Roosevelt's victory. If New York City's votes are excluded from the region's totals, Hoover would carry the area 50 percent to 47 percent. Political analyst Kevin Phillips explained the results this way: "Notwithstanding Roosevelt's gains, the Northeast was by far the most Republican section of the nation at the beginning of the New Deal. Roughly half of the Northeastern electorate voted for Herbert Hoover in 1932, and the GOP carried six of the eleven Northeastern states. Elsewhere in the country, Hoover won only one-third of the vote and no states. Even in the face of the Depression, the rural Yankee counties and urban silk-stocking precincts remained loyal to the party of their Establishment. The Democratic victories in New York and Massachusetts, for example, were the product of urban Catholic voting."[24]

Democratic Northeastern Presidential Voting, 1924–1932

State	Davis 1924	Smith 1928	Roosevelt 1932
Vermont	16%	33%	41%
Maine	22	31	43
New Hampshire	35	41	49
Massachusetts	25	50	51
Rhode Island	37	50	55
Connecticut	28	46	47
New York	29	47	54
Pennsylvania	19	34	45
New Jersey	27	40	50
Delaware	37	34	48
Maryland	41	42	62

Irish-Catholic Vote – New York County[25]
Districts Having Irish Population of 70% or Higher

	Democratic Vote	Republican Vote
1924	63%	25%
1928	82	18
1932	81	19

Italian Vote – New York County[26]
Districts Having Italian Population of 85% or Higher

	Democratic Vote	Republican Vote
1924	48%	44%
1928	77	23
1932	79	21

Italian Vote – Boston[27]
Districts Having Italian Population of 75% or Higher

	Democratic Vote	Republican Vote
1924	45%	35%
1928	95	5
1932	78	2

Chicago Ethnic Catholic Vote[28]
1932 Democratic Percentages

	Czechs	Poles	Italians
President	83%	80%	64%
Senator	81	76	59
Governor	81	75	57

Catholics voting in inner cities also gave the Democrats a large vote for members of the House of Representatives. In America's ten largest cities, Democrats won 75 percent of the House seats.[29]

* * * * *

On Inauguration Day, March 4, 1932, Roosevelt told a desperately frightened nation, that "the only thing we have to fear is fear itself – nameless unreasoning, unjustified terror which paralyzes needed efforts to convert retreat into advance. . . "

America's 14 million unemployed believed him and felt a sense of relief. FDR magnificently lifted America's spirit because he had the confidence and the ability to communicate his vision of the future. And in the first hundred days of his administration, the Congress blindly followed him and enacted legislation they hoped would help America's poor.

During the early days of the New Deal, many social Catholics voiced support for FDR's programs and argued that they were consistent with traditional Catholic social thought and with positions expressed in recent papal encyclicals. New York's Cardinal Hayes spoke for the Church when he said FDR was "crystallizing the sentiments of the Country in meeting the grave problems [of the depression]." At a Manhattan College commencement in June 1934, Hayes told the graduates, "We ought to rejoice that everything [Roosevelt] tries to do . . . will come to a happy success."[30]

America's Catholic press followed the hierarchy's lead. The conservative Brooklyn *Tablet* described the New Deal as "motivated by a Christian philosophy which moves forward in the right direction."[31] Liberal *Commonweal* declared "all Catholics who desire to give practical effect to the principles of social justice laid down by Pope Pius XI will see that Roosevelt's opportunity to lead . . . is likewise the Catholic opportunity to make the teaching of Christ apply to the benefit of all."[32]

Roosevelt knew that Catholics totaled one-sixth of the nation's population and that they represented the largest bloc of voters in many of America's major cities. Hence, to keep these Catholic voters within his political coalition, FDR stayed in close touch with their political and religious leaders.

FDR broke all records in the number of Catholics appointed to important governmental jobs. Catholics Jim Farley and Thomas Walsh were appointed, respectively, postmaster general and attorney general. Numerous other Catholics were appointed to significant posts, including Joseph P. Kennedy as the first chairman of the newly created Securities and Exchange Commission, which in retrospect was a classic case of putting a fox in charge of the hen house. The Brooklyn *Tablet* praised the president in December 1933 "for discarding past policies of refusing to recognize Catholics as suitable for important government positions."[33]

Catholics also supported the ill-fated National Recovery Administration (NRA) enacted in June 1933. The NRA was designed to establish guidelines for industries to "self-regulate," and Cardinal O'Connell of Boston urged every parish in his archdiocese to show their support for the NRA. The bishop of Syracuse, New York, John Duffy, told his flock that Roosevelt "has put into effect the principle announced by Pope Leo XIII forty odd years ago, that government has not only the right but the duty to assist in the formations of economic units."[34]

Catholic social reformer, Monsignor John A. Ryan, long-time director of the National Catholic Welfare Conference, was an important FDR supporter. Known as the "Right Reverend New Dealer," Ryan wrote in the May 1933 edition of *Dublin Studies* that FDR's banking reform, his AAA, NRA, and TVA taken together "constituted a more comprehensive and fundamental program of legislation than all the enactments of Congress during the preceding ten years."[35]

With the passage of these programs, particularly the Work Projects Administration (WPA), Roosevelt had plenty of jobs to hand out to America's inner cities. And the president knew that when it came to dealing with the Catholic political bosses, he was now in the catbird seat.

Franklin Roosevelt was described by one biographer, Conrad Black, as having perfected "mundane political arts – obfuscation, prevarication, flattery, sophisticated evasion and various forms of pandering." FDR, he continued, could exhibit an "amoral political genius" by which he would easily use and just as easily discard people and friends depending on the consequences of a given political decision.[36] Even his wife, Eleanor, recognized these character flaws and confessed in her memoirs that she too was merely "one of those who served his purpose."

When it came to the inner-city Catholic bosses, FDR applied "mundane political arts" with a vengeance. The president needed certain bosses to help in the execution of federal aid programs in their localities, and he would cherry-pick those who would get the credit. Loyalty meant nothing to FDR. He would easily dump those most true to him in favor of others, depending upon the political circumstances of the moment.

FDR "brain-truster" Rexford Tugwell would argue that Roosevelt, who had for decades been nursing a grudge against certain Catholic political machines (particularly in New York), wanted to use federal programs at least in part to put those bosses out of business. He contended that Roosevelt vowed to "show Curry, Ely, Hague, Cermak, Kelly, and Pendergast who was the paramount leader in the party." FDR intended to "steal [the bosses'] following, force *them* into subordination, make them *his* henchmen. He had begun to show how it could be done. A nationwide system of assistance for those who were dependent on the handouts of jobs, favors, food, shelter, or fuel would bring the bosses to heel. They could no longer trade help for votes."[37]

Boston mayor James Michael Curley, the only Massachusetts political leader to endorse FDR in 1932, was the first to experience the fickleness of Roosevelt. Curley, whose Massachusetts political career would span half a century and include one term as governor, four terms as mayor, and four terms in Congress, believed FDR would turn to him for advice on distributing the political swag. Like most big city mayors, he desperately needed people working in order to create a tax-revenue stream to support city services. But he was against direct welfare grants: "Work and Wages" was his slogan.[38] He proclaimed publicly that he opposed the "dole," which he believed would destroy a person's self-respect. "I would rather spend $10 to keep people working," he said, "than give $2 on the dole. People did not want handouts, they wanted work."[39]

But of the 150,000 federal jobs in Massachusetts, Curley was not allotted even one to fill. Instead, Roosevelt turned them over to former Smith supporters (and Curley's political enemies), U.S. Senator David Walsh and Governor Joseph Ely. Fidelity meant little to Roosevelt, and "by breaking off communications between Curley and the White House, and by refusing to supply money or jobs, he allowed the colorful Irishmen to wither on the vine."[40]

Over time, Roosevelt turned on Kansas City boss Thomas Pendergast too. But he could be generous: in Chicago, boss Edward Joseph Kelly, who had on one occasion proclaimed, "Roosevelt is my religion," was allowed to control all WPA jobs – approximately 600,000 between 1936 and 1940.

In New Jersey, FDR buried the hatchet with Jersey City Mayor Frank Hague, one of Al Smith's biggest supporters, and permitted his machine to control dollars from WPA and other programs. One of Hague's own men, William Ely, was appointed by Roosevelt as head of the WPA. As a result, approximately 100,000 WPA jobs annually found their way to New Jersey throughout the thirties.

Federal Relief for the Bosses: The WPA and the Cities, 1936[41]
(Worker listings are in thousands.)

	WPA Workers	City Employees	Registered Voters as % of City Employees	WPA Workers as % of Registered Voters	WPA Workers
New York	246.0	121.4	2,324.4	202.6	10.6
Jersey Cty	5.2	3.7	151.2	140.5	3.4
Albany	3.9	1.9	72.0	205.3	5.4
Chicago	68.4	29.5	1,503.2	231.9	4.6
Pittsburgh	20.8	5.3	246.5	392.5	8.4
Boston	26.0	13.6	305.6	191.2	8.5

While Roosevelt could as easily make peace with former foes and abandon former friends to further his political ambitions and agendas, there was one group he treated with straightforward contempt: New York's Tammany Hall.

After the 1932 Democratic Convention, Jim Farley, on behalf of FDR, negotiated a "truce" with Tammany Hall to ensure a united New York party behind the national ticket, and Tammany pulled out all the stops and delivered big for Roosevelt. Thanks to the help of the machine, Roosevelt's New York City vote total topped Al Smith's 1928 results.

When Roosevelt took office, however, he made it a political priority to pursue a plan that over time would destroy Tammany's power base.

To achieve this end, FDR executed a plan that would end boss control of New York City's executive branch. FDR instructed his allies to engineer a third-party candidate, prominent Democrat Joseph V. McKee, to enter the mayoral contest in 1933. The intent was to split the votes of the Democratic faithful between McKee, running under the banner of the "Recovery Party," and Tammany candidate, incumbent Mayor John O'Brien. The result would be the election of Republican renegade Fiorello LaGuardia. The plan worked, and for the remainder of his presidency, FDR fed billions in money and jobs to his favorite Republican mayor. Until the post-war period, Tammany was a toothless tiger.

Voting Percentages for New York City
1933 Mayoralty Election[42]

	City-Wide	Irish	German	Jewish	Italian
Republican (LaGuardia)	20.8	12.1	18.7	18.9	27.1
City Fusion (LaGuardia)	19.6	9.7	11.3	17.4	34.9
Total LaGuardia	40.4	21.8	30.0	36.3	62.2
Recovery (McKee)	28.3	39.5	45.4	22.7	11.3
Democratic (O'Brien)	27.2	36.9	22.5	31.9	23.7
Socialist (Charles Solomon)	2.9	1.3	1.6	5.6	2.0
Communist (Robert Minor)	1.2	0.4	0.3	3.3	0.7
Minor parties	0.1	0.1	0.2	0.2	0.1

In a 1968 essay titled "*Franklin Roosevelt and the Purge: The Impact of Urban Change in Political Parties*," author Richard Polenberg described the sad decline of Tammany during the New Deal years:

> During the 1930s, as Tammany Hall's political power waned, New York City Democrats bewailed the reversal of fortune suffered by their once-powerful machine. By 1938, Jeremiah T. Mahoney, who

had been the Democratic candidate for mayor a year earlier, reported: "Things in our local Democratic organization are at the lower ebb, and nobody seems to care much whether local organization progresses or dies." In the spring of 1939, Mahoney observed, the situation had not improved: "Tammany Hall is still plodding along at the bottom of the sewer. Nobody is doing anything to revive our old organization."[43]

* * * * *

While President Roosevelt could be ruthless with Catholic political leaders, he never lost sight of their Catholic constituents, and he made every effort to endear himself to them. To this end, he befriended the most powerful members of the American Catholic hierarchy, George Cardinal Mundelein of Chicago, New York's Patrick Cardinal Hayes, and Hayes's successor Archbishop Francis J. Spellman. The president frequently consulted them on foreign-policy matters, particularly on the Soviet Union and Mexico.

The Roman Catholic Church had been steadfast in its condemnation of atheistic communism and Russia's brutal totalitarian leaders, Lenin and Stalin. Prayers were said after every Mass for the "conversion of Russia." And when the White House floated a trial balloon on recognizing the Soviet Union, the bishops used the editorial pages of their diocesan newspapers to express their displeasure. America's leading Catholic newspaper, the Brooklyn *Tablet*, led the charge. When surplus cotton was sold to the Soviet government, the paper vigorously objected. "Dealing with Russia," wrote the *Tablet*, "is a blunder materially, morally and patriotically."[44]

The Knights of Columbus and the National Council of Catholic Men also vigorously opposed recognition. They warned their members that a godless state could never be trusted. In Massachusetts these organizations gathered 600,000 signatures on petitions condemning recognition.

At the request of the American bishops, a prominent Jesuit, Rev. Edmund Walsh, prepared a report for the president on religion in the Soviet Union. Walsh warned that "the Soviet Government undertakes to abolish religion itself, the God-idea in its every form and manifestation."[45] He concluded that if the United States recognized Russia without receiving some concessions on the religious liberty issue, it "would have the practical effect of helping the perpetual conditions that are a matter of public record."[46]

Sensing that Roosevelt's mind was made up on the Soviet issue, the Vatican's Pontifical Commission on Russian Affairs requested that the president at least seek assurance from the Soviet government that it would tolerate religious liberty for the Soviet populace. The ever-confident FDR told American churchmen, "I am a good horse dealer. . . ."[47] and promised to consider their concerns.

Just before the United States recognized the USSR in November 1933, Roosevelt did manage to get a small concession which he hoped would placate Catholics. Soviet Foreign Affairs Commissioner Maxim Litvinov agreed that American citizens who visited Russia would be free to practice their religion publicly. Even though the American hierarchy was not thrilled with the diplomatic crumb they were tossed, they realized this was all they were going to get, so to save face, they praised FDR "for defending the value of religion in society against Communist propaganda."[48]

On another front, having witnessed first-hand Woodrow Wilson's clashes with the Catholic Church over Mexican policies, Roosevelt kept close tabs on events in that volatile nation.

Angered by reports that the Mexican Government was responsible for the murder of scores of priests and nuns, the Knights of Columbus delivered a petition to the White House signed by 500,000 members demanding that the U.S. "make representations to the government of Mexico that unless evils . . . are ended forthwith, further recognition of the Mexican government will be withdrawn and diplomatic relations will be severed." Roosevelt, quickly replying, said that every person should "enjoy the free exercise of his religion according to the dictates of his conscience," but still refused to intervene, citing that the U.S. government had not received from any U.S. citizens, complaints that they were denied religious liberty while in Mexico.[49]

Unimpressed, Catholic newspapers blasted FDR for supporting Mexico's anti-clerical and anti-religious policies. But the hierarchy once again let Roosevelt off the hook. At the 1935 Notre Dame University commencement Cardinal Mundelein joined FDR on the dais and publicly praised him. Grateful for the Cardinal's support, the president went on to tell the graduates that the supreme rights we hold are "freedom of education and freedom of religious worship."[50]

The Cardinal's public comments helped mute Catholic criticism, and the Church settled for encouraging words and little action. For his part, Roosevelt did take at least one significant step: when the Mexican government's anti-clerical policies were at their zenith in 1935, the president canceled a summer visit there.

By early 1936, the White House was convinced that there would be minimal fallout from Catholic voters on foreign policy issues; hence the administration focused on domestic issues, including the rising influence of the Rev. Charles Coughlin.

Asked by his bishop to found a parish in Royal Oak, Michigan, Father Coughlin had built the Shrine of the Little Flower in 1926. After a local Ku Klux Klan chapter burnt a cross in his church yard, Coughlin requested a local radio station to give him broadcast time to help defuse the hostile situation. Recognizing that the priest had a natural talent for the new medium, station managers gave him a regular spot, and as the Depression deepened, Coughlin began to speak out on social and political issues. He condemned Hoover's inaction and the inequities of pure laissez-faire economics, and his audience grew to 40 million; his mail averaged 80,000 letters a week. His primary supporters were midwestern and eastern Irish, German, and Polish Catholics.

While Coughlin unabashedly voiced his support for Roosevelt in 1932, by 1936 he was disenchanted. He frowned upon recognition of the Soviet Union and criticized New Deal programs for being too modest in their aims. His messages became more radical as he blamed the nation's woes on Wall Street, international banking, Communists, and Jews.

Convinced that Roosevelt was an ungrateful political chameleon, Coughlin decided to punish him by forming the Union Party. North Dakota Congressman William Lemke became its candidate for president. In one public address Coughlin boasted: "As I was instrumental in removing Herbert Hoover from the White House, so help me God, I will be instrumental in taking a Communist out of the chair once occupied by Washington."[51] Coughlin told his radio audience that if Lemke did not receive 9 million votes he would go off the air.

Coughlin was not Roosevelt's only election-year Catholic problem. Al Smith was also disenchanted with the Roosevelt magic. An instinctive practitioner of subsidiarity, Smith was disturbed by the growing power of Washington's bureaucracies. Known for his efficient use of resources during his four terms as New York's governor, Smith found many New Deal programs to be wasteful. He told one audience that the reckless New Deal programs were designed by "one of the absent-minded professors [who] played anagrams with the alphabet soup."[52]

When Roosevelt took the nation off the gold standard, Smith feared the resurrection of the old Bryan wing of the Party. He referred to the devalued currency as "baloney dollars" and publicly demanded that the administration adhere to the Democratic Party's platform planks that supported both the gold standard and balanced budgets. Smith also warned FDR to purge his administration "of the counsels of the minority of bigots, fanatics, populists, demagogues, mountebanks and crack pots. . . who dragged religion and liquor into politics; the populists who blighted the party [with] free silver and other economic heretics [who were] without loyalty to person and principle [and] the mountebanks with their clownish antics and irresponsible millionaires and big business."[53]

Coughlin and Smith's dissension caused the *Tablet* to report that they sensed Catholic support for Roosevelt was slipping. The Boston *Pilot* also complained that New Deal radicals were trying to over-regulate the lives of individual Americans.[54]

Fearing that Catholic accusations that he was embracing extreme left-wing, Marxist agendas might stick in the minds of voters and hurt his re-election chances, Roosevelt hit the Communist issue head on in a September 1936 campaign appearance in Syracuse, New York:

> Here and now, once and for all, let us bury that red herring and destroy that false issue. . . . I have not sought, I do not seek, I repudiate the support of any advocate of Communism or of any other alien "ism" which would be fair means or foul change our American democracy. That is my position. It has always been my position. It always will be my position.[55]

As the charges of Coughlin escalated, Roosevelt refused to raise the cleric's profile by making any public comments. This did not stop FDR's friends in the hierarchy from speaking out, however. Cardinal Mundelein took the lead when he stated that Coughlin "is not authorized to speak for the Catholic Church nor does he represent the doctrine or sentiments of the Church."[56]

In October 1936, Papal Secretary of State Eugenio Cardinal Pacelli (later Pope Pius XII) made a social call on the president at his Hyde Park, New York, home during a tour of the United States. It is known that there were discussions about the U.S. sending an envoy to the Vatican, and historian Thomas Maier contends that an agreement was reached whereby Father Coughlin's activities would be reined in.[57]

Toward the end of the campaign, the Catholic press turned against Coughlin's political movement and praised the Roosevelt Administration's accomplishments. *Commonweal* magazine refuted accusations that the White House had Communist tendencies and argued that the New Deal was by its nature conservative because it attempted to restore to the people that "which greed and private and corporate dictatorship . . . have almost shattered."[58]

In New York, Catholic Charities director Father Bryan J. McEntegart (future archbishop of Brooklyn) applauded Social Security and stated that "planning" was permissible "as long as it follows the means suggested by Leo XIII of acting for the Common Good."[59]

Concerned more with bread-and-butter issues, American Catholic voters ignored foreign policy issues and charges of Marxist-Leninist plots and overwhelmingly supported Roosevelt for a second term. Roosevelt received 60.79 percent of the total vote, and it is estimated that he received between 75 percent and 81 percent of Catholic votes. The seven states with the largest number of Catholics as a percent of population came out for Roosevelt in numbers that surpassed the 1932 totals.

Seven Largest Catholic States – Percentage for Roosevelt

	1932	1936
New Mexico	62.8%	62.7%
Arizona	67.0	69.9
Rhode Island	55.1	53.0
Massachusetts	50.6	51.2
Maryland	61.3	62.4
California	58.4	67.0
Connecticut	47.4	55.3

Roosevelt easily carried America's largest cities, and in most cases, improved his numbers because most Catholics stuck with him and some Protestants who supported Hoover in 1932 now voted Democratic. Of the nation's cities that had populations that exceeded one hundred thousand, Roosevelt carried 104, while Republican Alf Landon carried a total of 2 cities.

Results in 13 Largest U.S. Cities

	Smith 1928	FDR 1932	FDR 1936	Lemke 1936
Baltimore	48%	61%	59%	0.006%
Boston	67	67	63	8.5
Chicago	47	55	62	2.7
Cleveland	46	50	65	7.3
Detroit	37	57	64	4.9
Los Angeles	29	57	67	1.3
Milwaukee	53	65	74	6.7
Newark	41	45	54	1.0
New York	62	70	75	–
Philadelphia	40	42	60	0.5
Pittsburgh	47	52	65	3.3
St. Louis	52	63	65	2.0
San Francisco	50	64	74	1.1

Most Catholics embraced Roosevelt because they believed he helped them to make inroads politically, socially, and economically. Roosevelt expert William Leuchtenburg explained Catholic enthusiasm this way: "[T]he newer ethnic groups in the cities swung to Roosevelt mostly out of gratitude for the New Deal welfare measures, but partly out of delight with being granted 'recognition.'"[60]

But some political experts did pick up some warning signs in the 1936 Catholic vote. There was a subset of Catholics who frowned upon FDR's recognition of the Soviet Union, his handling of the anti-Catholic Mexican government, and the radical growth of the U.S. government. These angry Catholics turned to the Union Party and William Lemke, who received 892,000 votes for 1.96 percent of the total. And while the Lemke candidacy fell short of Father Coughlin's goal of 9 million – Coughlin kept his word and went off the air, although only for seven weeks – it is important to note where those votes were cast. Lemke's name appeared on only thirty-four state ballots, and he did best in his home state of North Dakota where he received 13.4 percent of the vote. But in eastern states with large Catholic populations, he did pick up some support:

Lemke Support

Connecticut	3.2%
Illinois	2.3
Massachusetts	6.5
Minnesota	6.6
Michigan	4.2
Ohio	4.4
Rhode Island	6.3
Wisconsin	4.8

A careful review of the figures reveals that Lemke received 10 percent of the vote in thirty-nine counties nationwide. Samuel Lubell points out that twenty-one of these counties had Catholic populations over 50 percent, and in twenty-eight of these counties, Germans were the predominant ethic group. In Wisconsin and Ohio, thirty Catholic wards cast a plurality for Lemke. In Minnesota, Lemke's totals exceeded 15 percent in six heavily German-Catholic counties. Indeed the cities in which Lemke received more than 5 percent of the vote were all German- and Irish-dominated. Lemke did best in Cincinnati where he received 12 percent, in St. Paul with 11 percent, and in Dubuque at 9 percent.

These numbers indicate that there were pockets of Catholic voters who were concerned enough with the leftward drift of the national government and Roosevelt's "Anglo centrism" in foreign affairs to break with the Democratic Party. "As in 1920," observed political analyst Kevin Phillips, "foreign policy unhappiness gave the Republican abnormal strength in traditionally Democratic rural German Catholic counties."[61] And with war clouds gathering in Europe and in Asia, it was to be foreign-policy issues that would begin to dominate the second Roosevelt Administration.

*   *   *   *   *

Throughout the late 1930s, many Catholics of European descent had hoped that America would avoid confrontations and entanglements on the continent. Irish-, German-, Polish-, and Italian-Americans each had different perspectives on European events, but they were united in a call for American neutrality. And the various neutrality acts passed by Congress were enthusiastically endorsed by many Catholics.

Neutrality did not, however, stop America's Catholic hierarchy from speaking out against communism and fascism. Chicago's Cardinal Mundelein, who was of German descent, attacked Hitler's anti-Christian and anti-Jewish activities in May of 1937, calling Hitler "an inept paper hanger."[62] When the German press attacked the cardinal's comments, Al Smith, the American hierarchy, and Pope Pius XI all came to Mundelein's defense. During a trip to Chicago, President Roosevelt displayed his solidarity with Mundelein by dining at the Cardinal's residence – a first for an American president.

Even though they supported neutrality, most Catholics did not object to Roosevelt's call to expand our armed forces. In early 1939, Al Smith, after an inspection tour of Europe, announced his support for FDR's policies and warned American Catholics of the pending danger in Europe.

One area where Roosevelt was particularly sensitive to Catholic opinion was the Spanish Civil War that broke out in July 1936. FDR was aware that most U.S. Catholics sided with Francisco Franco in his fight to oust the atheistic forces of the "Loyalist" Republican government. Roosevelt tried to walk the fine line between Catholic opinion and the prevailing view of his administration – and of Eleanor – which supported the Loyalists. To avoid conflicts, he issued an executive order (that was codified by law in 1937) establishing an embargo on goods to Spain.

As the Civil War dragged on, American Catholics expressed their outrage at Loyalist atrocities that included the murdering of 5,255 priests, 2,492 monks, 12 bishops, and 283 nuns. The Gallup Poll reported that 58 percent of American Catholics supported Franco. Fordham University President Robert Gannon voiced agreement with British lecturer and author, the Catholic Hillaire Belloc, who on a visit to the university told the student body that the Civil War in Spain was a war for the "life or death of Christianity."[63]

Roosevelt refused to yield and when Eleanor Roosevelt and his liberal Secretary of the Interior Harold Ickes leaned heavily on him to help the Loyalists, the president dismissed them. Any change in policy would, he explained, would "mean the loss of every Catholic vote next fall."[64]

Roosevelt's woes increased when Germany invaded Poland in September 1939, and England and France declared war against the Nazis. American Catholics, like most of their fellow citizens, were leery about involvement in yet another European conflict. The new archbishop of New York, Francis Spellman, preached caution to the delegates attending the September 1940 American Legion Convention. He reminded them "that while our idealism of 1917 had been genuine, our democratic system was not transferable."[65] The Knights of Columbus reflected Catholic opinion when they approved a resolution in 1940 supporting non-intervention. Al Smith was criticized by numerous Catholics, including Father Coughlin and the anti-Communist editor of the *Tablet*, Patrick Scanlon, when on national radio he announced his support for Roosevelt's neutrality revisions.

Irish-Catholic pols Jim Farley, David Walsh, and Senator Francis Mahoney of Connecticut warned FDR that changes in the Neutrality Acts, which were advantageous to Britain, would anger many Catholics. Archbishop Spellman, on the other hand, who was working diligently to convince Roosevelt to appoint an envoy to the Vatican, tried to calm the situation by appealing to Catholic lawmakers to support the 1939 Neutrality Act. His efforts did help – Catholics in the House voted 41 "for" and 23 "against" the act; and in the Senate, seven out of eleven Catholics supported the president. When Roosevelt introduced the Selective Service Act – the draft – most Catholics supported the measure. Few Catholics had any moral objections to expanding U.S. armed forces.

During the early stages of the European war, ethnic-Catholic sensibilities came to the forefront just as they had during the Wilson Administration and the lead-up to American entry into WWI. Many Irish hated the pro-English attitude of the White House, while Germans and Italians were offended by the frequent verbal assaults on their former homelands. Many Italian-Americans were livid over remarks FDR made after Mussolini's army invaded France in 1940: "[T]he hand that held the dagger," the president said, "has struck it in the back of its neighbor."

As FDR began contemplating a third run for president, he knew he had to walk gingerly around these issues that concerned Catholics. To placate the hierarchy, he announced on Christmas Day 1939 his appointment of a personal representative to the Vatican, former U.S. Steel chairman Myron Taylor. But to avoid any Protestant backlash at the polls, FDR carefully described the position as a "personal" presidential post, not an official State Department assignment.

In 1940, after a conversation with FDR, Postmaster General Jim Farley became convinced that the president was eager to retire and return to Hyde Park at the end of his second term. So Farley began making plans of his own to run for the Democratic nomination. Farley believed that after years of personal contact with national party leaders, the issue of his Catholicism had been neutralized, and he could wage a successful fight for the top spot on the ticket.

Once Farley threw his hat into the ring, the press raised the specter of another 1928 debacle. One journalist reported a rumor that FDR said Secretary of State Cordell Hull would be labeled the "stalking horse of the Pope" if Farley were elected. Others commented that Protestant objections to Taylor's Vatican appointment proved there was still much concern in the nation over the fitness of Catholics to hold high public offices.

Shortly before his death in October 1939, Cardinal Mundelein invited Farley to his residence. In his memoir *Jim Farley's Story*, the postmaster general quotes this Mundelein remark:

> James, you have always been most frank and open with me, so that I feel entirely free in broaching a most confidential matter to you. It is my sincere feeling that a Roman Catholic could not be elected President of the United States at this time or for many years to come. I hope, therefore, that you will do nothing to involve the Catholics of the country in another debacle such as we experienced in 1928.[66]

After Farley described his reasons for running and his belief that FDR would not break the two-term tradition, the Cardinal replied, "I am satisfied he is going to run." An angry Farley chose to ignore the Cardinal's advice.

Not every Catholic agreed with Cardinal Mundelein: Catholic intellectual organs, including the Jesuit magazines *America* and the *Catholic World*, announced their opposition to a third term. Numerous bishops, the Catholic Truth Society, and the dean of Fordham sided with these journals. They believed that the destiny of the nation should not be dependent on one man. And Catholics, particularly in Massachusetts, were eager to support Farley for president.

There were, however, influential Catholics, including Joseph P. Kennedy, Archbishop Spellman, Msgr. Ryan, and leaders of the American Catholic Trade Union, who made it known that FDR was their man. To ensure that Democrats remained vigilant over Catholic sentiments, FDR engineered the appointment of Irish-Catholic Edward Flynn of the Bronx as national Democratic chairman. These Catholics helped crush Jim Farley's candidacy and orchestrated the "spontaneous" draft-Roosevelt movement at the convention.

The Democrats made every effort to cater to Catholic voter needs in 1940. Since Roosevelt was not wildly popular with Protestants, they could not permit a key component of his coalition to unravel. The 1936 Lemke vote proved there were disenchanted Catholics, and the Democrats did not want the virus to spread. Yet even though Roosevelt's opponent, Wendell Wilkie, was also an internationalist, some Catholic isolationists still turned to the Republican to register their displeasure with FDR.

The voter turnout on Election Day, November 5, 1940, was 80 percent – one of the highest in the nation's history. And while Roosevelt beat Wilkie, 54.7 percent versus 44.82 percent, an analysis of the figures shows that cracks were beginning to appear in the New Deal coalition.

Because FDR won over 70 percent of the southern vote, the total figures do not tell the full story. If the largest states of the Midwest and Northeast,

which represented 228 electoral votes are subtracted, Roosevelt received only
53 percent of the combined votes in these states:

	FDR 1936	FDR 1940	Electoral Votes
Massachusetts	51.2%	53.1%	17
New York	58.8	51.6	47
New Jersey	59.6	51.5	16
Pennsylvania	56.9	53.2	36
Ohio	58.0	52.2	26
Illinois	57.7	51.0	29
Wisconsin	63.8	50.2	12
Minnesota	61.8	51.5	11
Missouri	60.8	52.3	15
Michigan	56.3	49.5	19
Total			228

A shift of less than three percent of the vote in these states could have cost
Roosevelt the election. In cities where Catholics were the largest denomination, Roosevelt experienced significant slippage:

City	FDR 1936	FDR 1940	% of Pop. Catholic
Hartford	70.0%	65.0%	27%
Providence	62.7	62.1	52
Boston	69.9	63.3	40
Newark	72.6	62.2	45
New York	75.4	61.2	20
Pittsburgh	70.7	61.6	35
Baltimore	68.3	64.0	22
Philadelphia	62.1	60.0	27
Cleveland	76.5	69.9	32
Detroit	68.9	63.0	20
Chicago	66.9	58.5	26
Cincinnati	59.2	49.9	21
Milwaukee	82.1	64.1	29
St. Louis	67.0	58.1	25
St. Paul	73.8	58.1	29
New Orleans	91.3	85.7	38
San Antonio	73.5	70.8	29
Louisville	62.1	59.4	23
Denver	66.2	52.8	12
San Francisco	75.0	60.3	27
Los Angeles	71.3	61.1	11

This decline in support can be attributed to defections from Irish, Italian, and German communities over foreign policy issues. Overall, FDR's Catholic support dropped about 13 percent over the 1936 totals from about 81 percent to 68 percent.

Roosevelt Percentage Vote in New York City, by Ethnicity[67]

	City	Irish	German	Jewish	Italian
1932	66.4	75.7	62.7	72.2	80.5
1936	73.5	72.8	65.7	87.5	78.7
1940	60.9	56.0	41.8	88.5	42.2

Republican 1940 gains over 1936[68]

Irish Catholic	Suffolk (Boston), Massachusetts	+12%
– " –	Hudson (Jersey City), New Jersey	+12
German-Irish Catholic	Queens, New York	+20
Italian-Catholic	Richmond, New York	+18
– " –	Bergen, New Jersey	+14
– " –	Erie, Pennsylvania	+14

Increased Republican Support in German-Catholic Counties

	1936	1940
Clinton, Illinois	32%	62%
Putnum, Ohio	33	71

As results began to trickle in on election night, the ever-astute president quickly understood that he was not a shoo-in, and for a short while even thought he might lose his home state of New York. It is reported that FDR broke into a cold sweat and told the Secret Service to admit no one to his room. "I said anybody," he curtly told his guard.[69] Unlike 1932 and 1936, it was not until late in the evening that Roosevelt went out to his porch to greet neighbors and accept congratulations.

When America entered the Second World War in December of 1941, Catholics supported the president and vowed to fight as Americans. Over 4 million Catholic men served during the war, and it is estimated that a quarter to 35 percent of the total troops were Catholic.

Archbishop Spellman of New York, who served as military vicar for the armed forces, took the corps of 500 Catholic chaplains and transformed it into a force of 5,370 commissioned chaplains to minister the needs of Catholic troops. The first chaplain in U.S. history to receive the Congressional Medal of Honor was Father Joseph O'Callaghan. Sixty-six other Catholic soldiers were also awarded the nation's highest military honor, and no one could question the loyalty, patriotism, or heroism of American Catholics.

American Catholics had enthusiastically embraced Franklin Roosevelt's role as "Dr. New Deal" and "Dr. Win the War." But when it became obvious that victory over the Axis powers was inevitable, cracks in the Democratic coalition increased as many Catholics began to question the proposed policies of "Dr. Win the Peace."

Chapter 12
The Catholic Voter in the Age of Anxiety

After a dozen years spent fighting the Great Depression and the Axis powers, Franklin Delano Roosevelt was an exhausted and dying man. When he announced his intention to seek a fourth term in 1944, jittery Democratic leaders, concerned that the president would not live out the term, insisted that FDR dump his unpopular and very liberal vice president, Henry Wallace.

James Byrnes, the Supreme Court justice who resigned from the bench to become director of Economic Stabilization and Director of War Mobilization, was seriously considered as Wallace's successor, but was dropped from contention because he had been raised a Catholic and later had renounced his faith. In his stead, the compromise candidate promoted by political and union leaders was U.S. Senator Harry Truman of Missouri. Truman, who had made his mark in the Senate uncovering waste and corruption in war-time industries, was considered a safe choice for several reasons: he knew how to play political ball; he was from a border state; and – although he supported New Deal programs – he was not an extreme leftist. To avoid any floor fights at the convention, FDR went along with the choice.

In the early stages of the campaign FDR found himself behind in the polls against the 42-year-old Republican governor of New York, Thomas E. Dewey. Rumors abounded that the president was at death's door, and there was a growing sentiment that a younger, more vigorous man was needed to finish the war against the Axis. The rumors needed to be taken very seriously. So in order to silence his critics, FDR announced that he was an "old campaigner who loved a good fight," and he hit the campaign trail as vigorously as he ever had. On October 21st, Roosevelt capped off the campaign by driving in an open car fifty miles in the rain through New York's boroughs. His performance convinced the thousands cheering him along the broad boulevards of Brooklyn and Queens, the press who recorded the extraordinary event, and the millions who read the newspaper accounts that he was indeed fit for another four years in the White House.

By November, things were looking up for the president: American troops had liberated Paris and were racing to cross Germany's border. Douglas MacArthur had returned to the Philippines. And fifteen years after the start of the Depression, America was acknowledged as possessing the most powerful economy in the world.

Roosevelt's November 1944 electoral-college victory was decisive – 432 votes to Dewey's 99 votes. But his popular vote hit a new low of 53.39 percent. FDR's re-election rested on the fact that he could still muster 66 percent of the southern vote and 59 percent in America's major cities. Dewey, however, carried the remainder of the nation, with 52 percent of the vote.

Even though the inner-city vote provided the president's margin of victory in many states, Democratic pols were alarmed that the decline in urban votes they had experienced in 1940 had grown even larger by 1944. This drop in support was attributed to a backlash of disenchanted Polish and other Eastern European Catholic voters who believed their former homelands were being sold out by Roosevelt to placate Joseph Stalin.

Angriest of all were the Poles. War had been declared by England and France in 1939 because Poland's sovereignty had been violated by Germany and Russia, so for the Polish émigrés living in the West, a free Poland was "the moral condition of victory." And now after six long years of war, they sensed a repeat of 1918: As Wilson had abandoned his "Fourteen Points" to get his precious League of Nations, so FDR, they feared, was abandoning his 1941 "Atlantic Charter," which had stated that the U.S. "desires to see no territorial changes that do not accord with the freely expressed wishes of the peoples concerned," in order to secure support for his precious United Nations. The election results confirmed ethnic disenchantment:

FDR's 1932–1944 Results in 13 Largest U.S. Cities

	1932	1936	1940	1944
Baltimore	61%	59%	52%	43%
Boston	67	63	63	62
Chicago	55	62	55	57
Cleveland	50	65	62	59
Detroit	57	64	61	63
Los Angeles	57	67	58	56
Milwaukee	65	74	59	57
Newark	45	54	44	48
New York	70	75	61	61
Philadelphia	42	60	59	58
Pittsburgh	52	65	58	57
St. Louis	63	65	57	60
San Francisco	64	74	59	60

These declines after '36 were largely due to the erosion of Catholic support.

Most embarrassing was Roosevelt's poor showing in his home state of New York which he carried with only 52.3 percent of the vote. And outside of New York City, Dewey actually clobbered Roosevelt, receiving 57 percent of the total votes cast. For the first time in his four presidential campaigns, Roosevelt lost Ohio and Wisconsin, and a shift of less than 2 percent of the votes in the remaining states would have cost him the election:

	FDR 1936	**FDR 1940**	**FDR 1944**	**Electoral Votes**
Massachusetts	51.2%	53.1%	52.8%	17
New York	58.8	51.6	52.3	47
New Jersey	59.6	51.5	50.3	16
Pennsylvania	56.9	53.2	51.1	36
Ohio	58.0	52.2	49.8	26
Illinois	57.7	51.0	51.5	29
Wisconsin	63.8	50.2	48.6	12
Minnesota	61.8	51.5	52.4	11
Missouri	60.8	52.3	51.4	15
Michigan	56.3	49.5	50.2	19
Total				228

Roosevelt was comforted by the fact that he was the only man ever to be elected to the presidency four times. But he would not serve out the fourth term. On April 12, 1945, twenty-five days before Germany unconditionally surrendered, and fourteen weeks after his inauguration, Franklin D. Roosevelt died of a stroke at the age of 63.

* * * * *

As 12 million GIs were anxiously awaiting a return to civilian life, they looked to the little-known Harry Truman to lead them in the post-war era.

Born in Missouri in 1884, Truman had worked as a farmer and a bank clerk, and then in World War I as a captain of a regiment dominated by German and Irish Catholics, and finally as a haberdasher before being elected to his first office in 1922. He was a dedicated member of the Masons, and had flirted briefly with the Ku Klux Klan. He filled out the Klan application and paid the initiation fee but declined to take the oath when he realized the chapter was out to punish Kansas City Catholic political boss – Tom Pendergast. It was Pendergast who gave Truman his first chance to run for county judge and was to engineer his future election to the U.S. Senate.

In his first year as president, Truman had to deal with war-weary Americans, restless labor unions, work stoppages, meatless days, wage-and-price controls, high taxes, and a bleak post-war situation internationally. He also learned that he was not to have a honeymoon with the Catholic hierarchy.

Shortly after he moved into the White House, the American bishops ended their war-time silence and "condemned the proposed voting procedure of the United Nations because it rejected the equality of nations and gave a veto to the superpowers."[1] The bishops saw no alternative than to speak out because they believed the Soviet Union would manipulate the United Nations to keep their military presence in the "liberated" nations of Eastern Europe and to promote their ideological goal – world domination. "Every day makes more evident," the bishops declared, "the fact that there can be no meeting of minds between Marxism and Democracy."[2]

At first the American people thought Truman was not up to the job, and they expressed their doubts at the polls in the 1946 off-year congressional elections. Republicans won majorities in both houses of Congress for the first time since 1930. Democrats lost thirteen seats in the Senate and fifty-five seats in the House of Representatives. Of the eleven non-southern, Democratic incumbent senators, only four were reelected. The House figures were just as grim – outside the South, Democrats lost 40 percent of their seats.

Many of the lost House seats were in heavily Catholic areas: Philadelphia's six Democratic congressmen were defeated; in Chicago Democrats lost half their seats; in Detroit the loss was 40 percent; five out of seven Dems went down in Los Angeles; and in New York City five out of twenty-five Democrats went down in defeat.

In the face of such losses, Harry Truman was dismissed as a lightweight by the national press, as beatable by Republicans, and as a liability by members of his own party. But Truman refused to give up and planned domestic and foreign policy initiatives aimed at preserving enough of the New Deal coalition (particularly urban Catholics) to put him over the top in 1948.

On the domestic front, Truman addressed housing shortages and labor problems and championed issues that concerned returning GIs. He vigorously opposed the Taft-Hartley Act, which among other things terminated jurisdictional strikes and closed union shops. He vetoed the bill, but the veto was overridden.

But where Truman struck a real chord with Catholic voters was in his foreign policy. The president realized that "Uncle Joe" Stalin could not be charmed into withdrawing Soviet forces from the "liberated" nations of Central Europe, and that the Soviet dictator would not cooperate at the United Nations to help restore the war-torn world. As early as January 1946, Truman told Secretary of State George Marshall that he was "tired of babying the Soviets." To stop Stalin's advances, Truman began a get-tough policy.

In March 1946, Truman publicly greeted Winston Churchill at Fulton, Missouri, and sat next to the former Prime Minister as he delivered his famous anti-Communist "Iron Curtain" address. On May 22, 1947, the Greek-Turkish Aid Bill was signed into law by the president. In describing the need for this legislation, Truman told the American people: "I believe that it must be the policy of the United States to support free peoples who are resisting attempted subjugation by armed minorities or by outside pressures."[3] This approach became known as the Truman Doctrine.

At the June 5, 1947, Harvard commencement, Secretary Marshall proposed a massive aid package for all European nations that would prevent the Communists from assimilating all of war-devastated Europe. "Our policy is not directed," Marshall told the graduates, "against any country or doctrine, but against hunger, poverty, desperation, and chaos."[4] Reacting to the Communist seizure of Czechoslovakia in March 1948, Congress approved the plan. The Marshall Plan was a great success: the Italians and French excluded Communists from their coalition governments, and Austria removed itself from the Soviet sphere of influence. There were numerous other actions and events that strengthened Truman's anti-Communist and humanitarian credentials with Catholics including:

- The National Security Act of 1947, which unified the Armed Services and created the National Security Council and the Central Intelligence Agency.
- The Berlin Air Lift, which Truman commenced in June 1948 after the Soviets forbade all land access to Allied-occupied Berlin and which succeeded in making over 277,000 flights into Berlin and delivered over 2.5 million tons of food and other supplies.
- The Displaced Persons Act, which in June 1947 permitted 205,000 Europeans to enter the United States.
- The investigation of over 2 million federal employees in an effort to weed out Communist spies or sympathizers.

Still, in early 1948 most political pundits believed that the electorate would toss Harry Truman out of the White House in November. The media, convinced that New York governor Thomas E. Dewey would be the next president, devoted plenty of ink to speculations on Dewey's cabinet selections. The Republican nominee also believed that Truman had no chance; hence Dewey chose to stay above the political fray, said little, and adopted the British campaign model of simply "*standing*" for election.

In contrast, the tenacious Truman was *running* hard for another term.

The July 1948 Democratic National Convention resembled a three-ring circus. When the platform committee proposed and the convention supported a civil-rights plank, southern delegates bolted and formed the States Rights Democratic Party – or Dixiecrats – and nominated South Carolina governor Strom Thurmond for president. Democrats who opposed Truman's hard line against the Soviet Union also defected, and on July 25, 1948, the newly revived Progressive Party nominated former Vice President Henry A. Wallace as its presidential candidate.

But a determined Truman proved he had a better understanding of America's political landscape than all the pundits combined. For one thing, he knew that even after sixteen long years of Democratic rule, most Democrats could still not bring themselves to vote for the party of Herbert Hoover. That belief was reinforced in Truman's mind after he had a chance to watch his opponent's lackluster campaign style. Truman knew the haughty Dewey, who looked like the plastic groom on top of the wedding cake, would not appeal to blue-collar and farm Democrats.

The Dixiecrats were another matter. He knew they would drain off a significant piece of the southern vote, and yet the Democratic advantage was so huge in the South that even if Thurmond broke all third-party records and received as much as 30 percent of the vote, there would still be enough Democratic votes for Truman to carry most of the southern states by a plurality.

Finally Truman figured that Wallace's appeal would be limited to northeastern radical liberals and would either offend or frighten most Catholic voters. And he believed that his tough anti-communism would keep recalcitrant Catholics in the Democratic column.

Truman's political senses were right on target. Rank-and-file Catholics, who were staunch anti-Communists, looked with horror on the Progressive Party's platform. They viewed Henry Wallace as a troublemaker and a pawn of the Reds. The Association of Catholic Trade Unionists condemned the Progressive Party as "a new front for American Communists," and Church hierarchy publicized Wallace's statements accusing the Roman Catholic Church of being the key culprit in "stirring up trouble with Russia."[5]

Throughout 1948, Truman advanced his plan to bring back the Catholic vote. One important date in his plan was March 17, 1948. At the annual Friendly Sons of St. Patrick Dinner in New York City, over 4,000 men in tuxedos gathered to honor their patron saint and hear the keynote speaker, President Harry Truman. The presiding cleric, Francis Cardinal Spellman, warmed up the crowd with a rousing anti-Communist speech. Truman followed the cardinal and, playing to his audience, bluntly stated: "I do not want and I will not accept the political support of Henry Wallace and his Communists. If joining them or permitting them to join me is the price of victory, I recommend defeat. These are days of high prices for everything, but any price for Wallace and his Communists is too much for me to pay. I'm not buying."[6]

While Dewey was picking wallpaper for the White House, and the erratic Wallace was vehemently denying any domestic Communist threats, "Give-

'em-Hell" Harry barnstormed the nation and forged a bond with struggling lower- and middle-class Americans – particularly Catholics.

The election-day results stunned the pollsters, the pundits, and the Republicans: Truman beat Dewey 49.51 percent to 45.12 percent. Wallace flopped badly, receiving only 1.15 million votes, or a little over 2 percent. And 60 percent of the Wallace vote came from just two states, New York and California – mostly from extreme left-wingers and Communist sympathizers living in New York City and Los Angeles. The Dixiecrat movement also flopped, although not as badly as the Progressives. Thurmond managed to capture not only the 88 electoral votes of his home state of South Carolina, but he also carried Louisiana, Mississippi, and Alabama. Truman easily carried the remainder of the South.

Truman's read of the electorate was correct because, as Kevin Phillips noted, "he knew what the Republicans did not: that a normal Democratic majority now existed in the country."[7] And a key component of this majority was Catholic.

In analyzing the 1948 returns, Samuel Lubell concluded: "Truman received a record Catholic vote exceeding in some areas Al Smith's showing!"[8] Various Catholic groups united behind Truman: aging Father Coughlin supporters, Catholic union members, and anti-Communist Irish, Germans, and Eastern Europeans. Unlike FDR in 1940 and 1944, Truman won a majority of the votes in counties in Ohio and in Wisconsin where Union Party presidential candidate William Lemke had polled over 10 percent of the vote in 1936. In Boston, Irish Catholics, many of whom had been disenchanted with Roosevelt, came out in record numbers to support Truman.

Summing up the behavior of Catholic voters in 1948, Lubell wrote that:

> Although the strongest single factor behind this new Catholic voting solidarity seems to have been the end of the war and Roosevelt's death, it was certainly strengthened by Wallace's bolt and the removal of Communist influence from the Democratic party. Catholic unity also appears to have been bolstered by the Dixiecrat bolt, which also fortified the Negro attachment to the Democratic Party.[9]

* * * * *

But even as President Truman was savoring his come-from-behind victory, forces were gathering that over the next twenty years would unravel the Catholic component of the Democratic Party's winning coalition. The political perspective of the Catholic voting bloc would slowly change because of the impact of a number of issues, policies, and movements. Principal among them were: the Red Scare, the GI Bill of Rights and FHA/VA Housing programs, and the movement to reform the urban Democratic Party.

By 1950, China had fallen to the Communists; the Cold War in Eastern Europe was a stalemate; American troops were dying in South Korea; former State Department official, Alger Hiss, accused of espionage, was convicted of perjury; and a Manhattan Project scientist, Dr. Klaus Fuchs, was accused of being a Soviet spy. Historian Eric Goldman wrote that these events "loosed within American life a vast impatience of turbulent bitterness, a rancor akin to revolt. It was a strange rebelliousness, quite without parallel in the history of the United States."[10] Arthur Schlesinger, Jr., agreed and referred to the era as the "Age of Anxiety."

Reacting to America's fear of the Communist threat and nuclear war, Congress passed – over President Truman's veto – the 1950 McCarran Internal Security Act, which ordered Communist organizations to register, forbade members of the Communist Party from employment in Defense industries, and stopped individuals who had political roles in totalitarian countries from migrating to America.

The man who was to lead the charge against the "threat from within" first came to national prominence at a Lincoln Day Dinner in Wheeling, West Virginia. Wisconsin Senator Joseph McCarthy told an enthusiastic Republican audience:

> And ladies and gentlemen, while I cannot take the time to name all the men in the State Department who have been named as active members of the Communist Party and members of a spy ring, I have here in my hand a list of 205 – a list of names that were made known to the Secretary of State as being members of the Communist Party and who nevertheless are still working and shaping policy in the State Department.[11]

The accusation catapulted McCarthy to the front pages of America's newspapers and began one of the nation's most controversial periods. It also added to the American lexicon the phrase created by political cartoonist Herblock – "McCarthyism."

For over half a century historians and pundits have argued the merits of McCarthy's tactics, style, and especially his claims. And with the recent release of documents, particularly the archives of the Soviet Union, historians such as Arthur Herman are conceding that while McCarthy often overreached, he was also often right. But in the context of the time, Joe McCarthy's accusations caused tempers to flare and political sides to be chosen: those who loved McCarthy and those who despised him. Many Roman Catholics, particularly Irish, Germans, and Poles, quickly marched to the forefront in support of the senator. Gallup polls from 1951 to 1954 showed that a majority of Catholics, 56 percent, consistently had a positive view of McCarthy.

During the "Red Scare," Catholics took pride in displaying their anti-Communist sympathies. They reminded Protestants that historically, the Church was the foremost foe of the Marxist movement. They enthusiastically pointed to papal pronouncements denouncing godless, materialistic communism going back all the way to 1848.

Catholics viewed communism not merely as an economic prescription, but more fundamentally as a flawed philosophy of life. In 1948 the noted Catholic preacher, Monsignor Fulton J. Sheen (future archbishop and television star), explained the Church's position in his bestselling book *Communism and the Conscience of the West*:

> . . . communism is seen as the dehumanization of man by making him a social animal for whom an economic machine is the total meaning of existence. Communism represents an *active* barbarism outside Western civilization which has made inroads because of the *passive* barbarism within, which manifested itself in the general demoralization of society. . . . The basic struggle today is not between individualism and collectivism, free enterprise and socialism, democracy and dictatorship. These are only the superficial manifestations of a deeper struggle which is moral and spiritual and involves above all else whether man shall exist for the state, or the state for man, and whether freedom is of the spirit or a concession of a materialized society. It has not been given to every age in history to see the issue as clearly as it has been given to our own, for we have a double incentive to work for the peace and prosperity of the world: the first is the Gospel in its fullness, the second is the communism of Soviet Russia. The first teaches us that happiness comes from living rightly; the second, that misery comes from acting wrongly.[12]

For a people who had been treated for decades as political aliens, Catholics were delighted they could lead a cause that could be viewed as "Catholic and American."[13]

Catholic groups, particularly the Knights of Columbus and the Catholic Veterans Association, spoke out against Communist infiltration in America and Communist tyranny in occupied Europe.

Catholics condemned the Yalta Agreement and criticized the State Department's silence when Poland, Lithuania, Estonia, and Latvia fell under Soviet domination. They agreed with the August 20, 1951, *New York Times* editorial that stated "History will record that at Yalta, the United States repudiated some of its solemn obligations, yielded to Russian imperialism and gave way to appeasement. . . . The result of Yalta remains a triumph for Communist diplomacy."

Imprisoned Archbishops Aloysius Stepinac of Yugoslavia and Joseph Cardinal Mindszenty of Hungary became Catholic heroes. At a 1948 World Peace Rally, New York's Cardinal Spellman declared that Stepinac's only crime was "fidelity to God and Country."[14] In one year Spellman raised over $4 million to build a high school named after the embattled archbishop. From the pulpit of St. Patrick's Cathedral, Spellman told his congregation that Mindszenty was the prisoner of "Christ-hating Communists," and on the February 6, 1949, New York Archdiocese Day of Prayer for Mindszenty, 4,000 Catholic Boy Scouts marched down Fifth Avenue to participate in the ceremony. Classes that day at Fordham University stopped and 3,000 students prayed aloud the rosary.

In 1950, this Catholic fervor was energized by McCarthy. In a June 1950 editorial, the Brooklyn *Tablet* called on McCarthy's critics to "put up or shut up." The paper declared, "The time for being naïve about the substance of the McCarthy charges is long past. The presence of close to a hundred perverts in the State Department – even though [Alger] Hiss has been forced out and convicted and the perverts fired – justify [*sic*] a complete and thorough search for further evidences of the Communists' conspiracy within the departments of our government. That is the avowed objective of Senator McCarthy's efforts. . . . It is time for every Congressman and Senator to put up or shut up. If he (or she) cannot offer any better way of reaching and destroying the Communist conspiracy in our government than is being offered by Senator McCarthy, then at least, for the welfare of the United States, let him hold his peace and be silent!"[15]

Joseph Raymond McCarthy was born on a farm in Grand Chute, Wisconsin, on November 4, 1909. He received a law degree from Marquette University, a Jesuit institution, in 1935, was elected District Attorney of Shawano County in 1936, and served from 1940 to 1942 as a judge on the Wisconsin Circuit Court. During World War II, he attained the rank of captain in the U.S. Marine Corps.

Returning home, he shocked the Wisconsin political establishment in 1946 when he beat Robert M. Lafollette, Jr., in the Republican U.S. Senate primary. Dutch, German, Czech, and Polish Catholics, disgusted with the Yalta agreements and Soviet domination of Eastern Europe, put McCarthy over the top both in the primary and the November election. Many of his Catholic supporters were those who had broken with the New Deal in 1936 over foreign-policy concerns and had supported Union Party candidate William Lemke. Wisconsin's Catholics enthusiastically agreed with McCarthy's call for America to end "twenty years of treason."

By mid-1950, a Gallup poll indicated that McCarthy had hit a nerve with Catholics nationally: 49 percent believed his charges while only 28 percent believed he was grandstanding.[16]

McCarthy's message was even more appealing because it included the ironic claim that members of the Anglo-Saxon Protestant establishment – representatives of the very group that had long refused to accept the Americanism of Catholics – were the real subversives of the new Jerusalem. McCarthy delighted in the prosecution of Alger Hiss and the persecution of such State Department regulars as John Carter Vincent, John Stewart Service, and John Paton Davies, all of impeccable Yankee lineage. McCarthy did not blanch in naming Dean Gooderham Acheson and George Catlett Marshall, two of the most powerful members of the establishment in the United States, as front men for traitors; and McCarthy's assistants eventually accused the Protestant clergy of constituting the most serious Communist threat to America.[17]

For political pundits, the results in the 1950 Congressional elections would determine if McCarthy's crusade actually had legs, and the key test was in Maryland, where Senator Millard Tydings was running for re-election. Tydings, a leading critic of McCarthy, squared off against McCarthy enthusiast John Marshall Butler.

Since Maryland was America's first English-speaking Catholic settlement, all eyes were on the state's Roman Catholic population, which totaled about 20 percent. Senator McCarthy made three campaign appearances with Butler and accused Tydings of protecting traitors, "at a time when the survival of Western non-atheistic civilization hangs in the balance."[18]

McCarthy's office also helped raise money and prepared mailings for Butler. And their efforts paid off: On election day, Tydings lost by 40,000 votes, and Americans believed McCarthy had persuaded Maryland Catholics to take him down.

At that time, political analyst Louis Bean reported that Tyding's "greater losses" were "associated with the greater Catholic concentration" of voters.[19] He concluded that the larger a county's Catholic vote, the larger was Tyding's loss. *The New York Times* agreed: "The combination of the Catholic vote and the labor vote [made up] a large bloc of the sentiment that unseated [Tydings]."[20]

For the next four years, Joe McCarthy was to take his Catholic supporters on a kind of political rollercoaster ride. The growing McCarthy movement plus the rapidly declining popularity of President Truman, had the GOP chomping at the bit. After twenty years in the political wilderness, the Republicans believed they finally had an excellent shot at capturing the White House – and they believed that Catholic voters, despondent over the Communist menace, would join their cause.

*   *   *   *   *

While Republicans and Democrats were preparing for the 1952 presidential slug fest, they were mostly unaware that numerous public-policy initiatives were beginning to affect the very nature of the ethnic-Catholic neighborhoods.

Historically, first-generation Catholic immigrants who settled in America's ethnic neighborhoods worked in the community, often opening shops that provided services and commodities for their friends and neighbors. The second generation, for the most part, stayed in the neighborhood, took over the reins of the family business, and lived in neighborhood row houses. Members of the third generation often moved on; they became more well-educated, put on a gray flannel suit, and began working on the bottom rung of corporate or professional institutions. They moved out of the old neighborhoods and into higher rent districts in the cities or bought homes in suburbia.

But even with this upward mobility, ethnic neighborhoods continued to flourish because there was a continuous stream of new immigrants to replace those who had left and to work as laborers in neighborhood shops and plants. But during the 1930s this flow of new immigrants declined to a trickle, mostly due to the impact of the Johnson Immigration Act.

Passed by large majorities in the Congress, the Johnson Act was signed into law by President Calvin Coolidge on May 22, 1924. This law drastically reduced immigrant quotas from Eastern and Southern Europe. Its quota formula of ethnic-national composition of immigration was based on the census of 1890, and ensured that the annual admission of 150,000 immigrants would be primarily from Northern European countries. The April 13, 1924, *Los Angeles Times* headline summarized the law's implications:

Nordic Victory Is Seen In
Drastic Restrictions

Nativists, particularly Ku Klux Klan members, rejoiced over the bill's passage. And almost immediately the commissioner of immigration at Ellis Island happily reported "that virtually all immigrants now looked exactly like Americans."[21]

By the late 1940s the decline of new immigrants, the debut of the GI Bill of Rights, and the implementation of FHA/VA Housing programs were spelling doom for the old Catholic neighborhoods.

The GI Bill of Rights, signed into law by President Roosevelt in June 1944, was a program intended to thank World War II veterans for their service to the nation. It was also designed to lessen the impact that 12 million decommissioned GIs would have on the economy. Education and training programs, it was hoped, would slow down the absorption of these men into the job market and avert another depression.

The term "GI" meant "Government Issue" and it became a slang word applied to all World War II men in uniform. The "GI" Bill established veterans hospitals and vocational rehabilitation centers and provided guaranteed loans for veterans to purchase homes, farms, and businesses. And it also created the first educational voucher system: GIs could receive $500 a year to be applied to tuition at the college of their choice. They also received a $50 monthly allowance during their stints in school.

These educational allowances permitted thousands of inner-city Catholic GI's to advance far beyond the achievements of their immigrant forebears. Acquiring a college degree and an FHA/VA housing loan caused a mass exodus from the old cities to the fledgling suburbs.

When drafting these new policies and programs, New Deal social engineers made sure their fingerprints were all over the final documents. In the name of "urban planning," the Federal Housing Administration "encouraged banks to lend on millions of new low risk suburban homes while refusing to stake money on older city properties."[22] To ensure there were few exceptions in this anti-neighborhood lending program, FHA designed requirements on lot size, house width, and distance from adjacent homes that effectively eliminated categories of inner-city dwellings such as the sixteen-foot row house.[23] Historian Kenneth T. Jackson, in his award-winning work, *Crabgrass Frontier: The Suburbanization of the United States*, concluded that "Unfortunately . . . [these] programs hastened the decay of inner-city neighborhoods by stripping them of much of their middle-class constituency."[24]

One FHA manual actually informed lending institutions that "crowded neighborhoods lessen desirability [and] older properties in a neighborhood have a tendency to accelerate the transition to lower class occupancy." And to further insure policy compliance, federal tax-code changes gave developers incentives to build new structures in suburbia instead of improving old ones in city neighborhoods. Since most inner-city homes were disqualified from receiving loans, the mass exodus to "Levittown" settlements commenced.

Meddling federal social engineers were obsessed with "Americanizing" inner-city Catholic ethnics. World War II, they believed, began the process by placing millions of Catholic GIs in army camps with soldiers from all walks of life. To complete the assimilation they would now direct the ethnics into suburban communities that did not have Catholic social culture as their foundations.

To further their agenda, these big-government architects stripped away the planning powers of urban municipalities and directed the flow of federal dollars to big-time developers like the Levitts and master builders like New York's Robert Moses.

Moses's Pulitzer Prize-winning biographer, Robert Caro, points out that 250,000 New Yorkers were driven from their one- and two-family homes thanks to his policies. To destroy New York City neighborhoods, Moses built several elevated roadways (e.g., Brooklyn's Gowanus Parkway, the Cross-Bronx Expressway, and the Grand Central Parkway in Queens) right through the ethnic enclaves. "The ethnic neighborhood embodied everything Moses considered retrograde and to use his term, he took a 'meat-ax' to the neighborhood and chopped it to death."[25]

Other planners who strove to break up the cohesiveness of the Catholic neighborhoods included members of the Democratic Party's reform movement.

During the Progressive Era, the Republican Party had served as a refuge for social engineers who wanted to destroy the Catholic political machines and stop the flow of Catholic immigrants into the city neighborhoods. In the 1940s and 1950s, the social engineers found a new home, the Democratic Party.

As has been demonstrated in this work, the inner-city political machines reached the height of their powers in the 1920s. Yet even as they savored the presidential nomination of one of their own – Al Smith – the seeds of their destruction had been planted. The nativist movement cut off the machines' lifeline – immigration – with the passage of the 1924 restriction act. The New Deal resulted in the empowerment of a class of social planners equally capable of bold innovation and of exercising coercive political power. When Al Smith walked out of the 1936 Democratic convention, he was accused of sour grapes. But in a speech that fall, he revealed the real reason he had bolted: "The Regulars were out on a limb holding the bag, driven out of the party, because some new bunch that nobody ever heard of in their life before came in and took charge and started planning everything."[26]

The Democratic Party in America's major cities emerged in the late 1940s and 1950s as the new home for "social engineers." Searching for a new intellectual hero, they settled on the liberal Adlai Stevenson of Illinois. He was an odd choice – he had earned gentleman's C's at Princeton and Northwestern Law School, was more a socialite than an egghead, and, except for the Social Register, was not a particularly voracious reader.[27]

Furthermore, he wasn't even all that liberal: he opposed national health insurance, opposed revision of Taft-Hartley, opposed increases in the minimum wage and Social Security, and avoided civil-rights issues. Stevenson was, however, embraced by the new generation of reformers because he was, in Michael Barone's judgment, "the first leading Democratic politician to become a critic rather than a celebrator of middle-class culture – the prototype of the liberal democrat who would judge ordinary Americans by an abstract standard and find them wanting."[28] Liberal journalist Jack Newfield admitted in 1989: "Stevenson was a curious kind of hero. He was not a champion of the workers or the little guy. . . . Stevenson's appeal resided more in his intellect and wit, his patrician gentility, his melancholy dignity."[29] His cultural elitism and contempt for the blue-collar worker engendered a new generation of politicians whose roots were grounded not in the fragmented local politics which Franklin Roosevelt and his contemporaries had grown up with, but instead in the centralized national politics which had grown up with the large central government produced by Roosevelt's New Deal and wartime policies.

Taking advantage of the Democratic Party's internal struggle and the restlessness of the inner-city Catholics, in 1952 the Republican Party made a major play to win the Catholic vote. Since they were a minority party, Republicans knew that to win they had to co-opt a chunk of the New Deal Coalition – and Al Smith Catholic Democrats appeared to be the most likely voters they could peel away.

So when Republicans gathered at their 1952 convention in Chicago to nominate General Dwight David Eisenhower for president, they tailored parts of their platform to appeal to blue-collar Catholics.

Republicans knew, for instance, that Poles, who comprised 8 percent of first generation immigrants, were disenchanted with the Democrats, whom they blamed for giving America the Yalta agreements that had sold a free Poland down the river. Republicans also knew – or hoped – that Poles, who resided primarily in industrial areas, could provide margins of victory in elections in New York, Pennsylvania, Michigan, and Illinois. Hence they crafted platform language that would please Poles and other Eastern Europeans as well.

During the 1952 primary season, Eisenhower denounced the Yalta agreement on numerous occasions ("I swear upon my honor and integrity before God to work for the liberation of enslaved nations behind the Iron Curtain."), and he blessed the language of the Republican platform:

> Teheran, Yalta, and Potsdam were the scenes of those tragic blunders with others to follow. . . . The leaders of the Administration in power acted without the knowledge or consent of Congress or of the American people. They traded our overwhelming victory for a new enemy and for new oppressions and new wars which were quick to come. The government of the United States under Republican leadership will repudiate all commitments contained in secret understandings such as those of Yalta which aid Communist enslavement.[30]

To attract Irish-Catholic anti-Communists, Republicans promised:

> We have always recognized Communism to be a world conspiracy against freedom and religion. We never compromised with

Communism and we have fought to expose it and to eliminate it in government and American life.

A Republican President will appoint only persons of unquestioned loyalty. We will overhaul loyalty and security programs. In achieving these purposes a Republican President will cooperate with Congress. We pledge close coordination of our intelligence services for protecting our security. We pledge fair but vigorous enforcement of laws to safeguard our country from subversion and disloyalty. By such policies we will keep the country secure and restore the confidence of the American people in the integrity of our Government.[31]

During the fall campaign against Stevenson, Eisenhower took the high road and pledged, "I will go to Korea" if elected, while vice-presidential candidate Senator Richard Nixon took a less elevated path. Nixon was a proven anti-Communist who had helped to expose Alger Hiss, and he constantly reminded Catholic voters that the Democrats' "top administration officials have refused time and time again to recognize the existence of this fifth column . . . and to take effective action to clear subversives out . . . of our government."[32] Nixon also pointed a finger at Stevenson, whom he labeled "an appeaser," a "Ph.D. graduate of Dean Acheson's cowardly College of Communist Containment."[33] On one nationwide radio broadcast, Nixon asked: "Can such a man as Stevenson be trusted to lead our crusade against Communism?"[34]

Among Catholic Democrats Stevenson faced more serious problems than Nixon's attacks. For instance, Catholic Democratic ward leaders in Chicago regarded the divorcee as a "sanctimonious Lake Forest Presbyterian" and refused to lift a finger for him.[35] And this was in the candidate's home state.

Stevenson tripped up badly and offended many Catholics when, at a press conference, he ad-libbed his view on appointing an ambassador to the Vatican:

Stevenson: "I think I will not propose the appointment of an ambassador."
Reporter: "Why not?"
Stevenson: "I think the matter in this country has become – the feeling in this country is that it constitutes an official recognition of a religion – of a denomination – and this is highly incompatible with our theory of the separation of the church and the state, and so on. That is not to say that we must take advantage of the sources of information that are available at the Vatican, as at any other national capital, so to speak. I have not been able to see that there is any great disadvantage in the system that existed previously of a special representative of the President at the Vatican. This is a subject

that I have not heretofore discussed in the campaign. I may
have occasion to later. I haven't encountered it previously."

Reporter: "Since other nations do have representatives at the Vatican, is
there any inconsistency there, do you think?"

Stevenson: "Yes, I suppose there is."[36]

Stevenson's other major error was declining Cardinal Spellman's invitation to appear on the dais with General Eisenhower at the annual Al Smith Dinner. To skip a dinner dedicated to a great Catholic Democrat was bad enough, but to cede center stage to Eisenhower who gave a speech on foreign policy to a captive audience of New York's most distinguished Catholics was even worse.

To shore up the Catholic vote, the Republicans let loose their leading Irish politician, Joe McCarthy. Although Eisenhower and his key advisors found McCarthy to be a reckless bore, this did not stop them from encouraging him to stump in key Catholic regions.

McCarthy campaigned three times in Connecticut to help unseat Democratic Senator William Benton. In this state where 37 percent of the populace was Catholic, McCarthy hit hard, calling Truman, Acheson, and Benton "Commiecrats." Benton, who had won a 1950 special election by beating Prescott Bush (father and grandfather of future presidents) by only 1,000 votes, went down in flames – losing with 44 percent of the vote to McCarthy enthusiast and Roman Catholic, William Purtell. The Republican won because he was able to peel off a significant number of Catholic Democrats.

In the Massachusetts senate race, McCarthy had an impact simply by not appearing in the state. He declined to campaign for a man he despised, Republican Brahmin and incumbent senator Henry Cabot Lodge. McCarthy was buddies with Ambassador Joseph P. Kennedy and liked his son, Jack, who was Lodge's opponent. McCarthy knew that throughout America his popularity was probably highest among Massachusetts's 750,000 Irish-Catholics.[37] Thus by refusing to campaign for the Republican, he actually helped the Democrat, Congressman John F. Kennedy, beat Lodge by a razor-thin majority – even as Eisenhower carried the state in a landslide. Kennedy was spared the dilemma of taking a stand on McCarthy's anti-Communist probes which, depending on his answer, would have offended either his Irish supporters or his Harvard supporters.

On Tuesday, November 4, 1952, the Republican call to arms to end "Korea, Communism, Corruption" was endorsed by the American people: Eisenhower easily beat Stevenson with 55.13 percent of the vote versus 44.38 percent. Ike overwhelmingly carried the Electoral College with 442 votes to Stevenson's 89.

Catholics deserted the Democrats in numbers that had not been seen since the election of 1920. Overall, Catholic support for Eisenhower was about 46 percent. It is estimated that over 3 million ethnic Catholic voters switched to Eisenhower and that each group gave the "candidate a record-high percentage."[38]

German Catholics gave Eisenhower 73 percent of their votes, Poles and Irish over 50 percent. In Catholic families where there were no union members, 62 percent backed Ike. Reviewing the results, Democratic pollster Louis Harris concluded that "the shift of the German-American voter in 1952 (14 percent of the electorate) proved to be one of the decisive factors in the election of Dwight Eisenhower."[39]

Political analyst Kevin Phillips has pointed out that the Catholic sons and daughters of Al Smith's supporters who had moved to the newly built suburban areas outside New York City voted overwhelmingly Republican for president:

Suburban Voting in Predominantly Catholic New York Areas[40]
Eisenhower 1952

Pelham, N.Y.	84%
Orangetown, N.Y.	68
Babylon, N.Y	71
Smithtown, N.Y.	72
Oyster Bay, N.Y.	72
Yorktown, N.Y.	70

While Stevenson managed to carry most of the heavily Catholic-populated cities, his margins were down significantly when compared to Truman's 1948 results, and this decline helped Eisenhower carry every state in the Northeast and Midwest.

Democratic Vote in Major Cities
1948–1952

	Truman 1948	Stevenson 1952
Chicago	55%	50%
Cleveland	54	46
Boston	69	60
New York City	59	55

The 1952 election results indicated that Catholic attitudes were changing. Catholics who moved to suburbia were no longer dependent on inner-city Democratic machines and did not feel the need to remain loyal to the party of their parents. Germans, Poles, and other Eastern European ethnics who watched their former homelands fall under the Iron Curtain were disenchanted with Democratic foreign policy initiatives. As for the Irish, by 1950 only 10 percent of their population was first-generation. Third- and fourth-generation upwardly mobile Irish were losing the affection their forebears had had for the Democratic Party of the "good old days." Mrs. Emily Smith Warner, daughter of Governor Al Smith, exemplified this change of attitude when she endorsed and campaigned for Eisenhower.

The Eisenhower years were affectionately described by social critic Jeffrey Hart as the time "when the going was good." During his first term in office, Americans experienced peace abroad and prosperity at home. Internationally, Ike ended the war in Korea and avoided conflicts in Indo-China (Vietnam). His secretary of state's threats of atomic war ("brinkmanship") contained the Soviet Union and Communist China.

Domestically, Americans enjoyed unprecedented economic growth. The annual rate of inflation was a mere 1.5 percent and unemployment hovered at a low 3 percent. Personal income in Ike's first term grew by 20 percent. By 1956, 30 million more people had moved into suburban homes; televisions and automobiles had become necessities, not luxuries; and 60 percent of Americans had attained a middle-class standard of living.

As Catholics were busy advancing economically, they watched their hero, Joe McCarthy, self-destruct. His erratic behavior and his drinking caused his accusations to become more reckless and self-destructive. By 1954 (to the delight of Eisenhower and many Republicans) McCarthy had lost his hold on the American people. His final humiliation was his formal censure by the vote of his peers in the Senate on July 30, 1954.

By 1956, Americans were comfortable with Eisenhower's reassuring smile. In Ike's election rematch with Adlai Stevenson, American voters, including Catholics, confirmed they "liked Ike." Eisenhower's victory over Stevenson exceeded his win in 1952: He received 57.37 percent of the vote and 457 electoral votes versus Stevenson's 41.97 percent and 73 electoral votes.

Catholic Poles, Germans, Irish, Italians, and Eastern Europeans cast over 50 percent of their votes for Eisenhower. He carried the heavily Catholic populated cities of Chicago, Buffalo, Baltimore, and Jersey City. Michael Barone reports that "in 1956 [Eisenhower] made his biggest gains among Catholic voters."[41]

And this was most evident in New York City. In 1952, Ike had received 43 percent of the citywide vote while in 1956 he garnered 49.2 percent, losing the city by only 60,000 votes. While his vote totals declined in a few Manhattan "Silk Stocking" precincts and a few upstate Yankee towns, his totals increased in outer borough Catholic assembly districts. In fact, his best showings were in the thirteen districts heavily populated by Catholics:

Assembly District[42]	Eisenhower 1956
13th Queens (German-Irish)	80%
9th Brooklyn (Scandinavian-Irish-Italian)	80
2nd Richmond (Italian-Irish)	78
9th Queens (German-Irish)	76
1st Richmond (Italian-Irish)	75
3rd Queens (German-Irish)	74
12th Brooklyn (Italian-Irish)	73
10th Bronx (Italian-Irish)	70
20th Brooklyn (German-Irish)	70
3rd Brooklyn (Italian-Irish)	67
8th Brooklyn (Italian-Irish)	66

Eisenhower's vote also improved in New York suburban towns with significant Catholic populations:

Predominantly Catholic Suburban Voting[43]
Eisenhower

	1952	1956
Pelham, N.Y.	84%	86%
Orangetown, N.Y.	68	75
Babylon, N.Y.	71	76
Smithtown, N.Y.	72	77
Oyster Bay, N.Y.	72	73
Yorktown, N.Y.	70	72

Similar Republican improvements occurred in the heavily Catholic Chicago wards:

Ward	Dewey 1948	Eisenhower 1952	Eisenhower 1956
Irish 14th	22%	29%	39%
Italian 1st, 23rd	19, 28	26, 36	30, 47
German 43rd	44	51	56
Polish 32nd	23	33	45

It should be noted, however, that most Catholic voters who supported Eisenhower were ticket splitters. They returned to the Democratic ticket to support their local congressional candidates. As a result, Eisenhower was the first president since Zachary Taylor (1849) to win election and not carry party majorities in either house of Congress. Catholics, for the most part, were to remain loyal to local Democratic Party candidates for the balance of the century.

**Average Percent of Ethnic Catholics
Who Voted for a Democratic Congress, 1952–1970**

Irish	70
German	57
Italian	62
Polish	76
All[44] Americans	55

*   *   *   *   *

When Al Smith ran for president in 1928, Roman Catholics comprised 16 percent of the U.S. population. In the post-World War II era, Catholics were major contributors to the baby-boom, and by 1956 their numbers increased to 35 million, or 20 percent of the total population.

During the fifties, the Catholic Church prospered: over 60,000 priests served in parishes; 150,000 nuns were working in schools and hospitals; 12,000 religious brothers served in various Catholic ministries. Attendance in Catholic grammar schools, high schools, and colleges was rapidly growing to meet the needs of baby-boomers reaching school age.

Catholic historian Michael Perko has described the Church's position in the 1950s as the "Golden Age." "Politically and economically powerful," he wrote, "the Church exercised a role in American life previously unknown. No longer exclusively the preserve of a prosperous but insignificant minority, or of destitute immigrants, it had become a significant force of American society."[45]

With American Catholics moving up the economic ladder and being recognized as a viable political force, discussions revived in 1956 of a Catholic running for president, probably a Democrat. And one person paying careful attention to those discussions was the junior senator from Massachusetts, John F. Kennedy.

Chapter 13

The Campaign of 1960

When John F. Kennedy entered public life in 1946, he sought the same congressional seat, Boston's 11th District, that had previously been held by two of the city's most colorful Irish-Catholic politicians: by his own grandfather, John "Honey Fitz" Fitzgerald, who had also been mayor of Boston; and by James Michael Curley, also a Bean Town mayor, a governor of Massachusetts, and a prison inmate as well.

Despite Kennedy's Harvard education, his wealth, and the fact that he did not live in the district, many local pols believed his family ties in the old neighborhood would be enough for Jack Kennedy to carry the 11th. He was a war hero besides. But for the "Founding Father," Joseph P. Kennedy, who directed his son's campaign from behind the scenes, relying on the "Old Boy" network was simply not enough. To guarantee victory, he insisted on using his power and money to build an independent organization of loyal Kennedy men. He also used his muscle with the press and influence in the Church to make sure there were no unexpected roadblocks in executing the first stage of the Kennedy master plan. The people of the 11th who met the awkward young candidate (who was often in great pain due to a wartime back injury) were unaware that there were great plans in the works for JFK. The Kennedys were not satisfied to have him represent a little bit of real estate in the working-class part of Cambridge, or, for that matter, the whole of Boston as Grandpa Fitzgerald once had. No, Joe Kennedy's plans were to move beyond Massachusetts to every square mile of the whole forty-eight. When Jack was in the White House Joe would be content.

These dreams were fine, but still his more seasoned handlers wondered if the urbane, Choate- and Harvard-educated Jack Kennedy could relate to the district's Irish and Italian blue-collar citizens who spent their lives struggling to make ends meet. The rundown neighborhoods in which Kennedy was campaigning were very different from the Brookline, Bronxville, and Cape Cod communities in which he had been raised. To everyone's surprise, the novice candidate adapted easily to neighborhood campaigning.

Walking up and down the many flights of stairs in back-alley tenements, Kennedy saw for the first time the poor conditions in which his future constituents lived. Running on the slogan, "The New Generation Offers a Leader,"

Kennedy connected with veterans who were looking to move up the economic and social ladder, and after weeks of going door to door with the candidate, one of the early members of Kennedy's "Irish Mafia," Dave Powers, was able to say: "It was a strange thing, while Jack Kennedy was a completely new type of Irish politician himself, having come from such a different background, he was, at bottom, very Irish and he could never hear enough of the old Irish stories."[1]

After his election, Kennedy's congressional voting record reflected the anti-Communist, socially conservative views of his blue-collar, street-smart constituents. He was a cold warrior not afraid to promote his views, and on one occasion he sternly lectured a liberal intellectual:

> Soviet Russia, internally today, is run by a small clique of ruthless, powerful and selfish men who have established a government which denies the Russian people personal freedom and economic security. Soviet Russia today is a slave state of the worst sort. Soviet Russia today is embarked upon a program of world aggression. The freedom-loving countries of the world must stop Soviet Russia now, or be destroyed. The people in the United States have been far too gullible with respect to the publicity being disseminated throughout the world by the clever and brilliant Moscow propagandists.[2]

He was also unafraid to criticize decisions that came from a Democratic White House. Believing that the UN was a paper tiger, Kennedy publicly complained: "We should never have yielded to Russia and allowed the UN charter to embody the principle that a single veto by one of the big powers can stop action by the United Nations."[3] Kennedy did however enthusiastically support the Truman Doctrine and the Marshall Plan. He believed that the success of these programs helped keep the Soviets at bay. If the programs failed, he said, "the barriers would be down and the Red Tide would flow across the face of Europe and through Asia with new power and vigor."[4]

While he "possessed the affectation of a Brahmin" and accepted much of the liberalism of his Harvard associates, Kennedy also possessed an understanding of the social conservatism of his Roman Catholic constituents. Biographer Thomas Maier points out that JFK "acted as a stalwart supporter of the Church, both for calculated political reasons and out of his own convictions."[5] In a speech he gave in 1950 at Notre Dame, Kennedy sounded like a Thomistic scholar when describing the nature of man: "You have been taught that each individual has an eternal soul, composed of an intellect which can know truth and a will which is free. . . . Believing this, Catholics can never adhere to any political theory which holds that the state is a separate, distinct organization to which allegiance must be paid rather than a representative institution which derives its powers from the consent of the governed."[6] He also cautioned the graduates about "the absorbing hands of the great Leviathan" and warned against the "ever expanding power of the federal government." He even made a lucid statement on the principle of subsidiarity, when he said that "control over local affairs is the essence of liberty."[7]

But Kennedy could also be equivocal when it came to certain popular Catholic issues: After a public brawl erupted between Cardinal Spellman of New York and former First Lady Eleanor Roosevelt over the merits of direct federal aid to parochial schools, Kennedy took a "middle" position in order to avoid offending supporters on either side of the issue. To please liberals, he opposed such aid as unconstitutional. To placate the Church and his conservative constituents, he vigorously argued that Catholic students should receive direct aid for health services, transportation, and textbooks.

During congressional hearings on the 1947 Education Aid Bill, Kennedy became something of a folk hero to many Catholics when he took on Elmer Rogers, assistant to the Sovereign Grand Commander of the Southern Freemasons. During his testimony, Rogers had stated that the Catholic Church wanted a theocratic society and had ambitions "to be a world government." He declared that Catholic families were excommunicated if they did not send their children to parochial schools. An agitated Kennedy responded: "I never went to parochial school. . . . I am a Catholic and yet my parents were never debarred from the sacraments, so the statement is wrong." He also informed the witness that "I am not a legal subject of the Pope."

"There is an old saying in Boston," he went on, "that we get our religion from Rome and our politics at home, and that is the way most Catholics feel about it."[8] Commenting on the education-aid controversy, the Boston *Pilot* reported: "The principles are still clear but, unhappily, the prejudices remain powerful. . . . Standing out as a white knight against the crepuscular haze we are very proud of our own Congressman John F. Kennedy."[9]

*   *   *   *   *

Bored with the slow pace of the House of Representatives and anxious to execute the next step in the plan to reach the White House, Jack Kennedy decided to take on Massachusetts's leading Brahmin, Senator Henry Cabot Lodge, Jr., who was up for re-election in 1952.

Although Lodge had easily won three previous Senate elections, he was viewed as a weak campaigner with no effective statewide political organization. But poor campaigning is one thing; no campaigning is another. Lodge was overconfidently preoccupied with the presidential campaign of Dwight D. Eisenhower, in which he was serving as a senior advisor. He was spending little time tending to the needs of his commonwealth constituents.

So Jack Kennedy believed Lodge's seat was ripe for the taking and figured that if he beat so major a figure, he would receive instant national fame as a giant killer. And there was another reason the race was attractive: the Kennedys could settle an old family score. In 1916, Honey Fitz had lost a closely contested Senate race to Henry Cabot Lodge, Sr.

In the 1952 Senate campaign, the Kennedy family pulled out all the stops: Money, power, and pressure were applied on pols, newspapers, ands churchmen to promote Jack's candidacy.

One key issue in the race was, again, Joe McCarthy's anti-Communist crusade. The Kennedys knew McCarthy was immensely popular in Massachusetts, but – as in his first run for Congress – they did not want Jack to publicly embrace the Wisconsin firebrand because it might offend Harvard liberals.

It was a difficult situation: McCarthy had received political contributions from Joe Kennedy and had even dated Jack Kennedy's sister, Eunice. And Jack Kennedy was on record defending McCarthy: at a Harvard lecture a speaker had suggested that McCarthy and Alger Hiss were two sides of the same coin. Congressman Kennedy scolded him saying, "How dare you couple the name of a great American patriot with that of a traitor."[10]

Jack Kennedy had been elected three times to the House, and by now the famous Kennedy charisma was becoming an electoral steamroller, and the Lodge camp, seeing that they were in trouble, resorted to a desperate measure: they privately asked McCarthy to come to Massachusetts in support of Lodge. McCarthy, who had no use for his Senate colleague and no intention of betraying his friendship with the Kennedys, told Lodge's advisors that he would only come to Boston if the senator himself made a public request. McCarthy was confident the invitation would not be forthcoming. "[Lodge] will never do that," he told William F. Buckley Jr., "he'd lose the Harvard vote."[11]

McCarthy was right, and his absence undoubtedly had an impact. On election day, as Democrats lost both the presidency and control of Congress in Eisenhower's victory, the single Democratic highlight was John Kennedy's razor-thin upset over Henry Cabot Lodge: 1,211,984 votes versus 1,141,247 votes.

*   *   *   *   *

Throughout his first term in the U.S. Senate, Kennedy never lost sight of the end game – the presidency. And his first major move to achieve national recognition was at the 1956 National Democratic Convention.

The polls and the pols agreed that Adlai Stevenson would once again be the Democratic presidential nominee, and so all eyes turned to the number-two spot on the ticket. Ever since President Eisenhower's 1955 heart attack, the vice presidency had begun to receive more serious attention. And since Stevenson had lost a significant subset of Catholic voters in 1952, the political pros started talking up the case for a Catholic on the ticket as a way to regain their support.

So the Kennedy organization began promoting JFK as the most logical choice. To enhance their efforts, Kennedy aide Theodore Sorensen prepared a sixteen-page document that analyzed how essential Catholic voters were to Democratic victories at the polls. To make sure the study was not labeled as self-serving, Sorensen persuaded the Catholic chairman of Connecticut's Democratic Party, John M. Bailey, to circulate the study under his name – hence it became known as the "Bailey Memorandum."

The study was a remarkable document that drew on the work of election analysts Samuel Lubell and Louis Bean. It built on Lubell's belief that "Catholic voting strength [was] currently at its peak in view of the maturing of the offspring of the Italians, Poles, Czechs and other former immigrant elements."[12] The report pointed out that while the Catholic vote represented about 25 percent of the total pool of voters, 80 percent of them were located in the pivotal states of the North and Midwest. The electoral votes in these key states totaled 261, which was 5 short of the number needed to win.

Key Democratic-Catholic States

	A	B	C	D
New York	32%	40%	6.0%	45
Pennsylvania	29	39	3.0	32
Illinois	30	34	5.0	27
New Jersey	39	47	7.5	16
Massachusetts	50	57	4.4	16
Connecticut	49	55	5.9	8
Rhode Island	60	65	0.9	4
California	22	27	6.9	32
Michigan	24	30	5.8	20
Minnesota	24	27	5.6	11
Ohio	20	25	6.8	25
Wisconsin	32	38	11.2	12
Maryland	21	31	5.8	9
Montana	22	26	9.7	4
	(Needed to win: 266)			261

Key: A: Proportion of Catholics in adult population
      B: Estimated proportion of 1952 two-party vote made up of Catholic voters
      C: Eisenhower's margin over 50% of the 1952 two-party vote
      D: Electoral vote

Summary Analysis of Key Democratic-Catholic States

- In 1940, thirteen of these States with 240 electoral votes went Democratic, *without which the Democrats would have lost the election.*
- In 1944, twelve of these States with 221 electoral votes went Democratic, *without which the Democrats would have lost the election.*
- In 1948, eight of these States with 125 electoral votes went Democratic, *without which the Democrats would have lost the election.*
- In 1952, none of these States went Democratic, all 261 of their electoral votes went to Eisenhower, thus making possible the first Republican victory in twenty-four years.

The memo further argued that the turnout of Catholic voters in these major urban areas often determined the margins by which these states went Democratic:

Key Democratic-Catholic Cities

	A	B
New York City	38%	3.6%
Buffalo	62	8.6
Rochester	38	9.8
Albany	38	Not Available
Philadelphia	42	(gain) 8.0
Pittsburgh	46	5.0
Scranton	49	Not Available
Chicago	49	4.2
Newark-Jersey City	53	5.4
Trenton	46	Not Available
Boston	55	11.8
Hartford	59	Not Available
Baltimore	31	3.1
San Francisco	33	4.2
Los Angeles	22	5.2
Detroit	39	1.4
Minneapolis-St. Paul	30	9.0
Milwaukee	41	9.4
Cleveland	36	4.6
Cincinnati	25	5.5
Toledo	25	4.0

Key: A: Estimated proportion of 1952 two-party vote made up of Catholic voters
B: Decline in Democratic proportion of two-party vote from 1948 to 1952

Analysis of Voting Patterns of Key Democratic-Catholic Cities
1940–1952

- In 1940, without net margins in New York, Chicago, Hudson County (Jersey City), Philadelphia-Pittsburgh, Providence, and Milwaukee, the Democrats would have lost New York (47), Illinois (29), New Jersey (16), Pennsylvania (26), Rhode Island (4), and Wisconsin (12), or a total loss of 144 electoral votes.

- In 1944, without their net margins in New York, Hartford and New Haven, Chicago, Baltimore, Detroit, Hudson County (Jersey City), Minneapolis-St. Paul and Philadelphia, Democrats would have lost New York (47), Connecticut (18), Illinois (28), Maryland (8), Michigan (19), New Jersey (16), Minnesota (11), and Pennsylvania (35), or a total loss of 172 electoral votes – *and the Republicans would have won the election.*

- In 1948, without their net margins in Chicago, Los Angeles, Cleveland and Providence, the Democrats would have lost Illinois (28 electoral votes), California (25), Ohio (25), and Rhode Island (4), or a total loss of 82 electoral votes – *and the Republicans would have won the election.*

- In 1952, as shown on Table 2, the Democratic vote in all of the major cities except Philadelphia fell sharply, and these cities for the first time in twenty-four years did not contribute a single electoral vote to the Democrats, thus making possible the first Republican victory in twenty-four years.

The study went on to cite results of Gallup, Roper, and University of Michigan polling data which indicated that the shift of Catholic ethnics toward the Republicans in 1952 was decisive in determining the outcome of the election: Catholics who normally are 65 percent Democratic went 47 percent for Eisenhower, and Germans went 55 percent, Poles 50 percent and Irish 53 percent. Roper's polling concluded that if the trends continued "the important Irish and German voters, in particular, would become largely an independent group sharply affecting Democratic majorities in Northern cities."

Catholic "shifters" – as they were labeled by pollsters – totaled 7 percent of Eisenhower's national vote. And the memorandum reminded the Democrats that if Stevenson had held on to those Catholic votes he would have won the presidency.

	A	B	C	D
New York	35%	11%	11.0%	45
Pennsylvania	36	6	11.0	32
Illinois	31	9	9.3	27
Massachusetts	51	8	15.3	16
Connecticut	48	11	14.4	8
Rhode Island	63	15	18.9	4
New Jersey	40	13		16
California	23	12		32
Michigan	27	10		20
Minnesota	23	10		20
Ohio	21	12		25
Wisconsin	30	18		12
Maryland	27	10		9
Montana	21	16		4
	(Needed to win: 266)			261

Key: A: Estimated percent of Eisenhower vote in 1952 made up of Catholic voters

B: Proportion of Eisenhower vote constituting margin by which he carried state

C: Estimated percent of Eisenhower vote in 1952 made up of "normally Democratic" Catholic voters who shifted

D: Electoral votes

The report also listed examples of local Democratic Catholic candidates for Senate and Congress who managed to hold on to the Catholic vote and run ahead of the 1952 national ticket:

Examples of Democratic-Catholic Local Races – 1952

- Zablocki won in Milwaukee by 29 percent while Stevenson was losing by 4 percent.
- O'Brien won in Albany by 7 percent while Stevenson was losing by 9 percent.
- Delaney won in New York City by 2 percent while Stevenson was losing by 13 percent.
- Addonizio and Rodino won in Newark by 4 percent and 14 percent respectively while Stevenson was losing by 4 percent and 7 percent.
- Rabaut won in Detroit by 6 percent while Stevenson was losing by 2 percent.
- Dodd won in Hartford by 8 percent while Stevenson was losing by 1 percent.

The study concluded that in order to bring home these wayward voters, adding a Catholic to the national ticket would not only be helpful, it might make the difference between victory and defeat:

> If [a Catholic V.P.] brought into the Democratic fold only those normally Democratic Catholics who voted for Ike, he would probably swing New York, Massachusetts, Rhode Island, Connecticut, Pennsylvania, and Illinois – for 132 electoral votes. If he also wins the votes of Catholics who shifted to the Republicans in 1948 or earlier, he could also swing New Jersey, Minnesota, Michigan, California, Wisconsin, Ohio, Maryland, Montana, and maybe even New Hampshire – for a total of 265 electoral votes (needed to win: 266). Thus Ike could and would be defeated.

To enhance the case, the memo cited a recent Gallup poll (June 1956) which stated that three out of four respondents had said they would vote for a well-qualified Catholic – nominated by their party "for the Presidency itself." It also concluded that with a Catholic on the ticket, diminished Democratic margins in the South would not be enough to lose many electoral votes in that region and anyway would be offset by gains in the North.

As the Democratic convention in Chicago approached, Jack Kennedy began to take a serious interest in the V.P. spot, but – perhaps surprisingly – his father and some other advisors vigorously opposed the move. Convinced that Stevenson was a loser regardless of who was on the ticket, Joe Kennedy feared that if Jack accepted the second spot, he would be blamed by the Stevenson camp for the defeat.

By the time the delegates arrived in Chicago, whether or not to run appeared to be a moot question for JFK because the politically naïve Stevenson had decided he needed a southerner on the ticket.[13] Stevenson had failed to understand that if he recovered all the southern states he lost to Ike in 1952, he would pick up only 88 electoral votes and still be 89 short of victory.

Kennedy received national attention at the convention when on the first night he narrated a film celebrating the virtues of the Roosevelt-Truman years. *The New York Times* reported that Kennedy, with his "movie star" looks, had achieved instant celebrity status.[14]

On the second night of the convention, Stevenson, who was dead set against giving Kennedy the number two spot, nonetheless gave him the consolation prize: Kennedy was asked to place Stevenson's name in nomination. But then a remarkable thing happened. After his first ballot nomination, the Hamlet-like Stevenson, unable to make up his mind about who his running mate should be, asked the delegates to make the choice for him in an open vote.

It was too much for Jack Kennedy to resist. Going against the wishes of his angry father, JFK decided to make a run against the acknowledged front runner, Senator Estes Kefauver of Tennessee. The Kennedy team demonstrated its organizational skill by quickly pulling together an ad-hoc operation. Jack's brother, Bobby, along with John Bailey and Governor Abraham Ribicoff of Connecticut, raced through hotels, reaching out to key delegation chairmen. Coming up against thick-headed Catholic bosses who were leery about having one of their own on the ticket caused Ribicoff to remark, "I didn't think that the time would ever come where a Jew would have to stand up in a room full of Catholics to urge the acceptability of a Catholic."[15]

When Kefauver came up 200 votes shy of a majority on the first ballot, a Kennedy surge occurred on the second ballot. JFK came within 38 votes of the nomination (648 votes versus Kefauver's 551), but his momentum was short-lived: Kefauver's managers convinced several southern delegations to switch their votes, and it was enough to put the Tennessean over the top.

On national television, Jack Kennedy graciously accepted defeat and gave a rousing endorsement of the Democratic ticket. In defeat, he had won national recognition and was viewed by many Democrats as sure presidential material for 1960.

As he criss-crossed the nation campaigning for Stevenson in the fall, the self-deprecating Kennedy often told his audiences that, "Socrates once said that it was the duty of a man of real principle to avoid high national office, and evidently the delegates at Chicago recognized my principles even before I did."[16]

Shortly after Stevenson's 1956 defeat, Jack sat down with his father to discuss his presidential prospects for 1960. JFK listed the negatives: he would be just forty-two years old in 1960; only one U.S. Senator in the twentieth century had been elected president; and, of course, there was the Catholic question. After hearing Jack out, Joe gave a father-son lecture that concluded with these words:

> Just remember, this country is not a private preserve for Protestants . . . There's a whole new generation out there and it's filled with the sons and daughters of immigrants from all over the world and those people are going to be mighty proud that one of their own is running for President. And that pride will be your spur, it will give your campaign an intensity we've never seen in public life. Mark my word, I know it's true.[17]

With his father's blessing, Jack Kennedy was running and for the next four years, all of the Kennedy clan's energy, power, and money were directed toward winning the White House.

*   *   *   *   *

The age-old anti-Catholic issue, which was dormant during the Age of Roosevelt, was awakened in the post-war era. It was revived by a New York lawyer, Paul Blanshard, who authored a series of articles in 1948 that appeared in the left-wing journal, *The Nation*. Published in book form the next year by the Beacon Press, *American Freedom and Catholic Power* argued that loyalty to the Vatican prevented Catholics from being loyal to the United States. Church canon law, Blanshard contended, forbade Catholics from believing in the primacy of individual conscience, and the hierarchical organization of the Church stifled individual freedom.

Blanshard repeated many of the charges that were voiced during the heyday of the Know-Nothings and the APA. He simply replaced the crude words "Popery" or "Romanism" with the more grandiose "Catholic Power." He accused the pope of being an "idol" to whom "Catholic people are slaves who came to worship him." According to Blanshard:

> The Pope "has power to declare what is right and wrong by divine fiat," "the continuing corruption (by the Church) of human intelligence by systematically cultivated superstition . . . the devices for exploiting relics. . . . The most patent ecclesiastical frauds in the fields of relics and apparitions must be accepted without a murmur. . . . In the Catholic religious orders . . . recruiting, in fact, is largely based on the guilt feelings of youth and adolescence about sex, and the conviction of sin is systematically exploited to induce a commitment to the Religious vocation. . . . Monastery life is a mixture of selflessness and egotism, of religious fanaticism and social stupidity. . . . Priests are . . . encouraged to play upon the lowest superstitions of their people."[18]

He also argued that no true Catholic "can agree with the doctrine of Church-State separation in its American constitutional form and remain true to Vatican policy."

Blanshard's book, which went through six printings and sold 250,000 copies, pointed to Jack Kennedy's hometown, Boston, as a hotbed of Catholic insurrection. "Boston," he complained, "is aggressively Catholic largely because it is aggressively Irish, and it is aggressively Irish because its people have not quite overcome their sense of being strangers in a hostile land."[19] He accused other cities of being "Bostonized," by which he meant they were under papal control: Providence, Milwaukee, Buffalo, Newark, and San Francisco.[20]

Responding to his call for action, a group formed that named itself Protestants and Other Americans United for the Separation of Church and

State (POAU). Hiring Blanshard as their special counsel, the organization actively promoted his books and published pamphlets and a magazine, *Church and State*, which boasted 50,000 subscribers. POAU alleged that Catholics were using their growing influence to overthrow the government and create a religious state to be ruled by the pope. Defending the organization, the Alabama Ministerial Association proclaimed in June 1949 that POAU:

> . . . is thoroughly American. Any charge that this organization is unpatriotic, un-American and un-Christian is directed not only against the leaders of this organization but against the rank and file of Baptists, Methodists, Presbyterians, Episcopalians, Lutherans, and others who believe firmly in this principle [of separation of Church and State].[21]

Jack Kennedy knew he could not ignore groups like POAU, so part of his four-year presidential game plan was to personally defuse the issues they raised as best he could. So he rescinded his support of aid to parochial schools, reversed his support for diplomatic recognition of the Vatican, and went against the Church hierarchy by endorsing foreign aid to Communist Yugoslavia. He also portrayed himself as a sophisticated Harvard man who was totally different from the parochial Al Smith of 1928.

In March 1959, *Look* magazine commissioned Fletcher Knebel to write a major article titled "A Catholic in 1960." Kennedy happily cooperated with the author, believing it was a perfect opportunity to articulate his church-state positions to a national audience.

In his interviews with Knebel, Kennedy reiterated his support for public policies that were contrary to Church pronouncements, and he described his views on the Constitution. As Knebel wrote:

> "Whatever one's religion in his private life may be," he says, "for the officeholder, nothing takes precedence over his oath to uphold the Constitution and all its parts – including the First Amendment and the strict separation of church and state. Without reference to the presidency," he adds, "I believe as a senator that the separation of church and state is fundamental to our American concept and heritage and should remain so."[22]

Kennedy hoped his comments would eliminate Protestant concerns, which to some extent they certainly did. What he did not count on were Catholic concerns about his defensive view of his faith. Biographer Thomas Maier relates that "many [Catholics] thought Kennedy was striving too hard to dismiss his own cultural heritage:[23] The *Indiana Catholic and Record* cautioned that "Young Senator Kennedy had better watch his language." The remarks in *Look* article, the *Record* said, "have set Catholics fighting among themselves."[24] Ted Sorensen conceded that Kennedy had come across in Knebel's article as "a poor Catholic, a poor politician, a poor moralist and a poor wordsmith."[25] But despite this bump in the road, Kennedy stuck to the roadmap devised in 1956.

During the off-year election season in 1958, Kennedy's political mechanics organized a spectacular Massachusetts re-election campaign while Jack logged tens of thousands of miles campaigning for candidates across the nation. An incumbent president's party can usually expect to suffer dramatic losses in mid-term congressional elections, and 1958 was no different for Ike's Republicans, who were thrashed at the polls. The Republicans lost thirteen Senate seats, forty-seven House seats, and five governorships. Democrats made their greatest gains since 1936, and Jack Kennedy had a spectacular election night, garnering 73.2 percent of the vote: the largest margin of victory in his state's history.

Other Catholic politicians also made inroads in 1959. Catholic governors were elected in California, Hawaii, Pennsylvania, and Ohio. Four more Catholics were elected to the U.S. Senate, so that by January 1, 1959, twelve U.S. Senate seats, eight governors, and one hundred and two Congressmen were Catholics. Political scientist John Fenton concluded that "the 1958 elections lend substance to the notion that a Catholic candidate's religion would not be a serious political handicap. In fact, given the tendency of Catholics to discriminate more than Protestants on the basis of religion, and the concentration of much of the unreconstructed Protestant vote in the Democratic South (an automatic religious gerrymander), the outlook would seem to be happy for a Catholic candidate."[26]

*   *   *   *   *

When Jack Kennedy announced his candidacy for president of the United States in the Senate Caucus Room on January 2, 1960, he knew he could probably not win a brokered convention. The best way to prove his electability was in the primaries.

In 1960, there were just sixteen presidential primaries. Two (New Hampshire and Massachusetts) were not considered real contests, since they were in Kennedy's backyard and on his home turf. Others, such as California and Florida, had favorite sons who would be offended if anyone challenged them on their own states. That left about seven real contests, the first of which was Wisconsin.

In Wisconsin, he faced off with Minnesota senator Hubert H. Humphrey. Some pundits predicted the primary was a sure win for HHH, since it was next door to his home state. But the state's Catholic population was 31 percent, and the Kennedy camp viewed the race as competitive and hoped a victory in "Humphrey Country" would knock Humphrey out of the race.

As Kennedy campaigned in Wisconsin, he couldn't avoid the Catholic issue. The press buzzed around constantly questioning if he could make inroads in Protestant regions. Full-page newspaper ads suggesting Kennedy was controlled by the pope fueled the issue.

But on primary night, Tuesday, April 5, 1960, Kennedy easily beat Humphrey 56.5 percent to 43.5 percent. Good news, and yet the numbers had not broken as JFK had hoped. Humphrey carried the rural Protestant regions while Kennedy carried the heavily Catholic industrial areas that had once loved Joe McCarthy.

1960 Wisconsin Democratic Primary[27]
Top Ten Counties Carried by Kennedy

	Percent Kennedy	Percent Catholic	No. of Votes Kennedy	No. of Votes Humphrey
Brown	78.1	60.7	19,770	5,555
Portage	75.3	64.3	7,540	2,475
Outagamie	75.0	46.4	13,310	4,431
Calumet	73.1	58.6	2,754	1,011
Kewaunee	71.0	61.3	2,644	1,077
Maitowoc	70.2	47.8	12,428	5,280
Kenosha	65.0	34.6	13,397	7,223
Washington	64.9	45.2	5,517	2,983
Ozaukee	64.1	42.0	4,572	2,557
Oconto	64.1	29.3	3,234	1,807

1960 Wisconsin Democratic Primary[28]
Top Ten Counties Lost by Kennedy

	Percent Kennedy	Percent Catholic	No. of Votes Kennedy	No. of Votes Humphrey
Monroe	38.5	19.2	2,486	3,974
Buffalo	36.9	13.4	1,091	1,868
Barron	36.7	22.1	2,489	4,297
Eau Claire	36.6	13.3	5,137	8,885
Adams	34.6	7.4	543	1,024
Dunn	28.1	8.5	1,408	3,600
Jackson	27.8	8.0	1,085	2,821
Burnett	27.3	7.0	562	1,499
Polk	26.9	6.0	1,285	3,482
Vernon	21.4	7.4	1,294	4,756

After analyzing the Wisconsin results, pollster Elmo Roper revised his position expressed in a 1959 article, "The Myth of the Catholic Voter," writing ". . . this Spring's primaries suggested that with the Presidency at stake, religion had become a matter of much greater importance; and recent survey results confirm it's important for Catholics and non-Catholics alike."[29]

When asked on primary night what the results mean, Kennedy, who knew that he had to prove he was more than a Catholic candidate, replied: "It means that we have to do it all over again. We have to go through every [primary] and win every one of them – West Virginia, Maryland and Indiana and Oregon, all the way to the Convention."[30]

Kennedy racked up April primary victories in Illinois, Massachusetts, and Indiana, but for the pols and the press they were meaningless. It was a numbers game, and the Democratic nomination came down to the May 10th West Virginia primary.

And West Virginia's Catholic population was a mere 3 percent, "the smallest proportional Catholic population of any state" – as JFK often reminded the press. In the most Protestant of Protestant states, Kennedy decided upon the riskiest strategy imaginable: he would tackle the Catholic issue head-on in the hope that his opposition would be caught off-guard. The former Harvard football player knew that the best defense is a strong offense. So in a statewide television broadcast on the Sunday before the election, Kennedy answered questions about his faith put to him by emcee Franklin D. Roosevelt, Jr. Kennedy told the audience that as president he would swear to uphold the Constitution, which includes the separation of church and state. To violate that oath he said, "would be committing a sin against God." To illustrate the point, Kennedy, "raised his hand from an imaginary Bible, as if lifting it to God,' and repeating softly, said 'A sin against God, for he has sworn on the Bible.'"[31]

The gamble paid off: Kennedy's statement, plus his well-heeled organization, succeeded in making "tolerance" the key issue in the primary. To prove they really were open-minded, West Virginians handed Kennedy a stunning victory. He received 60.8 percent to Humphrey's 39.2 percent. *The New York Times* reported the next day, "If Senator Kennedy is to be turned down, those in control of the convention will be under heavy pressure to make a convincing demonstration that his religion was not officially responsible."[32]

Between May and the July convention, various "Stop Kennedy" cabals failed and he was nominated on the first ballot in Los Angeles. In his nationally televised acceptance speech on July 15, Kennedy first thanked the delegates and then addressed the religious issue:

> I am fully aware of the fact that the Democratic Party, by

nominating someone of my faith, has taken on what many regard as a new and hazardous risk – new, at least, since 1928. But I look at it this way:

The Democratic Party has once again placed its confidence in the American people, and in their ability to render a free, fair judgment.

And you have, at the same time, placed your confidence in me, and in my ability to render a free, fair judgment – to uphold the Constitution and my oath of office – and to reject any kind of religious pressure or obligation that might directly or indirectly interfere with my conduct of the Presidency in the national interest.

My record of fourteen years supporting public education – supporting complete separation of church and state – and resisting pressures from any source on any issue should be clear by now to everyone.

I hope that no American, considering the really critical issues facing this country, will waste his franchise by voting either for me or against me solely on account of my religious affiliation. It is not relevant. I want to stress what some other political or religious leader may have said on this subject. It is not relevant what abuses may have existed in other countries or in other times. It is not relevant what pressures, if any, might conceivably be brought to bear on me.

I am telling you now what you are entitled to know:

That my decisions on any public policy will be my own – as an American, a Democrat and a free man.[33]

As the campaign began, however, the religious issue haunted Kennedy. In early August, Protestant organizations in Michigan and Kentucky announced their opposition to electing a Catholic president.[34] Later in the month, twenty-five Baptist, Methodist, and Pentecostal ministers promised to "oppose with all powers at our command, the election of a Catholic to the Presidency of the United States."[35] Numerous other groups representing tens of thousands of Protestants voiced similar anti-Catholic oppositions to Kennedy.

The Kennedy team realized the issue was hemorrhaging when on September 7, an ad-hoc group of 150 Protestants led by the renowned Dr. Norman Vincent Peale issued a statement criticizing the Catholic Church and accusing it of being a "political as well as religious organization [that has] specifically repudiated, on many occasions, the principle sacred to us that every man shall be free to follow the dictates of his conscience in religious matters."[36]

Later that same day, POAU launched another political torpedo:

> . . . we cannot avoid recognition of the fact that one church in the U.S., the largest church operating on American soil, officially supports a world-wide policy of partial union of church and state wherever it has the power to enforce such a policy. In the U.S. the bishops of this church have specifically rejected the Supreme Court's interpretation of the separation of church and state.[37]

Kennedy realized once again that he could not ignore these diatribes, and he decided to confront the issue at a meeting of the Greater Houston Ministerial Association on September 12, 1960:

> I believe in an America where the separation of church and state is absolute – where no Catholic prelate would tell the President (should he be Catholic) how to act, and no Protestant minister would tell his parishioners for whom to vote – where no church or church school is granted any public funds or political preference – and where no man is denied public office merely because his religion differs from the President who might appoint him or the people who might elect him.
>
> I believe in an America that is officially neither Catholic, Protestant nor Jewish – where no public official either requests or accepts instructions on public policy from the Pope, the National Council of Churches or any other ecclesiastical source – where no religious body seeks to impose its will directly or indirectly upon the general populace or the public acts of its officials – and where religious liberty is so indivisible that an act against one church is treated as an act against all.[38]

While the Houston speech did appear to allay the fears of many, the anti-Catholicism in the campaign did not fade away. Instead it went underground, reappearing in pamphlets printed on basement presses. "The record shows," reported Professor Patricia Barrett, "that professional bigots were more active in 1960 than in 1928 and further their output was swamped by that of the more 'respectable' non-professional anti-Catholics. And the content of the bulk of the material published in 1960 was infinitely more sophisticated."[39]

The Fair Campaign Practices Committee reported that 392 different anti-Catholic pamphlets were published. Estimates of their estimated circulation are as high as 25 million. These brochures, pamphlets, and newspapers publicized issues that went back to the days of the Know-Nothings, e.g.,. that a Catholic's first allegiance is to the pope; that the Catholic hierarchy controls the lives of the faithful; that a Catholic president will establish a Catholic state; and that a Catholic president will force Catholic moral codes on all the American people.

Archbishop Karl Alter of Cincinnati, on behalf of the Church, refuted these charges:

> The fear that we as Catholics will use religious toleration here to gain the ascendancy in our country, and then, having achieved political hegemony, proceed to deprive our fellow citizens of freedom of speech in religion, freedom of conscience, or impose our convictions upon them willy-nilly, is utterly unwarranted by any doctrine of the Catholic Church, as well as by the consistent pronouncements of the American hierarchy. We seek no privileged status; we proclaim our full adherence to the provisions of the Constitution as of now as well as for the future.[40]

Kennedy's statements on the relation of church and state did not, however, sit well with all Catholics. And some members of the hierarchy (i.e., Francis Cardinal Spellman) were not pleased that by re-inventing himself and currying favor with liberals, Kennedy had discarded federal issues, such as aid to parochial schools, which were important to the Church.

America's leading Catholic thinker, John Courtney Murray, s.J., who had written extensively on the role of the Catholic Church in a pluralist society, was perturbed by Kennedy's attempt to sever any connection between one's religious and political creeds. "To make religion merely a private matter," Murray argued, "was idiocy." Murray "played on the Greek word *idiotes*, which originally signified a private person with no responsibility for public affairs and gradually came to mean a person who was irresponsible."[41] Assessing Kennedy's views, Historian William Miller has concluded: "The joke was that [Kennedy] turned out to be, in effect, our first Baptist president – one, that is, who defended a thorough-going separation more characteristic of that group than of his own church. . ."[42]

Dr. Robert Royal, president of the Faith and Reason Institute in Washington, D.C., made this observation about the Houston speech:

> Kennedy's speech to the Texas ministers was very clever and mostly right. But it was a strange concession for any Christian, let alone a Catholic, to say that he believed in an America "where no

religious body seeks to impose its will directly or indirectly" on
public matters. This means that religion should have no proper
public role – a view more suited to Nazi Germany, the old Soviet
Union, or modern France than to America. It is impossible to
understand the basis of American democracy, or something like
the civil rights movement, without religion. And since most
Americans take their moral bearings from their faith, it was
inevitable that conflicts over issues like abortion would confound
such pat separations. Kennedy seemed to suggest that religion is
fine for a politician so long as it's merely personal, though maybe
it should not be too personal for him either.[43]

Joe Kennedy, who had financially supported Church causes for decades,
was livid that the hierarchy was silent on his son's candidacy. He had expected that, at the very least, directions would have been given to parishes, *sotto
voce* if necessary, to get Catholics to the polls to support one of their own.

One reason for the lack of Church support was a fear of a Protestant backlash. According to Kennedy biographer Thomas Maier, America's leading
prelate, Francis Cardinal Spellman, "adopted a position in 1960 that he considered best for the Church rather than the interests of one family. Spellman
believed Richard Nixon would be more flexible to the Church's needs than
Jack Kennedy [because Nixon] was not handcuffed by his own words on the
separation of church and state. All the issues pressed by the Catholic hierarchy – funding for parochial schools, a U.S. ambassador at the Vatican, tough
stands on communism and sexual morality – would be likely pushed by
Nixon."[44]

As the 1960 Kennedy campaign progressed, there were certain ironies:
On the one hand, there were certain outspoken liberal journalists who had
used the anti-Catholic card against Joe McCarthy but were now supporting
Kennedy and attacking Catholic bashing. Murray Kempton described them
as "bigots who are our worst Catholic baiters." The left-wing *New Republic*,
for instance, criticized Protestant groups as bigots for their anti-Catholicism
in 1960, but a few years earlier had proclaimed Paul Blanshard's blatantly
bigoted book, *American Freedom and Catholic Power*, as "written with careful objectivity – a patient, honest attempt to break through a hush-hush
smokescreen. . ."[45] Writing in the *Indianapolis News* just a month before the
election, conservative columnist Ralph de Toledano commented that "it is an
irony of the situation that the most concerted attack on the Catholic Church
in the past decade came from liberals and leftists – many of whom now support Kennedy for their own good reasons – who made a best seller of Paul
Blanshard's book. . . . That Blanshard should have fanned the flames of

bigotry is not nearly so important as the reaction of the liberal gentry – now bleating that the GOP is anti-Catholic – to this vulgar rabble rousing book."[46]

The campaign of 1960 was one of the most exciting in America's history. John F. Kennedy and Richard M. Nixon, two attractive, talented, ambitious men, both in their forties and both World War II Navy veterans, criss-crossed the nation in search of votes. It was the first campaign to utilize television extensively. Millions of Americans were able to see and hear the candidates, and the sound bite was invented. When it came to this new medium, Jack Kennedy and his organization outpaced, outspent, and outclassed the Nixon operation.

On November 8, 1960, election day, a record-breaking 64.5 percent of eligible voters went to the polls, and John F. Kennedy was elected with 34.2 million votes (49.7 percent) to Richard Nixon's 34.1 million (49.6 percent). The electoral college broke 303 for JFK and 219 for Nixon.

The election was so close that if 12,000 votes had shifted in Illinois or Missouri or New Mexico or Hawaii, the outcome would have been reversed.

Throughout the campaign, Kennedy had stuck to the 1956 Bailey Plan, and this is why he won. Inner-city Catholic votes unquestionably provided his margin of victory. Theodore H. White, author of *The Making of the President 1960*, agreed: "There is no doubt that millions of Americans, Protestants and Catholics, voted in 1960 primordially out of instinct [and kinship]." Out of pride, 67 percent of Catholics who supported Eisenhower in 1956 swung back to Kennedy and boosted his total share of the Catholic vote to over 70 percent. Kennedy received about 70 percent of the Italian vote, 66 percent of Polish, 68 percent of the Irish and 50 percent of the German Catholic vote.

The results also proved that a significant number of Protestants had voted against Kennedy because of his religion. In fact, JFK was the first man elected president who *did not* receive a majority of the Protestant voter. IBM political analysts peg Kennedy's Protestant support at 46 percent while Gallup puts it at 38 percent. It is estimated that 4.5 million Protestant Democrats (mostly in the South) switched to Nixon. This was evident in the fact that Nixon's southern vote totals were actually higher than Ike's had been in 1956. Nixon managed to carry Florida, Virginia, Tennessee, and Kentucky, and he came within 1 percent of carrying Texas, South Carolina, and Missouri. Kennedy's southern numbers lagged behind Adlai Stevenson's, even as JFK ran 10 percent ahead of him in the Northeast.

Nixon's huge majorities in Iowa, Nebraska, and in North and South Dakota – formerly William Jennings Bryan country – were the result of Protestant distaste for Kennedy. Results there were similar to those in Milton County, Kentucky, where religious solidarity was most evident: in four

Protestant precincts, Nixon received 65 percent of the vote, and in five
Catholic precincts, Kennedy garnered 88 percent. The University of Michigan
Survey concluded "American Protestants were remarkably preoccupied by the
fact that Kennedy was a Catholic."[47] But then so were Catholics.

Democratic Presidential Vote in Six Predominantly Catholic Counties in Minnesota (percent)

County	1928	1932	1948	1952	1960
Mahnoman	69.5	86.8	78.6	54.1	67.9
Red Lake	67.9	84.4	74.9	58.1	73.3
Benton	53.5	74.6	63.1	40.2	55.8
Morrison	57.6	75.3	60.6	42.9	62.4
Scott	71.8	81.1	62.4	43.7	62.3
Stearns	71.4	80.3	60.0	35.2	58.3

Democratic Presidential Vote in Ten Predominantly Lutheran Counties in Minnesota (percent)

County	1928	1932	1948	1952	1960
Chippewa	36.4	66.7	60.2	41.8	48.2
Clearwater	38.5	76.1	70.5	51.5	59.9
Brant	45.1	70.2	57.1	40.2	51.0
Kittson	41.4	71.1	74.2	56.5	53.4
Lac qui Parle	39.7	67.6	61.3	41.2	50.5
Norman	29.8	73.3	65.7	44.5	52.6
Otter Tail	30.0	54.3	37.0	24.7	36.9
Pennington	32.3	69.4	65.9	50.7	55.6
Pope	33.0	67.9	60.6	39.9	48.5
Yellow Medicine	46.4	72.5	60.7	42.1	48.9
Total State	41.4	62.3	58.9	44.4	50.9

Jack Kennedy was saved by the urban vote in the rich electoral states of
Northeast and Midwest. In these regions he carried 78 percent of the Catholic
vote, 70 percent of the African-American vote, and 80 percent of the Jewish
vote. After reviewing the inner city vote tallies, pollster Elmo Roper concluded: "If there was a victim of religious prejudice it was Nixon more than
Kennedy. All but one of the states most heavily populated by Catholics went
for Kennedy."[48]

1960 Ethnic Catholic Vote in Key States[49]

| | Irish Voters | | Italian Voters | | Slavic Voters | | Spanish Voters | |
	Kennedy	Nixon	Kennedy	Nixon	Kennedy	Nixon	Kennedy	Nixon
Nation	75%	25%	75%	25%	82%	18%	85%	15%
Arizona							77	23
California							83	17
Colorado							75	25
Connecticut			72	28	77	23		
Illinois	73	27	80	20	73	27		
Indiana					79	21		
Maryland			74	26	85	15		
Mass.	80	20	87	13				
Michigan					90	10		
New Jersey			69	31	72	28		
New Mex.							70	30
New York	60	40	64	36	82	18	77	23
Ohio			83	17	88	12		
Penn.			78	22	78	22		
Rhode Isl.			78	22				
Texas							91	9
Wisconsin					83	17		

In New York, Kennedy's total was 52.6 percent. If it were not for the huge Catholic turnout in New York City where JFK received 62.8 percent and in Buffalo (64.9 percent), he would have lost the Empire State's 45 electoral votes, which comprised 15 percent of his total. The situation was the same in other key Kennedy states:

Kennedy Results

Chicago	63.6%	
Illinois	54.7	27 Electoral Votes
Newark	56.5	
New Jersey	50.4	16 Electoral Votes
Philadelphia	68.1	
Pennsylvania	51.2	32 Electoral Votes
Detroit	71.0	
Michigan	50.9	20 Electoral Votes
St. Louis	66.6	
Missouri	50.3	13 Electoral Votes

Democratic Vote in Selected Predominantly Irish
Precincts in Boston, 1956–1960[50]

	Low Income	Low to Middle Income	Middle Income	Upper-Middle Income
1956: President				
Stevenson	67.8%	55.2%	58.0%	38.8%
1960: President				
Kennedy	89.4	78.8	82.4	69.9

Democratic Vote in Selected Non-Irish
Precincts in Boston, 1956-1960[51]

	Italian	Yankee	African-American	Jewish
1956: President				
Stevenson	57.8%	33.5%	49.4%	8.6%
1960: President				
Kennedy	84.6	42.1	55.2	77.4

Michael Barone concludes that "these figures provide the firmest possible evidence for the irrefutable argument that the 1960 election split the nation along religious, which is to say cultural lines, not along lines of economic class."[52] Put another way: Kennedy's election was not a victory for liberalism, it was a victory for Catholicism.

Chapter 14
The Catholic Voter in the
Age of the Silent Majority

On Inauguration Day, January 20, 1961, American Catholics were understandably proud as they watched John Kennedy being sworn in as president of the United States. JFK was flanked by the first Catholic Senate majority leader, Mike Mansfield, and the first Catholic House majority leader, John McCormack. Catholics knew they had finally arrived. And when the young Cold Warrior told the tyrants in Moscow, Warsaw, East Berlin, Bucharest, and Budapest that "we shall pay any price, bear any burden, meet any hardship, support any friend, oppose any foe to assure the survival and success of liberty," the souls of every ethnic Catholic were stirred.

One thousand days later, on November 22, 1963, these same Catholics would weep to hear the news that their forty-six year old leader had been slain in Dallas. That weekend Catholics joined the entire nation in mourning, and on Monday the 25th they packed their parish churches to pray for the repose of Kennedy's soul.

But as proud as Catholics had been to have one of their own in the White House, proud as they were to see other Catholics rise through the ranks of the Democratic Party, there also increasing concern in ethnic neighborhoods throughout America about the elitist, left-wing drift of the party.

The first signs of this uneasiness were detected in 1960s election returns. Even though 78 percent of Catholics had cast their votes for Kennedy, the total was still below the 80 percent that Al Smith had received in 1928. In fact, Kennedy had enjoyed greater popularity with Jews, who gave him 82 percent of their votes – and this was quite obviously because he was a liberal.

And in many of New York City's Catholic, middle-class neighborhoods, Richard Nixon in had come close to winning or actually had won (see table on page 262).

The Irish, the largest subset of middle-class ethnic Catholics, were becoming the least-contented Democrats. In his work *Beyond the Melting Pot*, Daniel Patrick Moynihan explained it this way:

> The crisis for the conservative Irish came in 1960, when, for the

second time, an Irish Catholic ran for President. It turned out that for many the estrangement from the Democratic Party had gone too deep to be overcome by more primitive appeals. Alfred E. Smith, Jr., announced he was voting for Nixon. In fashionable Greenwich, Connecticut, the grandson of John H. McCooey of Brooklyn turned up ringing doorbells for the straight Republican ticket. Kennedy probably got little more than a bare majority of the Irish vote in New York City. The students at Fordham gave him as much, but it appears it was the Jewish students in the College of Pharmacy who saved that ancient Jesuit institution from going on record as opposed to the election of the first Catholic President of the United States.[1]

Assembly District[2]	Eisenhower 1956	Nixon 1960
13th Queens (German-Irish)	80%	64%
9th Brooklyn (Scandinavian-Irish-Italian)	88	60
2nd Richmond (Italian-Irish)	78	58
9th Queens (German-Irish)	76	56
1st Richmond (Italian-Irish)	75	55
3rd Queens (German-Irish)	74	59
12th Brooklyn (Italian-Irish)	73	53
10th Bronx (Italian-Irish)	70	49
20th Brooklyn (German-Irish)	70	45
3rd Brooklyn (Italian-Irish)	67	47
8th Brooklyn (Italian-Irish)	66	42

In the 1960s, a cultural revolt was brewing among a significant portion of the Catholic voting population. It was overlooked by the government bureaucrats and political commentators who remained under the influence of historians such as Charles Beard, Vernon Parrington, and Frederick Turner, who stressed that economic influences shaped political decisions. "What the purveyors of public policy forgot, or never understood, is that our society is what Catholic scholar Michael Novak calls a trinitarian polity. The underpinnings of this country are not merely a productive economic system and a representative political system, but also a system of moral and cultural values."[3] Novak joined a growing list of historians and sociologists who emphasized "that the energies shaping public life are emotional as well as rational, cultural as well as economic."[4] Historian Richard Hofstadter explained this in 1962:

> In our political life there have always been certain types of cultural issues, questions of faith and morals, tone and style, freedom

and coercion, which become fighting issues. To choose but one example, Prohibition was an issue of this kind during the twenties and early thirties. In the struggle over Prohibition, economic interests played only the most marginal role; the issue mobilized religious and moral convictions, ethnic habits and hostilities, attitudes toward health and sexuality, and other personal preoccupations.[5]

Most recently, political analyst Michael Barone, in *Our Country: The Shaping of American from Roosevelt to Reagan*, rejected the view that America's political history is the "story of progress on the road from nineteenth-century laissez-faire and isolationism to twentieth-century welfare statism and internationalism."[6] He argues that the person qua person makes a difference in the course of history, that actions based on cultural standards have had substantially greater impact on the political landscape than have economic ones. "The voting bases of the traditional Democratic and Republican Parties," Barone writes, "were primarily cultural; both drew allegiance from Americans who saw them not as promoters of their economic status, but as a protector of their way of life."[7] Although economics almost always plays a role in a person's political decision, nevertheless, an individual's cultural foundations cannot be ignored. Jeffersonians vs. Hamiltonians, Jacksonians vs. the Whigs, the Civil War, immigration restrictions, Prohibition, Civil Rights, Vietnam, and questions about the legalization of abortion or drugs – each of these battles for the soul of America has had a significant cultural impact.

Culture, which includes morals, beliefs, arts, laws, and habits, defines the community's purpose for being. "The formation of culture," writes British historian Christopher Dawson, "is due to the interaction of factors. It involves in varying degrees a community of work and a community of thought as well as a community of place and a community of blood."[8]

There exist in American society cultural elites who are contemptuous of working-class values. Their elitist views are not necessarily a function of wealth or schooling, but are attitudes of shallow sophistication that reject the fundamental democratic premise that people may be relied on to govern themselves. As Jeffrey Bell writes in his 1992 work *Populism and Elitism*: "Pessimism about people's ability to do well at this leads to a belief that the people should delegate the setting of standards to various elites, elected officials or more often in recent years, judicial and bureaucratic elites appointed by the elected officials and accountable only tenuously to the people."[9]

Older Catholic neighborhoods have often been the targets of the schemes of these social experimenters because it is these neighborhoods and the traditional values that they protect that prevent the elitists from dominating human behavior. Andrew Greeley has postulated that the cultural elites view the neighborhood as "a regression to more primitive and premodern ways of living. The neighborhood asserts the importance of the primordial, the local, the geographic, the familial against the demands of the bureaucratized, rationalized, scientific, corporate society. . . . The neighborhood is rejected by our intellectual and cultural elites because the neighborhood is not modern and what is not modern is conservative, reactionary, unprogressive, unenlightened, superstitious, and just plain wrong."[10]

Throughout the sixties, social engineers were advancing their agendas not only in the Democratic Party but in the Roman Catholic Church as well. In the aftermath of Vatican II, zealous young liberal bishops interpreted John XXIII's "aggiornamento" as a call to completely dismantle the very social foundations of the Church in America. So they looked to the same target as the political liberals: neighborhood ethnic parishes.

As this work has described, the Church in the late nineteenth and early twentieth centuries had in the spirit of subsidiarity permitted parishes to be founded by ethnic groups. "The Catholic Church," writes social critic E. Michael Jones, "had traditionally stated that each ethnic group had a right to organize its own parish, not that they had a right to take over the parishes of other groups."[11]

Suddenly post-Vatican II bishops discarded subsidiarity believing it was racist. These bishops lectured their flocks that the Church's long-time social policy encouraged segregation. And some bishops actively supported urban-planning programs that were dedicated to destroying the old neighborhoods.

Even America's leading conservative prelate, New York's Francis Cardinal Spellman, succumbed to the temptation. To implement plans to build Lincoln Center on Manhattan's West Side, master builder Robert Moses knew he would have to eliminate several Catholic parishes and their environs through the power of eminent domain. To avoid Catholic protests, he enrolled the support of Cardinal Spellman and the Jesuits of Fordham University. In exchange for the land needed to build Lincoln Center, Moses offered Fordham the chance to build a Manhattan campus. Cost of the property to Fordham? One dollar. The real price for the property? The dislocation of 7,000 mostly Catholic families along with the destruction of St. Matthew's Parish on West 68th Street.

"Don't let's spend too much time with an individual pastor who thinks his jurisdiction and membership may be somewhat reduced," Moses lectured his planners. "There must be adjustments in the churches," he told them, "to keep pace with adjustments of the general population."[12] New York's churchmen actually went along with this cynical view. Cardinal Spellman blessed the deal, and St. Matthew's was bulldozed to make way for Fordham's Graduate School, which included a School of Theology.

As these events unfolded in New York, the Democratic Party was becoming a captive of social planners in other major urban centers. In Los Angeles they were called the "California Democratic Council," and in Chicago the "Independent Voters of Illinois." These "Amateur Democrats," as political sociologist James Q. Wilson has labeled them, were viewed by the party's old-time Catholic regulars as "dilettantes," "outsiders," and "hypocritical do-gooders." The elitist reformers, on the other hand, described regulars as "hacks," "organization men" and "machine politicians."[13]

To grasp the cultural tensions between these opposing Democratic camps, a brief examination of the politics of the nation's largest metropolis, New York City, should be helpful.

In 1958, a year Democrats expected to sweep the mid-term elections nationally, Tammany Hall's grand sachem and State Party Chairman Carmine DeSapio, looked forward to the New York Democratic convention that he believed would nominate a winning slate and further enhance his reputation as kingmaker. This Lower East Side Italian-American, who had taken control of the machine in 1950, anticipated re-electing a governor and electing a U.S. Senator in 1958.

To consolidate and maintain his power, DeSapio implemented what was later called the "big-tent" theory. He supported neighborhood regulars in local races while encouraging liberals to run in major races. In 1954, he was responsible for the election of Governor Averell Harriman, and he organized Robert F. Wagner's New York mayoral victories in 1953 and 1957. DeSapio viewed himself as nothing more than a political mechanic. "The extent of his ideological commitment," according to Daniel Patrick Moynihan, "may be measured by his pronouncement to the Holy Name Society Communion Breakfast of the New York Sanitation Department that 'there is no Mother's Day behind the Iron Curtain.'"[14]

At the 1958 Buffalo Convention, DeSapio pushed renowned Manhattan District Attorney Frank Hogan for the U.S. Senate nomination. In DeSapio's judgment, the ticket needed an Irish-Catholic to balance the WASP Harriman and the Jewish candidate for comptroller, Arthur Levitt.

Liberal reformers, including Eleanor Roosevelt and Herbert Lehman, were appalled by the "boss-controlled" convention. Hogan's nomination and Governor Harriman's passive acceptance of the "balanced" ticket were unacceptable. To the reformers, ethnic ticket balancing was a corrupt act.

In the fall, hordes of liberal Democrats deserted their ticket. And on election night, while, nationally, Democrats picked up thirteen slots in the Senate, forty-seven House seats and nine governorships, Harriman lost to Nelson Rockefeller by 593,000 votes, and Republican Congressman Kenneth Keating beat Hogan by 132,000 votes.

After the 1958 electoral debacle, New York's reform Democrats began to make moves to capture the soul and machinery of their party. As James Q.

Wilson has observed, these "Amateur Democrats" were in an "ideal situation to recruit candidates on the basis of their commitment to a set of policies. . . . The party would be held together and linked to the voters by a shared conception of the public interest. . . . Private interests, which for the professional are the motive force of politics, the amateur would consider irrelevant, irrational or immoral."[15]

In 1963, reformer Edward I. Koch scored a major upset by beating the last "tiger" of Tammany Hall, DeSapio himself, for Greenwich Village District Leader. Other reformers throughout New York began to conquer their local organizations. The reformers were appalled by the parochial attitudes and the political ethics of the lower classes. "Patronage" had entirely pejorative connotations; clubhouse beer parties and picnics were frivolous.

Surveying the battles between liberal reformers and neighborhood regulars, Daniel Patrick Moynihan concluded that "the divergence is cultural in a broad sense." "The Reformers," he wrote, "are people with what is called a high rate of upward mobility. Not so the Regulars who incline to stay near the old neighborhoods, speaking with the old accents, even after they have become rich and successful. . . . The liberals live in silk stocking Republican neighborhoods and they have virtually no connection with the working class."[16]

The regulars, losing assault after assault, managed to hold on to their local patronage judgeships and bureaucratic jobs in borough-halls but ceded state legislature, city council, and congressional seats. Reformers such as Elizabeth Holtzman, Robert Abrams, Herman Badillo, Shirley Chisholm, Edward Koch and Allard Lowenstein began their political careers by challenging "regular" legislative incumbents.

By 1961, one could detect discontent among New York City's ethnic voters. Although Mayor Robert F. Wagner was reelected to a third term in November by deserting the "bosses" who had created him and embracing the reformers, there was a third-party movement led by Comptroller Lawrence Gerosa that Catholic neighborhoods found attractive.

Gerosa, a Catholic, had been elected comptroller on Wagner's ticket in 1953 and was reelected in 1957. But a bitter feud developed between the two men during their second term, and in 1961 Wagner dumped Gerosa from the ticket. Gerosa believed that Wagner had sold out the neighborhood folks who had first elected him, so he decided to run for mayor as an independent on the "Citizens Party" ballot. This race "was the culmination of the conflict between the party's culturally conservative wing dominated by Catholics and the liberal wing dominated by Jews."[17] The electorate that supported Gerosa lived in blue-collar, Catholic-ethnic areas. His message that the reformers were driving working-class Democrats out of their party hit a nerve, and Gerosa received 14 percent of the total 320,000 votes, mostly from Catholics.

There were other Catholics concerned that both New York's Democratic *and* Republican Parties were dominated by elitist liberals. J. Daniel Mahoney and Kieran O'Doherty, both lawyers from Queens County, began holding meetings in 1961 to discuss the feasibility of establishing an alternative political organization, a New York Conservative Party.

This new party, whose charter would serve the political ideals of New York's "street corner conservatives," would be a vehicle for right-minded New Yorkers to circumvent the major parties. They could devote their energies to promoting candidates who embraced conservative principles and to provide visibility for conservatives who might otherwise be silenced.

Having survived court challenges, the Conservative Party introduced its candidate for governor, David Jaquith, in the fall of 1962. Jaquith was president of a Syracuse steel-fabricating firm. Kieran O'Doherty, co-founder of the party, was nominated to run for the U.S. Senate against Jacob Javits.

Despite efforts to label them as radical "John Birchers," the conservative candidates did appeal to a significant number of voters. Jaquith received 141,887 votes and O'Doherty 116,151. In Buffalo, Albany, Syracuse, and New York City, the votes they received came primarily from Catholic neighborhoods, and since the gubernatorial candidate had received over 50,000 votes, the Conservative Party became, by law, a permanent part of New York's political structure.

The rightward movement of New York's ethnic Catholics continued in 1964. Although Barry Goldwater received only 31.3 percent of the ballots cast in New York and lost the state by 2.7-million votes, political analysts revealed some interesting voter trends.

According to analyst Kevin Phillips, Barry Goldwater's appeal to segments of the New York populace was based on cultural issues. Phillips concluded.

> . . . the restless black ghetto impinged on Catholic trade unions and neighborhoods; rising taxes for escalating welfare bore down on small home-owners; soaring crime rates jeopardized blue-collar and middle-class lives; new sociological concepts hamstrung the police and undermined the neighborhood school; and new hiring policies and political realities disrupted the Catholic political clubhouses and municipal bureaucracies. More than any other Northeastern religious group, Catholics tended to inhabit the socio-economic "combat zone," confronting the Democratic Party with the cruel dilemma of aborting its ideological thrust or alienating the loyalties of its largest bloc of longtime supporters.[18]

In 1964, Goldwater actually won a majority of New York's white Catholics. In the blue-collar sections of Queens, Staten Island, Brooklyn, and the Bronx, many Catholic neighborhoods gave solid majorities to the Arizona senator.

Catholic Presidential Voting Trends in New York City
1960-64[19]

Assembly District	Nixon 1960	Goldwater 1964
10th Bronx	49%	45%
Italo-Irish	**60**	**65**
Italian	**56**	**56**
9th Bronx	29	25
Irish	**44**	**42**
8th Bronx	30	27
Irish	**46**	**48**
7th Bronx	26	20
Italian	**40**	**44**

Also, in the substantially Catholic working-class suburbs, Goldwater ran well ahead of his 31.3 percent state total:

New York Catholic
Suburban Voting Trends

Town	Goldwater 1964
Scarsdale	35%
Pound Ridge	44
Pelham	59
Orangetown	41
Babylon	43
Smithtown	45
Oyster Bay	42
Yorktown	42

This conservative trend among Catholics in ethnic neighborhoods was tested again in New York City's 1965 mayoral race. Political polemicist and *National Review* founder William F. Buckley Jr., decided to take on the Republican-Liberal candidate John V. Lindsay and Democrat Abraham Beame. Congressman Lindsay, who represented the Upper East Side's "Silk Stocking" district, had an Americans for Democratic Action voting record of 100 percent and was considered one of the most liberal members of the House of Representatives.

The Buckley-Lindsay-Beame campaign was legendary – particularly for the debates where Buckley's wit and charm captivated the city. Buckley lost, but the 13.4 percent of the vote he received was significant. His highest percentages came from mostly white, ethnic Catholic neighborhoods.

Buckley's Top Vote in Catholic Ethnic Neighborhoods[20]
By Assembly District

AD	County	Buckley %	Description
94	Bronx	27.1	Parkchester-City Island-Pelham Bay
23	Queens	26.8	Ridgewood-Glendale
60	Kings	26.7	Bay Ridge
64	Richmond	26.7	Fox Hills-Richmond-Tottenville
25	Queens	24.7	Woodhaven-Ozone Park
29	Queens	24.1	Hollis-Queens Village-Bellerose
31	Queens	23.8	Richmond Hill-Jamaica
27	Queens	23.1	Bayside-Douglaston-Little Neck
65	Richmond	22.2	West Brighton Pt.-Richmond-Travis
93	Bronx	21.6	Woodlawn-Baychester-Morris Park
61	Kings	21.5	Brooklyn Heights-Prospect Park
59	Kings	21.4	Bay Ridge-Bath Beach

According to the Louis Harris Voter Profile Analysis (VPA), the ethnic breakdown of the mayoral race was the following (by electoral district):

Ethnic Group[21]	ED	Lindsay	Beame	Buckley
Jewish (Manhattan)	7	49.3%	47.1%	3.4%
Jewish (Kings-Bronx)	5	34.8	61.1	3.6
Italian	7	40.7	40.1	17.8
Irish	4	40.4	37.5	21.9
Other Catholic (Central European)	4	33.5	39.5	26.2
German (Lutheran)	2	50.4	22.5	26.3
"WASP"	5	60.9	15.9	22.6
African-American	5	42.4	54.9	1.1
Puerto Rican	1	24.5	72.4	2.9

The trend of white Catholic ethnics moving out of the Democratic and into the conservative fold continued in 1966. Reacting to the programs of Lyndon Johnson's Great Society, to questions about Vietnam policy, and to racial unrest in the cities, New York voters turned to the Conservative Party and endorsed candidates throughout the state. Governor Nelson Rockefeller managed to win a third term, but only with a plurality of 44.8 percent of the vote. More significantly, Conservative candidate Paul Adams out-polled Liberal Party candidate Franklin Delano Roosevelt, Jr., 510,000 (8.5 percent) to 508,000 (8.4 percent).

A major cultural battle was waged in New York City that November as well. Mayor Lindsay had promised in his 1965 campaign to institute a Civilian Review Board to examine brutality charges against city police. He kept his pledge, and on May 2, 1966, appointed four civilians to the board that also included three police deputy inspectors. Police commissioner Vincent Broderick assailed the decision as a "cruel hoax, this bromide, this palliative of an independent civilian review board."

Opposition to the board became a rallying cry for Catholic conservatives fed up with rampant crime and violence. A petition to put a referendum on the ballot, which was permitted by Municipal Home Rule Law, was sponsored by the Conservative Party and the Policeman's Benevolent Association (P.B.A.). The Review Board was decisively defeated in the election:

1966 New York City Civilian Review Board Vote

	Abolish	Keep
Manhattan	168,391	234,485
Bronx	235,310	128,084
Brooklyn	414,133	201,336
Queens	426,821	191,787
Richmond	63,083	12,800
	1,307,738 (62.9%)	768,492 (37.1%)

The Catholic vote against the Board averaged 80 percent in ethnic neighborhoods.

*   *   *   *   *

New York Catholics were not alone in their distrust of the Democratic Party's ascendant social engineers. Ethnic Catholics in Boston, Chicago, Philadelphia, Scranton, St. Louis, and the rapidly growing outer-city suburban districts were upset over many of the Great Society's social programs. And while most of them remained registered with the Democratic Party, surveys showed that their loyalty was weakening.

The Party's left wing rationalized that this trend was based on economics: as Catholic Democrats achieved middle-class status, they thumbed their noses at their benefactors. Future Speaker of the House Tip O'Neill, who held John Kennedy's old congressional seat, declared on one occasion: "I go out and campaign among those guys whose parents went to school on the G.I. Bill, got their first house on F.H.A. housing, whose life has been made by these Democratic programs. Then they go out and make $20,000 a year and start voting Republican."[22]

Catholic-Democratic Party Affiliation[23]
1952–1978

	A	B	C	D	E	F	G	H
1952	29%	27%	12%	7%	7%	10%	8%	0%
1954	24	27	13	7	6	12	8	4
1956	25	26	9	11	7	13	8	3
1958	31	25	10	9	5	10	7	3
1960	33	30	9	8	3	9	6	1
1962	34	24	9	7	5	11	8	2
1964	31	27	11	9	5	8	8	0
1966	25	30	10	14	4	12	5	1
1968	23	29	13	10	8	10	6	1
1970	22	30	12	13	6	12	5	0
1972	19	31	13	12	10	8	6	1
1974	25	25	13	15	6	11	5	0
1976	18	32	14	11	9	9	7	1
1978	17	32	16	12	7	10	4	2

Key: A: Strong Democrat   E: Independent Republcan
            B: Weak Democrat   F: Weak Republican
            C: Independent Democrat   G: Strong Republican
            D: Independent Independent   H: Apolitical

Myopic reform Democrats could not see that working-class ethnic Catholics in the sixties no longer felt wanted in the Democratic Party. As James Q. Wilson described in the *Amateur Democrat*, the reformers preoccupation with "small-d democracy," integration, "good" candidates, and liberalism "[were] simply irrelevant to the major preoccupations of both the lower classes and those middle-class representatives of ethnic groups. . . ."[24] These old-line Democrats were concerned with more than economics. They feared rampant neighborhood crime, the decline of traditional values, quotas, soaring welfare costs, the defense of freedom abroad, and respect for the American flag at home. Both the inner city's working classes and the ethnic suburbanites began to feel alienated by the Democratic Party's ideology and the constituencies it embraced. "Before the sixties fairness had meant that a person received what his sweat earned him. The family that emerged from Ellis Island to work six days, twelve hour shifts in sweat shops deserved to move up. It had played by the rules. Just so, the less industrious did not deserve to do so well."[25] These voters who lived by this code were frightened by what they perceived to be a new fairness doctrine in the Democratic Party that meant not equality of opportunity but equality of result. The reformers labeled these old-fashioned views racist, but as Senator Joe Lieberman of Connecticut (a

Democrat who was elected by going against the ideological tide of his party) points out, "The average white voter is not racist. The average white voter is protective of what he has. . . . There is a sense of injustice here that is beautiful. It's more [the working class saying] 'You [Democrats] are making a fool of me. What am I, a chump? I'm breaking my back, my wife is, too. And you're going to give my money to these people who don't even work and are pulling the wool over your eyes. What are you, fools?"[26]

This was even true in the Kennedy's backyard. Boston Catholics were angered by accusations from radical left-wing students, feminists, and civil rights activists that practicing their traditional beliefs was racist or selfish. Boston historian Thomas O'Connor described the clash this way:

> Slowly and painfully, Irish Catholics worked their way up the social and economic ladder, taking the meanest of jobs and the smallest of opportunities to establish a place for themselves in a hostile environment. After a century of struggle, with little or no assistance from private agencies or governmental institutions, surviving only through the self-sacrifice of their family members and the generous patronage of their own political representatives, by the middle of the twentieth century many of the Boston Irish had finally "made it. . . ." Most Irish Catholics resented it furiously therefore, when black leaders denounced them as bigots, defined "their" city of Boston as "the most racist city in America," and demanded that the government assure them access to better jobs, better housing, and better schools. This was asking for "too much, too soon," objected the Boston Irish. Nobody had helped *them*, they protested. Nobody had given *them* jobs, provided *them* with houses, made the schools easier for *their* children. They did all these things themselves, through persistent hard work – and it took them more than a century.[27]

As the election of 1968 approached, unrest in the nation's cities and campuses, the failure of the Great Society to ameliorate inner-city tensions (1967 was the worst year ever for race riots), and a sense of futility about the Vietnam War caused many Catholic Democrats to look elsewhere for leadership that addressed their concerns.

*   *   *   *   *

In 1968, two Catholics, Eugene McCarthy and Robert Kennedy, campaigned for the Democratic presidential nomination, believing they were lightning rods for voter discontent over Lyndon Johnson's Vietnam War policies. But the true concerns of many ethnic Catholics were missed by these politicians and by most of the media. Pollster Richard Scammon realized these voters were motivated by social issues more than foreign policy. "This included," says Scammon, "deep concern about crime, race, narcotics, alien-ation. It also included a feeling against the dissent and disruption engendered by the Vietnam protesters."[28] This evolving attitude of a large subset of voters, particularly glum and rattled inner-city and suburban Catholics, played into the hands of two other presidential candidates that year: George Wallace and Richard Nixon.

Governor George Wallace of Alabama had made his national debut when in his 1963 inaugural address he had pledged "segregation today, segregation tomorrow, segregation forever." Later that year he made national headlines when he kept his pledge to "stand at the school house door," and tried to block the admission of two African-American students to the University of Alabama. The national media wrote him off as a crank, failing to understand that this Southerner, racist though he was, had a keen political antenna and sensed a mood change in the American people as early as 1964. Deciding to test the political waters, he entered the 1964 Democratic primary in Wisconsin against President Johnson.

The pundits were certain that, in the aftermath of the Kennedy assassina-tion, Johnson's popularity was unassailable, so when the results of the April 7th primary were tallied they were stunned by the results: Wallace received 33.8 percent of the vote, and he went on to receive 29.8 percent in the Indiana primary, and 42.7 percent in the Maryland face-off. Wallace "backlash" votes came primarily from Italians and Poles in Milwaukee, Catholic mill laborers in Gary, and Catholic steelworkers in Baltimore. While the media preferred to write off these protest voters as racists, Wallace and smart pollsters thought otherwise. There was a growing anger among white middle-class voters, including Catholics, who believed that their way of life and the ideals that guided them were threatened with extinction.

Feeding on this fear during the next four years, Wallace transformed him-self from a regional racist into a national populist. Calling for a return to the traditional lifestyle that had existed prior to the fad of radicalism, Wallace lec-tured audiences on the sanctity of the family, the virtues of hard work and self-reliance, and on the preservation of neighborhoods.

In an interview with James Jackson Kilpatrick in 1967, Wallace described his pulse reading of the American public:

> What are the issues going to be in 1968?. . . . Schools, that'll be one thing. By the fall of 1968, the people of Cleveland and Chicago and Gary and St. Louis will be so god-damned sick and tired of Federal interference in their local schools, they'll be ready to vote for Wallace by the thousands. The people don't like this tri-flin' with their children, tellin' 'em which teachers to have to teach in which schools, and bussing little boys and girls half across a

> city just to achieve 'the proper racial mix.' . . . I'll give you anoth-
> er big one for 1968: law and order. Crime in the Streets. The peo-
> ple are going to be fed up with the sissy attitude of Lyndon
> Johnson and all the intellectual morons and theoreticians he has
> around him. They're fed up with a Supreme Court that . . . it's a
> sorry, lousy, no-account outfit. . . . Housing? Sure, that'll be an
> issue . . . any time the Federal government lays down the law for
> people . . . fixing the terms and conditions on which they can sell
> their own homes. . . . Folks won't stand for it. And there's nothing
> about the sale of private housing in the Constitution either . . . .[29]

In 1968, Wallace decided to skip the Democratic Party primary route and
created the American Independence Party. In the aftermath of the assassination
of Robert Kennedy, Wallace's numbers were on the rise: polls placed him at 16
percent in June and 21 percent by mid-September. Pollster Richard Scammon
had it right: "The Democratic Party had lost touch with the mainstream of the
American electorate, which was white, middle-aged, and working/middle
class."[30] According to Scammon, somewhere between a "fifth and a third of the
electorate . . . [was] up for grabs largely on the basis of the social issue."[31]

The other man watching the 1968 political drama unfold was Republican
Richard Nixon. The former vice president was listening to a young political
demographer, Kevin Phillips, who convinced Nixon there was a political
realignment in the works that made possible an "emerging Republican majority." According to Professor Dan Carter, author of *The Politics of Rage*,
Phillips "grasped the political significance of the growth of the conservative
sun belt and recognized the political dynamite embedded in the social and cultural conflicts that dominated the 1960s. . . . [Phillips] emphasized the essential conservatism of first generation and second generation European immigrants and he was perfectly willing to take advantage of the anti-intellectual-
ism that Wallace had brilliantly illuminated . . ."[32]

After the riotous 1968 Chicago Democratic convention that nominated
Hubert Humphrey for president, both Nixon and Wallace shot up in the pub-
lic-opinion polls. For one brief moment in September, the pollsters had
Humphrey coming in third.

But with the media now covering the Wallace's campaign full-time, many
pro-Wallace Americans began to have second thoughts. They watched the night-
ly news and saw Wallace rallies turning into brawls. And Wallace himself diminished in appeal the more one saw and heard him. One woman told political analyst Samuel Lubell in late October: "I wanted to vote for Wallace, just so the
politicians will wake up and realize that people won't go along with what we
have now. But I've found out a lot about him and I'm afraid he might win."[33]
While many people, including large numbers of blue-collar Catholics, enjoyed

hearing Wallace's verbal assaults against "pointy-headed . . . brief-case bureaucrats who are trying to run your lives," and even though they gave him standing ovations after he told them that "if any demonstrator lies down in front of my car when I'm president, that'll be the last car he lays down in front of,"[34] they felt uneasy when it came to actually casting a vote for this "shoot from the hip" politician. By mid-October, polls reflected that Wallace could no longer sustain support, particularly in densely populated Catholic areas. Some of his supporters went back home to the Democratic Party but most transferred to Nixon.

In the words of Michael Barone, Richard Nixon "was a man with little charm, who did nothing to nurture friendship, who had neither money nor much in the way of connections, who seemed ill-suited to a political career."[35] Yet he was the man who filled the political void after the collapse of the Great Society, the man who provided the voice for the "Silent Majority." It was Nixon who forged the Republican realignment of northern blue-collar ethnic Catholics and southern whites. Herbert Parmet, in *Nixon and His America*, described his appeal to the Catholic working class:

> Nixon personified the children of the New Deal generation who regained confidence in American capitalism. They rediscovered the values that seemed to have gone askew. Nixon keenly reflected the priorities that were especially important to those we may identify as the working middle class. They saw in Nixon not a figure of glamor at all, but someone closer to the real gut: a guardian of their intent to secure a piece of the American turf, or their idea of the American dream, and to do so without losing out to those who insisted on changing the rules in the middle of the game by grabbing advantages not available to earlier generations. This was not only the coming of age of the great middle-class majority; we must also understand it as a process of acculturation and assimilation by generations of immigrants. They achieved their security, had faith in the American dream, and contributed a conservative, stabilizing force in the context of American traditionalism.[36]

Nixon was perceived as the protector of the interests of these second- and third-generation ethnics while the Democratic "elitist heirs" of Adlai Stevenson scorned them.

On November 5, 1968, Richard Nixon was elected the 37th President of the United States, receiving 43.42 percent of the vote versus Humphrey's 42.72 percent and Wallace's 13.53 percent. The Electoral College totals were Nixon, 301 votes; Humphrey 191, and Wallace 46.

In 1960, JFK had garnered 78 percent of the Catholic vote and Lyndon Johnson, running on the Kennedy record in 1964, had managed to hold on to

76 percent. But in 1968 there was serious slippage – only 59 percent of Catholics cast their votes for Humphrey, with 33 percent going for Nixon and 8 percent for Wallace. The Catholic swing toward Nixon and Wallace was most evident in New York:

Catholic-Dominated New York City Neighborhoods[37]

AD Neighborhood	Nixon	Humphrey	Wallace
49th Brooklyn (Bay Ridge)	61%	32%	7%
50th Brooklyn (Bay Ridge)	60	33	7
58th Richmond (Staten Island)	58	33	9
30th Queens (Elmhurst, Ridgewood)	56	34	10
20th Queens (Cambria, Hollis)	56	36	8
28th Queens (Woodhaven)	55	36	9
59th Richmond (Staten Island)	53	38	9
80th Bronx (Parkchester, Throgs Neck)	50	41	9
34th Queens (Sunnyside, Maspeth)	50	41	9
29th Queens (South Ozone Park)	49	42	9
22nd Queens (Douglaston)	51	44	5
85th Bronx (Morris Park, Pelham Bay)	49	45	6
32nd Queens (Steinway, Woodside)	48	45	7
33rd Queens (Astoria, Long Island City)	47	45	8
53rd Brooklyn (Gowanus)	44	47	9
86th Bronx (Baychester)	45	48	7
38th Brooklyn (East New York)	44	48	8
35th Brooklyn (Greenpoint)	41	50	9
Citywide (68 AD's)	34	61	5

Vote for Nixon Catholic-Dominated[38] (New York Metro Areas)

	1960	1968
New Haven County, Connecticut	42%	45%
Bridgeport, Connecticut	36	42
Richmond County, New York	56	62
Oneida County (Utica), New York	48	54
Passaic County (Passaic and Paterson), New Jersey	45	52
Yonkers, New York	51	55
Hudson County (Jersey City), New Jersey	39	42
Clinton County, New York	45	53
Franklin County, New York	49	55
Orangetown, New York	48	60
Babylon, New York	55	62
Smithtown, New York	57	65
Oyster Bay, New York	53	57
Yorktown, New York	60	60

Support for Nixon was higher in suburban areas that were populated by Catholic ethnics and lower in the more liberal Republican "silk stocking" areas. This trend was not isolated to the Northeast. In America's heartland, Catholics provided the margin of victory for Nixon in Michigan, Wisconsin, Ohio, Illinois, and Indiana. Kevin Phillips points out the GOP's greatest gains were in midwestern counties dominated by German Catholics.[39]

Vote for Nixon in German-Catholic Dominated Areas

	1960	1968
Kewaunee, Wisconsin	48	63
Clinton, Illinois	48	63
Dubois, Indiana	38	47
Putnam, Ohio	53	68
Huron, Michigan	62	70

Irish-Catholic Votes in Key States – 1968[40]

	Humphrey	Nixon	Wallace
New Jersey	45%	51%	4%
New York	45	48	7
Pennsylvania	45	41	13

Italian-Catholic Votes in Key States – 1968[41]

	Humphrey	Nixon	Wallace
New Jersey	42%	40%	18%
New York	42	49	9
Ohio	65	19	16
Pennsylvania	57	34	9

While Slovak-Catholics remained the most loyal to the Democratic Party, there was still a significant decline in their 1968 Democratic totals versus 1964:

Slovak-Catholic Vote in Key States,[42] 1964–1968

	Johnson	Goldwater	Humphrey	Nixon	Wallace
Illinois	67%	33%	49%	35%	16%
Indiana	74	26	57	27	16
Michigan	86	14	76	11	13
New Jersey	75	25	49	37	14
New York	84	16	71	20	9
Ohio	86	14	66	17	17
Pennsylvania	79	21	65	26	9
Wisconsin	85	15	68	19	13

In 1968, approximately 15 million conservative Democrats – Protestants in the South and Catholics in the North and Midwest – deserted their party in favor of either Nixon or Wallace. Most distressing to Democratic pollsters, the voting strength of the Catholic suburbs outside America's twelve largest non-Southern cities was growing rapidly – and voting Republican. The old New Deal coalition had unraveled, and for the first time ever suburban votes outnumbered city votes cast:

**Total Vote Cast in the Twelve Largest Non-Southern Cities[43]
And Suburbs, Presidential Elections 1952–1968**

	Cities	Suburbs
1952	10,324,000	6,284,000
1956	9,643,000	7,080,000
1960	9,636,000	8,264,000
1964	9,274,000	8,519,000
1968	8,112,000	8,591,000

Reviewing the results, many leftist Democrats blamed their losses on racism. This was political tunnel vision, and it would dominate the Democratic Party's thinking for the next generation. But not everyone bought the party line. Super liberal Teddy Kennedy saw the discontent of Boston voters and conceded that the culture of resistance being registered at the polls – particularly in the Catholic wards where the Wallace vote was 9 percent – was not to be blamed on race. Most Wallace voters, Kennedy, admitted, "are not motivated by racial hostility or prejudice." Rather he explained, it was they "who bear the burdens of a draft that defers the better off, are unable to afford higher education, but are not poor enough for scholarships." It was they, according to Kennedy, who carried the brunt of the taxes for an "established system [that] has not been sympathetic to them."[44]

When he took office in January 1969, Richard Nixon inherited an unpopular and seemingly endless war, student unrest over the draft, an ailing economy, a hemorrhaging federal budget that was attempting to finance "guns and butter" – a war and an expanding welfare state – as well as rampant crime, and inner-city racial tensions. While dealing with all these issues, Nixon always kept one eye on middle-class reactions, particularly among Catholics. Nixon believed that if they were content with his performance, in the 1972 election he might affect a realignment of farm-belt evangelicals, southern right-wingers, and inner-city and suburban Catholics. Simply stated, his goal was to transform the old FDR coalition into a new Nixon coalition.

In the off-year election of 1970, Nixon decided to speak out on the themes recommended by his in-house analyst Kevin Phillips: "law and order," "pornography," and "old fashioned patriotism."[45]

One contest that intrigued Nixon was New York's three-way Senate race between Republican-Liberal incumbent Charles Goodell, Democratic Congressman Richard Ottinger, and Conservative James L. Buckley, brother of William F. Buckley Jr.

Jim Buckley had made his first run as the Conservative Party's candidate in 1968 against liberal Republican Senator Jacob Javits and Democrat Paul O'Dwyer. In this race, Buckley had received 1.1 million votes (19 percent of the total) and actually outpolled or came close to outpolling the Democrat Paul O'Dwyer in counties with large Catholic populations.

	O'Dwyer	Buckley
Nassau	130,185	128,893
Rockland	17,243	15,435
Suffolk	70,781	83,223
Westchester	78,468	65,309
Queens	216,782	180,831
Richmond	25,738	33,111

In the blue-collar Catholic Queens neighborhoods of Maspeth, Glendale, and Ridgewood, Buckley actually won:

Maspeth-Glendale-Ridgewood 1968 U.S. Senate Results:

Javits (R-L)	16,847	36.3%
O'Dwyer (D)	12,249	26.4
Buckley (C)	17,308	37.3

By 1970, conservatives in New York and the White House were convinced that a right-wing wind was blowing in left-wing New York. Gearing up to run for a fourth term, even Nelson Rockefeller began to remold himself as a conservative. To soften his liberal image, he declared war on drugs and crime. "With a conservative administration controlling the federal government, Rockefeller [went] further right. He warned of a 'grave financial crisis' and called for a halt to new programs and an across-the-board cut in state spending of five percent."[46] He also asked the nation's new conservative hero, Vice President Spiro Agnew, to campaign for upstate. An amazed President Nixon, recalling that Rockefeller had told him in 1958 and in 1966 to keep out of his campaigns, stated: "Isn't that something! They're really reading the tea leaves, aren't they?"[47]

To fill the U.S. Senate vacancy created by the assassination of Robert F. Kennedy, Rockefeller had appointed Congressman Charles Goodell of Jamestown. Rockefeller figured that Goodell, who was acceptable to conservatives, would keep the "right" happy in 1970.

But Senator Goodell had other ideas. Upon arriving in the Senate, he became a "liberal dove." Condemning his Republican president, he demanded immediate withdrawal from Vietnam and voted with liberal Democrats on social programs.

Political consultant F. Clifton White (creator of the "Draft Goldwater" movement) convinced Jim Buckley that he could win in a three-way race, and Buckley agreed to make another run for the Senate.

While Rockefeller was battling Democratic-Liberal Arthur Goldberg, Buckley took on Ottinger and Goodell. Numerous Republican leaders and state legislators deserted Goodell for Buckley. As *The New York Times* reported on October 22, 1970: "White House Repudiates Goodell." Nixon all but embraced Buckley, and Vice President Agnew called Goodell the "Christine Jorgenson" of the Republican Party. ("Miss" Jorgenson was a man who had recently undergone a sex-change operation.)

Endorsed by the New York *Daily News* and the Gannett newspaper chain, Buckley won the three-way race with 39 percent of the vote.   Rockefeller scored his biggest victory to date, beating Goldberg by 742,000 votes. The front page of the *New York Post* titled its lead story, "Rocky's Turn to Right Did It." The article stated:

> Rockefeller managed to arrange a tacit truce with the state's Conservative Party, a tactic that persuaded many Republicans to push for a ticket of Rockefeller and James L. Buckley, the Conservative Party Senate candidate.
>
> The Republican Governor, who won an unprecedented fourth four-year term in Albany, wooed the conservative Italian and Irish New York City voters to offset the large Jewish turnout here for Goldberg.[48]

Analyzing the Buckley candidacy, loser Charles Goodell made this observation: "He [Buckley] came through as a person of whom a hard hat could say, 'I'll vote for him. He's against the labor laws, he's against all the things we believe in, but he's for safety in the streets and for patriotism.'"[49] Like Nixon in 1968, Buckley appealed to blue-collar, "hard-hat" Catholics, who were part of the "silent majority," and he easily carried their neighborhoods.

Samuel Lubell confirms that Buckley drew the support of Catholic construction workers, truck drivers, as well as white-collar employees, sundry salesmen, and company executives. According to Lubell, 80 percent of New York's policemen voted for Buckley and nearly 70 percent of his backing was Catholic.

In the election of 1970, the Republican law and order campaign was successful only in New York, Maryland, and Tennessee. But gaining two U.S. Senate seats and losing only nine House seats was not a bad outcome for an incumbent president's party in an off year election. Nevertheless, the results proved that while Northern Catholics and Southern Conservatives could be moved by national issues to vote Republican in presidential and senate races, they were not yet ready to desert Democratic candidates on the local level. Congressmen, state legislators, and town and city representatives were more like neighbors, were closer to their constituents, and more in tune with their frustrations.

Nixon accepted these facts, and for the next two years executed a plan designed to increase his stature among northern Catholics and Southern conservatives. He was less concerned with his standing in the Republican Party.

To enhance support in ethnic neighborhoods, Nixon befriended up-and-coming Philadelphia politician, Catholic Frank Rizzo. His record as the city's police commissioner had energized enough of South Philadelphia's ethnic Catholics to elect Rizzo mayor in 1971. Reacting to Rizzo's victory, Bob Haldeman, Nixon's Chief of Staff, wrote in his diary on November 3, 1971, that Nixon "wants to be sure that we pound home the fact that the mayor's race proves our political strategy, that the place for us is not with the Jews and the Negroes, but with the white ethnics and that we have to go after the Catholic thing."[50]

As the 1972 presidential campaign got underway, it appeared that events were breaking Nixon's way: On May 15, George Wallace was taken out of the presidential race when an attempted assassination crippled him. And at the Democratic National Convention in July, the portion of Roosevelt's coalition that remained in the Democratic Party – the left wing element – took control of the convention and nominated one of their own, Senator George McGovern.

As the 1972 campaign proceeded, Nixon reminded political assistant Chuck Colson about the "silent majority" voters: "The Italian labor leaders who have moved with us, the Italian political leaders who have moved with us, [Cardinal] Krol [of Philadelphia] and the Polish group, etc. All these are of the very first priority at this time. . . . In other words, the blue-collar issues and the Catholic issues, where McGovern simply cannot be appealing to them as we are."[51]

The president spent plenty of time cultivating these ethnic Catholic voters. He appointed Poles, Hungarians, Irish, and Italians to high profile posts. On Columbus Day 1971, he spent 90 minutes with Aldo Moro, Italy's Foreign Minister, and accepted from the Sons of Italy their Marconi Award. On a presidential trip to Ireland, he traced his family's roots. When visiting Chicago, he had interviews with Polish newspaper editors and the heads of Polish fraternal orders. At the White House, Poland's famous Pozzan Boy's Choir serenaded President and Mrs. Nixon. Nixon also came out publicly for aid to parochial schools and against funding of abortion.

Accompanying the Nixon campaign, journalist Theodore White reported, "He turns up in Philadelphia with Cardinal Krol to support Federal aid to Catholic schools; he writes a letter to Cardinal Cooke of New York opposing abortion; he rejects quota hiring and downplays the Philadelphia Plan of minority hiring on federally financed projects."[52]

As the election results poured in on the evening of Tuesday, November 7, there could be no doubt that the Democratic coalition forged by Franklin Roosevelt had completely disintegrated. Richard Nixon carried forty-nine states for a total of 538 electoral votes to McGovern's one state and the District of Columbia for a total of 17 votes. Nixon garnered 47.2 million votes (60.69 percent) to McGovern's 29.2 million (37.53 percent).

Among Catholics, Nixon's victory was staggering. He carried 59 percent of the Catholic vote – a new record for a Republican. In the blue-collar states of New Jersey, Pennsylvania, Ohio, Indiana, and Missouri, Nixon received 60 percent of the vote. Poles in Detroit, Pittsburgh, Buffalo, and Lackawanna, Pennsylvania; the Italians in Philadelphia, Boston, and Chicago; the Irish in New York and Boston; the Germans in St. Paul and Milwaukee – each group overwhelmingly endorsed Richard Nixon.

Presidential chronicler Theodore White gave this analysis of the Catholic turnout in the Northeast:

> In Eastern industrial states, Catholics had achieved a rough voting parity with Protestants in the electorate; and now, by the CBS analysis, in the election of 1972 the once heavily Democratic Catholics had gone Republican for the first time in any American Presidential election. Nixon spoke to them. Rhode Island, the most heavily Catholic state in the Union, had gone against Nixon by two to one in 1968; in 1972 Rhode Island voted for him. Even Providence County, which had gone for Hubert Humphrey by 70 percent in 1968, gave Nixon a majority in 1972. All through the East, the same way: Hudson County, New Jersey; Allegheny County (Pittsburgh), Pennsylvania; Albany and Erie counties (Buffalo), New York; Hartford County, Connecticut – all heavily Catholic, and all, utterly out of previous political character, voted for the Republican Protestant from Yorba Linda, California.[53]

Northeastern Counties with Urban Catholic Voters
1960–1972

County	Nixon 1960	Nixon 1968	Wallace 1968	Nixon 1972
Androscoggin, Maine	36%	28%	1%	50%
Bristol, Massachusetts	33	30	4	45
Suffolk, Massachusetts	25	18	6	33
Providence, Rhode Island	33	28	4	42
Oneida, New York	48	51	5	70
Albany, New York	40	38	4	55
Richmond, New York	57	55	9	74
Hudson, New Jersey	39	37	10	61
Middlesex, New Jersey	42	42	10	63
Lackawanna, Pennsylvania	38	39	3	56

In New York, where Senator James Buckley served as the key Nixon spokesman, voters gave Nixon 57.3 percent of their vote and he came within eighty thousand votes of carrying New York City.

Nixon Support in Heavily Catholic
New York City Assembly Districts, 1972

Queens	Percentage	Brooklyn	Percentage
25 AD	67.2	47 AD	56.1
31 AD	72.0	49 AD	77.3
33 AD	80.2	50 AD	73.9
35 AD	70.1	51 AD	64.6
36 AD	61.5	58 AD	62.7
37 AD	73.4		
38 AD	80.5		

Bronx	Percentage	Staten Island	Percentage
80 AD	78.2	60 AD	78.5
85 AD	52.0	61 AD	73.1
86 AD	58.9	62 AD	64.2

It is interesting to note that while Nixon was carrying the Catholic blue-collar neighborhood of Ridgewood, Queens, George McGovern won in the fashionable, Anglo-Saxon Republican "silk stocking" district on Manhattan's Upper East Side.

And the Catholic vote that overwhelmingly supported Nixon did not reward his party. Republicans lost two seats in the Senate, although they picked up twelve seats in the House. Ethnic-Catholic Democrats were ticket splitters, and it would take another decade before they would be pulling the lever for Republicans in local elections.

"Nixon versus McGovern," wrote historian Herbert Parmet, "divided the country along not only the so-called social issues but also ethnic, class and cultural lines."[54] The losers, McGovern and his liberal supporters, were, according to Kevin Phillips, associated with "middle class reformism and permissivism of avaricious economic, diplomatic, sociological and sexual hues."[55]

One Italian-American Democrat, Mario Cuomo, viewed the wreckage of 1972 and conceded that McGovern had driven away the blue-collar worker, "who felt alienated by a new Democratic Party which he thought neither understood nor related to him."[56]

Chapter 15

The Catholic Voter in the Age of Reagan

During the 1970s, ethnic Catholics were perplexed and shocked by the social upheavals within their religious and political institutions. In addition to watching their political hero, Richard Nixon, self-destruct in the downward spiral of Watergate revelations, there were numerous and profound post-Vatican II liturgical and devotional changes that severely disrupted religious life. And there was the January 1973 *Roe v. Wade* decision, in which the Supreme Court extended the so-called constitutional right to privacy, invalidated all state prohibitions on abortion and made abortion on demand the law of the land.

Immigrants who had brought with them from Old World to New a commitment to the rock-solid doctrines of the Catholic faith were now bombarded by zealous innovators, who in the name of Vatican II discarded, tampered, revised, or eliminated ceremonies and doctrines that had been practiced and cherished for generations.

Bishops, priests, nuns, theologians, and canon lawyers questioned Church certitudes and papal authority. Some declared independence from the magisterium and interpreted Church doctrine according to their whims. They questioned all matters, even the divinity of Christ.

There were young priests who sought degrees in social work instead of theology, who believed their call was eliminating social injustice, not saving of souls. Instead of praying and tending to parishioners, many pursued careers as activists: in the civil-rights movement, the War on Poverty, and in the anti-war movement. They stood by Cesar Chavez and his United Farm Workers, formed the Campaign for Human Development, and generally launched the Church's equivalent of the Great Society.

Ethnic Catholics, whose families supported Catholic higher education for over a century, were shocked in July 1967 when twenty-six educators from ten Catholic colleges signed the so-called "Land O'Lakes" Document. In it they declared their independence from the Vatican in running their schools. Crucifixes were taken down from classroom walls in order to appear secularized. Dissent was the order of the day – faculty members took pride in questioning Church doctrine in the classroom.

Those bishops desperate to appear "with it" allowed dissenters within their dioceses to subvert the Church. Apostasy was fostered, with dissenters condemning or ridiculing papal and ecclesiastical teachings on contraception, and later, ordination of women, and homosexuality.

Vacillating bishops, rebellious priests and nuns, and revisionist-theologians caused confusion in parishes, in Church grammar schools, and on Catholic campuses. It has been estimated that in 1960, 75 percent of America's 40 million Catholics went to Mass weekly and that 85 percent made their annual Easter duty. By 1980 the statistics had a marked change:

* Only 25,000,000 Catholics attended Sunday Mass, a figure 17 percent lower than that of 1960, even though by virtue of natural increase the Catholic population was 25 percent larger.
* Baptisms declined by 500,000, indicating an unusually low Catholic birthrate.
* The Sacrament of Penance was virtually wiped out, evidence of a lessened sense of sin.
* The 5,000,000-student Catholic school system [was] cut in half by attrition and leakage, with questions increasingly raised about the Catholic quality of what is left.
* Seminarians studying for the priesthood were below 6,000, one quarter of the 1960 number.[1]

The ethnic Catholic was bewildered by the new social order that promoted secular ideologies such as Marxism, Darwinism, Freudianism, and behaviorism – all of which denied man's spirituality and declared him free of all moral constraints.

Catholics found it hard to understand – and most could not accept – that in these ideologies man is reduced to an individual without intrinsic value: he is not a person in the traditional sense, just the highest animal on the evolutionary scale. For these ideologues the human person is irrelevant. Universal ideas and absolute values are meaningless because man's existence has no spiritual dimension. Without personhood, the concept of liberty (freedom to do what one ought to do) becomes absurd, since for the modernist freedom means license to do whatever is desired. Values are reduced to taste; the common good is disregarded in favor of the collective good or individual good.

In this new social order, rights became the weapons of self-interest; responsibility based on a moral hierarchy became anathema. By the 1980s, the following notions infiltrated every aspect of society:

* Poverty programs promulgated victimism, "it's not your fault" attitudes;
* In sex-ed programs, the family was defined as a group of people

who lived together; condoms were distributed to children; illegitimate births, single parent families, and homosexuality were portrayed as normal "alternative" life styles;

* In judicial systems, punitive sanctions were rejected and in place of guilt and punishment, tolerance and understanding were being espoused.

These notions also affected the Church, so that by 1980 researchers would find that among Catholics:

* three out of four approved sexual intercourse for engaged couples.
* eight out of ten approved of contraception.
* seven out of ten approved of legalized abortion.
* four out of ten did not think the pope is infallible.[2]

Of all the tumult in the tumultuous '70s, however, it was the Supreme Court's 1973 decision in *Roe v. Wade* that shook the average Catholic to his core. In this decision, the Court ruled that the Texas abortion law that forbade any abortions, except when the life of the mother was threatened, was unconstitutional. While the court paid lip service to the view that the states had some interest in regulating abortion in the final trimester, that interest could be trumped by a woman whose doctor recommended the abortion based on the mother's "health." The court defined "health" to include emotional health which opened the door to abortion on demand at any time during pregnancy.

Roe v. Wade was the most blatant example so far of the success of legal positivism. The Supreme Court chose the same rationale used by the Nazis: that an innocent human being can be declared a non-person and deprived of life if "its" existence is merely inconvenient or deemed *unfit* by those presently holding judicial or legislative power. *Roe v. Wade* was the catalyst for many ethnic Catholics to mobilize as a political force in the public square.

* * * * *

In the aftermath of the *Roe v. Wade*, the American people were embroiled with the lengthening shadow of the Watergate affair. The cover-up of a second-rate burglary destroyed the Nixon administration, and on August 9, 1974, he became the first man ever to resign the presidency.

Upon being sworn-in as the nation's 38th President, Gerald Ford calmed the nation with his style and rhetoric. After only a few weeks in office, however, Ford was caught in a political whirlwind. Liberal Democrats despised him after he pardoned Nixon, and conservative Republicans were appalled at his appointment of Nelson Rockefeller to fill the vice-presidential vacancy.

Although during the first year of his presidency Ford had proved his conservative credentials by containing the growth of government and by vetoing fifty-three spending measures, the right wing of his party was still not satisfied. Conservative Ronald Reagan, former two-term governor of California, announced his intention to challenge the incumbent president, and a great donnybrook commenced within Republican ranks.

Meanwhile, on the Democratic side, a former one-term governor of Georgia, Jimmy Carter, was running for president as a political outsider pledged to represent the American people instead of the Washington establishment.

As the 1976 presidential conventions drew near, the Catholic voter (and therefore the abortion issue) became a major concern to both parties. The Roman Catholic Church had a long history in opposing abortions as "unspeakable crimes" that destroyed innocent human life. In 1968, the American bishops reminded the nation that abortion "was contrary to Judeo-Christian traditions inspired by love for life, and Anglo-Saxon legal traditions protective of life and the person."[3]

Immediately after the announcement of the Supreme Court's *Roe v. Wade* opinion, Philadelphia's John Cardinal Krol, president of the National Conference of Catholic Bishops (NCCB), stated it was "bad logic and bad law." The NCCB also told the faithful that "every legal possibility . . . be explored to challenge the opinion of the United States Supreme Court decision which withdraws all legal safeguards for the right to life of the unborn child."[4] The NCCB went one step further in November 1973. They made it very clear that they "considered the passage of a pro-life constitutional amendment a priority of the highest order."

Hearing this strong message, politicians in both parties frantically sought means to "finesse" the emerging pro-life issue. In the summer of 1972, when radical left-wing forces had taken over the machinery of the Democratic Party, that party's platform committed to every conceivable right including: "The right to be different, to maintain a cultural or ethnic heritage or lifestyle, without being forced into a compelled homogeneity . . ." They promised empowerment to those without rights: "Children, the mentally retarded, mentally ill and prisoners."[5] Still, there was one "right" presidential candidate Senator George McGovern managed to keep out of the platform, namely, a pro-abortion rights plank.

Fearing a Catholic backlash, McGovern told his feminist supporters that although he supported a woman's "right to choose," he thought it a matter of conscience best left to the states. He also said he could not support abortion-on-demand.[6] The other major candidates vying for the Democratic nomination also opposed abortion. Hubert Humphrey said, "I'm not for it." Senator Edmund Muskie, a Catholic, stated, "It compromises the sanctity of life."

Even the Rev. Jesse Jackson viewed abortion "as too nice a word for something cold, like murder."[7] McGovern's first choice for vice president, Senator Thomas Eagleton of Missouri, was also pro-life. (Eagleton, who was forced to step aside because he failed to disclose that he had once received psychiatric help, was the last pro-lifer ever nominated on the national Democratic ticket.)

Richard Nixon, on the other hand, was ahead of the Democrats on the pro-life issue. After New York's Republican-controlled State Legislature passed a liberalized pro-abortion bill in 1970 that was signed into law by Republican governor Nelson Rockefeller, President Nixon wrote to Terence Cardinal Cooke, Archbishop of New York, expressing his thoughts on the subject. Conceding that abortion "is a matter for state decision outside Federal jurisdiction," nevertheless he told the Cardinal, "I would personally like to associate myself with the convictions you deeply feel and eloquently express."[8]

While in 1972 abortion was not a key issue, by the 1976 presidential election it was, and every candidate was expected to articulate clearly his position. Yet, knowing that abortion was a political hot potato, candidates hedged. Jimmy Carter, for instance, had encouraged the Georgia plaintiffs in the *Roe v. Wade* companion suit, *Doe v. Bolton*, to pursue their case. He had also written an introduction to *Women in Need*, a pro-abortion book. And as governor he had supported Georgia family-planning programs that included abortion.[9] On the national campaign trail, however, Carter played a different tune: In Iowa, in which a half-million Catholics resided in 1976, he told Catholic clergy that he "opposed abortion as a matter of personal conviction and though he would not support a constitutional amendment banning abortion, he would support a national statute regulating abortion."[10] On another occasion while campaigning in Iowa, when a pro-lifer asked him if he "would support a constitutional amendment uniformly applying to all states the anti-abortion ban in Georgia law voided by the Supreme Court, [Carter] 'whispered . . . under certain circumstances, I would.'"[11]

When reporters later asked for clarification, Carter said he "opposed a constitutional amendment but would favor any law not in conflict with the Supreme Court decision that would restrict abortions through better-planned parenthood, availability of contraceptive devices, and improved adoption procedures."[12]

When the 1976 Democratic Convention passed a pro-abortion plank, the president of the NCCB, Archbishop Joseph Bernardin of Cincinnati, received national coverage when he criticized the Democrats for "opposing protection of the life of the unborn and endorsing permissive abortion."[13]

Sensing a "Catholic Problem," Carter gave an exclusive interview to the National Catholic News Service (NCNS) clarifying his position. The wording of the plank (which had been drafted by Carter staff members), "was not," he told the NCNS, "in accordance with my own desires. . . . The insinuation of the plank's opposition to citizen effort to amend the Constitution as inappropriate is what I object to."[14]

Archbishop Bernardin, who in 1976 believed the abortion issue was of primary concern over any other social issue, had this reaction to Carter's comments:

> Despite [Governor Carter's] personal opposition to abortion, we regret that he continues to be unsupportive of a constitutional amendment to protect the life of the unborn. His reiteration of this stance reveals an inconsistency that is deeply disturbing to those who hold the right to life to be sacred and inalienable. . . . The pro-abortion plank of the Democratic platform remains seriously objectionable.[15]

Realizing that both Carter and Ford were vying for the Catholic vote, the NCCB invited the presidential candidates to meet with them and discuss key issues. Both readily agreed. Carter advisor Stuart Eizenstat stated that Carter "needed desperately to win the northern blue-collar voter. . . . The bishops could affect that vote at the margin, and it is at the margin, after all, that elections are won and lost."[16]

The Ford camp agreed to the NCCB meeting because they were convinced that the Watergate mess had stalled the "Emerging Republican Majority" in the South. Believing that southern Nixon-Democrats would vote for Carter out of regional pride, the only swing group available was ethnic Catholics.

In August 1976, when Carter met with the bishops, he told them he agreed with them on numerous issues and told them that he believed abortion was immoral. Convinced that their only differences on abortion were matters of strategy, Carter hoped his views would be "minimally acceptable" to the bishops. Carter's hopes were dashed when he heard Archbishop Bernardin's public response to his plea:

> We have called for a constitutional amendment that will give the maximum protection possible to the unborn. Despite contrary positions, there is no other way to correct the serious situation that now exists. If there is an agreement that abortion is a moral evil because it violates a person's most basic right, then the only logical conclusion is that something must be done to correct the evil, and the only remedy is a constitutional amendment. It is for this reason that, on behalf of the Conference of Catholic Bishops, I issued a statement on June 23 expressing strong disagreement –

> indeed outrage – with the abortion plank in the Democratic plat-
> form.
>
> . . . We . . . repeat, today with all the moral force we can
> muster, the need for a constitutional amendment to protect the life
> of the unborn. Indeed, without such a remedy, the effort to pro-
> mote other human life causes for individual and social betterment,
> about which we are all concerned, is seriously weakened.[17]

While Ford's staff was jubilant, Carter's staff believed their man had been "sandbagged."

When the bishops met Ford at the White House for the president's inter-view, it was known that he was mushy on abortion, and that his feminist wife, Betty Ford, was a vocal proponent of a woman's right to choose abortion. But thanks to the demands of the Reagan forces at the 1976 Republican Convention, a plank calling for a constitutional amendment to ban abortion was added to the GOP's platform.

Ironically, this plank saved the day for Ford – he was able to point out to the bishops that his party's platform was similar to the position of the NCCB. He told the bishops that he found abortion to be immoral and that he support-ed an amendment returning the right to the states to end abortions.

After the meeting, Bernardin told the press, "relative to the abortion deci-sion we are encouraged that the President agrees on the need for a constitu-tional amendment. We urged him to support an amendment that will give the maximum protection possible to the unborn."[18]

While the bishops did not endorse anyone for president, the press cover-age over the next twenty-four hours implied they were with Ford. And that's how many ethnic Catholics interpreted it as well.

Gerald Ford began the fall campaign fifteen points behind Carter. But by early October he was rapidly closing that gap. Since he could not assume that many southern states would go his way, he devoted significant time to the Midwest states rich with ethnic-Catholic voters.

In a September 15th speech at his alma mater, the University of Michigan, President Ford promised Catholics "new tax breaks for parents sending their children to parochial schools,"[19] and by early October opinion polls revealed that this strategy was working thanks to the shifting of the Catholic vote, the gap between Carter and Ford was closing.

Since Carter could not compete on the abortion issue, he decided to employ another tactic to attract back Catholic support. The desperate Carter adopted the liberal misperception that the world view of neighborhood white Catholics was driven by racism, not the social doctrine of subsidiarity, and declared his opposition to open-housing projects, saying, "I see nothing wrong with ethnic purity being maintained."

America's two leading Catholic social critics, Andrew Greeley and Michael Novak, condemned Carter for siding with the extreme leftist, anti-Catholic wing of the Democratic Party which labels inner-city Catholics as bigoted low-lives. Novak bluntly told the press:

> Carter is no Robert Kennedy, nor even a Hubert Humphrey, uniting both the whites and blacks of Gary, and Pittsburgh, and Chicago, under one set of symbols and policies. On the contrary, Carter reinforces the perceptions that the Democrats are interested in "affirmative discrimination" against working-class and white-collar Catholics.[20]

But it was a major misstatement at the October 1976 presidential debate that took Carter off the hot seat and stopped Ford's momentum. In discussing the Helsinki Accords, which legalized Soviet control of the so-called Captive Nations, President Ford said: "There is no Soviet domination of Eastern Europe and never will be under a Ford administration."

Advisors in both camps gasped when they heard this statement – they knew it could decide the election. One political aide recalled, "I kept thinking of the Alliance of Poles Hall in Cleveland and how they might be throwing beer bottles at the screen by then."[21]

Carter, grasping the magnitude of Ford's statement, replied: "I would like to see Mr. Ford convince the Polish-Americans and the Czech-Americans and the Hungarian-Americans in this country that those countries don't live under the domination and supervision of the Soviet Union behind the Iron Curtain."[22]

The election went down to the wire with Jimmy Carter edging out Gerald Ford with 50.1 percent of the vote to 48 percent. The Electoral College was just as close with Carter carrying twenty-three states plus the District of Columbia with 297 electoral votes to Ford's 240 electoral votes from twenty-seven states. In Missouri, Ohio, and Pennsylvania, states Carter barely carried, the Catholic votes made the difference. Nationally, Jimmy Carter received 57 percent of the Catholic vote to Ford's 42 percent. Election analyst Robert Teeter concluded that the defection from the GOP ticket of Eastern European Catholics had cost Ford the election.[23]

*   *   *   *   *

Carter's election was a result of the Watergate mess, southern pride, and Gerald Ford's misstatement about Eastern Europe. Political analysts, including Kevin Phillips and Michael Barone, looked upon Carter's victory as a fluke – or as historian Clarence Carson called it – an "interlude." Shortly after he took office, leaders of both parties realized that the president and his top staff possessed a self-righteous arrogance that would render them politically impotent. Journalist Victor Lasky summed up the views of many in Washington when he wrote:

> Rarely in the history of the Republic has there been an occupant of the Oval Office who demonstrated so quickly an inability to conduct even the simplest affairs of the state. . . . He is perceived both at home and abroad as a politician of limited and uncertain talents, a well-meaning man whose power derives far more from the office he lucked into than the qualities of personal leadership he has been able to exert.[24]

By 1979, gasoline prices had skyrocketed, inflation was out of control, the economy was a shambles, interest rates were at all-time highs, unemployment was hitting highs not seen since the Depression, and respect for America overseas had reached new lows.

Then on November 3, 1979, Iranian students seized sixty-three Americans at the United States Embassy and held them hostage for 444 days. Carter's ineptitude in handling the hostage crisis contributed to his unpopularity. Also, his weak foreign policy prompted the Soviet Union to invade Afghanistan in 1979. Carter, who believed that U.S. intrusion, not Soviet expansion, was the root of world tensions, was suddenly shocked that the Communists could be so aggressive and brutal. With polls showing that Carter was losing the support of the American people, the self-righteous president unsuccessfully tried to change the tide by blaming *his* shortcomings on "America's malaise."

Concerned that the Democratic Party would lose its reputation as the bastion of liberalism, Senator Edward Kennedy challenged the incumbent president's right to another term. Kennedy, who regarded himself the keeper of the liberal flame, was at odds with the Catholic Church on abortion. He took pride in supporting women's right to choose, federal financing of abortion, and, in later years, partial birth abortion.

While the Carter-Kennedy battle was splitting the Democratic Party, Ronald Reagan was locking up the Republican nomination and pursuing a winning coalition in which ethnic Catholics were a key component.

Reagan and his key advisors understood that Catholics were comfortable in aligning themselves with a coalition leader who respected their traditional working-class values. To cement this coalition, Reagan ran on a platform that pledged to restore America's traditional morals at home and its strength and respect abroad, and that pledged to reject redistributive politics at home. Reagan aide Richard Darman described the voters that found Reagan's view of America's future appealing:

[They were] people who were not poor but who were often lower-middle class or working class. They were people with just enough money to stick their heads up, look around, and feel certain feelings. They were people who always thought someone or something was keeping them from getting ahead, from achieving in some way. They were resentful. It is partly a resentful movement. But they were also hopeful. They believed in America and the American dream; they came from people who packed up in Europe or wherever and took a dangerous journey across the ocean, often alone, in search of a better life. That is not the action of someone who is demoralized or driven into helplessness by circumstances. It is a profoundly hopeful act.[25]

In this nutshell, Darman described many Roman Catholics.

Catholics did not rally around Ted Kennedy as they did his brother a generation earlier. They found both Ted Kennedy's private and public lives to be embarrassing. Working-class Catholics blamed Ted Kennedy and his ilk for permitting the left-wing counter-culture to seize control of the Democratic Party. They agreed with journalist Theodore White's observation that these Democratic "social engineers" were destroying their party because they pursued a program that would produce "not equality of opportunity, but equality of result stipulated in goals, quotas, and entitlements, based not on excellence or merit, but on bloodlines."[26]

While Carter beat Kennedy for the nomination, he lost control of the party platform, which was drafted by radical leftists. As a result, the platform endorsed homosexual orientation as a civil right, Medicaid funding of abortion, and the denial of party financial support to any Democrat who opposed the Equal Rights Amendment.

When they forced their radical abortion stand on the Democratic Party, extreme left-wing delegates intentionally ignored the results of the 1978 Congressional elections. In that year, three U.S. senators and twenty-three congressmen lost their seats because they were active proponents of legalized abortion and the Equal Rights Amendment.

In Iowa, for example, pro-life Catholics organized opposition to pro-abortion Senator Dick Clark. Pro-life squads followed Clark around the state and over three hundred thousand flyers were distributed after Sunday Masses at every Iowa Catholic Church. Pro-life Republican Roger Jepsen edged out Clark 51.1 percent to 47.9 percent, thanks to the Catholic activists.

*   *   *   *   *

Ronald Reagan opened his campaign over the Labor Day Weekend on Liberty Island in New York Harbor with the Statue of Liberty serving as a backdrop. With his shirt sleeves rolled up, Reagan began his race for the

White House by appealing directly to the ethnic-Catholic voters. In his remarks that day, he lauded the true grit of millions of immigrants who had passed through Ellis Island.

This soft-spoken former Democrat invited Catholics to follow his lead into the Republican Party. Portraying himself as the antithesis of cultural liberalism, Reagan stressed the themes of "work, family, neighborhood, peace and freedom." He told Catholic voters:

> The secret is that when the Left took over the Democratic Party we took over the Republican Party. We made the Republican Party into the Party of the working people, the family, the neighborhood, the defense of freedom, and yes, the American Flag and the Pledge of Allegiance to one Nation under God. So, you see, the Party that so many of us grew up with still exists except that today it's called the Republican Party.[27]

Reagan also hit a chord with Catholics when he spoke fondly of New Deal programs and harshly about the Great Society social experiments. Reagan, who four times had voted for FDR, still admired the former president and copied his style. Reagan's frequent call for a "Rendezvous with Destiny" was lifted from Roosevelt's 1936 acceptance speech.

President Carter's re-election campaign was in shambles. He was burdened with a pro-abortion, pro-gay rights platform that was costing him Catholic and southern votes. In addition to being upset with the Democrats' stand on social issues, many Catholics were angry because they were hurting economically. Over 250,000 blue-collar automobile industry jobs were wiped out during the Carter years. In Flint, Michigan, unemployment hit 25 percent. Many ethnic Catholics were forced to move out of Michigan, Pennsylvania, and Ohio in search of employment. In the late seventies, it was estimated that 1.5 million had moved to the Sunbelt.[28]

Throughout the fall, the Carter campaign made gaffe after gaffe. On one occasion, during a stopover in the Parma section of Cleveland, Carter could not understand the awful reception he received from the Slovak neighborhood. It turns out the president was not informed that his Justice Department had accused the ethnics of being racists because for three generations those neighborhood folks were selling their houses to family members and friends. Historian Kenneth Heineman pointed out: "The possibility that Catholic families might want to remain close to childhood, parish and kin was not even worth contemplating."[29]

As the Communists were slaughtering the populace of Afghanistan and cracking down on Poles seeking freedom, Carter's naïve view that Russia was no longer a threat also offended many Catholics. This comment Carter made at the 1977 Notre Dame graduation was now haunting him: "We are now free of that inordinate fear of Communism which once led us to embrace any dictator who joined us in our fear."[30]

Carter's appeal to racism also failed. His comment that Reagan's election "would divide black and white, Christian and Jew" was severely criticized. The president was so unpopular in Catholic circles that at the prestigious Al Smith Dinner, he was booed by New York's leading Catholics.

Ronald Reagan closed his 1980 campaign with these questions:

> Are you better off than you were four years ago? Is it easier for you to go and buy things in the stores than it was four years ago? Is there more or less unemployment in the country than there was four years ago? Is America as respected throughout the world as it was? Do you feel that our security is as safe, that we're as strong as we were four years ago?[31]

On November 4, 1980, the American people gave a resounding "No" to the inquiry. Millions of Democratic Catholics and Southerners rejected Carter and overwhelmingly supported Reagan.

Carter received only 41 percent of the vote, which was the greatest rejection of an incumbent president since Herbert Hoover. The voters also tossed out of office old-line liberal senators: George McGovern, Frank Church, and Birch Bayh went down in flames. The GOP picked up thirteen U.S. Senate seats and gained a majority in that body for the first time since 1952.

Reagan carried the Catholic vote 49 percent to Carter's 42 percent, with Independent candidate John Anderson receiving 7 percent.[32] Reagan made his greatest electoral inroads among ethnic Catholics – Irish, Italian, Poles, and Slovaks supported him overwhelmingly.

Irish Catholic Support in Largest States – 1980

	Reagan	Carter	Anderson
New York	53%	35%	12%
California	64	28	8
Texas	65	31	4

Italians, who had voted Democratic in every presidential election except 1972, were now solidly in the Republican camp:

Italian-Catholics in Key States

	Reagan	Carter	Anderson
New York	57%	37%	6%
New Jersey	60	33	7
California	64	26	10

While the Eastern European vote gave Carter a slim majority in Pennsylvania, Ohio, and Maryland, they deserted him in the other states that contained significant Slovak populations:

Polish-Slovak Catholic Votes in Key States – 1980

	Reagan	Carter	Anderson
Michigan	49%	44%	7%
New Jersey	60	29	11
Connecticut	44	41	15
Texas	62	33	5
Illinois	49	39	12

Many Catholic voters sent a strong message in 1980 that they had had it with the Democratic Party's radical social agenda, appeasement policies toward the Communists, and failed economic policies. Analyst Michael Barone concluded that Carter was rejected in 1980 because "the cultural segment of America, which was emotionally most inclined to see Jimmy Carter as its kind of American, had decided he was not; its members felt at the least disappointed, and in some cases betrayed."[33]

One area that was a microcosm of 1980 Catholic defections was Macomb County, Michigan. This heavily Catholic, blue-collar Detroit suburb of 700,000 people deserted their party and became Reagan Democrats.

According to National Demographics and Lifestyles, a corporation that analyzes trends in metropolitan areas, Macomb County is one of America's most typical middle-class populations. "Football is big there, wine tasting is not. The 'in' leisure sport is bowling, not tennis. They shop at Kmart, not Neiman Marcus. Breakfast is bacon and eggs, not croissants and champagne."[34]

Macomb County, Michigan, Vote for President
1960–1988

	Republican	Democratic	Independent
1960	36.9%	62.8%	–
1964	25.3	74.5	–
1968	30.4	55.2	14.4%
1972	62.7	34.9	–
1976	51.2	46.9	–
1980	51.9	40.4	7.7
1984	66.2	33.3	–
1988	60.3	38.8	–

The hard-core union, blue-collar Democrats of Macomb County deserted their party because they were disillusioned over cultural issues: busing, drugs, crime, and abortion.

* * * * *

Sworn in as America's oldest president, the sixty-nine-year-old Reagan told the nation: "Our Government has no special power except that granted it by the people. It is time to check and reverse the growth of government which shows signs of having grown beyond the consent of the governed."

Throughout his first term, Reagan outwitted the Washington establishment led by House Speaker Tip O'Neill. Because they believed Reagan was a lightweight, Democrats constantly underestimated his resiliency, devotion to principle, powers of political persuasion, and ability to negotiate. Time and again, the "inept" Reagan managed to get the biggest piece of the political pie.

President Reagan signed into law America's largest tax cut, fired the nation's striking air-traffic controllers, enhanced government deregulation of industries, ended runaway inflation, and got the stagnant economy to flourish.

The president also improved our international standing by articulating a hard line against the "evil empire," the Soviet Union. He committed the resources needed to win the arms race and called for the building of "star wars," the Strategic Defense Initiative. Our armed forces successfully expelled a Marxist coup in Grenada, and the president worked closely with Pope John Paul II to bring down the Iron Curtain.

Cognizant of America's cultural divide, President Reagan rejected the culture of death in favor of the defense of life. Admitting that his greatest public mistake had been to sign a liberal abortion bill while he was governor of California, President Reagan published an article, "Abortion and the Conscience of the Nation," on the tenth anniversary of *Roe v. Wade*. In the essay he reminded the nation that "regrettably we live at a time when some persons do not value all human life. They want to pick and choose which individuals have value. . . . In other words, quality control."[35]

Throughout his first term, Reagan's popularity hit all-time highs. Millions of people, whose faith in America's institutions had been shaken in the 1970s, felt a renewed confidence under Reagan. According to liberal pollster Stanley Greenberg, Reagan knew how to speak to the forgotten middle class:

> Reagan reached out to ordinary people: he touched them first with his essential honesty and then with his heartfelt proposal to lift their financial burden by cutting tax rates. He sought to restore faith in the market and in entrepreneurship in order to allow people once again to believe that American business could lead

America to a new age of growth and prosperity. For a moment, it all seemed quite magical; it was, as the campaign ad suggested, "morning in America."[36]

Rank-and-file Roman Catholics were very high on Reagan. They approved of his economic plans as well as his opposition to abortion and communism. They were also pleased that in his 1983 State of the Union Address, he supported a constitutional amendment for school prayer and called for a tuition tax credit for parents with children in parochial schools.

This Catholic contentment with Reagan did not sit well with many of the left-wing bishops who were appointed in the 1960s and 1970s. One extremist, Seattle's Archbishop Raymond Hunthausen, announced his support for unilateral U.S. disarmament and urged Christians to refuse to pay 50 percent of their federal income tax. He told his flock to withhold the money spent on "nuclear murder."

While the bishops approved the Republican stance against abortion, for most of them their hearts were with the Democratic Party on many other issues. To prevent abortion from being the premier Catholic issue, Archbishop Bernardin promoted the "seamless garment" approach to dealing with the great controversies of the day:

> I am convinced that the pro-life position of the church must be developed in terms of a comprehensive and consistent ethic of life. . . . The principle which structures both cases, war and abortion, needs to be upheld in both places. It cannot be successfully sustained on one count and simultaneously eroded in a similar situation. . . . I contend the viability of the principle depends upon the consistency of its application.[37]

This position was also held by the NCCB Administration Committee:

> Abortion and the need for a constitutional amendment to protect the unborn are among our concerns. So are the issues of unemployment, adequate educational opportunity for all, an equitable food policy both domestic and world wide, the right to a decent home and healthcare, human rights across the globe, intelligent arms limitation and many other social justice issues. . . . The Catholic Bishops of the United States have often publicly stated – and we here reaffirm – deep commitment to the sanctity, dignity, and quality of human life at all states of development, as well as to legislation and public policy which protects and promotes these values in all contemporary contexts.[38]

Although many bishops, for example Cardinal Humberto Medeiros of Boston and New York's Archbishop O'Connor, rejected this approach and insisted that the premier life issue was abortion, the liberals' approach opened the door for the bishops to get involved in protesting the nuclear arms race.

Believing that the anti-abortion, or right-to-life, argument should be extended to "the same level of commitment to other threats of human life," the NCCB issued, "The Challenge of Peace: God's Promise and Our Response," on May 3, 1983. The paper "condemned a defense policy based either on first use of counterforce nuclear weapons or on second strike countervalue attacks, each of which said the bishops, by threatening the lives of millions, violated Jesus' peaceable injunctions and the principles of Catholic just-war theory."[39]

The liberal media applauded this criticism of Reagan Administration policies and gave the "dovish" bishops unprecedented coverage. In the May 5, 1983 *New York Times*, two full pages were devoted to text and commentary on the bishops' "challenge." The liberal media, which had so often criticized the Catholic hierarchy for violating the separation of church and state by speaking out on other issues (i.e., gay rights and abortion), were now in the thrall of episcopal wisdom.

The same cannot be said of Catholics, however. Many were displeased by the bishops' statement. The leader of pro-deterrence Catholics, Michael Novak, in his *Moral Clarity in the Nuclear Age*, "stressed the concrete circumstances the United States currently faced." "No doubt," Novak wrote, "deterrence was far from perfect, but the particulars of the contemporary situation made it the least of the available evils in the context of Soviet ambitions, ideology and the historical experience of Soviet respect for strength and contempt for conciliation."[40]

Hoping that the liberal positions of the bishops reflected the sentiments of rank-and-file Catholics, Walter Mondale chose as his running mate, the first woman V.P. candidate, Italian-American Congresswoman Geraldine Ferraro of Queens, New York City. A so-called "pro-choice Catholic," Ferraro was a favorite of NOW, Jane Fonda, and Speaker Tip O'Neill.

As the fall campaign began, Ferraro dominated the news because of allegations concerning her family's financial connections and her views on abortion. The new archbishop of New York, John O'Connor, set the ground work for a clash with Ferraro when in June 1984 he said in a press conference, "I do not see how a Catholic in good conscience can vote for an individual expressing himself or herself favoring abortion."[41] Most concluded that O'Connor was pointing his finger at Catholic voters who supported Governor Mario Cuomo, U.S. Senator Daniel Patrick Moynihan, and Congresswoman Ferraro. When he refused to back off his statement, *The New York Times* took this shot at O'Connor:

> It might as well be said bluntly: . . . the . . . effort to impose a reli-
> gious test on the performance of Catholic politicians threatens the
> hard-won understanding that finally brought America to elect a
> Catholic President a generation ago.[42]

O'Connor pushed the political envelope further when after the Democratic Convention he said that a letter Ferraro had sent to fifty Catholic congressmen concerning a group called *Catholics for a Free Choice* had, "said some things about abortion relevant to Catholic teachings which are not true."[43] He was referring to a line in the letter which stated that "[Members of Catholics for a Free Choice] show us that the Catholic position on abortion is not monolithic and that there can be a range of personal and political responses to the issue."[44]

The political heat on Ferraro increased when, in September, seventeen New England bishops publicly criticized Catholic politicians who claimed that while they "personally opposed" abortion, they were against imposing their moral beliefs on others, and thus supported federal and state tax dollars to pay for abortions. The bishops concluded: "To evade the issue of abortion under the pretext that it is a matter pertaining exclusively to private morality is obviously illogical."[45]

While Ferraro continued to defend her "personally-I-have-always-been-against-abortion" position, *The New Republic*'s Charles Krauthammer pointed out the inconsistency of her position:

> When Geraldine Ferraro . . . says she's "personally opposed" to
> abortion, she means this: I wouldn't have one myself and I would-
> n't want my children to have one, but I won't go around telling
> people whether to have one or not. Unfortunately, Ferraro is con-
> fusing belief with practice. If a person says, "I refuse to own
> slaves, but I won't go around telling others what to do," it is cor-
> rect to say that he does not practice slavery, but can one really say
> he is opposed to it?[46]

Mario Cuomo, Tip O'Neill, Ted Kennedy, and others did come to Ferraro's defense: Cuomo delivered a major address at the University of Notre Dame defending the "I-personally-oppose-but . . ." position. Senator Kennedy accused Archbishop O'Connor of "blatant sectarian appeals" and argued that not "every moral command" could become law. In his book, *God Is A Conservative*, historian Kenneth Heineman pointed out that Kennedy's statement implied "that anyone who opposed Ferraro and abortion was a religious bigot."[47]

All these pro-abortion rationalizations were too much for some members of the Democratic Party. Former New York governor Hugh Carey complained that liberals were "gloating and gleeful that their party will kill more fetuses than the other party." Governor Cuomo was criticized by former Minnesota Senator and liberal icon, Eugene McCarthy, who said that "abortion is a legitimate public issue and far from sectarian, since more than just Catholics oppose it."[48]

All this controversy did not help the foundering Mondale campaign, and his plan to attract Catholics back to the party with the Ferraro choice appeared to be backfiring.

Taking advantage of the chaos, Ronald Reagan reached out to disaffected Catholics. In Waterbury, Connecticut, a Catholic town of factory workers that had hosted John F. Kennedy's last campaign appearance in 1960, Reagan said: "You know, I was a Democrat once. . . . The only abandoning I see is the Democratic leadership abandoning the good and decent Democrats of the JFK and FDR . . . and Truman tradition."[49]

Mondale and many others in the Democratic Party failed to grasp that across the nation Catholic priests regularly preached that *Roe v. Wade* was inherently evil – it approved the taking of unborn life. It was the murder of a child. For average church-going Catholics in 1984, abortion was one matter on which they could not compromise. As a result, the most visible Catholic politicians in 1984 – Mario Cuomo, Edward Kennedy, and Geraldine Ferraro – were viewed more as traitors than champions.

In contrast, Ronald Reagan was pro-life. He also had an attitude and a demeanor as president that enhanced his support among Catholics. They were pleased when, after a long trip home from China, the president had stayed in Alaska an extra night to meet Pope John Paul II at the Fairbanks International Airport. They were impressed that Reagan stood on their side of the barricades in the brewing culture wars. And they were delighted that Reagan stood up for them and fought the tyranny of big government and the big taxes needed to support it. A blue-collar worker in the Northeast put it best: "The Democratic Party has been good to me – Social Security, G.I. Bill, student loans. The Democratic Party made me middle class. But Reagan will keep me middle class."[50]

On election day the American people overwhelmingly re-elected President Reagan. He carried forty-nine states with 525 electoral votes, the largest total ever received. Mondale carried only his home state of Minnesota (49.7 percent v. Reagan's 49.5 percent) and the District of Columbia, and he lost every voting bloc except African-Americans, Jews, and liberal journalists.[51]

Sixty-one percent of Catholic voters cast their ballots for Reagan. Mondale's gamble with Geraldine Ferraro failed. Robert McElvaine's observation in a *New York Times* op-ed piece that the selection of Ferraro "could neutralize Mr. Reagan's attempt to convince the American people that St. Peter was a registered Republican"[52] was wrong. Historian Kenneth Wald has pointed out that among Catholics, "the defections from the Democratic Party appeared to have been highest among those . . . most deeply involved in parish life."[53] The fact that Reagan handily carried Ferraro's Ninth Congressional District with 57 percent of the vote confirmed Wald's contention.

And the shift of Catholics to Republican ranks appeared on the rise: whereas in 1980 only 17 percent of Catholics considered themselves Republican, by 1986 that number had grown to 26 percent. Liberal Pollster Stanley Greenberg pointed out that a 1980 "28 point Democratic [voter registration] advantage among Catholics was cut nearly in half to 15 points."[54]

* * * * *

Throughout the eighties, Ronald Reagan successfully pursued policies that curbed inflation, restored long-term productivity growth, strengthened our defense system, and preserved a humane social safety net.

The success of his policies caused inflation to drop to 1.9 percent in 1986 from a high of 13.5 percent in 1980; the prime rate to drop to 8.5 percent from 21 percent in 1980; and disposable income to grow 46 percent between 1980 and 1986. In addition, from 1981 to 1986, American net worth was up 39 percent. Mr. Reagan risked huge deficits when he decided to increase spending to boost our sagging defense system. This strategy culminated with the Soviet decision to bargain seriously at the disarmament conferences.

Reagan also promoted a public philosophy that consisted of these three fundamental ideas:

> The first of those ideas concerned the nature of a free society. The central feature of such a society, said Reagan, is not competition between individuals, but a voluntary and reciprocating association among them. Human beings are one another's partners, capable of combining their strengths and talents and obliged to do so if they are to solve their problems and promote undertakings of significance. The secret of human prosperity in a free society is the art of teaming up.
>
> The second of Reagan's core ideas was that human nature is not perfectible. It consists of a divided self, with hate and love inextricably mixed. Every individual, of whatever culture or status, has both the capacity for cruelty and the free will to overcome the countless temptations to hate and to hurt. No one is an angel, but no one has to be an evil beast.
>
> The third of Reagan's ideas concerned human worth. The ethical measure of individuals, he insisted, is not the consequences of

their actions but the magnitude of their efforts to resist their worse selves and uphold their better selves. In other words, what matters about individuals is whether they try to do their best with what they have. Not their material but their spiritual achievements count: effort is what merits honor.[55]

Reagan's philosophy of man plus his economic and fiscal policies led to an era of renewal in America that pleased many Catholic voters. In viewing his two terms, George Will pointed out that "the nation needed what he delivered – confidence and a sense that government could act decisively . . . in accordance with a clear vision."[56]

As President Reagan's second term was winding down, he managed to maintain his popularity with the American people. His approval ratings in 1988 hovered at 60 percent. And, as the 1988 elections approached, voters had to decide which of the candidates hoping to succeed Reagan would maintain the economic prosperity and the social calm they had enjoyed throughout the 1980s.

Republicans turned to Vice President George Bush to head their ticket, because they believed he would be the next best thing to an actual third Reagan term. Bush did have some negatives: He was viewed by many on the right as a "wimp" and a "preppy" child of privilege whose family were members in good standing of the old Eastern-establishment wing of the Republican Party. But the ambitious Bush was malleable and gave his political guru Lee Atwater a free hand to portray him as the candidate of "faith, family and flag."[57]

The Democrats faced a serious problem – a weak stable of wannabees. The condition of the Democratic Party was summed up by Richard Nixon:

> The Democrats face a traumatic dilemma. In 1972, they could excuse McGovern's loss by the fact that he was not a mainstream Democrat. [In 1984], they had an establishment Democrat, Mondale, campaigning on traditional Democratic issues and appealing to the old Democratic coalition of minorities, labor, the disadvantaged, etc., which proved unbeatable for Roosevelt, Truman, and Johnson. What [that] election demonstrated is that there just aren't enough voters in those groups to make a majority. [58]

To most Americans, liberalism was no longer a philosophy for uplifting the average struggling American, but rather a narcissistic attitude now believed by old segments of the FDR coalition. Liberalism was "self-involved . . . [and] responsible for cultural decay, a rising crime wave, racial polarization and a weakening of America abroad."[59] At the 1988 Democratic Convention, Congressman Peter Kostmayer of Pennsylvania sought to down play this cultural divide when he told delegates: "Just shut up gays, women, environmentalists. Just shut up. You'll get everything you want after the election. But just for the meantime, shut up so that we can win."[60]

Hoping to sidestep the liberal stigma, the Democrats turned to Governor Michael Dukakis of Massachusetts. Although Dukakis was definitely a man of the left and a proud card-carrying member of the ACLU, he came across as a man devoid of philosophical foundations who applied legalistic and technocratic formulas to governing. Dukakis's theme was "Competence, Not Ideology."

Known as "Michael the Harvard Techie," Dukakis was uncomfortable in public. He possessed little political charm, and he could not project any warmth or compassion. During the summer of 1988, instead of overseeing the organizing of a campaign that would take on the Republican assault team, he seemed more concerned about his backyard vegetable garden. He scolded his wife for forgetting to water the dying cucumber patch. To many Democrats, Dukakis was not the successor to FDR, Truman, and JFK, but the heir of Henry Wallace and George McGovern. Journalist Fred Barnes wrote in the *New Republic*: "All [Dukakis] cares about is that the pipeline is neat and shiny and clean. But me, I don't care if the pipeline is cracked and rusty as long as the right result comes out the other end."[61]

Tin-eared Dukakis supporters did not realize that their candidate actually carried plenty of baggage that the Republicans would use to turn the campaign into one based on cultural issues. Numerous decisions by Governor Dukakis came back to haunt him including:

* His veto of a law requiring students to say the Pledge of Allegiance.

* His support of weekend furloughs for convicted violent criminals. One such convict, Willie Horton, raped a woman while on furlough.

At the Republican Convention, Mr. Bush drew a line in the sand on these cultural issues: In his acceptance speech he defined his support for the Pledge of Allegiance, the death penalty, and school prayer, proclaiming, "My opponent says no, but I say yes!"[62]

Dukakis's early seventeen-point lead in the polls quickly began to dissipate as Republicans bashed him on the social issues. And the polls revealed the validity of their strategy. An ABC News/*Washington Post* poll revealed in mid-October that 67 percent believed that "preserving the values of the

American family" was very important. The Pledge of Allegiance was very important to 45 percent of the respondents.[63]

Bush beat Dukakis in November, receiving 53.4 percent of the vote to 45.6. The Republican carried forty states for 426 electoral votes to the Democrat's ten states and the District of Columbia for a total of 111 electoral votes.

While Bush did not receive the level of Catholic support Reagan had in 1988, he did carry a majority – 51 percent to Dukakis's 49 percent.

The Bush Campaign strategy to stress social issues clearly hit the mark. All voters, including Catholics, put abortion, the death penalty, and drug abuse at the top of their lists of concerns:

Important Issues in the 1988 Presidential Vote[64]

Item	% Mentions		
	All Voters	**White Catholics**	**Non-White Catholics**
Abortion	29%	29%	21%
Death Penalty	24	24	15
Illegal Drug Problem	23	25	24
Dukakis/Bush Debates	23	26	35
My Candidate's Political Party	21	21	18
Education	20	20	24
Health Care	19	21	20
Social Security	17	19	18
Environmental Problems	17	18	16
College Costs	11	12	16
Pledge of Allegiance	11	9	6
Prison Furloughs	11	11	5
Foreign Competition	11	13	10
Quayle for Vice President	11	12	8
Bentsen/Quayle Debate	10	11	12
My Candidate's Personality	10	10	9
Iran-Contra Affair	10	10	11
None of These	10	10	9
Bentsen for Vice President	9	10	11
ACLU stand	8	7	3
Capital Gains Tax	7	7	5

Reviewing vote totals in the Age of Reagan, Gallup pollsters concluded that Catholics had become "a two-party church." Catholics were still considered legitimate swing voters, and Gallup gave a final note on nearly a century of American electoral politics: "One thing is clear, no Democrat will ever be elected president without heavy Catholic support, and no candidate, Democrat or Republican, can take the Catholic vote for granted."[65]

Chapter 16

The Catholic Voter in the Twenty-First Century

Most of this book has been devoted to describing the political history of European Catholic immigrants. From 1780 through 1924, millions of these Catholics reached America's shores with only the clothes on their backs. They turned to their parishes and neighborhood confrères and together helped one another to become part of the nation's mainstream.

In the second half of the twentieth century, these Catholics were members of America's "greatest generation." John Kennedy described these World War II veterans in his inaugural speech as those to whom had been passed the torch of leadership. They were ". . . born in this century, tempered by war, disciplined by a hard and bitter peace, proud of our ancient heritage – and unwilling to witness or permit the slow undoing of those human rights to which this nation has always been committed, and to which we are committed today at home and around the world."

But by the 1990s the influence of ethnic Catholics from Europe and the British Isles was on the decline. They were aging, leaving the old neighborhoods and the new suburbs for retirement settlements in the South or the West. And they were dying too. In the last decade of the twentieth century, members of the WWII generation were passing away at the rate of one thousand a day.

During the post-war era, many Catholics had achieved middle-class status and became assimilated into mainstream America. As sociologist David Carlin has written, they were:

> . . . no longer what they had once been. They were no longer immigrants or the children of immigrants. They were no longer poor and badly educated. In short, they were no longer marginal Americans. Instead, they were now three or four generations away from Europe and Quebec; they had done their fair share of patriotic fighting and dying in World War II; they had become middle class; they had moved to the suburbs; they were sending their kids to college. In short, except for their religion, they were just like everyone else; they had become fully Americanized.[1]

However, many of the Catholic children and grandchildren of the "greatest generation" no longer practiced or even respected the moral teachings of the Church. By the end of the twentieth century, many Catholic "yuppies" found Church doctrine embarrassing, and, to be accepted by the "beautiful people" who dominated America's urban enclaves, had became "cafeteria" Catholics – keeping the Catholic doctrines they liked and rejecting those they found inconvenient. Not only do these "Catholics" ridicule their Church, they even permit anti-Catholicism to be the "last acceptable prejudice."

They reject the Church's teaching on abortion, promiscuity, birth control, homosexuality, euthanasia, and cloning. They accept the utilitarian position that one should be free to do "one's own thing" so long as it doesn't harm others.

Cafeteria Catholics in public life were often the first at the Communion rail on Christmas, St. Patrick's Day, and Easter, but during the rest of the year they preached the politics of "pluralism" and "diversity." Catholics such as New York governor George Pataki, who had called for the Republican Party to drop the pro-life plank from its platform in 2000, and both Massachusetts senators, Ted Kennedy and John Kerry – to name only a few – subscribe to this approach. By 2004 approximately 70 percent of the Catholic members of the U.S. Congress had cast pro-abortion votes.

This split between practicing Catholics and cafeteria Catholics has caused considerable confusion. Pollsters and politicians have begun to wonder if Catholics can still be recognized as an actual voting bloc.

Polling research now distinguishes church-going Catholics from the nominal or cafeteria Catholics. While it is true that during the Reagan-Bush years a majority of Catholics from both these groups voted Republican, they did so for different reasons. Most practicing Catholics went for Reagan because of his stands on cultural issues, whereas many nominal Catholics voted Republican purely for economic reasons. The latter group lives by the fashionable maxim, "I am socially progressive and economically conservative."

But the effect on voting patterns caused by the divisions between traditional ethnic Catholics and progressive cafeteria Catholics pale in comparison with the political impact wrought by the rapid increase in America's Hispanic population. After the federal government ended quotas on immigrants from Latin America in 1978, there was a huge surge in Hispanic immigration:

Latin American Immigration

1961–1970	1.1 million
1971–1980	1.7 million
1981–1990	3.0 million
1991–1996	4.7 million

One-third of these Hispanics live in California, while most of the others reside in Texas, New York, Florida, Illinois, and New Jersey.[2]

For deserted inner cities, the influx of Hispanics from numerous Latin American countries has been a boon – they have strengthened the quality of urban areas, repopulating communities, schools, and transit systems. They have refurbished deserted homes and reintroduced neighborhood shops and restaurants. In his study, *New People in Old Neighborhoods*, Louis Winnick has written that this new wave of immigrants has revitalized neighborhoods with "an ethic of work and family that shrinks the Protestant ethic to apathy."

These Hispanics, of whom 80 percent are Catholic, are becoming a political force just as the European Catholics were in the nineteenth and twentieth centuries.

In part because they have settled in inner cities that have always been Democratic, more than 70 percent of Mexican-Americans and Puerto Ricans have become registered Democrats. Inner-city Democratic organizations have given them the same opportunities the old political machines gave the Irish a century ago, namely, entry to the government jobs that put them on the road to middle-class status. Notable exceptions are the large Cuban communities found in Florida and Union City, New Jersey, which are Republican. Because they immigrated for political reasons, Cubans are more attracted to the anti-Communist Cold War reputation of the Republican Party. Hence over 70 percent of these Cubans are registered in the GOP.

Hispanic share of the 1992 statewide vote in selected states[3]

State	Total Vote	Latino Vote	% Latino of Statewide Vote
Arizona	1,728,000	156,000	9.0
California	11,789,000	1,135,000	9.6
Colorado	1,688,000	136,000	8.1
Florida	5,772,000	411,000	7.1
Illinois	5,650,000	171,000	3.0
New Jersey	3,572,000	173,000	4.8
New Mexico	675,000	172,000	25.5
New York	7,613,000	382,000	5.0
Texas	6,817,000	927,000	13.6

Hispanic Voting, 1980–1992[4]

	Democrat	Republican
1980	56%	37%
1984	66	34
1988	70	30
1992	60	24

For the most part Hispanics are liberal on economic issues but somewhat conservative on cultural issues. A 1992 Latino National Political Survey showed that support for capital punishment was high and support for quotas was low:

	Mexican	**Puerto Rican**	**Cuban**[5]
Support for quotas for jobs/college	31.3%	33.9%	18.2%
Support for capital punishment	65.4	53.1	69.7
Abortion should *never* be permitted	20.2	22.3	11.7

Hispanics may soon comprise the Catholic Church's largest ethnic group in the United States. If so, they will also be one of the nation's most significant voting blocs.

What are politicians to make of this change in the Catholic population? Parties and pollsters alike have recognized that Catholics, as Catholics, are no longer a cohesive political force and approach them as several separate groups with different political hot buttons

Pollster Sydney Greenberg summed it up this way:

> The result is that Catholics are very much up for grabs. For some parts of the Catholic community, Reagan settled the issue of aspirations and values, but in fact, a majority of the New Deal-generation Catholics remained Democratic into the nineties. The Catholic male baby boomers became Republicans with Reagan, but the women did not. And the youngest generation of Catholics are dividing along general lines, deepening the parity, with the men strongly Republican and the women strongly Democratic as both have come of age. By the end of the century and this era, Democrats and Republicans had reached parity in party identification in this very fragmented community.[6]

Political analyst, John Morgan, contends there are now five groups of Catholic voters:

* Urban, ethnic blue-collar types found in the Northeast and Midwest. They are typically Democratic but socially conservative.
* Suburban Catholics who for the most part are third-generation Irish and Italian. They are found in Long Island and outside of Chicago, Cleveland and Milwaukee and St. Louis. They are more attached to the Republican Party.
* Midwest German and Polish Catholics who are very conservative but not wedded to the Republican Party. They serve as

swing voters in Wisconsin, Iowa, Minnesota, Michigan, Ohio, and Missouri.

* Hispanics, who are basically Democratic. In Morgan's judgment, for Republicans to attract Hispanic votes, they should appeal to their more socially conservative side.

* Cafeteria Catholics who, for the most part, have fallen away from the Church. Morgan estimates that 20 percent of Catholics fall into this category.[7]

What follows is an attempt to describe how Republicans and Democrats may try to woo these different blocs.

*   *   *   *   *

During the 1988 presidential election, George H. W. Bush made only one New York City campaign stop – in Ridgewood, Queens. He appeared at a Catholic high school before an audience of blue-collar locals and hundreds of "New York's Finest," who conferred on him the endorsement of their union, the Patrolmen's Benevolent Association.

Bush's advisors understood the significance of this appearance; they knew that throughout the twentieth century, blue-collar Catholic neighborhoods have been America's political battlegrounds, and that the right appeal to the cultural values of voters in these neighborhoods has been decisive in national elections.

Claiming to be the rightful heir to Ronald Reagan, George H. W. Bush had to prove that – at least in spirit – he was a member of the neighborhood. Hence in his acceptance speech he declared:

> An election that is about ideas and values is also about philosophy. And I have one.
>
> At the bright center is the individual. And radiating out from him or her is the family, the essential unit of closeness and of love. For it is the family that communicates to our children – to the twenty-first century – our culture, our religious faith, our traditions and history.
>
> From the individual to the family to the community, and on out to the town, to the church and school, and, still echoing out, to the country, the state, the nation – each doing only what it does well, and no more. And I believe that power must always be kept close to the individual – close to the hands that raise the family and run the home.
>
> I am guided by certain traditions. One is that there is a God and He is good, and His love, while free, has a self-imposed cost:

We must be good to one another. . . .

And there is another tradition. And that is the idea of community – a beautiful word with a big meaning, though liberal Democrats have an odd view of it. They see community as a limited cluster of interest groups, locked in odd conformity. In this view the country waits passive while Washington sets the rules.

But that's not what community means – not to me.

For we are a nation of communities, of thousands and tens of thousands of ethnic, religious, social, business, labor union, neighborhood, regional and other organizations, all of them varied, voluntary, and unique.

The Bush strategy of attracting Catholic votes by appealing to their cultural values may have been triumphant at the polls in 1988, but after watching his performance in the White House many culturally conservative Catholics began to question Bush's commitment to their traditional beliefs. Mr. Bush had boasted that "I'm getting this vision thing down pretty good," but to many Catholics he was a liberal in conservative clothing; one who could talked the Right's talk, but who walked the walk of the Left's social engineers.

By 1991 President Bush seemed to have fallen in line with the heirs of Republican progressivism – at least on domestic issues. Wall Street Republicans – Bush's life-long friends, allies, and supporters – were embarrassed by the party's new blue-collar constituency, as perhaps was the president himself. Certainly there was a whiff of elitism in his management style. *The New York Times* referred to his approach as "the Patrician's Way." Journalist Maureen Dowd reported: "Playing beneath the surface of President Bush's words about the budget crisis was a flicker of impatience. It was a characteristic reaction for a patrician who was bred to believe in the Establishment way of operating. . . . He offers the image of himself as a leader bred to rule." Trying to play down the elitist charge, Bush once protested to aides, "I haven't worn a button-down shirt in 20 years."[8]

There was further evidence of elitist influence: In 1990 the Republican National Committee urged a softer abortion line, homosexuals participated in the signing of the Hate Crime Statistics Act, he fudged on his no-tax pledge, and quietly signed the Comprehensive AIDS Resources Emergency Act.

Bush surrounded himself with establishment types who evicted Reagan "true believers" from the executive branch. This new crowd possessed a political tin-ear and didn't understand that the Republican Party was no longer the party of Thomas Dewey, Nelson Rockefeller, and John Lindsay – even in New York, where the party was controlled by a pro-life Italian-Catholic, U.S. Senator Alfonse D'Amato. He had knocked off long-term liberal-Republican Senator Jacob Javits in the 1980 primary and went on to win in the general election. Re-elected in 1986, Senator D'Amato reflected the demographic change in New York's Republican Party.

The *New York Times* reported in March 1992:

> Demographic profiles compiled from Marist Institute voter surveys show that the typical New York Republican voter is a conservative; white Roman Catholic, more than 40 years old with an income of at least $41,000. The surveys found that 90.3 percent of Republicans polled were white, 51.6 percent Catholic and 36.4 percent Protestant. Forty-nine percent called themselves conservatives, compared with 34.4 percent who said they were moderate and 16.6 percent who said they were liberal. Almost 35 percent were 60 or older and 30 percent between the ages of 41 and 60. Another 30 percent were between 25 and 40.[9]

One local Long Island pol described the shift this way: "The Republican Party is a suburban blue-collar party now. The high WASPs have moved left. They're Democrats now. We used to be a progressive Protestant party. Now we're a conservative Catholic party. There's no better manifestation of this change than Al D'Amato."[10]

Because the Bush administration misunderstood the cultural politics of the era, the nationally syndicated columnist and former member of the Nixon and Reagan administrations, Roman Catholic Patrick Buchanan, decided to challenge the president in the 1992 Republican Primaries.

Buchanan complained that Bush "has come out of the closet as an Eastern Establishment liberal Republican" and "has sold us down the river again and again."[11] In New York, Mike Long, Chairman of the Conservative Party and a Roman Catholic, echoed Buchanan's cries: "They say 'Read my lips, no new taxes,' and we get taxes. They say, 'No quotas,' and we get a quota bill. . . . With Buchanan in the race, it's going to be a wide-open ball game. We [the Conservative Party] are not going to be so fast to move into an endorsement position of the president. . . . It is very clear that Bush's retention of the [Conservative] Party line in 1992 is in jeopardy. If Buchanan does well in New Hampshire's notoriously quirky primary, you could be witnessing a one-term president."[12]

Bush also encountered other problems on his road to a second term: The 1990 recession severely affected white- and blue-collar workers alike. "Baby Boomers" were hit the hardest experiencing a 27 percent wage loss.[13] Blue-collars, particularly those in the automobile industry, blamed their economic woes on Bush instead of on the flood of cheaper Japanese imports.

Bush annoyed many Catholics by his leftward tilt on social issues, but he also suffered from the loss of another major issue, one that for several generations had brought Catholic voters closer to the GOP – the Cold War. Thanks to the efforts of President Reagan, the Iron Curtain had fallen in the first year of the Bush Administration and we had won the Cold War. Millions of Eastern European nations and former Soviet republics now established democratic governments, which was wonderful news for everyone – except for President Bush. By 1992, aging white, ethnic Catholics were focused on cultural issues, on many of which George Bush appeared by to be on the wrong side.

Pat Buchanan, who understood the importance of cultural and blue-collar economic issues, reached out to these disenchanted Catholics. The insurgent candidate struck a chord when he harped on the loss of manufacturing jobs to overseas competition. In New Hampshire, where unemployment was double the national figures, Buchanan told audiences, "Mr. Bush, you recall, promised to create 30-million jobs. He didn't tell you he would be creating them in Guangdong Province, Yokohama, or Mexico."[14] He also pounded away at the social issues including the National Endowment of the Arts, which he condemned for "subsidizing both filthy and blasphemous art."[15] Buchanan hit particularly hard the Bush quota bill which rankled many Reagan Democrats:

> Mr. Bush promised he would veto a quota bill, and then . . . he caved in. . . . Now if you belong to the Exeter-Yale GOP club, that's not going to bother you greatly because, as we know, it is not their children who get bused out of South Boston into Roxbury, it is not their brothers who lose contracts because of minority set-asides, it is not the scions of Yale and Harvard who apply to become FBI agents and construction workers and civil servants and cops, who bear the onus of this reverse discrimination. It is the sons of middle America who pay the price of reverse discrimination advanced by the Walker's Point [Bush's Kennebunkport home] GOP to salve their social consciences at other people's expense. If I am elected, my friends, I will go through this administration, department by department, agency by agency, and root out the whole rotten infrastructure of reverse discrimination, root and branch.[16]

In the New Hampshire primary, Buchanan scored 37 percent – a big number for a candidate running against his party's incumbent president. The Bush White House panicked, because, as journalist Tom Rosenstiel pointed out, "no president in this century had won in November if a challenger in his party had earned 37 percent or more."[17]

Buchanan knew he was not going to dethrone George Bush, but he figured a good showing would force the Republican convention to appease him. The need to keep him happy became evident to the Bush camp when they learned that 14 percent of the convention delegates were Catholic and 40 percent were Evangelical Christians.

On the Democratic side, political heavies believing Bush was a shoo-in for a second term stayed on the political sidelines. This happenstance opened the way for second-tier candidate, Governor Bill Clinton of Arkansas, to run away with the nomination.

*   *   *   *   *

William Jefferson Clinton was the hero of the Democratic Leadership Conference (DLC), a centrist group that preached that their party had lost the confidence of the American people because it had strayed too far to the left. For them, Clinton personified the New Democrat – the sort of moderate who could put together a winning coalition. Working with the DLC, Clinton was able to overcome charges that he was a Vietnam draft-dodger and a philanderer. He was able to survive the primary season because he adopted the DLC's core philosophy. Throughout 1992 he stressed:

* That he was a "different Democrat," that neither liberalism nor conservatism were working; that we needed a "third way" in order to "reinvent government;" and that both parties were brain dead.
* That government programs had to be based on "reciprocity," honoring those who "played by the rules," which meant "No More Something for Nothing," an astonishing line coming from a Democrat with solid ties to the liberal wing of that party.
* That he believed America should "end welfare as we know it."
* That he believed that an erosion of "personal responsibility" was at the root of many of our national problems.[18]

To further his appeal to cultural conservatives and to prove he was not a captive of the left, Clinton came out in favor of the death penalty and took on Jesse Jackson. When Jesse Jackson said Clinton "again exposed a character flaw" for condemning the Sister Souljah rap song lyrics that called on blacks to kill whites, Clinton condemned the song and made it clear that Jackson was not in consideration as a running mate. Dismissing Jesse Jackson underscored Clinton's contention that he was not a prisoner of the old Democratic Party.

The 1992 Democratic National Platform also reflected the thinking of Clinton and his DLC colleagues – some sections read like Ronald Reagan had ghost-written them:

* "We honor business as a noble endeavor";
* "Governments don't raise children, people do";
* "Welfare should be a second chance, not a way of life";
* "The simplest and most direct way to restore order in our cities is to put more police on the streets";
* "We reject both the do-nothing government . . . as well as the big government theory. . . "[19]

Clinton Democrats tried to placate every group out there except for one – the pro-lifers.

The Commonwealth of Pennsylvania, whose twenty-three electoral votes represented the fifth largest bloc in 1992, was represented at the Democratic Convention by its Irish-Catholic governor, Robert Casey. Governor Casey, who was re-elected to a second term as governor in 1990 with 68 percent of the vote, was a classic Al Smith Democrat – supportive of New Deal Programs but socially conservative. Uneasy about the direction his party had taken in the eighties, he was seen sporting a lapel button that read, "I want my party back."

At platform hearings, he urged his party to "reexamine its position on abortion in the context of the Democratic Party's historic and noble mission of protecting the powerless." His views were not only ignored, but at the convention party chairman Ron Brown even denied Governor Casey the opportunity to address the delegates. Reacting to this decision, political analyst Ben Wattenberg wrote: "The idea that Governor Bob Casey of Pennsylvania, who is pro-life, was not able to get a time to speak at the Democratic Convention was outrageous. Equally outrageous was that the press did not make an issue of his muzzling. (I say this as a pro-choice supporter.)"[20]

When the Republicans met in Houston, Catholic delegates led by Phyllis Schlafly and Christian Coalition delegates controlled the platform hearings and made sure the pro-life plank matched the one found in Reagan platforms. And at the convention, former president Reagan, understanding the importance of the cultural issues, ridiculed the newly found values of the Democrats:

> They put on quite a production in New York a few weeks ago. You might even call it slick. A stone's throw from Broadway, and how appropriate. Over and over they told us they were not the party they were. They kept telling us with a straight face that they're for family values, they're for a strong America. They're for less intrusive government.
> And they call me an actor![21]

To get Pat Buchanan back on the Republican reservation, Bush advisors granted him prime time in return for an endorsement. Buchanan rocked the convention when he described the culture wars in America:

> My friends, this election is about much more than who gets what. It is about who we are. It is about what we believe, it is about what we stand for as Americans. There is a religious war going on in our country for the soul of America. It is a cultural war, as critical to the kind of nation we will one day be – as was the Cold War itself.

> And in that struggle for the soul of America, Clinton and Gore are
> on the other side, and George Bush is on our side. And so, we have
> to come home – and stand beside him.

The liberal media were outraged over the traditional values talk. *Newsweek* described the convention as "wall-to-wall ugly."[22] Liberal columnist Tom Wicker wrote in the August 20, 1992, issue of *The New York Times*, "Fire, brimstone and sexual weirdness: Right-wing Republicans declare a religious war 300 years after Salem's witch trials."[23] Historian Kenneth Heineman points out that Bush's White House staffers, "most of whom favored unrestricted abortion and gay rights . . . wilted."[24]

*   *   *   *   *

One surprise factor in the 1992 presidential sweepstakes was the emergence of Ross Perot as a viable independent candidate. The Texas billionaire and eccentric conspiracy theorist began his quixotic campaign by articulating opposition to the ever-increasing federal budget deficit. He was not, however, a single issue candidate. He spoke in favor of marital fidelity, hard work, deferred gratification, and discipline. He boasted that his own employees were expected to wear dress shirts and ties, to abstain from alcohol while on the job, and to be drug-free. He was also pro-gun, in favor of welfare reform, and opposed to ending the ban on homosexuals in the military. He favored abortion but called for liberal restrictions.

The Clinton camp knew their man was weak on the cultural issues, so they hammered away at the economy as the fall campaign progressed, blaming all of America's financial and economic woes on Bush. The Bush campaign, shell-shocked by the criticism they had received from their establishment friends concerning the Buchanan-Christian Coalition convention follies, fell for the Clinton bait. They chucked the cultural issues and chose to debate on Clinton's terms, arguing that the recession was over and the economy was improving.

The Clinton machine was delighted. The Democratic campaign slogan became: "It's the economy, stupid." With Bush fighting on their turf, Democrats were confident that enough disgruntled voters (e.g., Catholics) would move to Perot, split the Republican base, and hand Clinton a plurality victory.

Clinton's operatives focused on the Catholic vote, particularly among Hispanics and Catholics living in industrial towns hard hit by the recession. And this strategy appeared to be working: *The Wall Street Journal* headline reported on September 14, 1992, "Catholic Voters, Core of the 'Reagan Democrats,' Returning to Their Party Amid Economic Fears."

To allay Catholic fear that he was a nativist, the Baptist Clinton told a gathering at Notre Dame University that as an undergraduate at Georgetown University he had learned the "common ground that Baptists and Catholics could walk together."[25] To further enhance this image, special events for Clinton were hosted in ethnic neighborhoods. Boston's Irish mayor, Ray Flynn, and New York's Italian governor, Mario Cuomo, pitched in to woo the ethnic Catholic vote.

The strategy to win by a plurality worked – Bill Clinton was elected the 42nd president of the United States with 43 percent of the vote. President Bush came in second with 37.4 percent and Ross Perot received the highest number of votes ever cast for a third party candidate – 19.7 million for a total of 18.9 percent.

Clinton ran far behind the congressional Democrats who garnered 55 percent of the vote. Nevertheless, with Perot siphoning off millions of normally Republican voters, Clinton won decisively in the Electoral College receiving 370 votes to Bush's 168 and Perot's 0.

Clinton's base consisted of seniors (fearful of Medicare cuts), African-Americas (Clinton would even be called "America's first black president"), and Jews (the most liberal of all voting groups), but he also did extremely well among the post-World War II electorate. One should note that by 1992, 60 percent of the eligible voters were born after 1945. They didn't experience the Great War or the Depression or even the sacrifices of World War II, and they had no real allegiance to any party. Their votes shifted depending on who appealed best to their outlook on life. And in 1992, Bill Clinton and his wife Hillary, themselves Baby Boomers, fit the bill.

The Catholic vote in 1992 comprised about 25 percent of the national total, with large concentrations in the following states:

State	Catholic % of Population
Connecticut	42
New Jersey	42
New York	40
Illinois	31
Pennsylvania	30
Wisconsin	27
California	25
Michigan	24
Ohio	20
Missouri	16

Clinton managed to carry each of these states. By picking off segments of the Catholic vote, he confirmed the *Wall Street Journal's* analysis: "To be sure, the Catholic vote, which represents about a quarter of the November electorate, isn't monolithic. The group is split by ethnic heritage, generations, education level and between the huge blocs that speak English and Spanish."[26]

	Clinton	Bush	Perot[27]
National Vote	43.0%	37.4%	18.9%
Generic Catholic Vote	44	35	21
White Catholic:			
Practicing	39	41	20
Cafeteria	44	33	21
Hispanics	62	24	14

What do these results prove? That unlike the Evangelical Christian vote, which went decidedly for the Republican Party, the Catholic vote is not a "lock" for either party.

About 3 million Catholic voters deserted Bush in 1992 – mostly cafeteria Catholics. Analyst Geoffrey Layman, in his work *The Great Divide*, concluded that "the majority of Democratic Catholics were non-regular Church attenders."[28] What was most interesting is that a significant number of white Catholics, who were disgusted with both Bush and Clinton, voted for Perot in numbers greater than his national percentage of 18.9 percent:

State[29]	All Perot Voters	Catholics (White)	Perot Catholic Margin
Arizona	24%	29%	+5
California	21	25	+4
Connecticut	23	24	+1
Florida	20	23	+3
Georgia	13	20	+7
Illinois	17	16	-1
Kentucky	14	18	+4
Louisiana	12	12	0
Maryland	14	12	-2
Massachusetts	23	26	+3
Michigan	20	25	+5
Minnesota	24	24	0
Missouri	22	26	+4
New Jersey	16	20	+4
New Mexico	17	16	-1
New York	16	18	+2
Ohio	21	25	+4
Pennsylvania	18	21	+3
Texas	22	21	-1
Virginia	14	16	+2
Washington	24	24	0
Wisconsin	22	25	+3

* * * * *

Once he took over the reins of government, Clinton discarded his conservative rhetoric and moved to the extreme left. In his first month in office, he infuriated many Catholics when he lifted the ban on fetal-tissue research and announced he would permit homosexuals to openly integrate into the armed forces. To please abortion advocates he also lifted the "gag rule" that prohibited clinics that received federal dollars from providing abortion material. He also made good on his litmus test promise by appointing two pro-abortion Supreme Court justices: Ruth Ginsburg and Stephen Breyer. Clinton further alienated traditionalists when, in September 1993, his Justice Department filed a brief with the U.S. Supreme Court endorsing a legal approach that would emasculate child pornography laws and make it more difficult to convict pedophiles. Also, the May 1994 sexual harassment suit filed by Paula Jones did not improve the Clinton character gap.

On "it's the economy, stupid" issues, Clinton broke his promises to initiate a middle-class tax cut and to "end welfare as we know it." Finally, Hillary Clinton's "Big Brother" plan to reform health care, which would have nationalized America's medical profession, frightened large segments of the electorate.

As the 1994 congressional elections approached, polls showed that many Americans were infuriated with the administration's lunge to the left. One poll showed that 72 percent of Americans did not want their children to grow up to be like Clinton. The president's scores were low in the "Strong," "Effective," and "Ethical" categories.

Other polls began to show that what mattered now were values and not the economy. In October 1995, an NBC/*Wall Street Journal* poll showed that 54 percent believed "the social and economic problems that face America are mainly the result of a decline in moral values while only 34 percent believed it was a result of financial pressures."[30] In 1994, Republicans ran aggressively against Clinton Democrats and the values they represented. Representative Newt Gingrich of Georgia reminded the voters that "no civilization can survive with 12-year olds having babies, with 15-year olds killing each other, with 17-year olds dying of AIDS, with 18-year olds getting diplomas they can't even read."[31]

The 1994 election results were a major earthquake on the political seismograph. For the first time in over a half-century, Republicans captured a majority in both houses of Congress, gaining fifty-two House seats, eight Senate seats, and eleven governorships as well. Old-time liberals, including House Speaker Tom Foley of Washington and New York Governor Mario Cuomo, were booted out of office.

In the 1994 mid-term elections, no Republican incumbent – governor, senator, or representative – was defeated. Reflecting on the results, Walter Dean Burnham – America's leading expert on political realignment – stated that 1994 was "the most consequential off-year election in one hundred years."[32]

What was most amazing about the results was that for the first time Catholics cast a majority of their votes for Republican congressional candidates:

Catholic Congressional Vote History[33]

	1980	1982	1984	1986	1988	1990	1992	1994
Democrat	59%	63%	58%	55%	55%	54%	57%	48%
Republican	41	37	42	45	45	46	43	52
GOP Margin	-18	-26	-16	-10	-10	-8	-14	+4

Republican pollster John McLaughlin concluded that "if a majority of Catholics had not voted for Republican candidates for the House in [1994], Dick Gephardt would most likely be Speaker of the House."

While the total Catholic vote was 52 percent Republican, the breakdown tells a different story: 56 percent of white, practicing Catholics voted Republican versus 46 percent of white, cafeteria Catholics, and Catholic Hispanics cast just 32 percent of their votes for Republican candidates. Overall, however, analyst Joseph Barrett pointed out that in 1994, "For the first time [Catholics] not only voted Republican, they voted Republican at a rate higher than the national average."

National Opinions of Catholic Voters[34]
November 1994

Ideology

Liberal	Moderate	Conservative	DK/Refuse
16.9%	39.4%	39.9%	4.0%

Party Affiliation

Republican	Democrat	Independent	Other	DK/Refuse
36.7%	35.5%	19.0%	0.8%	8.1%

Voting Behavior

Always Democrat	Usually Democrat	Ticket Splitters	Usually Republican	Always Republican	DK/Refuse
4.0%	24.2%	29.8%	26.6%	6.0%	9.3%

President Clinton was devastated by the 1994 election results. At one press conference, the vultures in the media pressed Clinton to rationalize his relevance. The politically crippled president told them, "The Constitution gives me relevance. The power of our ideas gives me relevance. . . . The president is relevant here, especially an activist president."[35]

* * * * *

Clinton was willing to do whatever it would take to become the first Democrat since FDR to be elected to a second term. So he attentively listened to his political pollster, Dick Morris, who informed him that taking credit for a robust economy wasn't enough. Clinton would have to outflank the presumptive 1996 GOP nominee, Senator Robert Dole, on the social issues.

Clinton readily agreed to follow Morris's prescriptions, and over the next two years Clinton:

* Signed legislation that forbade gay marriages;
* Became a law-and-order advocate supporting teenage curfews and mandatory drug tests for teens applying for a driver license;
* Admitted the private sector, not the federal government, was best suited to drive the economy;
* Supported Republican Welfare Reform that limited benefits.

With Republican support strong in southern and western states, Clinton knew that to win in 1996, he would once again have to carry the electoral-rich states that were home to large numbers of Catholic voters. In 1992, a plurality of Catholics had voted for him because he ran as a "New Democrat," code for "not liberal." But he had betrayed them, and the 1994 results proved that knew he had, but that did not stop Clinton from trying to win them back.

Clinton knew he could not appeal to most Catholics on the issues of abortion and school vouchers, but he did look to once again chip away at the vote by appealing to ethnic and cafeteria-Catholic concerns. His active role in the Northern Ireland accords was an attempt to appeal to Irish Americans. Similar appeals were made to Eastern Europeans and Italians on issues that concerned them. The president created a White House office dedicated to seeking the Catholic vote, and he played his Georgetown University card, and made inroads with left-wing Jesuits and their followers. Mrs. Clinton also reached out to "Dorothy Day" left-wing Catholics who controlled Catholic Charities, the Catholic medical and child-care industry. (Dorothy Day was a radical left-wing activist and professed anarchist who had gained fame in the 1930s and '40s.)

While Clinton was running to the right, Senator Bob Dole, who feared a repeat of the 1992 "traditional values" convention, started moving to the left. As Senate majority leader, Dole had been a brilliant insider who understood the mechanics of shepherding legislation, but he had little sense of the culture wars being fought across America. Having spent his entire political career running for office in the small Protestant state of Kansas, he had no clue as to the thinking of inner-city and suburban Catholics. In addition to his political tin-ear, Dole was a poor campaigner and public speaker. He excelled at mumbling in cryptic "Senatese" sentences that contained legislative jargon that made no sense to the electorate.

Dole also felt a need to placate liberal pro-abortion Republicans in the Northeast, such as Governor Christine Todd Whitman of New Jersey and Governor William Weld of Massachusetts. When the GOP convention blessed the pro-life platform plank, Dole back-pedaled and told the press that platforms don't mean much; that, as he said, "it was only a moral issue."[36] Despite the fact that he had always been pro-life, Dole proved he was another Republican who craved the endorsement of *The New York Times* editorial page. At first he justified his leftward lurch by saying that he had "grown," but when he caught flak from the Republican Right for his comments, the hapless Dole said, "I'm willing to be another Ronald Reagan if that is what you want."[37]

Dole's vice-presidential pick, Jack Kemp, was very much aware of the importance of social issues, particularly to practicing Catholics. Kemp, the former professional football star who for eighteen years had been a Congressman representing the blue-collar, Catholic city of Buffalo, New York, reached out to that constituency and beyond during the campaign. In the dying steel towns in Pennsylvania, Michigan, and Ohio, Kemp touted his support for vouchers for parochial school students and his opposition to partial-birth abortion. "I can't imagine our nation," he told them, "being that city on a hill if we continue to allow the partial-birth abortion strategy to continue in America."[38] Kemp was unafraid to condemn Clinton's veto of the partial-birth ban. He agreed with the Catholic Church's hierarchy's public condemnation of the Clinton veto: "Your action . . . takes our nation to a critical turning point in its treatment of helpless human beings inside and outside the womb. It moves our nation one step further toward acceptance of infanticide."[39]

The presidential campaign of 1996 cost $800 million, double the 1992 figure. The turnout, however, was the lowest since records were kept: 54.2 percent of the voting population went to the polls.

The Republican effort to paint Clinton as a character-flawed liberal failed, and he became the first Democratic president to be elected to a second term since Franklin Roosevelt in 1936:

	Clinton	**Dole**	**Perot**
Percentage	49.2	40.7	8.4
Popular Votes	47.4 million	39.1 million	8 million
Electoral Votes	379	159	0

Because of the low turnout, the Catholic vote totaled about 28 percent – higher then the national number:

	Clinton	**Dole**	**Perot**[40]
Generic Catholic Vote	54%	31%	7%
White Practicing Catholic	39	52	9
White Cafeteria Catholic	57	31	12
Hispanic Catholic	75	19	6

Bill Clinton's strategy to appeal to subsets of Catholics succeeded. He easily won the cafeteria-Catholic and the Hispanic-Catholic vote. In a post-election poll taken during November 7–10 by McLaughlin and Associates, the results revealed that, overall, 63 percent of all Catholics had a favorable opinion of Clinton versus a 51 percent favorable opinion for Dole (and – a portent of things to come – just 24 percent for Newt Gingrich). Democrats, according to the poll, also received 52 percent of the Catholic vote in congressional races.

* * * * *

President Clinton, who planned in his second term to build an impressive legacy, found his presidency derailed by his sexual conduct in what became known as "Zippergate."

Special Prosecutor Kenneth Starr presented to the Congress on September 9, 1998, a 445-page report that "included detailed descriptions of sexual conduct including incidents of oral sex, in and just outside of the oval office."[41] In his report, Starr proposed eleven possible grounds for impeachment, about half of them instances of the president lying under oath.

What was remarkable was that large segments of the American population were not upset with the president's conduct. Even after the House of Representatives formally impeached Clinton on December 19, 1998, his popularity remained well over the 50 percent mark.

Throughout Zippergate, Catholic voters were split on the scandal. Practicing Catholics were appalled by Clinton's behavior, and many believed the only responsible act was for the president to resign his office. According to liberal Stanley Greenberg, these white, practicing Catholics represented 10 percent of the voting population as the twenty-first century began. In Greenberg's view, these Catholics are "those most committed to and identified with the church and most likely to bring their Catholic identity into politics. They trace their families back to Europe, dominated by Ireland (21 percent), Germany (19 percent), Italy (15 percent), and Poland (9 percent)."[42] On the other hand, baby-boomer cafeteria Catholics viewed Clinton as one of their own and merely made light of his behavior. So long as his exploits were sexual and between consenting adults, they didn't care – holding the president to a higher standard was rejected. The baby-boomer Catholics accepted the arguments of Ted Kennedy and other cafeteria-Catholic politicians that there must be a separation of public and private morality.

One of the founders of the modern conservative movement, William F. Buckley Jr., himself a practicing Catholic, concluded that the boomer generation's reaction to the Clinton scandals confirmed a "growing national tendency to corruption or hedonism; an insensitivity to suffering, a callousness that breeds ugliness of behavior."[43]

As the 2000 election approached, the emerging presidential candidates represented the nation's great political divide: Democrat Albert Gore insisted that he would maintain the Clinton prosperity, while Republican George W. Bush pledged to restore character and integrity to the Oval Office.

Bush, the Texas governor, was a born-again Christian who left America's leading mainline faith – the Episcopal Church – to become a Methodist. According to biographer Bill Minutaglio, when Bush entered public life he crafted "a 'personal responsibility' manifesto that suggested that Texans would be better served by turning to God, not government, to improve their social standing."[44]

As the Bush camp began to plan its 2000 presidential strategy, it was understood that in a close election the Catholic vote still mattered. They were willing to concede the cafeteria Catholics to Mr. Gore, but not the practicing Catholics or Hispanic Catholics. Mr. Bush's advisors believed that his "personal responsibility" manifesto could make the difference between victory and defeat. In Bush's surprise 1994 gubernatorial victory in Texas, he had received only 24 percent of the Hispanic vote, but in his spectacular 1998 re-election, a special effort was made to win over these voters, and the efforts had paid off: results in the Hispanic community shocked all the pundits: he received 49 percent of their votes (and 68 percent overall). This was the highest vote total ever received from Hispanics by a Republican, and helped Mr. Bush become the first Texas governor to be elected to a second four-year term.

He had achieved Latino support by spending significant time in Hispanic neighborhoods during in his first term. He spoke to these constituents in fluent Spanish, supported government aid to legal immigrants, and opposed U.S. troops at the Mexican border.

To raise his profile with Hispanic communities across America during the presidential campaign, Bush promoted "compassionate conservatism," a domestic-policy strategy that stressed the needs of poor could be best served by local churches, community leaders, and ordinary citizens rather than "Big Brother" in Washington. He also supported parental notification legislation regarding teen abortion, and advocated a ban on adoption by gays and lesbians. Bush preached a new brand of subsidiarity.

Just as the Bush campaign was beginning to implement its grand strategy in 2000, it stumbled. Governor Bush addressed the student body at Bob Jones University in South Carolina, an institution known to promote anti-Catholic prejudice. The school website contained rhetoric that disparaged the Catholic Church as the "mother of harlots" and as an "ecclesiastic tyranny." The pope was described as the "Archpriest of Satan."

At first the Bush campaign defended the appearance, despite receiving criticism from both Democrats and Republicans. The candidate's own silence on the subject annoyed a Roman Catholic congressman from Long Island, Peter King, who complained to the *New York Post* that "by going to [Bob Jones University] and being silent, [Bush] gives approval."[45]

During this same period, Republican Speaker of the House, Dennis Hastert, passed over a Catholic priest for House chaplain, and accusations hit the air waves that anti-Catholic Republicans had prevented the appointment of Father Timothy J. O'Brien, who would have become the first Catholic to hold the position. This was the last thing the Bush camp needed to have dominate the news.

Suddenly, Dan Rather, Tom Brokaw, Al Sharpton, Alan Dershowitz, and Maureen Dowd "found the ugly specter of anti-Catholicism lurking in Republican showdowns."[46] Democrats suddenly came to the defense of Catholics, despite the fact that over the years they had refused to criticize the desecration of the Communion host by homosexuals in protests at St. Patrick's Cathedral or the anti-Catholic smears made by pro-abortion groups. Kate O'Beirne wrote in the *Wall Street Journal* that "Democrats have discovered anti-Catholicism. Seeing a chance to exploit tensions in the Republican base and to make a play for Catholic swing voters, they have been tarring Republicans as anti-Catholic bigots. . . ."[47]

Bush's opponent for the Republican presidential nomination, Arizona Senator John McCain, took advantage of this chaos and approved a "Catholic Voter Alert" phone campaign in the heavily Catholic-populated state of Michigan. "The voice," according to columnist Robert Novak, "claimed Governor Bush sought support from anti-Catholic bigots in winning the South Carolina primary."[48] The "Catholic Voter Alert" probably boosted underdog John McCain's unexpected 11 point victory in the February 22 primary.

To avoid offending Evangelical Christian voters in the February 19 South Carolina Primary, the Bush camp remained silent on the Bob Jones University flap. Yet after the Michigan Primary defeat and the release of a *Wall Street Journal* poll which "showed the GOP trailing among Catholics in both the presidential and congressional votes,"[49] the Bush campaign went into damage-control mode.

Turning to Mike Long, the Roman Catholic chairman of the New York Conservative Party, Bush operatives asked for help in getting a letter of apology to the ailing Archbishop of New York, John Cardinal O'Connor. On February 27, one week before the critical New York primary, a letter of apology was delivered to the Cardinal:

> Your Eminence:
>
> A few weeks ago, I visited Bob Jones University in South Carolina to address its students and outline the reasons I'm seeking the presidency. Some have taken – and mistaken – this visit as sign that I approve of the anti-Catholic and racially divisive views associated with that school. . . .
>
> Criticism should be expected in any political campaign. What no American should expect – and what I will not tolerate – is guilt by association. I reject racial segregation – in our laws, in our hearts and in our lives. And I reject religious intolerance – because faith is defined by grace and hope, not fear and division. . . .
>
> In my speech to the students, I emphasized that I am a uniter, not a divider, and that Americans can work together for the good of all. On reflection, I should have been more clear in disassociating myself from anti-Catholic sentiments and racial prejudice. It was a missed opportunity, causing needless offense, which I deeply regret.[50]

And at a press conference in Austin, Texas, that same day Mr. Bush said:

> I got back off the road. I thought long and hard about the speech I gave. . . . I started thinking about the impressions about me that just weren't true. I couldn't believe that anybody would think I'm an anti-Catholic bigot. I regret not having got up there and spoken from my heart.[51]

The New York *Daily News* reported the next day that, "Bush's *mea culpa* to the leader of 2.4 million New York Catholics was classic damage control, Bush sources say – an eleventh-hour attempt to stop the hemorrhaging to Bush's stumbling campaign."[52]

To further counter the damage, Republicans in the House of Representatives planned to vote on bills of interest to Catholic voters: education savings accounts, partial- birth abortion ban, and "a resolution condemning some abortion-rights activists for advocating a downgrading of relations with the Vatican."[53]

The strategy worked, and by the end of April George Bush was acknowledged as the presumptive presidential nominee of the Republican Party.

As for Bush's vice-presidential spot, names of nominal Catholics were being urged, including Governor Thomas Ridge of Pennsylvania and Governor George Pataki of New York. Many analysts asked, however, if Bush would take the risk of upsetting what was expected to be a harmonious convention by recommending a pro-abortion or cafeteria-style Catholic vice president.

As far as many Republican Catholics were concerned, George Pataki was unacceptable. He was not only pro-abortion, but pro-funding of abortion, and pro-gay rights. Pataki had granted homosexual state employees in New York domestic-partnership rights and had called for the GOP to drop the pro-life plank in 2000.

Tom Ridge posed a greater problem. Pennsylvania, unlike New York, was a key swing state. Putting Ridge on the ticket could have made the difference in what was shaping up to be a close presidential election. Yet for many conservatives, Ridge was "not a conservative who happens to be pro-choice; he's a liberal Republican who happens to have done a handful of conservative things as governor."[54] As a member of Congress, Ridge had a reputation for being anti-defense: he had opposed the MX missile, supported a nuclear freeze, and opposed funding to Nicaragua's Contras.[55]

If nominated, Ridge had another problem that would have immediately become front-page news: Bishop Donald Trautman, the governor's hometown ordinary (Erie County), had prohibited the governor from speaking on Church property. Trautman took seriously the statement adopted by the National Conference of Bishops in 1998: "Catholics who are privileged to serve in public leadership positions have an obligation to place their faith at the heart of their public service, particularly on issues regarding the sanctity and dignity of human life."[56]

To his credit, Ridge did not whine about separation of church and state but admitted the bishop was "stating what a man of the Church should state," and he conceded, "I've created my own problem."[57]

Bush avoided controversy and chose a member of the GOP establishment as vice president, Dick Cheney, and did not tinker with the pro-life platform plank. On the Democratic side, however, religion became a front-page topic when Democratic presidential nominee Al Gore chose a pro-abortion, Orthodox Jew, Senator Joseph Lieberman of Connecticut, as his running mate.

Suddenly, the liberal media, usually the guardians of secular America, began praising Lieberman's call for a greater role for religion in public life. Nationally syndicated columnist Michael Medved (also an Orthodox Jew) was quick to point out that "Republicans who cite God a lot get pilloried as budding Ayatollahs. But when a Democrat like Mr. Lieberman does it, no one minds."[58]

Catholics who spoke of religion in the public square did not get off as easy in 2000. In a major article in *Columbia*, a Knights of Columbus magazine, Bishop James T. McHugh explained to the organization's 1.7 million members: "Why your understanding of Church teaching matters when you mark your ballot." He reviewed the teachings in the 1998 bishops' statement: "Living the Gospel of Life: A Challenge to American Catholics" and the September 1999 document, "Faithful Citizenship: Civic Responsibility for a New Millennium." He reminded his readers that these documents "highlighted a number of issues that have both social and moral implications for the United States – issues that Catholics should take into consideration in their choice of candidates."[59]

Bishop McHugh wrote that "Catholic officials who persist in their actions and statements contrary to the Gospel of Life should not be invited:

* To leadership positions in the diocese, parish or other Church agencies or organizations.
* To receive any type of honor or public recognition by Church agencies or organizations.
* To serve as a chairperson or committee member of major Church celebrations or events, including fundraising programs.
* To exercise any liturgical ministry or public role in the celebration of the Mass or other sacraments.
* To public lectures, gatherings, or other events where the speaker is given positive recognition or approval to be speaker at graduation ceremonies, anniversary celebrations and so forth.[60]

Living up to his position, Bishop McHugh created a gale-wind of controversy when he announced on October 3, 2000, that he was canceling twenty candidate forums that were to be held on Long Island Church property. The political left was apoplectic. Bishop McHugh was condemned as another Grand Inquisitor for actually adhering to and enforcing Church pronouncements. Kelli Conlin, Executive Director of the National Abortion and Reproductive Rights Action League in New York, was outraged by the cancellation and stated, "It seemed . . . they were afraid parishioners would be exposed to another point of view."[61] But Bishop McHugh stood his ground and dismissed the criticism: "The reason for this is that it would be foolish and counterproductive to provide a platform to those who favor or support a public policy of abortion on demand or of euthanasia or assisted suicide."[62]

As the campaign of 2000 came down to the wire, pollsters predicted it would be the tightest election since the Cleveland-Blaine race of 1884. Each candidate was cognizant that in a close election every swing group – no matter of what size – could make the difference in determining the outcome. As a result, the Catholic vote was much in play in 2000. Both sides knew that in the last quarter century, the candidate who carried the Catholic vote had won the election.

Al Gore, who as a Tennessee Congressman had "opposed federal funding and said abortion was arguably the taking of a human life,"[63] was now "pro-choice" and actively sought cafeteria-Catholic votes by appealing to their support of various liberal poverty and social programs. George Bush, on the other hand, was aggressively seeking the votes of practicing Catholics and Hispanics. He said he would sign a bill banning partial-birth abortion and boasted that his favorite Supreme Court justice was pro-life Catholic Antonin Scalia.

The presidential election of 2000 proved that the nation was evenly divided:

	Bush	Gore
Total Votes	50,456,169	50,996,116
Percentage	47.9	48.4
Electoral Votes	271	267

And the Catholic voters were just as divided as they were during the Clinton years:

	Bush	Gore
Generic White Catholic Vote	51%	46%
White Practicing Catholics	57	43
White Cafeteria Catholics	41	59
Hispanic Catholics	24	76

As political analyst, Michael Barone has written:

> More than half, 54%, of Bush's voters were more observant Protestants or Catholics; only 15% were blacks, Hispanics or non-Christians. More than half of Gore's voters, 51%, were blacks, Hispanics or non-Christians; only 20% were more observant Protestants or Catholics. Although they may be uncomfortable with the fact, Americans increasingly vote as they pray – or don't pray.[64]

Writing in the Spring 2001 edition of *The Public Interest*, social critic Gertrude Himmelfarb agreed with Barone's observation:

> One might speculate that the Republican electorate was becoming more religious, but it is more probable that a religious electorate was simply responding to a candidate who was more overtly (and convincingly) religious, both in his policies and personal history, than either his predecessor or his opponent.[65]

Generic Catholic Vote – 2000 Election[66]

State	Catholics	General Election		Catholic Vote	
		Bush	Gore	Bush	Gore
Rhode Island	64%	32%	61%	35%	62%
Massachusetts	49	33	59	32	62
Connecticut	42	39	56	42	54
New Jersey	42	40	56	51	47
New York	40	35	60	40	56
Wisconsin	32	48	48	47	50
Illinois	**31**	**43**	**55**	**45**	**53**
Louisiana	31	53	45	57	41
California	30	41	54	40	56
Pennsylvania	**30**	**46**	**51**	**46**	**50**
New Hampshire	28	48	47	47	49
Minnesota	27	46	48	51	42
Vermont	25	41	51	48	47
Nevada	24	49	46	46	52
New Mexico	**24**	**47**	**48**	**33**	**65**
Michigan	**23**	**46**	**51**	**50**	**48**
North Dakota	23	61	33	54	42
Texas	23	59	38	67	32
Nebraska	22	62	33	58	38
South Dakota	22	61	37	53	46
Hawaii	20	38	56	35	60
Ohio	**20**	**50**	**46**	**50**	**47**
Maine	19	44	49	44	50
Iowa	18	48	49	41	55
Maryland	17	40	57	43	54
Missouri	**17**	**51**	**47**	**55**	**44**
Arizona	16	50	45	43	52
Kansas	16	57	38	60	39
Delaware	15	42	55	44	51
Montana	15	59	33	60	36
Colorado	14	51	42	42	53
Florida	**14**	**49**	**49**	**52**	**44**
Indiana	13	57	41	46	51
Idaho	10	68	28	64	33
Kentucky	10	57	41	54	44
Oregon	10	48	46	48	49
Washington	10	45	50	40	56
Wyoming	10	69	28	58	40

continued on page 333.

State	Catholics	General Election		Catholic Vote	
		Bush	Gore	Bush	Gore
Alaska	9%	59%	28%	65%	31%
Virginia	8	52	45	61	37
West Virginia	6	52	46	40	58
Georgia	5	55	43	56	41
Mississippi	4	58	41	N/A	
Oklahoma	4	60	38	N/A	
Utah	4	67	26	N/A	
Alabama	3	56	43	N/A	
Arkansas	3	50	46	47	52
North Carolina	3	56	43	64	35
South Carolina	3	55	40	N/A	
Tennessee	3	51	48	53	39

Bold: Key Swing States

It is interesting to note that in the key battleground states (Illinois, Pennsylvania, New Mexico, Ohio, Missouri, and Florida), the candidate who carried the Catholic vote won the given state. The only exception among "swing states" was Michigan.

* * * * *

Because George W. Bush lost the popular vote and had to rely on a Supreme Court decision to attain the presidency, he knew his first task was to heal and unite the divided nation. And Catholics were high on Bush's list of groups to whom he would reach out.

Eight months after being sworn in, Bush legitimized his presidency in the eyes of the American people by his leadership in the aftermath of 9/11. Although the president has spent most of his time since that tragic event serving as commander-in-chief, he and his advisors have continued to keep a watchful eye on America's political pulse.

It is obvious that in key battleground states in 2004, practicing Catholics can once again decide the outcome of the presidential race. Hence, throughout Bush's term, serious overtures have been made to Catholic voters.

Shortly after being sworn in, the president met with leaders of Catholic Charities to announce his support of legislation that would permit taxpayers who do not itemize to separately deduct charitable contributions. On March 17, Mr. Bush celebrated the feast of St. Patrick with Republic of Ireland officials. Later that month, numerous cardinals and bishops were invited to the White House to hear the president praise the Catholic educational system. One month later, Bush dedicated the Pope John Paul II Cultural Center in

Washington, D.C. and spoke passionately of "the innocent child waiting to be born."[67]

The president culminated his 2001 Catholic campaign by appearing as the keynote speaker at the University of Notre Dame Commencement. In the speech, he praised the basis of Catholic Social teaching, subsidiarity:

> Our task is clear, and it's difficult. We must build our country's unity by extending our country's blessings. We make that commitment because we're Americans. Aspiration is the essence of our country. We believe in social mobility, not social Darwinism. We are the country of the second chance where failure is never final. And that dream has sometimes been deferred. It must never be abandoned.
>
> We are committed to compassion for practical reasons. When men and women are lost to themselves, they are also lost to our nation. When millions are hopeless, all of us are diminished by the loss of their gifts.
>
> And we're committed to compassion for moral reasons. Jewish prophets and Catholic teaching both speak of God's special concern for the poor. This is perhaps the most radical teaching of faith that the value of life is not contingent on wealth or strength or skill, that value is a reflection of God's image. . . .
>
> Compassion often works best on a small and human scale. It is generally better when a call for help is local, not long distance. Here at this university you've heard that call and responded. It is part of what makes Notre Dame a great university.
>
> This is my message today. There is no great society which is not a caring society, and any effective war on poverty must deploy what Dorothy Day called the weapons of the spirit. There's only one problem with groups like the South Bend Center for the Homeless: There aren't enough of them.
>
> It's not sufficient to praise charities and community groups. We must support them, and this is both a public obligation and a personal responsibility. . . .[68]

Throughout his first four years, President Bush initiated and promoted programs and policies that appealed to Catholics. He reversed pro-abortion Clinton executive orders, proposed faith-based initiatives, voucher experiments, and limits on stem-cell research. He also signed into law the ban on partial-birth abortion.

Since the Bush machine expects another close election in 2004, it is their hope that these overtures to practicing Catholics will make a difference, particularly in the Commonwealth of Pennsylvania.

Pennsylvania, whose Catholic population stands at 30 percent, is an unusual northeastern state. While Philadelphia and its suburbs tend to be more liberal, the western city of Pittsburgh and its environs are politically and culturally more conservative. And as the locals describe it, the area between Pittsburgh and Philadelphia is basically Alabama. The farming, coal-mining, and the old industrial towns such as Bethlehem, are predominantly pro-gun and pro-life. These culturally conservative regions provided the votes that elected in 1994 and reelected in 2000, the Catholic and nationally recognized pro-life U.S. Senator, Rick Santorum. The presence of this culturally conservative voting bloc also explains how, in the April 2004 Republican senatorial primary, an unknown insurgent, Congressman Pat Toomey, a pro-life Republican, came within a nose of beating the long-time liberal incumbent, Arlen Specter.

With the entire Republican establishment supporting him, including President Bush and Senator Santorum, Specter barely mustered 51 percent of the vote. Toomey, who was outspent 5 to 1, organized grassroots pro-life activists, who swarmed the state, going door to door in search of votes. And even though Toomey lost, receiving 49 percent of the votes, it sent shock waves through the liberal pro-abortion, Republican establishment.

Because of this cultural split, electorally, Pennsylvania has swung back and forth over the years:

Pennsylvania Presidential Votes

	Republican	Democratic
1980	49.6%	42.5%
1984	53.3	46.0
1988	50.7	48.4
1992	36.1	45.1
1996	40.1	49.2
2000	46	51

Pennsylvania has about 4 million Catholics out of a population of 12.2 million. Many of these Catholics are blue-collar workers who, for generations, have worked in the Commonwealth's steel mills and coal fields. According to political analyst Michael Barone, these regions are "full of strong-belief Catholics and Protestants and hunters who do not want their guns taken away."[69]

Abortion is a key issue in Pennsylvania, and election results prove it. When Congressman Tom Ridge ran for governor in 1994, he was elected with only 45 percent of the vote – that's because a Pro-Life Independent candidate received 13 percent of the vote. Meanwhile, pro-life Congressman Rick

Santorum beat incumbent Democratic Senator Harris Wofford with 49 percent of the vote. In 2000, the victor of the Democratic U.S. Senate primary was pro-life Congressman Ron Klink, who Santorum easily beat in the general election, 52 percent to 46 percent. It is interesting to note that in 2000 the Democratic Party, which had listed Santorum as their #1 target for defeat, deserted Klink in the general election because he was pro-life and pro-gun.

The Bush White House fully grasped Pennsylvania's voting volatility and has seriously courted the populace, particularly the Catholics. By early 2004, President Bush had made over thirty visits to the commonwealth.

*   *   *   *   *

The first years of the twenty-first century were a tough period for Catholics. The scandal of sexual abuse by priests and the subsequent cover-ups and large monetary payoffs to victims of the abuse shocked even the most observant and conservative Catholics. The faithful were appalled to learn that over a fifty-year period 4,392 priests had abused 10,000 victims. They were angered by the revelation that 81 percent of these perverse acts were committed by homosexual priests against teenage boys.

And there was an angry backlash. Bernard Cardinal Law of Boston was pressured to resign because it appeared he swept scandal under the rug. Milwaukee Archbishop Rembert Weakland abandoned his job on May 24, 2002, when newspapers revealed a homosexual relationship and hush money payments totaling $400,000.

Throughout 2002 and 2003, American Church leaders were paralyzed. In the mad rush to explain and defend their policies in dealing with wayward priests, they lost their collective voice when it came to moral issues confronting the nation.

Sensing weakness, extreme secular humanists aggressively pursued their political agendas, and they scored many major victories. In New York, for instance, cafeteria Catholic George Pataki embraced "hate-crime" legislation and domestic-partner benefits advocated by homosexual groups, and the governor created a special class of citizens when he signed the state's Gay Rights Law. Pataki went along with legislation that repealed a "conscience clause" on state abortion services, thus forcing religious medical institutions to violate their commitment to the sanctity of human life.

In 2003, the Massachusetts Supreme Court ordered that state's legislature to revise its laws to permit gay marriages, and pandemonium broke out across the nation. The mayors of San Francisco and New Paltz, New York, blatantly ignored existing laws (and their oaths to uphold them) and began performing gay marriages.

Liberal ideologues, who believe that duly elected legislators are not enlightened enough to pass progressive legislation the political left approves, applauded the Massachusetts court for usurping legislative authority and enforcing politically correct social policy.

But practicing Catholics, conservative Protestants, and many observant Jews were outraged by these attacks on the sanctity of marriage. They feared that if civil law permits gay marriages, their priests, ministers, and rabbis might lose the ministerial exemption which permits religious institutions not to marry or hire homosexuals.

While liberal pundits were dancing in the streets over the prospects of legally sanctioned gay marriages, pollsters detected a popular revolt brewing. Writing in the April 5, 2004 issue of *The Weekly Standard*, analyst Mark Stricherz made this observation:

> Those most opposed to gay marriage are the white working class. Over the years this group has been referred to as Joe Sixpack, Reagan Democrats, NASCAR dads, and waitress moms. But their ideology remains roughly the same – economically liberal and culturally moderate or conservative. And while the media tend to dismiss them, they represent a crucial voting bloc. Indeed, both McInturff and Democratic pollster Stanley Greenberg have found independently that this group will vote to oppose gay rights.
>
> This group, according to McInturff, consists of Democratic men, seniors, union members, and residents of Bush-leaning swing states. Subsequent polls have revealed another development: Many of these voters live in the battleground states of the Rust Belt and Midwest.[70]

Public Opinion Strategies, a polling firm, revealed in January 2004 that in a presidential race, if a Democrat supports gay civil unions, Bush would pick up an additional 12 percent of the voters. Exit polls taken during the March Ohio presidential primary revealed that over 70 percent of Democrats opposed gay marriages and civil unions.[71]

It didn't take the White House long to figure out that if they equivocated or ignored the gay marriage issue they risked alienating their base voters – practicing Catholics and evangelical Protestants. Hence, in February 2004, President Bush publicly endorsed a constitutional amendment preserving marriage between a man and a woman.

With the nation still evenly divided as the 2004 election cycle began, turning out the base vote became the strategy of both Republicans and Democrats. And the Bush team had to know that to keep practicing Catholics in their camp (who represent 9 percent of the total voting population), they could not weaken on key social issues.

An intensive polling and focus group study, performed by the Greenberg

Quinlan Rosner Research group between November 2001 and July 2003, tells why:

	All Voters	Devout[72] Catholics
Percent of All Voters	**100**	**9**
Party Alignment		
Democrat	46	46
Republican	46	48
Margin	0	R + 2

Thermometer	**Degrees**	
NRA	**51.3**	**47.6**
Warm	42	37
Cool	36	37
Net	+6	0

Pro-Life Groups	**49.8**	**65.4**
Warm	38	58
Cool	38	20
Net	0	+38

Clinton	43.1	38.7
Warm	38	33
Cool	49	55
Net	-11	-22

Which Party Is Better on the Issues

Keep America Strong	**All Voters**	**Devout Catholics**
Democrats	23	22
Republicans	53	54
Net	R + 30	R + 32
On Your Side		
Democrats	40	38
Republicans	35	38
Net	R + 3	0
The Economy		
Democrats	40	38
Republicans	43	46
Net	R + 12	R + 11

Which Party Is Better on the Issues

	All Voters	Devout Catholics
Education		
Democrats	43	38
Republicans	35	38
Net	D + 8	0

Practicing Catholics, for the most part, lean toward the culturally conservative Bush, but they can't be taken for granted.

* * * * *

In 2004, Catholics were confronted with the prospects of a major political party nominating for the first time in over forty years, a presidential candidate who professed to be Roman Catholic, Senator John F. Kerry of Massachusetts.

The race of 2004 was significantly different from 1960. In public life, Senator Kerry had to take positions on social issues that Senator John F. Kennedy never had to think about: abortion, government funding of abortion, parental consent for teen abortions, rights of unborn victims of violence, partial-birth abortion, stem-cell research, euthanasia, assisted suicide, civil unions and marriages for homosexuals. And on each of these issues, Senator Kerry took public positions that were contrary to the teachings of his Church.

While John Kerry was raised a Catholic, served as an altar boy, and told *Time* magazine in April 2004 that he is a "believing and practicing Catholic," his public pronouncements and Senate voting record places him in the category of cafeteria Catholics. Senator Kerry has a 100 percent NARAL pro-choice rating and has pledged to stop any nominee to the U.S. Supreme Court who opposes *Roe v. Wade*.

When in March 2004 Kerry became the presumptive presidential nominee of the Democratic Party, many Catholics, particularly the bishops, realized they had a serious problem on their hands. Faith and Reason Institute president, Dr. Robert Royal, had this take on the bishops' dilemma:

> With the Kerry candidacy, several chickens came home to roost. The American Catholic bishops had largely looked the other way for decades while Catholic politicians like Kerry and fellow Massachusetts Senator Teddy Kennedy went from "personally opposed" to radical advocacy of abortion rights. Fears that criticism of and perhaps even ecclesiastical penalties for such politicians would create a backlash ignored the fact that the bishops had already thrown away much of their influence through neglect. Lay men and women had gotten used to seeing politicians who called

themselves Catholic publicly flouting basic Catholic principles. Several bishops stood up in early 2004 to say that the usual deal would not be in place this time around. But there remained a reluctance among the bishops as a body – and especially among laymen at the bishops' conference – to take the final step and require any politician running for office and Kerry most notably among them, either to support Church teaching on line-in-the-sand issues like abortion or stop calling themselves Catholic.[73]

The "Catholic Issue" began to make national headlines in March 2004 when Kerry compared himself to Jack Kennedy in 1960 and stated, "I don't tell Church officials what to do, and Church officials shouldn't tell American politicians what to do in the context of our public life."[74] Kerry also resorted to this cliché: "It is not appropriate in the United States for a legislator to legislate your personal beliefs for the rest of the country."[75] Writing in the April 26, 2004, issue of *The Weekly Standard*, J. Bottum made this observation concerning the Kerry revisionist view of the Kennedy position: "John F. Kennedy's promise that he would accept no orders from religious officials in the performance of his office has devolved into the idea that religious officials may not even instruct believers in the tenets of their faith."[76]

In April, it became apparent that the Vatican was carefully monitoring the Kerry candidacy. One Vatican official told *Time*, "People in Rome are becoming more and more aware that there's a problem with John Kerry and a potential scandal with his apparent profession of his Catholic faith and some of his stances, particularly abortion."[77]

United States bishops began to feel the heat from the faithful to exhibit leadership. Columnist Maggie Gallagher opined that if the bishops didn't chastise Catholics who "dissent from the Church's core teachings on things like abortion . . . it is hard to see how the next generation of Catholics can avoid concluding the Church is just not serious."[78]

As many Catholics are aware that the Vatican and the National Catholic Conference have always spoken out forcefully about Catholics in public life. In November 2002, for instance, Pope John Paul II released a commentary on "The Participation of Catholics in Political Life," which bluntly stated that "lawmaking bodies have a grave and clear obligation to oppose any law that attacks human life." The pope also noted that Catholic politicians must understand "that a well-formed Christian conscience does not permit one to vote for a political program or individual law which contradicts the fundamental contents of faith and morals."

Bishops hesitant to defend the faith were reminded of their own September 2003 pastoral statement, *Faithful Citizenship: A Catholic Call to Political Responsibility*, which states that abortion "is never morally acceptable."

And some bishops stepped forward and performed their episcopal duties: Archbishop Raymond Burke of St. Louis told the *St. Louis Post Dispatch*, "I would have to admonish [Kerry] not to present himself for communion."[79]

Senator Kerry's own archbishop, Sean O'Malley of Boston, who allowed Kerry to receive communion at his 2003 installation Mass, told *Time* in 2004 that Catholic politicians who publicly oppose Church positions "shouldn't dare come to communion."[80]

Reacting to the April 4 *Time* article, *The New York Times* reported on April 6 this comment by Kerry:

> I'm not a church spokesman. I'm a legislator running for president. My oath is to uphold the Constitution of the United States in my public life. My oath privately between me and God was defined in the Catholic church by Pius XXIII and Pope Paul VI in Vatican II, which allows for freedom of conscience for Catholics with respect to these choices, and that is exactly where I am. And it is separate. Our constitution separates church and state, and they should be reminded of that.[81]

To many, Kerry's comments were both wrong and misleading. Of course there was no Pius XXIII, but statements by Pope *John* XXIII, Pope Paul VI, and Vatican II documents contradict the senator's statement:

"Human life is sacred – all men must recognize that fact. From its very inception it reveals the creating hand of God. Those who violate His laws not only offend the divine majesty and degrade themselves and humanity, they also sap the vitality of the political community of which they are members." – John XXIII, *Mater et Magistra* (para. 194)

> "... to speak to rulers of nations. To you most of all is committed the responsibility of safeguarding the common good. You can contribute so much to the preservation of morals. We beg of you, never allow the morals of your peoples to be undermined. The family is the primary unit in the state; do not tolerate any legislation which would introduce into the family those practices which are opposed to the natural law of God." Paul VI, *Humanae Vitae* (para. 23)

> "... the political community and public authority are founded on human nature and hence belong to the order designed by God, even though the choice of a political regime and the appointment of rulers are left to the free will of citizens. It follows also that political authority, both in the community as such and in the

representative bodies of the state, must always be exercised within the limits of the moral order and directed toward the common
good." Second Vatican Council, *Gaudium et Spes* (para. 74)

The political heat continued to increase. On the day Planned Parenthood
broke its own precedent and endorsed a presidential candidate for the first
time – John Kerry, of course – Nigerian Cardinal Francis Arinze, Vatican
Prefect of the Congregation for Divine Worship and the Discipline of
Sacraments, told the media that a Catholic politician who supports abortion
"is not fit" to receive communion.[82] The Cardinal made the additional point
that "the Catholic Church exists in the United States and there are bishops
there. Let them interpret it."[83]

But the president of the U.S. Conference of Bishops, Wilton D. Gregory,
made what seemed to be a comment meant to give politicians such as John
Kerry some breathing room:

> . . . Cardinal Arinze's statement made clear that each diocesan
> bishop has the right and duty to address such issues of serious pas-
> toral concern as he judges best in his local church, in accord with
> pastoral and canonical norms.[84]

The editorial response of the liberal New York *Daily News* was even
stronger:

> Francis Cardinal Arinze, who issued the directive from the
> Vatican, didn't mention Kerry by name – but even if he had, the
> church has every right to declare what its moral teachings are and
> how it desires its flock to follow them.[85]

Following Rome's advice, more bishops stood up for Church teachings.
In May 2004, the bishops of Camden and Trenton, New Jersey, declared that
the state's governor, James McGreevey, a former altar boy, "is not a devout
Catholic because of his stance on several political causes that are opposed by
the Church, including domestic partnership for gay couples, abortion rights
and the use of human stem cells in medical research."[86] McGreevey was told
he would be refused communion.

That same week, a five-page pastoral letter penned by Newark
Archbishop John Myers appeared in his archdiocesan newspaper, *The
Catholic Advocate*. The archbishop asked that all Catholic public officials
who promote abortion "spare the Church *scandal* by opting not to seek communion when they attend mass."[87]

Undeterred by criticism that he had violated "separation of Church and State," Archbishop Myers made it clear that he was doing his duty by offering guidance to the 1.3 million Catholics in the Newark Archdiocese: "My position as a pastor and a teacher is to help people understand, not to get involved in politics directly."[88]

At least one New Jersey politician, state senator Bernard Kenny, Jr., made a remarkable act of conscience: After meeting with Archbishop Myers to discus the pastoral letter, the senator told the press he was leaving the Roman Catholic Church. "I don't argue with the Church's right to exercise its prerogative," he said. "But I'm not comfortable going to Mass and being denied communion, which is the cornerstone of the entire liturgy. I view it as a form of ostracism based on my political beliefs."[89] Of course it may be that Mr. Kenny has ostracized himself from the Church.

Not every American bishop had the fortitude of the New Jersey Ordinaries. Theodore Cardinal McCarrick, Archbishop of Washington, D.C., who serves as Chairman of the National Bishops Conference Task Force on Catholic Participation in Catholic Life, met privately with Senator Kerry for 45 minutes on April 15, 2004. Political columnist Robert Novak reported that the cardinal was lobbied by Kerry "against being denied Holy Communion as an unswerving pro-choice abortion advocate."[90] McCarrick's comments on the matter, that appeared a week later in his archdiocesan newspaper, *The Catholic Standard*, appalled many Catholics: While asserting abortion "may be primary," he added that "people who are with us on one issue" may be "against us on many other issues." McCarrick concluded: "All these things will have to be weighed very carefully." Intentionally or not, he was following the lead of liberal, pro-choice Democrats in providing cover for Kerry among traditional Catholics.[91]

By mid-May 2004, prominent Catholic laymen and Catholic organizations had begun publicly to criticize Cardinal McCarrick. In a full-page advertisement published in *The Washington Times* and other periodicals, the American Life League's "Crusade for the Defense of Our Catholic Church" asked Cardinal McCarrick:

"ARE YOU COMFORTABLE NOW?"

The passion and suffering of Christ are examples of the "comfort" faithful Catholics should expect in this world.

On April 17, 2003, Pope John Paul II made it clear that bishops have an obligation to deny Holy Communion to Catholics demonstrating "outward conduct which is seriously, clearly and steadfastly contrary to the moral norm."

Despite the counsel of both Christ and the Holy Father, Cardinal Theodore McCarrick of Washington, D.C. made this statement on April 27, 2004, concerning Catholic politicians who openly support legalized abortion:

"I have not gotten to the stage where I'm comfortable in denying the Eucharist."

Comforting words for John Kerry, Nancy Pelosi, Ted Kennedy and the 68 other pro-abortion "Catholic" politicians in Congress.

But cold comfort for the 1.3 million babies surgically aborted every year.

YOU CAN'T BE BOTH CATHOLIC AND PRO-ABORTION!

Another group taking action was the newly formed "Catholic Citizenship" run by one of America's leading lay Catholic voices, former Boston mayor Ray Flynn. Unlike the failed "Catholic Campaign for America," which never advanced beyond hosting cocktail parties in fashionable urban neighborhoods, "Catholic Citizenship" intends to register practicing Catholic voters, distribute voting profiles on candidates, publish a "Faithful Citizenship Guide," and establish a "Campaign to Build a Culture of Life." If the bishops refuse to lead, this group may fill the void and lead a Catholic counter-revolution.

* * * * *

As the presidential primary season ended and Democrats and Republicans were preparing for their national conventions in Boston and New York respectively, the American Catholic bishops were dominating the political news.

In the spring and summer of 2004, the distribution of Holy Communion to recalcitrant Catholic politicians was the major issue confronting Church leaders. Many bishops were under pressure to avoid any showdowns with pro-abortion politicians, and pundits were predicting backlash among the faithful if bishops dared to deny communion to John Kerry or any other elected official.

Democratic National Chairman, Terry McAuliffe (a graduate of the Catholic University of America), gave this warning in April: "If I went to my local church in Virginia and was denied communion, I'd be very upset about that. I doubt it will come to that. I think it would be a huge mistake for the Catholic Church."[92]

In late May, forty-eight Catholic Democrats in the House sent a letter to the Archbishop of Washington, D.C., Theodore Cardinal McCarrick, complaining about bishops who were threatening to deny communion. They warned that such actions could "revive latent anti-Catholic prejudice." One signer, Representative Rosa DeLauro (D-CT) said, "I just don't think that the Eucharist ought to be used as a political weapon."[93]

In early June, Senator Richard Durbin (D-IL), speaking on behalf of pro-abortion Catholics in Congress, donned the "seamless garment" and argued, in a report titled "Evaluating the Votes and Actions of Public Officials from a Catholic Perspective," that these Democrats give greater support to United States Conference of Catholic Bishops (USCCB) agenda than most pro-life Catholic Republicans.

Attempting to equate life issues with other social issues (i.e., minimum wage) Senator Durbin argued: "None of us can expect to measure up perfectly against the Church's full agenda of political engagement. What Catholic politicians can hope to see, however, is an attempt to evaluate their work comprehensively, not on the basis of only a narrow slice of the Church's teachings."[94]

After a review of the Durbin report, the Catholic League for Religious and Civil Liberties issued this statement: "Durbin has even gone so far as to say that the 'right to religious belief and the separation between church and state' may be *compromised* by bishops who impose sanctions on pro-abortion lawmakers. This is ironic, coming from the senator who on the Judiciary Committee enforced a *de facto* religious test barring pro-life Catholics from the federal bench. The fact of the matter is that the bishops have not only the right but the duty to speak on moral issues that play out in the public sphere; and Durbin's inflammatory rhetoric is a blatant attempt to muzzle them."

Defending Senator Durbin and the 48 pro-abortion Catholics in Congress, a *New York Times* editorial asserted that "threats by some bishops to deny communion to Catholic politicians who support abortion rights" are "deeply hurtful." The *Times* went on to warn Catholic churchmen that "any attempt to make elected leaders toe a doctrinal line when it comes to their public duties raises multiple risks. Breaching the church-state line that is so necessary to protect religious freedom is one. Figuring out when to stop is another."[95]

In counterpoint, William F. Buckley Jr. (himself a practicing Catholic) attacked the *Times* editorial for its flawed reasoning:

> If we have a separation of church and state, then the right of the Church is to decide who does and who does not receive communion. If you are saying that a member should be given communion even if he counsels laws that violate rights believed by the Church

> to be universal, then you are not arguing the separation of church
> and state. You are arguing the supremacy of the state. State
> believes abortion okay, therefore, Church must not discriminate
> against anyone who also says it is okay. [96]

It could be construed as hypocritical for the Left to portray the American
bishops as stepping over the line and violating separation of church and state
because they spoke out on controversial public issues. These critics chose to
ignore that in the 1960s, the Left lauded the bishop of New Orleans for
excommunicating racist Catholics for opposing the civil rights movement.
And liberals applauded when the bishops criticized Ronald Reagan's nuclear
and fiscal policies in "The Challenge of Peace" (1983) and "Economic Justice
for All" (1986).

What the Left failed to grasp is that bishops, as shepherds, have a duty to
their flocks to offer guidance on the Church's moral teachings. They also have
an obligation to correct any person – especially a Catholic politician – who
misleads or sows confusion about Church doctrine. Clergy of all faiths explain
to their co-religionists how their religions apply in the temporal world.
Catholics are no different.

In a closed-door meeting at their June 18 meeting in Denver, the
American Catholic bishops approved 183 to 6 a resolution they hoped would
clarify the situation. "Catholics in Public Life," as the document was called,
concluded that pro-abortion politicians are cooperating in evil. They did not,
however, approve a national policy on denying communion; that was left to
the discretion of the local ordinary. But the document did call on the Catholic
community to deny awards, honors, and platforms to Catholic politicians who
"act in defiance of our fundamental moral principles."[97]

The bishops also forcefully articulated their belief that:

> The separation of church and state does not require division
> between belief and public action, between moral principles and
> political choices, but protects the right of believers and religious
> groups to practice their faith and act on their values in public life. [98]

"Catholics in Public Life" was a compromise statement that placated leftist clerics led by Cardinal McCarrick and Los Angeles archbishop, Cardinal
Roger Mahony. As early as April, McCarrick set the tone when he told Fox
News, "every archbishop has the right to make his own decision in his own
area [and] many of us would not like to use the Eucharist as part of the sanc-
tion."[99]

In a similar vein, Cardinal Mahony declared at the bishops conference:
"The Archdiocese [of Los Angeles] will continue to follow Church teaching

which places the duty on each Catholic to examine their [*sic*] consciences as to their worthiness to receive Holy Communion. That is not the role of the person distributing the body and blood of Christ."[100]

Ethics and Public Policy Center senior fellow and biographer of John Paul II, George Weigel, termed the decisions of the bishops as "a last gasp effort to hold on to the tattered seamless garment." Weigel told *National Review Online*: "We now know, because Kerry has demonstrated it, that the seamless garment metaphor, whatever truths it embodies within it, becomes in the hands of politicians an excuse [to oppose church teaching on life issues]. Why are we trying to stitch the thing together again?"

In the final hours of the American bishops conference, rumors abounded that the content of a Vatican statement clarifying communion issues was purposely not disclosed because it refuted the McCarrick/Mahony position.

Indeed, when "Worthiness to Receive Holy Communion – General Principles," written by the Vatican's Joseph Cardinal Ratzinger (the future Pope Benedict XVI) was finally released, it confirmed the suspicions of many of the Catholic faithful. Archbishop Raymond Burke of St. Louis, in Rome when he read the statement, said he "was stunned by the text, because we hadn't received it." "I personally was irritated," said Omaha Archbishop Elden Curtiss. "I think his point of view should have been expressed right from the beginning, and clarified."[101]

The Vatican's statement, which flatly contradicted Cardinal Mahony's June 19 statement, succinctly described the obligations of lay Catholics and the "ministers of Holy Communion." Ratzinger described numerous situations when a priest would have no alternative but to deny communion, and he directed priests to meet privately with any Catholic who publicly supports abortion and euthanasia laws, and to offer instruction in Church teaching. The pastor's job is to inform the public servant "that he is not to present himself for Holy Communion until he brings to an end the objective situation of sin and warning him that he will otherwise be denied the Eucharist." Ratzinger also explained that a priest who denies communion is not judging the condition of the individual's soul but "is reacting to the person's public unworthiness to receive Holy Communion due to an objective situation of sin."

Ratzinger's statement also pulled the rug out from under the proponents of the "seamless garment" argument by making it perfectly clear that not all moral issues have the same moral weight as abortion and euthanasia. "There may be," he declared, "a legitimate diversity of opinion even among Catholics about waging war and applying the death penalty, but not, however, with regard to abortion and euthanasia." When it comes to abortion, death penalty, or the war in Iraq, only abortion is intrinsically wrong because it destroys *innocent* human life.

On the death penalty and the war, Ratzinger confirmed that the Church

does not hold a univocal view. While it is true that Pope John Paul II and the
U.S. bishops oppose the death penalty, they have never decried the *Church's*
stand on capital punishment. In fact, in a 1980 pastoral letter, the American
bishops insisted that "the state has the right to take the life of a person guilty
of a serious crime." Catholics are free to oppose using the death penalty in
particular situations, but Catholics are not free to condemn it in the name of
the Church as *always* morally wrong.

Similarly, while the Vatican opposed the U.S. invasion of Iraq, Catholics
are free to use prudential judgment in determining if it was just. The U.S.
Conference of Catholic Bishops (USCCB) has stressed that "reasonable people can disagree about the necessity of using force" to overthrow Saddam.

Looking for loopholes, leftist Catholics zeroed in on Ratzinger's last
paragraph which stated:

> When a Catholic does not share a candidate's stand in favour of
> abortion and/or euthanasia, but votes for that candidate for other
> reasons, it is considered remote material cooperation, which can
> be permitted in the presence of proportionate reasons.

The Rev. Andrew Greeley led the way, declaring that Catholics could, in
good conscience, vote for Kerry because the right-wing Ratzinger said so. In
his nationally syndicated column, Greeley quoted that final paragraph and
concluded: "It is as close to an official statement on the subject as one is likely to get. It says that Catholics are not obliged to vote on one issue, no matter
how important the issue might be. They may vote for Kerry 'for other reasons'
so long as they are not supporting him merely for his pro-choice stance. . . .
This ought to settle the matter."[102]

But as with the flawed June 2004 bishop's statement, quoting only one
paragraph of the statement and not properly explaining the phrase "propor-
tionate reasoning" allowed Greeley to mislead his readers. Dr. Robert Royal,
president of the Washington-based Faith and Reason Institute, had this reaction to Greeley's pronouncement:

> Some liberal American Catholics, like Fr. Andrew Greeley, chose
> deliberately to misunderstand then Cardinal Ratzinger's directive
> about voting for pro-abortion Catholics only for "proportionate
> reasons." Democrats and their hangers-on tried to spin this as
> meaning if they were good for "the poor," meaning they passed
> out other people's money, they had equal moral footing. In fact, as
> anyone who follows these issues in the Church knows, propor-
> tionate reasons means serious offenses against life such as a

massacre or genocide, and even then abortion is killing 1.2 million Americans alone a year, so it would have to be a rather large massacre or genocide intended by some pro-life Republicans that would explode their moral superiority on abortion per se.

The Ratzinger statement did not, however, stop USCCB bureaucrats from promoting the Democratic Party's social agenda.

To play down Senator Kerry's association with the proponents of abortion and euthanasia, the USCCB's Office of Government Liaison carefully crafted a presidential-candidate questionnaire that took the "seamless garment" arguments to new lengths.

The questionnaire, which was sent out to the presidential candidates without the formal approval of the U.S. bishops, attempted to give equal moral weight with the paramount issues of life to such issues as broadcast licensing, a $7-per-hour minimum wage, housing vouchers, immigration quotas, gun control, and farm subsidies. The forty-one questions resembled a high-school true-false exam on which one has to achieve a 65 percent grade (twenty seven correct out of forty-one questions) to pass.

John Kerry could take this quiz, answer wrong the eight questions covering abortion, marriage/homosexual unions, physician-assisted suicide, embryo research and human cloning, and still get a better grade than he earned at Yale. His grade would have been 82.9 percent – a "B" in most schools.

When the questionnaire leaked out, prominent lay Catholics objected. They pointed out that neither the Ten Commandments, nor the Sermon on the Mount, nor the 900-page Official Catholic Catechism made any reference to a $7 minimum wage. In his 1891 encyclical letter, *Rerum Novarum*, for instance, Pope Leo XIII did call for fair wages and working hours – but neither Leo nor his successors ever published a dollar-per-hour schedule to be hung on the wall of church vestibules. The same is true with regard to farm subsidies, refugee quotas, and each of the other 13 non-life issue categories.

Catholic bloggers complained that the USCCB questionnaire was a sham and demanded that it be retracted and the reckless behavior of the USCCB's lay bureaucrats be curtailed.

Culture of Life Foundation president Austin Ruse explained that "some people will tick through these like a scorecard and say, 'in a majority of cases we voted with the Church.' . . . That is exactly how it will be used." Ruse additionally commented:

> The lay staff of the Bishops conference may believe that immigration and abortion have the same status. But that is not the teaching of the body of Bishops, nor is it the teaching of the Holy

See. In an absolutely proper exercise of their authority, the Church hierarchy has consistently taught the centrality of the abortion issue, over and above all others. Some on the lay staff do not like that and it shows in their legislative priorities and in the current questionnaire.

The questionnaire was withdrawn on Friday, September 3, 2004.

* * * * *

Members of Democratic salons in New York and Los Angeles expected John Kerry to come out swinging against his Church's hierarchy. Many hoped he would throw down the gauntlet and attend Mass at a church that *would* deny him Communion. An altar-rail confrontation, they believed, would be the catalyst for a voter backlash of millions of men and women of good will, who would be appalled by the unenlightened Roman Catholic Church.

Many leftist Democrats were delighted that bishops throughout the country continued to speak out on controversial issues as the fall presidential campaign began in earnest. They were pleased with the August announcement by the bishops of Atlanta (GA), Charleston (SC), and Charlotte (NC) that unless pro-abortion Catholic politicians publicly recant they would be denied Communion. Newark's archbishop, John Myers, received major headlines from "old" media after the publication of a September 17, 2004 *Wall Street Journal* op-ed essay. In his piece, the prelate reminded Catholics:

Abortion and embryo-destructive research are different. They are intrinsic and grave evils; no Catholic may legitimately support them. In the context of contemporary American social life, abortion and embryo-destructive research are disproportionate evils. They are the gravest human rights abuses of our domestic politics and what slavery was to the time of Lincoln. Catholics are called by the Gospel of Life to protect the victims of these human rights abuses. They may not legitimately abandon the victims by supporting those who would further their victimization.

Archbishop Raymond Burke also raised eyebrows when he stated in an October pastoral letter that "not only are Catholics morally obligated to vote . . . but they must do so in accordance with the moral teachings of the Church."

To add fuel to the fire, *The New York Times* published an op-ed piece titled "Voting Our Conscience, Not Our Religion" in which author Mark Roche, employing the familiar "seamless garment" approach, concluded that Catholics in good conscience should vote for Kerry:

In many ways, Catholic voters' growing political independence has led to a profusion of moral dilemmas: they often feel they must abandon one good for the sake of another. But while they may be dismayed at John Kerry's position on abortion and stem cell research, they should be no less troubled by George W. Bush's stance on the death penalty, health care, the environment and just war. Given the recent history of higher rates of abortion with Republicans in the White House, along with the tradition of Democratic support of equitable taxes and greater integration into the world community, more Catholics may want to reaffirm their tradition of allegiance to the Democratic Party in 2004.

Roche, whose bio in the *Times* piece was "Dean at the University of Notre Dame," inferred he spoke for the Church and threw in the questionable statistic that abortions had gone up under the pro-life Bush Administration versus the pro-abortion Clinton years. (The allegation, which created a stir in the media, was exposed in 2005 as bogus.) William McGurn, a *New York Post* columnist, saw through the ruse: "I'm fairly confident that the name the *Times* wanted on its pro-Kerry op-ed page was not Mark Roche but Notre Dame's. . . . Had Mark Roche been a dean at Indiana University, nobody would have paid attention."[103]

Reacting to the Roche article, Brooklyn's Bishop Nicholas DiMarzio blasted the author, complaining that this "Dean of a major Catholic University, confused the issue of conscience and, in fact, told people how to vote." "This," he continued, "is something that none of us particularly likes."

DiMarzio reminded Catholics that conscience is "not some type of free-wheeling optional determinate of our action" but instead must be informed. The bishop went on to demonstrate that there is "a hierarchy of values" regarding life and that one cannot equate poverty issues to abortion or euthanasia.[104]

The *Times* then published an op-ed piece by the Archbishop of Denver, Charles Chaput, in which he challenged Catholics (including politicians) to stand up for their beliefs:

> Words are cheap. Actions matter. If we believe in the sanctity of life from conception to natural death, we need to prove that by our actions, including our political choices. Anything less leads to the corruption of our integrity. Patriotism, which is a virtue for people of all faiths, requires that we fight, ethically and nonviolently, for what we believe. Claiming that "we don't want to impose our beliefs on society" is not merely politically convenient; it is morally incoherent and irresponsible.[105]

Whether the archbishop's piece was added for balance or to further excite liberals is a matter for debate.

A very important symbolic shot across the bow of the Kerry campaign was the September 17 announcement that he would not be invited as a speaker/dais guest to the nation's premiere annual Catholic political event, New York's Al Smith Dinner.

For over half a century, the dinner has been a command performance for presidents and would-be presidents. Past speakers have included John F. Kennedy and Richard M. Nixon in 1960, Ronald Reagan and Jimmy Carter (1980), George W. Bush and Al Gore (2000). That the Alfred E. Smith Memorial Foundation (chaired by New York's Edward Cardinal Egan), dedicated to honoring the memory of the first Catholic Democratic nominee for president, declined to invite the third Catholic Democratic presidential nominee, shattered any illusions Democratic pols may have had concerning the attitudes of many of Mr. Kerry's Catholic confreres.

As the campaign progressed, the Left still believed that their assaults on the bishop's so-called "meddling" in the electoral process would prove to be a big boost to their candidate. And many were confused about why the Kerry campaign wasn't pounding home this "freedom of conscience" theme more vigorously.

Throughout the summer and early fall of 2004, John Kerry ducked most opportunities to talk about his commitment to the tenets of his Church. Silence appeared to be the best policy, because his campaign did not want to risk inciting a backlash from practicing Catholics. Such a backlash could doom Kerry's candidacy because, unlike non-practicing "Cafeteria" Catholics, who are concentrated in northeastern and far-western states that Kerry was expected to easily carry, practicing Catholics were major voting blocs in the key battleground swing states of Wisconsin, Pennsylvania, Ohio, and Missouri. When jobs disappeared in these traditionally industrial states, Yuppie Catholics moved to "Kerry Country" – Boston, Chicago, New York, Los Angeles, while older practicing Catholics chose to live out their lives in these rust-belt regions.

Democrat political pros knew that practicing Catholics, like most Americans, considered the war on terrorism the number one issue, but they also knew that in a close election, (which the 2004 race was expected to be) the issues and voters along the margins matter. A slight shift of 1 or 2 percent of voters who are, for instance, pro-life or anti-gay marriage could decide the election in the closely contested rust-belt states.

Kerry supporters did not want to energize these marginal voters in the swing states by advertising that their candidate voted six times to keep partial-birth abortion legal and opposed federal legislation requiring parental consent for teens seeking abortions. They did not want it well known he was pro-gay rights and represented the state that was the first to permit same sex marriages. Implementing this strategy became more imperative when the results came out that 71 percent of Missouri's voters supported an August 2004 state constitutional amendment forbidding same-sex marriages.

To avoid public clashes, the Kerry campaign stressed economic issues that might appeal to rust-belt, blue-collar Catholics. This may explain why by early October only 23 percent of Americans knew Kerry was a baptized Catholic whereas 90 percent knew Kennedy was Catholic in 1960.

This approach seemed to make sense for Kerry because as a survey of religion and politics published by the Bliss Institute of the University of Akron revealed, practicing Catholics were not in tune with the thinking of Democrats:

* 93% believed it is important that a president have strong religious beliefs;
* 88% believed organized religious groups should stand up for their beliefs;
* 50% believed that the U.S. has a special role in the international arena;
* 65% believed the U.S. can engage in preemptive war;
* 76% believed abortion should always be illegal or legal in few circumstances;
* 71% supported traditional marriage.

Northeastern and far-western pundits, who did not understand this strategy and thought they were doing Kerry a favor by clashing with the Catholic hierarchy, were disgruntled and began putting heat on their candidate to speak out. *The New York Times* published an above-the-fold article (10/7/04) titled, "Kerry and Religion. Pressure builds for a Public Discussion." And every time Kerry or his handlers tried to placate their extreme left-wing base, thy seemed to shoot themselves in the foot.

In June, the Kerry camp had to gag their Director of Religious Outreach, Mara Vanderslice, when the Catholic League revealed that she was active "in the Earlham Socialist Alliance, a group that supports the convicted cop killer Mumia Abu-Jamal and openly embraces Marxism-Leninism. After graduating, Mara spoke at rallies held by ACT-UP, the anti-Catholic group that disrupted Mass at St. Patrick's Cathedral in 1989 by spitting the Eucharist on the floor. In 2000, she practiced civil disobedience when she took to the streets of Seattle in a protest against the World Trade Organization. In 2002, she tried to shut down Washington, D.C. in a protest against the IMF and the World Bank."[106]

Kerry was also criticized for turning to the former Boston congressman, Jesuit Robert Drinan for advice. "This was the same Drinan who had to retract a 1997 op-ed piece in *The New York Times* that supported President Clinton's veto of the partial-birth abortion ban."[107]

The Democratic National Committee hired as its Senior Advisor for Religious Outreach, the Rev. Brenda Bartella Peterson, who had signed an *amicus* brief asking the Supreme Court to delete the words "under God" from the Pledge of Allegiance. A member of the extreme left-wing group, Clergy Leadership Network, which takes no position on abortion, Rev. Peterson was quoted in saying that, "paying taxes is a way of loving your neighbor." Exposed by the Catholic League on August 2, Peterson resigned her post on August 4.

Another can of worms was opened when the Director of the Boston Common Paulist Center (where Kerry often attended Sunday Mass) praised the Senator for aligning "with the social justice aspects of our ministry." Conservative bloggers responded to this endorsement by exposing Paulist Center practices as more Unitarian than Roman Catholic. It was revealed that during Masses celebrated at the Paulist Center, sections of the Nicene Creed referring to "Our Lord" and "the One Holy Catholic and Apostolic Church" are deleted because the phrases are viewed as *too* controversial. This Paulist Center (note that it is called a *Center* and not a Church) advertised that they serve "those persons searching for a spiritual home and those who have been alienated from the Catholic Church."[108]

The Center may have been a safe haven for Kerry to receive Communion but its schismatic practices did not sit well with practicing Catholics.

His religious advisors were not his only problem. Whenever Kerry spoke out on his religious beliefs or his relationship with his Church, he often left himself wide open for criticism.

In his autobiography, Kerry wrote that "there are absolute standards of right or wrong. They may not always be clear but they exist, and it is our duty to honor them as best we can." Fine words, but apparently in Kerry's world, the absolute standard, "Thou shall not kill," did not apply to the unborn.

Senator Kerry told *Catholic Digest* that his "commitment to equal rights and social justice . . . is not simply a matter of political fashion or economic and social theory but a direct command from God." Once again, Kerry appeared to be deaf to God's call for social justice for the unborn.

Kerry dug a deeper hole when he explained to the *Washington Post* that "I oppose abortion . . . I believe life does begin at conception. [But] I can't take my Catholic belief, my article of faith and legislate it on a Protestant or Jew or an Atheist." In the second debate when asked by a town hall participant how he can support federally financed abortions, he reaffirmed that stand claiming that even through he is a "practicing" Catholic, he had no choice but to support pro-abortion legislations because, "I can't take what is an article of faith for me and legislate it for someone who doesn't share that article of faith."

To suggest that a Catholic can't vote his conscience on important issues was viewed by many Catholics and members of other faiths as morally and intellectually incoherent. By its very nature, a senator's vote in favor of any piece of legislation *requires* an act of faith that it is the best policy to impose on all the American people – including those who don't share the legislator's "faith" in the issue. Reacting to the Senator's comment, *National Review* editor Rich Lowry wrote: "This is a sophomoric relativism that ignores the fact that our most important laws have a moral underpinning."

In the third presidential debate (October 13, Tempe, Arizona) Senator Kerry continued to contradict himself. When asked about Catholic bishops' comments on the potential sinfulness of voting for a pro-abortion, pro-unlimited stem cell research candidate, Kerry gave his standard answer:

> I respect their views. I completely respect their views. I am a Catholic. And I grew up learning how to respect those views. But I disagree with them, as do many. I believe that I can't legislate or transfer to another American citizen my article of faith. What is an article of faith for me is not something that I can legislate on somebody who doesn't share that article of faith. I believe that choice, a woman's choice is between a woman, God and her doctor. And that's why I support that. Now I will not allow somebody to come in and change Roe v. Wade. The president has never said whether or not he would do that. But we know from the people he's tried to appoint to the court he wants to. I will not. I will defend the right of Roe v. Wade.[109]

Instead of giving up the rest of his allotted time, the Senator insisted on elaborating his religious views:

> Now with respect to religion, you know, as I said I grew up a Catholic. I was an altar boy. I know that throughout my life this has made a difference to me. And as President Kennedy said when he ran for president, he said, I'm not running to be a Catholic president. I'm running to be a president who happens to be Catholic. Now my faith affects everything that I do and choose. There's a great passage of the Bible that says What does it mean my brother to say you have faith if there are no deeds? Faith without works is dead. And I think that everything you do in public life has to be guided by your faith, affected by your faith, but without transferring it in any official way to other people. That's why I fight for equality and justice. All of those things come out of that fundamental teaching and belief of faith. But I know this: that President Kennedy in his inaugural address told of us that here on earth

God's work must truly be our own. And that's what we have to – I
think that's the test of public service.[110]

After pointing out how he could not impose his religious views on others,
Kerry went on to contradict himself, stating that "everything you do in public
life has to be guided by faith." A stupefied Rich Lowry had this to say the next
day on *NR Online* –

> Kerry presented diametrically opposed views on the role of moral-
> ity in public life within about 30 seconds. He went on to say that
> his environmentalism and his poverty-fighting measures were
> borne of his faith. In other words, his faith affects everything –
> including his position on whether the minimum wage should be
> $5.15 or $7 an hour – but not how he legislates concerning life
> issues, because it would be wrong to legislate his morality,
> although he does it all the time.

In an attempt to clarify his support of the doctrine of separation of church
and state, Kerry took his campaign to the pulpit in Florida's Mount Hermon
A.M.E. Church on Sunday, October 24. In his "sermon," Kerry further confused Catholics by taking a shot at many leaders of his own church:

> I know there are some bishops who have suggested that as a pub-
> lic official I must cast votes or take public positions, on issues like
> a woman's right to choose or stem cell research, that carry out the
> tenets of the Catholic Church. I love my church; I respect the bish-
> ops; but I respectfully disagree.[111]

While the Kerry Campaign was foundering over religious values, the
Bush camp was humming along, implementing political-action plans to reach
out to millions of Evangelical Protestants and Roman Catholics.

After analyzing the 2000 presidential returns, Bush's political architect,
Karl Rove, realized that about 5 million Evangelicals, who agreed with the
president on social issues, had stayed home on that earlier Election Day.

Like many analysts, Rove also recognized that in 2004 voter concern for
moral-values issues was on the rise – particularly when it came to issues like
abortion and same-sex marriage. The fact that eleven states in 2004 were to
have referendums on the ballot to mandate that marriage could only be
between a man and a woman, confirmed the polling data.

Reacting to this phenomenon, Rove developed a simple two-part plan for
the 2004 election:

1. To keep red states in the GOP column and to increase the popular vote

turnout, a massive grassroots effort was implemented to bring out millions of Evangelicals by reminding them to vote their values.

2. To carry closely contested swing states and to decrease Democratic margins, a grassroots plan was executed in key rust-belt states to energize white, blue-collar, practicing Catholic voters. In parts of the South and the Southwest, "a vote your moral values" plan was initiated to attract Hispanic Catholics.

It was at this time that the Republican National Committee created KerryWrongForCatholics.com and organized 55,000 volunteers to bring out Catholic voters for Bush.

Unlike Senator Kerry, President Bush was not uneasy when it came to expressing his faith in public. On Bill O'Reilly's FOX News show, the President told his host that religion "is an important part of my life" and "means strength and calm in the face of the storm." He also casually explained to *Catholic Digest*: "I don't hide the fact that I am influenced personally by my faith."[112]

In August, Bush appeared in Dallas at the Knights of Columbus convention as the keynote speaker. He boasted to this crowd of Catholics that during his first day in office he restated President Reagan's "Mexico City Policy" which stopped U.S. money from being spent to promote abortion internationally. He also told the cheering delegates that he signed into law the Born Alive Infants Protection Act (which protects children who survive an abortion); the Unborn Victims of Violence Act; and the ban on partial-birth abortion. On the issue of stem cell research, he said: "Human life is a creation of God – not a commodity to be exploited by man."

Concerning the role of religion in the public square, Bush did not fear to tell his listeners that, the state "should never be the church, and the church certainly should never be the state. But the state should never fear the good works of the church."[113]

Reminding the audience that his brother, Florida Governor Jeb Bush, was a member of their fraternal organization, he said, "Jeb knows, as I do, that your works of mercy are making our society more compassionate, changing the lives of millions of citizens."

After a tumultuous standing ovation for the President, Knights of Columbus chief, Carl Anderson, turned to Bush and said, "Thank you for restoring moral integrity to the office of President."[114]

In the Presidential debates, Mr. Bush described his faith in clear terms that could be grasped by all Americans. When asked about same-sex marriage, he did not equivocate:

> I believe in the sanctity of marriage. I think it's very important that
> we protect marriage as an institution between a man and a woman.

I proposed a constitutional amendment. The reason I did so was because I was worried that activist judges are actually defining the definition of marriage. And the surest way to protect marriage between a man and woman is to amend the Constitution. It has also the benefit of allowing citizens to participate in the process. After all, when you amend the Constitution state legislatures must participate in the ratification of the Constitution.

Without hesitation, President Bush told the American people that "every being counts and every person matters." He showcased the pro-life legislation he signed into law and promised he would continue to "promote a culture of life."

And in the closing minutes of the last presidential debate he explained how religion is an essential part of his private and public life:

Religion is an important part. I never want to impose my religion on anybody else. But when I make decisions I stand on principle. And the principles are derived from who I am. I believe we ought to love our neighbor like we love our self. That's manifested in public policy through the faith-based initiative where we've unleashed the armies of compassion to help heal people who hurt. I believe that God wants everybody to be free. That's what I believe. And that's one part of my foreign policy. In Afghanistan, I believe that the freedom there is a gift from the Almighty. And I can't tell you how encouraged I am to see freedom on the march. And so my principles that I make decisions on are a part of me. And religion is a part of me.[115]

* * * * *

On November 2, 2004, President George W. Bush was re-elected to a second term receiving 51.1 percent of the vote and 274 electoral votes.

The Karl Rove strategy to energize the GOP base appeared to have worked. Fifty-nine million Americans cast their ballots for the Bush-Cheney ticket – a record breaking turnout.

Bush was the first presidential candidate to receive over 50 percent of the popular vote since 1988. In forty-five of the fifty states, Bush's vote totals were higher than his 2000 count. Bush received 8 million more votes than he had in 2000. Bill Clinton's vote, for instance, between his elections in 1992 and 1996 increased by only 2.5 million.

Other 2004 election facts:
* Bush's percentage of total votes was greater than any Democratic presidential candidates total since 1968;

* Bush was the first GOP President to have second term majorities in the House and Senate since 1924;
* Not since F.D.R.'s 1936 second term victory has a president picked up seats in both the Senate and House of Representatives.[116]

The Republican strategy to increase the turnout of Evangelical supporters in the South and Catholics in the Rust Belt and South West exceeded all expectations. Political analyst Michael Barone made this observation concerning the turnout:

> It turns out that the increase among Bush voters was greater by a really big margin . . . . In the safe Bush states, Bush turnout was up 21 percent; Kerry turnout up only 12 percent. In the safe Kerry states – and here's some fascinating numbers – Bush turnout up 16 percent; Kerry turnout up only 5 percent, and Kerry turnout actually down in New York City and New York metropolitan area – 9/11 I think has some effect there in any case.[117]

In the election of 2004, Methodist George Bush actually carried the total Catholic vote over baptized Catholic John Kerry 52 percent to 47 percent. Senator Kerry was the first Catholic presidential nominee not to carry a majority of his co-religionists.

Generic Catholic Vote – 2004 Election [118]

State	Catholics %	General Election Bush %	General Election Kerry %	Catholic Vote Bush %	Catholic Vote Kerry %
Alabama	8	63	37	n/a	n/a
Alaska	17	62	35	67	31
Arizona	23	55	44	52	47
Arkansas	6	54	45	57	42
California	28	45	54	35	63
Colorado	19	52	47	52	46
Connecticut	48	44	54	53	47
Delaware	31	46	53	53	47
Florida	28	52	47	57	42
Georgia	10	58	41	69	31
Hawaii	30	45	54	49	51
Idaho	13	68	30	60	40
Illinois	36	45	55	44	56
Indiana	18	60	39	56	43
Iowa	23	50	49	46	53
Kansas	22	62	37	61	39

Generic Catholic Vote – 2004 Election [118]

State	Catholics %	General Election Bush %	General Election Kerry %	Catholic Vote Bush %	Catholic Vote Kerry %
Kentucky	21	60	40	57	43
Louisiana	38	57	42	68	31
Maine	26	45	54	40	58
Maryland	24	43	56	57	41
Massachusetts	44	37	62	49	51
Michigan	29	48	51	49	50
Minnesota	28	48	51	49	50
Mississippi	10	60	40	80	19
Missouri	22	54	46	50	49
Montana	24	59	39	56	43
Nebraska	22	66	33	67	32
Nevada	25	51	48	47	52
New Hampshire	38	49	50	52	47
New Jersey	44	46	53	58	41
New Mexico	32	50	49	38	61
New York	42	40	58	51	48
North Carolina	9	66	44	60	40
North Dakota	25	63	36	62	36
Ohio	26	51	49	55	44
Oklahoma	9	66	34	66	34
Oregon	11	48	52	42	58
Pennsylvania	35	49	51	49	51
Rhode Island	57	39	60	40	59
South Carolina	10	58	41	62	37
South Dakota	25	60	39	63	36
Tennessee	9	57	43	52	47
Texas	21	61	38	51	49
Utah	5	71	27	n/a	n/a
Vermont	31	39	59	48	52
Virginia	15	54	45	63	36
Washington	16	46	53	37	62
West Virginia	10	56	43	53	46
Wisconsin	32	49	50	48	52
Wyoming	19	69	29	54	45

Bush's increased Catholic support represented 2.5 million additional votes. It is estimated that of the 32 million Catholics who voted in 2004, 17 million cast their ballots for Bush.

The University of Akron's post election poll, sponsored by the Pew Forum on Religion & Public Life, revealed that 72 percent of "traditionalist" Catholics voted for Bush. This was a dramatic increase over the 56 percent who voted for the President in 2000.

The efforts of 55,000 volunteers who distributed 76-million voter guides to practicing Catholics in 12 battleground states appeared to have paid off.

This Catholic turnout for Bush contributed to the margin of victory in key battleground states and helped to narrow the Kerry margins in Blue states, thus assuring a popular vote majority for the President.

Key Swing States

	General Vote			Catholic Vote	
	2000	2004	Increase	2000	2004
	Bush %	Bush %	Bush %	Bush %	Bush %
Florida	48.85	52.22	+3.4	52	57
New Mexico	47.85	50.11	+2.3	33	38
Ohio	49.97	50.96	+1.0	50	55
Pennsylvania	46.43	48.62	+2.2	46	49
Wisconsin	47.61	49.33	+1.7	47	48

Practicing Catholics were the decisive factor in numerous swing states. In Ohio, for instance, 65 percent of them voted for Bush, and in Florida the President's support from practicing Catholics reached 66 percent. Working-class Catholics, many of whom were of Eastern European origins, stuck with the President, because they agreed with him on cultural and moral issues. These issues were more important to them then their economic woes.

Even in Kerry's home state of Massachusetts, one of America's bluest states, there was a significant shift in the Catholic vote. In 2000, Catholics for Bush totaled 32 percent of the state's electorate while in 2004 his total was 49 percent. In raw numbers this increase represented 166,000 additional Catholic votes for Bush in Massachusetts (622,000 versus 456,000 in 2000).

Former Democratic mayor, Ray Flynn, who founded the organization Liberty, Life and Family to register and motivate Catholic voters, while visiting numerous parishes in his home state sensed a shift in the loyalties of old-line Catholic Democrats. "The [Democratic] party," he said, "thinks that just because a guy's an electrician or works for the gas company, he will be a traditional Democrat who will ignore culture issues, but that's not true any longer."[119]

The Massachusetts State Supreme Court decision permitting same sex marriages also contributed to voter backlash against John Kerry.

"Massachusetts," Flynn explained, "was the perfect example of how lay Catholics should respond to the challenge of defending our values."

The most significant Bush gains were in the Hispanic communities, which are 70 percent Catholic. Republicans continued to expand their record of attracting Hispanics. In 1996, 21 percent of Hispanics had voted for Bob Dole; 34 percent had voted for Bush in 2000; and in 2004, 41 percent of Hispanics cast their ballots to re-elect the President. Hispanics, who represented 10 percent of the 2004 electorate, cast 12 million of their votes for Bush – a 2.4-million increase over 2000's totals. Reviewing these returns, former Clinton political consultant Dick Morris concluded: "More Hispanics voted Republican for a variety of factors, including Bush's efforts to cultivate them, his proposals to legalize guest workers, and his conservative position on social values, which was of special importance to religious Catholic Hispanics." Leslie Sanchez, President of the Impacto Group, a Republican communications research firm, agreed with Morris: "There is no doubt Hispanics share many of the values of the Republican Party."[120]

Concerned about this trend, Mickey Ibarra, former Chairman of the Democratic National Committee's Hispanic Caucus, publicly criticized his party:

> If [Howard] Dean, as Chair of the Party, does not recognize this need and provide the required leadership to reverse the loss of market share among Hispanic voters, a Democratic loss in the 2008 election is inevitable, as is the permanent decline of the Democratic Party . . . .The Hispanic vote is up for grabs. The alleged Democratic lock on this constituency is a myth. The King has no clothes.[121]

2004 Hispanic President Vote in Key States

State	Hispanic Vote %	Bush %	Kerry %
California	21	32	63
Nevada	10	39	60
Arizona	12	43	56
New Mexico	32	44	56
Colorado	8	30	68
Texas	20	49	50
Florida	15	56	44

In the election of 2004, Catholics were part of a growing voting population who considered the moral and cultural issues the most important factor in their electoral decision-making process, 22 percent of the voting population in 2004. The power of this bloc explains in part the increased support for George Bush as well as the overwhelming opposition to same-sex marriages in eleven state referendums.

Most important issue [122]

Percentage who said		Who they voted for:	
		Bush %	Kerry %
22%	Moral values	79	18
20%	Economy/jobs	18	80
19%	Terrorism	86	14
15%	Iraq	25	74
8%	Health care	22	78
5%	Taxes	56	44
4%	Education	25	75

Social Issue [123]

Abortion	Bush %	Kerry %
Legal in all cases	25	74
Illegal in all cases	78	22
Gay Unions		
Support gay marriage	22	76
Support gay civil unions, not marriage	52	47
Oppose any legal recognition	70	29
Religion		
Attend services more than once a week	64	35
Attend a few times a month	51	49
Never attend services	35	63
Protestant/other Christian	59	40
Catholic	52	47
Jewish	24	75

Moral Value Vote – 2004 Election[124]

State	Moral Values Voters %	General Election	
		Bush %	Kerry %
Alabama	n/a	n/a	n/a
Alaska	29	78	19
Arizona	22	81	18
Arkansas	33	92	8
California	17	70	29
Colorado	24	83	16
Connecticut	n/a	n/a	n/a
Delaware	n/a	n/a	n/a
Florida	20	80	19
Georgia	24	88	12
Hawaii	n/a	n/a	n/a
Idaho	n/a	n/a	n/a
Illinois	19	80	20
Indiana	24	85	14
Iowa	22	87	12
Kansas	n/a	n/a	n/a
Kentucky	26	93	7
Louisiana	21	86	12
Maine	18	69	29
Maryland	18	70	28
Massachusetts	16	39	59
Michigan	19	82	16
Minnesota	24	77	21
Mississippi	n/a	n/a	n/a
Missouri	24	86	12
Montana	n/a	n/a	n/a
Nebraska	n/a	n/a	n/a
Nevada	17	75	23
New Hampshire	17	67	31
New Jersey	13	62	36
New Mexico	23	80	18
New York	12	66	33
North Carolina	24	89	11
North Dakota	n/a	n/a	n/a
Ohio	23	85	14
Oklahoma	29	90	10

| State | Moral Values Voters % | General Election | |
		Bush %	Kerry %
Oregon	22	78	21
Pennsylvania	18	80	19
Rhode Island	n/a	n/a	n/a
South Carolina	23	88	12
South Dakota	25	88	11
Tennessee	28	89	10
Texas	n/a	n/a	n/a
Utah	n/a	n/a	n/a
Vermont	20	50	47
Virginia	22	87	13
Washington	20	74	24
West Virginia	25	88	11
Wisconsin	21	82	16
Wyoming	n/a	n/a	n/a

November 2004 Referendum Supporting Traditional Marriage

State	Yes %	No %
Arkansas	75	25
Georgia	77	23
Kentucky	75	25
Michigan	59	41
Mississippi	86	14
Montana	66	34
North Dakota	73	27
Ohio	62	38
Oklahoma	76	24
Oregon	57	43
Utah	65	35

The "Michael Moore" wing of the Democratic Party and old time party elites were enraged over the election results and the voter-profile studies. Many portrayed Mr. Bush as a "thug" and "killer" in league with bin Laden, accused him of Nazi-like policies, warned that rape would be legal if he were re-elected; and said that like the half-witted Fredo in *The Godfather*, should be shot. They were shocked that a majority of Americans rejected their counsel.[125]

The New York Times favorite "anti-Catholic" Catholic writer, Garry Wills, wrote on the November 4 op-ed page that "many more Americans believe in the Virgin Birth than in Darwin's theory of evolution." *The Times* Maureen Dowd accused Republicans of dividing America "along fault lines of fear, intolerance, ignorance and religious rule." E.J. Dionne of *The Washington Post*, blamed Kerry's defeat on "the exploitation of strong religious feelings." Ronald Dworkin wrote in the *New York Review of Books* that Bush's alliance with the religious Right has already "proved a serious threat to America's commitment to social inclusiveness."

Thomas Frank, author of *What's the Matter with Kansas*, looked upon the GOP "vote your values" strategy as a corporate Wall Street cover up: "The culture wars, in other words, are a way of framing the ever-powerful subject of social class. They are a way for Republicans to speak on behalf of the forgotten man without causing any problems for their core big-business constituency."[126]

In a letter to supporters, House Democratic Minority Leader Nancy Pelosi blamed her party's defeat on Catholics. "The Democratic message," she wrote, "was eclipsed by so-called values pronouncements . . . As a devout Catholic, I observe with great regret the intervention of some Catholic bishops who joined evangelical leaders in the political arena." According to Pelosi, these outspoken bishops blurred the separation of Church and state "and that is wrong."[127]

The elites in the Democratic Party felt no blame for the loss. It was inconceivable to them that their views were out of the mainstream. Columnist George Will summed up the distain these Democrats had for the judgment of the majority of Americans:

> A small but significant, because articulate, sliver of the Democratic Party seems to relish interpreting the party's defeat as validation. This preening faction reasons as follows: the re-election of George W. Bush proves that 51 percent of the electorate are homophobic, gun-obsessed, economically suicidal, antiscience, theocratic dunces. Therefore to be rejected by them is to have one's intellectual and moral superiority affirmed.[128]

Some Democrats, such as Thomas Frank, who profess to prefer actually winning elections – still believe that the way to achieve victory is to have the right message: one that stresses economics: "To short-circuit the Republican appeals to blue-collar constituents, Democrats must confront the cultural populism of the wedge issues with genuine economic populism. They must dust off their own majoritarian militancy instead of suppressing it; sharpen the distinctions between the parties instead of minimizing them; emphasize the contradictions of culture-war populism instead of ignoring them; and speak forthrightly about who gains and who loses from conservative economic policy."[129]

Frank, like other economic determinists, finds it inconceivable that religious values can transcend the desire for wealth or status. For people like Frank, values are a mere side-show in the battle for materialistic gain: Religion is the opium of the people.

Or is there another explanation?

Shortly after the election, *Washington Times* columnist Suzanne Fields described the attitudes of millions of average Americans on Election Day:

> The culture wars are about the values of common sense that underwrite traditions that have undergirded Judeo-Christian moral codes for centuries. The culture wars are about how we raise our children, what the schools teach them, how we teach them what's right and what's wrong. The marriage amendments, after all, merely attempt to protect the tried and true status quo. The culture wars are about how the political culture reinforces, or contradicts, the popular culture. The voters understood that last week and the elites didn't.[130]

Proof that cultural issues took precedence over monetary ones was most evident in a state Bush narrowly failed to carry, the Commonwealth of Pennsylvania. Republican George Bush, to the surprise of many pols in the Keystone State, carried (or nearly carried) the overwhelmingly Democratic, economically depressed coal and steel regions while he actually lost the wealthy Republican "Main Line" counties to John Kerry.

	Bush %	Kerry %
Pennsylvania	48.6	50.8
Republican Counties		
Bucks	48.3	51.5
Delaware	42.4	57.2
Montgomery	44.0	55.5
Democratic Counties		
Schuylkill	54.6	44.8
Lehigh	48.5	50.8
Northampton	49.0	50.1
Westmoreland	55.9	43.5

These results can only be explained in cultural terms. Pro-life, pro-gun, blue-collar Democrats living in poorer regions voted for Bush while pro-abortion, white-collar Republicans from affluent areas supported Kerry. Economics and class warfare had nothing to do with the decisions made by these Pennsylvanians in the ballot booth.

The Almanac of American Politics editor Michael Barone explained it this way: "So moral values, that's part of our politics, but I think what's interesting here – and it's unsettling to many people – is that religious belief, degree of religious observance, moral values or principles, if you will, seems to be the real cleaving demographic in this electorate, and it has been really since the 1980s, or has emerged as such in the 1980s . . . . In fact, the more anti-abortion candidate has won six of the eight presidential elections held since the Roe v. Wade decision, which I think sort of negates the assumption that you can't oppose abortion and win a presidential election. It's happened three-quarters of the time."[131]

Some Democrats in the post-election period lectured the Party's progressive intelligentsia that it was time for them to at least attempt to appeal to the cultural views of ordinary Americans. At a February 2005 House Democratic retreat, University of California professor George Lakoff, author of *Don't Think of an Elephant! Know Your Values and Frame the Debate*, told the assembly that Republicans "talk about tort reform, but nobody talks about the tort justice system." In an interview with *The New York Times*, Lakoff said, "I urged them to talk in details of their values but they're not used to talking that way. They're used to talking in terms of programs and that's a disaster."[132]

Lakoff believes that culturally conservative Democrats could be wooed back into the Democratic fold if the Party changes its jargon, not its ideology. He suggests, for instance, that to rehabilitate the image of the Party's largest contributors – trial lawyers – they should be referred to as "public protection" attorneys. "Environmental protection" should be known as "poison-free communities."[133]

A memo titled *Reclaiming the White Catholic Vote* prepared by Democracy Corps (a political tactics group founded by Democratic consultants James Carville and Bob Shrum and pollster Stanley Greenberg) conceded that pro-life sentiment is growing among Catholic voters and was "a factor in the recent losses and one of the blockages for Democrats, at least in the mid-west."

The Democracy Corps poll revealed that 49 percent of white Catholics were less likely to vote for a candidate who is denied Communion by their local bishop. Polling data also indicated that abortion is not a fading issue:

> Although the pro-life position is strongest among seniors, Catholics' current pro-life position does not appear likely to lessen

with time. While middle-age Catholics lean toward keeping abortion legal, voters under 30 are more pro-life; 53 percent believe abortion should be illegal in most cases.

With 55 percent of white Catholics polled admitting they were more inclined to support a pro-life Democratic candidate, the memo recommended that the Party should present themselves as one that "[b]elieve's in a woman's right to choose but believes all sides should come together around the common goal of preventing and reducing the number of abortions, with more sex ed, including abstinence, access to contraception, and more adoption."[134]

Reading these political tea leaves, New York Senator Hillary Clinton shook the foundations of the liberal establishment when, in early 2005, she called on Democrats to be more tolerant of the beliefs of those who oppose abortion.

The question Democrats will face in the coming election cycle will be whether they are willing to risk alienating organizations like NARAL and Emily's List, who have deep pockets, in order to attract pro-life Catholics. Planned Parenthood president Karen Pearl sees the rise of a third party movement if Democrats betray pro-abortion forces. "When the day is done," Ms. Pearl told *The New York Times*, "I don't believe they will backslide."[135]

In his 1996 memoir, the late pro-life Democrat Governor Bob Casey of Pennsylvania warned:

> Many people discount the power of the so-called "cultural issues" – and especially of the abortion issue. I see it just the other way around. These issues are central to the national resurgence of the Republicans, central to the national implosion of the Democrats, central to the question of whether there will be a third party. The national Democrats may, and probably will, get a temporary bump in the polls – even, perhaps, one more national election victory – from their reactive strategy as the defenders of the elderly and poor who rely on Medicare and Medicaid. But the Democrats' national decline – or better, their national disintegration – will continue relentlessly and inexorably until they come to grips with these values issues, primarily abortion.

Writing shortly after the 2004 election, *New York Post* columnist (and now Bush speechwriter) William McGurn referred to the plight of the Democratic Party as "Bob Casey's Revenge." McGurn believes that Governor Casey's 1992 warning (when he was denied a speaking slot at the Democratic National Convention because he was pro-life) that his Party risked becoming "little more than an auxiliary of NARAL," has come to pass.

While McGurn agrees with George Lakoff that if America's two Party system is to endure Democrats must renew their relationship with people of faith, particularly practicing Catholics, he contends that they must go beyond the fine tuning of political slogans:

> They have much to ponder, as do all Americans who truly care about life, for it should be clear that a Democratic Party in its current shape is not healthy for America. We need pro-life Democrats to be able to breathe again. This means that we need a Democratic leadership that doesn't demand that Democrats vote against, among other things, judicial nominees whose only crime is their "deeply held" personal beliefs or a suspected skepticism toward the one dogma in the Democratic Party: that while all other Supreme Court decisions are malleable and must bend to the social and political agenda of the day, *Roe v. Wade* is holy writ.[136]

* * * * *

It has been the contention of this book that for most of our nation's history, the American Catholic voter has been an important contributor to the electoral process. For almost two centuries, the Catholic faithful have united to defend their political turf – their parishes and neighborhoods – and have tried to fend off political assaults from nativists, progressives, eugenicists, and reformers.

In the twenty-first century, practicing Catholics in the public square are quickly learning that while the opposition's rhetoric may sound more sophisticated or scientific, the level of distaste for Catholicism is the same as in previous eras. Catholics are still viewed by the secular humanists as public villains and in their salons, anti-Catholicism is still an acceptable prejudice.

Today secular humanists are ecstatically confident they have the political upper hand and are busily writing obituaries for the Catholic Church in America. But now as in the past their prejudices blind them from several realities: While the number of practicing Catholics has declined in recent decades, the faithful still represent approximately 9 percent of the total popular vote. Since the bulk of these voters reside in key swing states, Catholics will continue to have a major impact at the polling booth and may determine election results.

The other point the secular humanists miss is this: regardless of the Church's size, the faith will endure because it has always endured, its members still standing on the solid 2,000-year-old rock of St. Peter. And the Church's faithful in America will continue to adhere to the tenets of Christ and, like St. Paul at the beginning of the Church, will "fight the good fight" to ensure that their voices are heard in the public square.

Endnotes

Chapter 1
"The Free Exercise Thereof . . ."

1 Williams, Michael, *The Shadow of the Pope*, p. 26.
2. Ibid., p. 27.
3 Ibid., p. 25.
4 Ibid., p. 26.
5 Ibid., p. 27.
6 Ellis, John Tracy, *American Catholicism*, p. 23.
7 Ibid., p. 25.
8 Ibid., p. 21.
9 Ibid., p. 26.
10 Leckie, Robert, *American and Catholic*, p. 30.
11 Williams, p. 30.
12 Perko, F. Michael, s.j., *Catholic and American*, p. 58.
13 Leckie, p. 32.
14 Ibid., p. 32.
15 McAvoy, Thomas T., *A History of the Catholic Church in the United States*, p. 17.
16 Ibid.
17 Williams, p. 24.
18 McAvoy, p. 24.
19 Klein, Milton M., *Politics of Diversity*, p. 24.
20 Metzger, Charles H., s.j., *Catholics and the American Revolution*, p. 22.
21 Ibid., p. 6.
22 McAvoy, p. 28.
23 Metzger, p. 8.
24 Ibid., p. 11.
25 Ibid., p. 14.
26 Ibid., p. 7.
27 Ibid., p. 10.
28 Ibid., p. 20.
29 Williams, p. 32.

30 Ibid., pp. 31–32.
31 Metzger, p. 26.
32 Ibid., p. 30.
33 Ibid., p. 37.
34 Ibid., p. 43.
35 Ibid., p. 40.
36 Leckie, p. 41.
37 Williams, p. 34.
38 Metzger, p. 20.
39 Ibid.
40 Leckie, p. 42.
41 Ibid., p. 49.
42 Ibid.
43 McDermott, Scott, *Charles Carroll of Carrollton*, p. 129.
44 Maynard, Theodore, *The Story of American Catholicism*, p. 115.
45 McDermott, p. 129.
46 Leckie, p. 50.
47 McDermott, p. 138.
48 Ibid., p. 134.
49 Ibid., p. 135.
50 Walsh, James, *Education of the Founding Fathers of the Republic*, p. x.
51 Sheldon, Garrett Ward, *The Political Philosophy of Thomas Jefferson*, p. 43.
52 Ibid., p. 30.
53 Marlin, George J., *The Politician's Guide to Assisted Suicide, Cloning, and Other Current Controversies*, pp. 36–41.
54 Marino, Anthony J., *The Catholics in America*, p. 43.
55 Marlin, pp. 36–41.
56 Ibid.
57 Ibid.
58 Maynard, p. 117.
59 Leckie, pp. 51–52.
60 Williams, pp. 36–37.
61 Odegard, Peter H., *Religion and Politics*, p. 30.
62 McDermott, p. 187.
63 Metzger, p. 276.
64 McDermott, p. 149.
65 Ibid., pp. 151–52.
66 Azar, *Twentieth Century in Crisis*, p. 213.
67 Maynard, p. 159.
68 Leckie, p. 55.

Chapter 2
First Stirrings:
The Catholic Voter and the Election of 1800

1 Shaw, Richard, *Dagger John*, p. 7.
2 Williams, p. 44.
3 Maynard, p. 154.
4 Williams, p. 42.
5 Shaughnessy, Gerald, *Has the Immigrant Kept the Faith?* p. 56.
6 Ibid., p. 57.
7 Maynard, p. 155.
8 Shaughnessy, p. 57.
9 Williams, p. 48.
10 Ibid.
11 Carson, Clarence, *A Basic History of the United States*, Vol. 2, p. 112.
12 Ibid., p. 137.
13 Ibid.
14 Ibid., p. 132.
15 McDermott, p. 208.
16 Leckie, p. 73.
17 McDermott, p. 207.
18 Ibid.
19 Ibid., p. 213.
20 Boller, Jr., Paul F., *Presidential Campaigns*, p. 8.
21 Schlesinger, Arthur, Editor, *History of U.S. Political Parties*, Vol. 1, p. 17.
22 Weisburger, Bernard, A., *America Afire*, p. 110.
23 Boller, p. 10.
24 Ibid.
25 Schlesinger, Arthur, *History of American Presidential Elections*, Vol. 1, p. 118.
26 Boller, p. 11.
27 Ibid., p. 12.
28 McDermott, p. 215.
29 Ibid.
30 Ibid.
31 Fox, Dixon Ryan, *The Decline of Aristocracy in the Politics of New York, 1801–1840*, p. 9.
32 Ibid., p. 143.
33 Kelly, Robert, *The Cultural Pattern in American Politics*, p. 123.
34 Ibid., p. 78.
35 Fox, p. 76.
36 Williams, p. 55.

37 Ibid.
38 Mushkat, Jerome, *Tammany*, p. 25.
39 Ibid.
40 Schlesinger, *History of American Presidential Elections*, Vol. 1, p. 108.
41 Boller, p. 18.
42 Werner, M.R., *Tammany Hall*, p. 22.
43 Schlesinger, Vol. 1, p. 109.
44 Kelly, p. 126.
45 McDermott, p. 215.
46 Ibid.
47 Kelly, p. 126.

Chapter 3
The Catholic Voter in the Age of Jefferson and Jackson

 1 Adams, James Truslow, *Dictionary of American History*, Vol. 3, p. 171.
 2 Boorstin, Daniel J., *The Lost World of Thomas Jefferson*, p. 156.
 3 Sheldon, p. 108.
 4 Craycraft, Kenneth R., Jr., *The American Myth of Religious Freedom*, p. 75.
 5 Ibid.
 6 Shaughnessey, p. 70.
 7 Boller, p. 23.
 8 Ibid., p. 24.
 9 Carson, Vol. 1, p. 96.
10 Schlesinger, Arthur, *History of U.S. Political Parties*, Vol. 1, p. 125.
11 Ibid.
12 Novak, Michael, *The Spirit of Democratic Capitalism*, p. 132.
13 Handlin, Oscar, *The Uprooted*, p. 24.
14 Billington, Ray Allen, *The Protestant Crusade, 1800–1860*, p. 395.
15 Shaughnessey, p. 120.
16 Billington, p. 43.
17 Ibid., p. 44.
18 *National Interest*, Winter, 1999.
19 Fox, p. 310.
20 Lipsky, George, *John Quincy Adams: His Theory and Ideas*, p. 78.
21 Ibid., p. 79.
22 Schlesinger, *History of U.S. Political Parties*, Vol. 1, p. 577.
23 Ibid., p. 579.
24 Ibid., pp. 587–88.
25 Guimstead, David, *Notions of the American Culture*, p. 87.
26 Fox, p. 74.
27 Remini, Robert V., *Martin Van Buren*, p. 36.

28 Fox, p. 74.
29 Remeni, Robert, *The Election of Andrew Jackson*, p. 81.
30 Ibid., p. 194.
31 Schlesinger, *History of American Political Parties*, Vol. 1, p. 582.
32 Billington, p. 67.
33 Ibid.
34 Ibid., p. 69.
35 Williams, pp. 66–67.
36 Billington, p. 87.
37 Leckie, *American and Catholic*, p. 156.
38 *New York Observer*, October 20, 1827.
39 Billington, p. 128.
40 Ibid., p. 130.
41 Ibid., p. 143.
42 Ibid., p. 145.
43 Ibid.
44 Leckie, p. 117.
45 Billington, p. 147.
46 Ibid., p. 148.
47 Ibid., p. 150.
48 Ibid., p. 152.
49 Ibid., p. 156.
50 Ibid., p. 174.

Chapter 4
The Catholic Voter Versus the Nativist Voter

1 Connelly, James F., *The History of the Archdiocese of Philadelphia*, p. 170.
2 Ibid., p. 172.
3 Ibid., p. 175.
4 Billington, p. 271.
5 Ibid., p. 222.
6 Connelly, p. 180.
7 Billington, p. 230.
8 Ibid., p. 231.
9 Greeley, Andrew, *The Catholic Experience*, p. 107.
10 Ibid.
11 McAvoy, Thomas, *A History of the Catholic Church in the United States*, p. 164.
12 Holt, Michael, *The Rise and Fall of the American Whig Party*, p. 117.
13 Maynard, p. 279.

14   Holt, p. 118.
15   Sibley, Joel, *Political Ideology and Voting Behavior in the Age of Jackson*, p. 132.
16   Graft, Henry F., *The Presidents*, p. 145.
17   Holt, p. 191.
18   Benson, Lee, *The Concept of Jacksonian Democracy*, p. 221.
19   Remini, Robert, *Daniel Webster*, p. 599.
20   Ellis, John Tracy, *American Catholicism*, pp. 64–65.
21   Holt, p. 192.
22   Ibid.
23   Benson, pp. 171–72.
24   Kelly, Robert, *The Cultural Patters in American Politics,* p. 172.
25   Ibid., p. 174.
26   Holt, p. 204.
27   Ibid.
28   Ibid., p. 205.
29   Ibid.
30   Schlesinger, Arthur, *History of American Presidential Elections*, Vol. 2, p. 798.
31   Holt, p. 266.
32   Ibid., p. 697.
33   Ibid., p. 674.
34   Ibid., p. 730.
35   Richter, *Religion and the Presidency*, p. 37.
36   Holt, p. 775.
37   Ibid., p. 746.
38   Billington, p. 381.
39   Leckie, p. 157.
40   Maynard, p. 304.
41   Shaw, p. 290.
42   Ibid., p. 291.
43   Ibid.
44   Billington, p. 417.
45   Schlesinger, *History of American Presidential Elections*, Vol. 3, p. 1025.
46   Billington, p. 424.
47   Current, Richard, *The Political Thought of Abraham Lincoln*, p. 83.
48   Billington, p. 428.
49   Richter, p. 44.
50   New York *Daily Times*, October 6, 1856.
51   Rayback, Robert, *Millard Fillmore*, p. 407.
52   Ibid.
53   Holt, p. 967.

Chapter 5
The Catholic Voter in the Age of Lincoln

1 Leckie, p. 167.
2 Maynard, p. 344.
3 Ibid., p. 348.
4 Ibid., p. 349.
5 Luebke, Frederick, *Ethnic Voters and the Election of Lincoln*, p. 7.
6 Kelly, p. 194.
7 Ibid., p. 194.
8 Ibid.
9 Cogley, John, *Catholic America*, p. 50.
10 Luebke, p. xiii.
11 Ibid., p. 153.
12 Ibid., p. 174.
13 Ibid., p. 216.
14 McPherson, James, *Battle Cry of Freedom*, p. 223.
15 McAvoy, p. 185.
16 Gibson, Florence, *The Attitudes of the New York Irish toward State and National Affairs,* p. 110.
17 *Irish American*, June 30, 1860.
18 Dohen, Dorothy, *Naturalism and American Catholicism*, p. 141.
19 Ibid., pp. 139–40.
20 O'Brien, David, *Public Catholicism*, p. 67.
21 Ibid.
22 Gibson, p. 159.
23 Ibid.
24 McGreevey, John, *Catholicism and American Freedom*, p. 73.
25 O'Brien, p. 68.
26 Wittke, Carl, *The Irish in America*, p. 144.
27 Shaw, p. 362.
28 Ibid., p. 365.
29 Ibid., p. 367.
30 Ibid., p. 369.
31 Morris, Charles, *American Catholic*, p. 78.
32 *Harper's Weekly*, August 1, 1863.
33 Katz, Irving, *August Belmont*, p. 119.
34 Ibid., p. 135.
35 McGreevy, p. 73.
36 Wittke, pp. 135–36.
37 Marino, p. 58.
38 Ibid., p. 52.

39 McAvoy, p. 188.
40 Marino, p. 53.
41 Leckie, p. 172.
42 Marino, p. 53.
43 Maynard, p. 371.
44 Gibson, p. 173.

Chapter 6
The Catholic Voter in the Gilded Age:
The Golden Years.

1 Higham, John, *Strangers in the Land*, p. 26.
2 Ibid., p. 29.
3 Kleppner, Paul, *The Cross of Culture*, p. 99.
4 Ibid.
5 Ibid., pp. 96–97.
6 Coleman, Charles, *The Election of 1868*, p. 304.
7 Schlesinger, Arthur, *History of American Presidential Elections*, Vol. 3, p. 1271.
8 Burnham, Walter Dean, *Presidential Ballots, 1836–1892*, p. 101.
9 McGreevy, pp. 108–9.
10 Schlesinger, *History of American Presidential Elections*, Vol. 3, p. 1260.
11 McGreevy, p. 93.
12 Kleppner, p. 117.
13 *Pastoral Letters of the United States Catholic Bishops*, Vol. 1, p. 224.
14 Kleppner, p. 117.
15 *The Nation*, July 4, 1867.
16 *Harper's Weekly*, October 5, 1872.
17 Kleppner, p. 116.
18 Ibid.
19 *Boston Pilot*, October 27, 1873.
20 *New York Herald*, December 21, 1875.
21 Ibid., December 27, 1875.
22 Katz, *Belmont*, p. 204.
23 Schlesinger, *History of American Presidential Elections*, Vol. 4, p. 1315.
24 Morris, Charles, *American Catholic*, pp. 78–79.
25 Lipset, Seymour Martin, et al., *The Politics of Unreason*, p. 73.
26 McAvoy, p. 228.
27 Ibid.
28 High, Stanley, *The Church in Politics*, p. 1.
29 McGreevy, p. 91.
30 Smith, Jean, *Grant*, p. 176.

31 McGreevy, p. 92.
32 Ibid.
33 Higham, p. 28.
34 Ibid., p. 28.
35 McGreevy, p. 109.
36 Schlesinger, *History of American Presidential Elections*, Vol. 4, p. 1442.
37 Staffer, A.P., "Anti-Catholicism in the United States" (Doctoral Thesis, Harvard), p. 77.
38 Ibid., p. 81.
39 Kleppner, pp. 115–16.
40 Staffer, p. 81.
41 Schlesinger, *History of American Presidential Elections*, Vol. 4, p. 1494.
42 Richter, p. 50.
43 Barnard, Harry, *Rutherford B. Hayes and His America*, p. 274.
44 Clancy, Herbert J., *The Presidential Election of 1880*, p. 214.
45 Ibid.
46 Wasson, W.W., *James A. Garfield: His Religion and Education*, pp. 140–41.
47 Ibid.
48 Clancy, p. 173.
49 Richter, p. 52.
50 Ibid., p. 36.
51 Summers, Mark, *Rum, Romanism, and Rebellion*, p. 283.
52 King, James, *Facing the Twentieth Century*, p. 408.
53 *New York Times*, November 3, 1885.
54 Ibid.
55 Summers, p. 292.

Chapter 7
The Catholic Voter in the Gilded Age:
The Silver Years

1 Gibson, p. 413.
2 *Irish American*, September 1, 1888.
3 *Irish World*, June 30, 1888.
4 Nevins, Allan, *Grover Cleveland: A Study in Courage,* p. 431.
5 *Boston Evening Transcript*, October 1, 1888.
6 Schlesinger, *History of American Presidential Elections*, Vol. 4, pp. 1681–83.
7 Ibid.
8 Gibson, p. 420.
9 Nevins, p. 412.

10 Schlesinger, *History of American Presidential Elections*, Vol. 4, p. 1641.
11 Ibid.
12 Ibid., p. 1,652.
13 Morgan, Thomas, *Roman Catholic and Indian Affairs*, p. 6.
14 Williams, Hal, *Years of Decision*, p. 6.
15 *Boston Standard*, October 2, 1892.
16 *Cincinnati Enquirer*, November 7, 1892.
17 Williams, R. Hal, p. 66.
18 Schlesinger, *History of American Political Parties*, Vol. 5, p. 1787.
19 Smith, Page, *History of America*, Vol. 12, p. 536.
20 Tarbell, Ida, *The Nationalizing of Business*, p. 246.
21 Turner, Frederick Jackson, *The Frontier in American History*, p. ii.
22 Hofstadter, Richard, *American Political Tradition*, p. 184.
23 Ibid.
24 Ibid., p. 188.
25 Ibid.
26 Ibid., p. 191.
27 Jones, Stanley L., *The Presidential Election of 1896*, p. 37.
28 Hofstadter, *American Political Tradition*, p. 187.
29 Jones, p. 291.
30 Hofstadter, Richard, *The Age of Reform*, p. 34.
31 Lubell, Samuel, *The Future of American Politics*, p. 38.
32 Schlesinger, *History of American Presidential Elections*, Vol. 5, p. 1873.
33 Phillips, Kevin, *William McKinley*, p. 17.
34 Morgan, Wayne, *William McKinley and His America*, p. 158.
35 Ibid.
36 Morgan, Wayne, *From Hayes to McKinley*, pp. 517–18.
37 Jones, *The Presidential Election of 1896*, p. 290.
38 Schlesinger, *History of American Presidential Elections*, Vol. 5, p. 1827.
39 Lynch, Margaret, *In the Days of McKinley*, pp. 76–77.
40 Key, V.O., *Politics, Parties and Pressure Groups*, p. 171.
41 Morgan, *McKinley and His America*, p. 248.
42 Phillips, *McKinley*, p. 79.
43 Ibid., p. 80.
44 Ibid., p. 81.
45 *New York Times Book Review*, October 5, 2003, p. 24.
46 Morgan, *From Hayes to McKinley*, p. 528.

Chapter 8
The Rise of the Urban Catholic Voter

1 See Shaughnessy for Catholic population figures.

2 Ibid.
3 Marlin, pp. 22–23.
4 See Shaughnessy for Catholic population figures.
5 Marlin, pp. 22–23.
6 Greeley, Andrew, *Neighborhood*, p. 133.
7 Thomas, John L., s.j., *The American Catholic Family*, p. 113.
8 Novak, p. 10.
9 Olson, James S., *Catholic Immigrants in America*, p. 12.
10 Ibid.
11 Olson, p. 123.
12 Thomas, p. 406.
13 Greeley, Andrew, *The American Catholic*, p. 216.
14 Olson, p. 115.
15 Greeley, *The American Catholic*, p. 228.
16 Erie, Steven P., *Rainbow's End*, p. 18.
17 Plunkitt, George Washington, *Plunkitt of Tammany Hall*, pp. 33–34.
18 Ellis, John Tracy, *The Life of James Cardinal Gibbons.* Vol. 2, p. 110.
19 *Omaha Morning World Herald*, October 26, 1891.
20 Ibid.
21 Higham, p. 57.
22 Ibid., p. 54.
23 *Patriotic American*, October 22, 1892.
24 Lipset, p. 92.
25 Ibid.
26 Levine, Edward M., *The Irish and Irish Politicians*, p. 96.
27 Plunkitt, p. 22.
28 Marlin, George J., *Fighting the Good Fight: A History of the New York Conservative Party*, p. 16.
29 Novak, p. 231.
30 Stave, Bruce, *The New Deal and the Last Hurrah*, p. 6.
31 Greeley, Andrew, *The Irish Americans*, p. 160.
32 Hofstadter, Richard, *Social Darwinism in American Thought*, p. 51.
33 Ibid., p. 60.
34 Ibid., p. 50.
35 Haller, Mark H., *Eugenics*, p. 6.
36 Parmet, Herbert, *Nixon and His America*, p. 6.
37 Marlin, *The Politician's Guide to Assisted Suicide, Cloning, and Other Current Controversies*, p. 132.
38 *New York Herald*, April 6, 1888.
39 *Ave Maria*, June 6, 1896.
40 *New York Times*, March 1, 1898.

41   Reuter, Frank, *Catholic Influence on American Colonial Policies, 1898–1904,* p. 7.
42   *New York Herald*, April 6, 1888.
43   Reuter, p. 7.
44   Ibid., p. 14.
45   Ibid.
46   Ibid.
47   Ibid., pp. 45–46.

Chapter 9
The Catholic Voter in Peace and War

1   Hofstadter, Richard, *American Political Tradition*, p. 219.
2   Dalton, Kathleen, *Theodore Roosevelt, A Strenuous Life*, p. 81.
3   Dyer, Thomas G., *Theodore Roosevelt and the Idea of Race*, p. 126.
4   Ibid.
5   Pickens, Donald, *Eugenics and the Progressives*, p. 119.
6   See Marlin, *The Politician's Guide to Assisted Suicide, Cloning, and Other Controversies*.
7   Harbaugh, William, *Power and Responsibility*, p. 223.
8   Dyer, p. 127.
9   Reuter, p. 127.
10 Ibid., p. 109.
11 Ellis, John Tracy, *The Life of James Cardinal Gibbons*, Vol. 1, p. 110.
12 The Boston *Pilot*, October 25, 2002.
13 Reuter, p. 134.
14 Ibid., p. 133.
15 Ibid., p. 122.
16 Ibid.
17 Ibid., p. 135.
18 Ibid., p. 134.
19 Ibid., p. 135.
20 Ibid., p. 136.
21 Ibid., p. 139.
22 Maynard, p. 539.
23 Ibid.
24 Koenig, Louis, *Bryan: A Biography of William Jennings Bryan*, p. 455.
25 Ibid., p. 435.
26 Schlesinger, *History of American Presidential Elections*, Vol. 5, p. 2089.
27 Fleming, Thomas, *The Illusion of Victory*, p. 13.
28 Brands, H.W., *T.R.: The Last Romantic*, p. 19.

29 Schlesinger, Arthur, *History of American Presidential Election*, Vol. 6, p. 2151.
30 Richter, p. 64.
31 McAvoy, Thomas T., *Roman Catholicism and the American Way of Life*, p. 228.
32 Ibid., pp. 227–28.
33 Brands, p. 29.
34 Link, Arthur, *Wilson*, Vol. 1, p. 496.
35 Weiss, Nancy, *Charles Francis Murphy, 1858–1924: Respectability and Responsibility in Tammany Politics*, p. 71.
36 Link, *Wilson*, Vol. 2, p. 496.
37 Reedy, George, *From the Ward to the White House*, pp. 102–3.
38 Link, Vol. 2, p. 499.
39 Ibid., p. 500.
40 Heckscher, August, *Woodrow Wilson*, p. 277.
41 Blum, John Morton, *Joe Tumulty and the Wilson Era*, p. 89.
42 Ibid., p. 92.
43 Maynard, p. 539.
44 Fleming, p. 65.
45 Ibid.
46 Reedy, p. 103.
47 Schlesinger, *History of American Presidential Election*, Vol. 6, p. 2073.
48 Blum, p. 106.
49 Ibid.
50 Blum, pp. 106–9.
51 O'Brien, David J., *Public Catholicism*, p. 152.
52 Ibid.
53 Carson, *A Basic History of the United States*, Vol. 4, p. 201.
54 Fleming, p. 349.
55 Ibid., p. 351.
56 Ibid., p. 374.
57 Ibid., P. 371.
58 Ibid., p. 363.
59 Ibid., p. 404.
60 Ibid., p. 405.
61 Ibid., p. 412.
62 Ibid.
63 Sinclair, Andrew, *Prohibition*, Jacket cover.
64 Schlesinger, *History of American Presidential Election*, Vol. 6, p. 2373.
65 Fleming, p. 462.
66 Ibid.
67 Ibid., p. 463.

68 Ibid.
69 Schlesinger, *History of American Presidential Election*, Vol. 6, p. 2384.
70 Fleming, p. 491.
71 Ibid., p. 470.

Chapter 10
The Campaign of 1928

1   Barone, *Our Country*, p. 9.
2   Weiss, p. 22.
3   Barone, p. 8.
4   Weiss, p. 75.
5   Caro, Robert, *The Power Broker*, p. 94.
6   Williams, Michael, p. 132.
7   Lay, Shawn, *Hooded Knights on the Niagara*, p. 43.
8   Williams, Michael, p. 141.
9   Murray, Robert, *The 103rd Ballot*, p. 247.
10 Jackson, Kenneth T., *The Ku Klux Klan and the City*, p. 239.
11 Schlesinger, Arthur, *History of American Presidential Election*, Vol. 6, p. 2487.
12 Odegard, p. 47.
13 Ibid., p. 55.
14 Handlin, Oscar, *Al Smith and His America*, p. 4.
15 Smith, Alfred E., *Progressive Democracy*, pp. 254–69.
16 Ibid.
17 Ibid.
18 Schlesinger, *History of American Presidential Elections*, Vol. 7, p. 2597.
19 Smith, Alfred E., *Campaign Addresses of Governor Alfred E. Smith*, pp. 43–60.
20 Williams, Michael, p. 196.
21 Ibid., p. 196.
22 Ibid., p. 197.
23 Ibid., p. 201.
24 Slayton, Robert, *Empire Statesman*, p. 310.
25 Ibid.
26 Ibid., p. 312.
27 Ibid., p. 316.
28 Burner, David, *The Politics of Provincialism*, p. 202.
29 Slayton, p. 315.
30 Finan, Christopher, *Alfred E. Smith, The Happy Warrior*, pp. 212–13.
31 Lubell, Samuel, *The Future of American Politics*, p. 34.
32 Josephson, Matthew, et al., *Al Smith: Hero of the Cities*, p. 397.

33 Lubell, p. 45.
34 Ibid.,, pp. 36–37.
35 Phillips, Kevin, *The Emerging Republican Majority*, p. 151.
36 Allswang, John M., *A House for All Peoples*, p.42.
37 Burner, p. 243.
38 Bruce M. Stave, *The New Deal and the Last Hurrah*, p. 196.
39 Ibid., p. 211.
40 Ibid., p. 222.
41 Lichtman, Allan J., *Prejudice and the Old Politics*, p. 53.
42 Shannon, William, *The American Irish*, p. 181.
43 Lubell, pp. 38–39.
44 Burner, pp. 242–43.

Chapter 11
The Catholic Voter in the Age of Roosevelt

1 Freidel, Frank, *Franklin D. Roosevelt: A Rendezvous with Destiny*, p. 20.
2 Ibid.
3 Ibid.
4 Flynn, George Q., *American Catholics and the Roosevelt Presidency*, p. 3.
5 Miller, Nathan, *F.D.R., An Intimate History*, p. 86.
6 Ward, Geoffrey, *A First-Class Temperament*, p. 252.
7 Black, Conrad, *Franklin Delano Roosevelt*, p. 56.
8 Ward, p. 255.
9 Freidel, *Franklin D. Roosevelt: A Rendezvous with Destiny*, p. 298.
10 Ward, p. 252.
11 Ibid.
12 Ibid.
13 Miller, p. 123.
14 Ibid.
15 Caro, Robert, *The Power Broker*, p. 283.
16 Ibid.
17 Handlin, Oscar, *Al Smith and His America*, p. 140.
18 Allswang, John M., *The New Deal and American Politics*, p. 72.
19 Caro, p. 285.
20 Ibid.
21 Mitgang, Herbert, *Once Upon a Time in New York*, pp. 107–8.
22 Flynn, p. 16.
23 McGreevy, p. 151.
24 Phillips, Kevin P., *The Emerging Republican Majority*, p. 59.
25 Burner, p. 235.

26 Ibid., p. 230.
27 Ibid., p. 243.
28 Allswang, *A House for All Peoples*, p. 42.
29 Burner, p. 251.
30 Flynn, p. 37.
31 Brooklyn *Tablet*, May 13, 1933.
32 Flynn, p. 42.
33 Ibid., p. 54.
34 Ibid., p. 79.
35 Broderick, Francis L., *Right Reverend New Dealer: John A. Ryan*, p. 212.
36 Black, p. 16.
37 Tugwell, Rexford, *The Brains Trust*, p. 371.
38 Beatty, Jack, *The Rascal King*, p. 269.
39 Ibid., p. 265.
40 Dorsett, Lyle W., *Franklin D. Roosevelt and the City Bosses*, p. 28.
41 Erie, p. 130.
42 Bayor, Ronald H., *Neighbors in Conflict*, p. 42 .
43 *New York History*, July 1968, p. 307.
44 Flynn, p. 127.
45 Ibid., p. 138.
46 Ibid.
47 Ibid.
48 Ibid., p. 162.
49 Ibid., p. 169.
50 Ibid., p. 204.
51 Handlin, p. 174.
52 Ibid., p. 175.
53 Flynn, p. 201.
54 Ibid., p. 205.
55 Shannon, p. 317.
56 Maier, Thomas, *The Kennedys,* p. 109.
57 Flynn, p. 218.
58 Ibid., p. 222.
59 Leuchtenburg William E., *Franklin D. Roosevelt and the New Deal*, p. 184.
60 Phillips, p. 339.
61 Flynn, *Roosevelt and Romanism*, p. 13.
62 Ibid., p. 37.
63 Cook, Blanche Wiesen, *Eleanor Roosevelt*, Vol. 2, p. 504
64 Flynn, *Roosevelt and Romanism*, p. 67.
65 Farley, James A., *Jim Farley's Story*, p. 174.
66 Ibid., p. 175.

67   Bayor, p. 147.
68   Phillips, p. 62.
69   Barone, p. 143.

Chapter 12
The Catholic Voter in the Age of Anxiety

1   Flynn, George Q., *Roosevelt and Romanism*, p. 223.
2   Ibid.
3   Carruth, Gorton, *Encylopedia of American Facts and Dates*, p. 534.
4   Reeves, Thomas C., *Twentieth-Century America*, p. 143.
5   Walton, Richard J., *Henry Wallace, Harry Truman, and the Cold War*, p. 48.
6   Ibid., p. 205.
7   Phillips, Kevin, *The Emerging Republican Majority*, p. 65.
8   Lubell, Samuel, *The Future of American Politics*, p. 211.
9   Ibid., pp. 212–13.
10 Reeves, Thomas C., *The Life and Times of Joe McCarthy*, p. 147.
11 Ibid., p. 224.
12 Sheen, Fulton J., *Communism and the Conscience of the West*, p. 9.
13 Crosby, Donald F., s.j., *God, Church and Flag, Senator Joseph R. McCarthy and the Catholic Church, 1950–1957*, p. 8.
14 Gannon, Robert I, *The Cardinal Spellman Story*, p. 338.
15 Crosby, p. 3.
16 Ibid., p. 53.
17 Fuchs, Lawrence H., *John F. Kennedy and American Catholicism*, p. 128.
18 Crosby, p. 72.
19 Ibid., p. 73.
20 Ibid., p. 74.
21 Higham, p. 325.
22 Jones, E. Michael, *The Slaughter of Cities*, p. 200.
23 Ibid., p. 188.
24 Jackson, Kenneth T., *Crabgrass Frontier*, p. 206.
25 Jones, p. 200.
26 Moynihan, Daniel P., *Coping*, p. 54.
27 Martin, John Bartlow, *Adlai Stevenson of Illinois*, p. 111.
28 Barone, *Our Country*, p. 254.
29 Newfield, Jack, et al., *City for Sale*, p. 107.
30 Wytrwal, Joseph A., *Poles in American History and Tradition*, p. 408.
31 Schlesinger, Arthur, *History of American Presidential Elections*, Vol. 8, p. 3286.
32 Ibid., p. 3233.

33 Ibid., p. 3246.
34 Ibid., p. 3246.
35 Martin, p. 618.
36 Ibid., p. 681.
37 Crosby, p. 112.
38 Parmet, Herbert S., *The Democrats: The Years after F.D.R.*, p. 99.
39 Harris, Louis, *Is There a Republican Majority*, p. 89.
40 Phillips, p. 62.
41 Barone, p. 292.
42 Phillips, p. 161.
43 Ibid., p. 181.
44 Greeley, Andrew M., *The American Catholic*, p. 94.
45 Perko, p. 269.

Chapter 13
The Campaign of 1960

 1 Maier, Thomas, p. 203.
 2 White, John Kenneth, *Still Seeing Red*, p. 45.
 3 Ibid., p. 45.
 4 Ibid., p. 28.
 5 Maier, p. 203.
 6 Ibid., p. 268.
 7 Dallek, Robert, *An Unfinished Life*, p. 143.
 8 Ibid., p. 146.
 9 Maier, p. 303.
10 Dallek, p. 162.
11 Maier, p. 272.
12 To review a complete copy of the "Bailey Memorandum," see Victor
    Lasky's *JFK: The Man and the Myth*, Appendix B..
13 Dallek, p. 206.
14 Ibid.
15 Martin, Ralph G., *A Hero for Our Time*, p. 107.
16 Dallek, p. 205.
17 Maier, p. 284.
18 O'Neill, James M., *Catholicism and American Freedom*, p. 270.
19 Blanshard, Paul, *American Freedom and Catholic Power*, p. 28.
20 Ibid., p. 84.
21 Creedon, Lawrence P., et al. *United for Separation*, p. 2.
22 Odegard, p. 193.
23 Maier, p. 319.
24 Ibid.
25 Ibid., p. 320.

26 Fenton, John H., *The Catholic Vote*, p. 85.

27 Ibid., pp. 128–29.

28 Ibid.

29 *The Saturday Review*, November 11, 1960.

30 White, Theodore H., *The Making of the President – 1960*, p. 94.

31 Barone, p. 324.

32 Maier, p. 335.

33 Schlesinger, *History of American Presidential Elections*, Vol. 9, p. 3541.

34 *New York Times*, August 4, 1960.

35 *New York Times*, August 24, 1960.

36 Barrett, Patricia, *Religious Liberty and the American Presidency*, p. 14.

37 Ibid., p. 15.

38 Ibid., p. 161.

39 Ibid., p. 3.

40 Ibid., p. 43.

41 *U.S. Catholic Historian*, Fall 2003, p. 40.

42 Hurley, Mark J., *The Unholy Ghost*, p. 81.

43 Interview with Dr. Robert Royal, President of Faith and Reason Institute, Washington, D.C., February 2004.

44 Maier, pp. 348–49.

45 Lasky, p. 488.

46 Ibid., p. 489.

47 Maier, p. 355.

48 *Saturday Review*, December, 1960.

49 Levy, Mark R., *The Ethnic Factor*, pp. 230–31.

50 Dawidowicz, Lucy S., et al., *Politics in a Pluralist Democracy*, p. 12.

51 Ibid., p. 13.

52 Barone, *Our Counry*, p. 334.

Chapter 14
The Catholic Voter in the Age of the Silent Majority

1 Moynihan, Daniel P., *Beyond the Melting Pot*, p. 272.

2 Phillips, Kevin, *The Emerging Republican Majority*, p. 161.

3 *Policy Review*, Fall 1991, p. 18.

4 Kelly, Robert, *The Cultural Pattern in American Politics*, p. 7.

5 Hofstadter, Richard, *The Radical Right*, p. 99.

6 Barone, *Our Country*, p. ii.

7 Ibid., p. 30.

8 Dawson, Christopher, *Dynamics of World History*, p. 5.

9 Bell, Jeffrey, *Populism and Elitism*, p. 26.

10 Greeley, Andrew, *Neighborhood*, p. 119.

11 Jones, E. Michael, *The Slaughter of Cities*, p. 373.
12 Ibid., p. 359.
13 Wilson, James Q., *The Amateur Democrat*, p. 2.
14 Moynihan, Daniel P., *Coping*, p. 60.
15 Wilson, James Q., p. 18.
16 Moynihan, *Coping*, p. 58.
17 McNickle, Thomas, *To Be Mayor of New York: Ethnic Politics in the City*, p. 175.
18 Phillips, p. 166.
19 Ibid., p. 167.
20 Buckley Jr., William F., *The Unmaking of a Mayor*, pp. 326–30.
21 Ibid.
22 Edsall, Thomas, et al., *Chain Reaction*, p. 5.
23 *American National Election Data Sourcebook*, p. 95.
24 Wilson, James Q., p. 58.
25 Brown, Peter, *Minority Party*, p. 82.
26 Ibid., p. 85.
27 O'Connor, Thomas H., *The Boston Irish*, p. 294.
28 Scammon, Richard M., et al., *The Real Majority*, p. 94.
29 White, Theodore H., *The Making of the President – 1968*, p. 346.
30 Curtis, Dan T., *The Politics of Rage*, pp. 377–78.
31 Ibid., p. 378.
32 Ibid., p. 379.
33 Lubell, Samuel, *The Hidden Crisis in American Politics*, p. 61.
34 Barone, *Our Country*, p. 450.
35 Ibid., p. 317.
36 Parmet, *Nixon and His America*, p. viii.
37 Phillips, Kevin, *The Emerging Republican Majority*, p. 173.
38 Ibid., p. 171.
39 Ibid., p. 353.
40 Levy, Mark R., *The Ethnic Factor*, p. 231.
41 Ibid.
42 Ibid.
43 Lubell, Samuel, *The Hidden Crisis in American Politics*, p. 98.
44 Siegel, Fred, *Troubled Journey*, p. 201.
45 Carter, p. 428.
46 Kramer, Michael, and Roberts, Steve, *I Never Wanted to Be Vice President of Anything*, p. 334.
47 Ibid., p. 346.
48 *New York Post*, November 4, 1970.
49 Markmann, Charles, *The Buckleys*, p. 300.
50 Haldeman, H.R., *The Haldeman Diaries*, p. 370.

51 Parmet, *Nixon and His America*, p. 579.
52 Ibid., p. 630.
53 White, Theodore H., *The Making of the President – 1972*, p. 344.
54 Parmet, p. 629.
55 Ibid.
56 White, John Kenneth, *The New Politics of Old Values*, p. 83.

Chapter 15
The Catholic Voter in the Age of Reagan

1 Kelly, George A., *Keeping the Church Catholic with John Paul II*, pp. 19–20.
2 Kelly, George A., *The Battle for the American Church*, p. 457.
3 Byrnes, T., *Catholic Bishops in American Politics*, p. 55.
4 Ibid., p. 57.
5 Heywood, Steven, *The Age of Reagan*, p. 356.
6 Ibid., p. 356.
7 Ibid., pp. 341–42.
8 White, Theodore H., *The Making of the President – 1972*, p. 236.
9 Heywood, p. 494.
10 Ibid., p. 495.
11 Witcover, Jules, *Marathon, The Pursuit of the Presidency, 1972–1976*, p. 206.
12 Ibid., p. 207.
13 Byrnes, p. 72.
14 Ibid.
15 Ibid., p. 72.
16 Ibid., p. 70.
17 Ibid., p. 75.
18 Ibid., p. 77.
19 Witcover, p. 183.
20 Heineman, Kenneth J., *God Is a Conservative*, p. 84.
21 Witcover, p. 598.
22 White, John Kenneth, *Still Seeing Red*, p. 183.
23 Ibid., p. 184.
24 Lasky, Victor, *Jimmy Carter: The Man and the Myth*, p. 4.
25 White, John Kenneth, *The New Politics of Old Values*, p. 60.
26 White, Theodore H., *American in Search of Itself*, p. 135.
27 White, *The New Politics of Old Values*, p. 147.
28 Heineman, p. 69.
29 Ibid., p. 120.
30 Ibid., p. 93.
31 Barone, Michael, *The Almanac of American Politics – 1982*, p. xviii.

32 Election results data is from the polling firm of Fabrizio, McLaughlin.
33 Barone, Michael, *Our Country*, p. 577.
34 Brown, p. 29.
35 Reagan, Ronald, *Abortion and the Conscience of the Nation*, p. 2.
36 Greenberg, Stanley B., *Middle Class Dreams*, p. 131.
37 Byrnes, p. 115.
38 Ibid., pp. 83–84.
39 Allitt, Patrick, *Catholic Intellectuals and Conservative Politics in America, 1950–1985*, p. 290.
40 Ibid., pp. 294–95.
41 Hentoff, Nat, *John Cardinal O'Connor*, p. 78.
42 *New York Times*, September 15, 1984.
43 Hentoff, Nat, *John Cardinal O'Connor*, p. 81.
44 Schlesinger, Arthur, *History of American Presidential Elections Supplement*, p. 302.
45 Henry, William A., III, *Visions of America*, p. 232.
46 Hentoff, p. 82.
47 Heineman, p. 141.
48 Ibid., p. 142.
49 Greenberg, *Middle Class Dreams*, p. 141.
50 Will, George F., *The New Season*, p. 123.
51 Heineman, p. 149.
52 Byrnes, p. 128.
53 Wald, Kenneth D., *Religion and Politics in the United States*, p. 238.
54 Greenberg, p. 142.
55 Muir, William Ker, Jr., *The Bully Pulpit*, p. 2.
56 Will, p. 128.
57 White, *The New Politics of Old Values*, p. 154.
58 Ibid., p. 71.
59 Radosh, Ronald, *Divided They Fell*, p. 200.
60 White, *The New Politics of Old Values*, p. 162.
61 Ibid., p. 160.
62 Ibid., p. 164.
63 Ibid., p. 157.
64 Guth, James L., et al., *The Bible and the Ballot Box, Religion and Politics in the 1988 Election*, p. 177.
65 Ibid., p. 188.

Chapter 16
The Catholic Voter in the Twenty-First Century

  1 Carlin, David, *The Decline an d Fall of the Catholic Church in America*, p. 51.

2 Barone, Michael, *The New Americans*, pp. 156–57.

3 DeSipio, Louis, *Counting on the Latino Vote*, p. 69.

4 Ibid., p. 31.

5 Ibid., p. 53.

6 Greenberg, Stanley, *The Two Americans*, p. 178.

7 From an Address by pollster John McLaughlin on "The Importance of the Catholic Vote."

8 Marlin, George, "The Politics of Ethnic Values," *Crisis*, May 1991.

9 *New York Times*, March 1, 1992.

10 Ibid.

11 Goldman, Peter, *The Quest for the Presidency 1992*, p. 318.

12 Marlin, *Fighting the Good Fight*, pp. 293–94.

13 Heineman, p. 184.

14 Ibid., p. 189.

15 Ibid.

16 Germond Jack W. and Witcover, Jules, *Mad as Hell*, pp. 235–36.

17 Rosenstiel, Tom, *Strange Bedfellows*, p. 108.

18 Wattenberg, Ben J., *Values Matter Most*, p. 42.

19 Ibid., p. 45.

20 Ibid., p. 47.

21 Ibid., p. 53.

22 Heineman, p. 201.

23 *New York Times*, August 30, 1992.

24 Heineman, p. 201.

25 *Wall Street Journal*, September 14, 1992.

26 Ibid.

27 Results are compiled from the pollster firm, John McLaughlin & Associates. DeSipro in *Counting on the Latino Vote* and Brewer in *Relevant No More?*

28 Layman, Geoffrey, *The Great Divide*, p. 107.

29 Barrett, Joseph A. and Tobin, Robert W., "Patterns of Change in the U.S. Catholic Vote."

30 Wattenberg, pp. 111–12.

31 Ibid., p. 394.

32 White, J.K., *Still Seeing Red*, p. 224.

33 Data from pollster John McLaughlin.

34 Ibid.

35 White, J.K., p. 231.

36 Heineman, p. 239.

37 White, J.K., p. 241.

38 Heineman, p. 242.

39 Ibid., p. 240.

40 Data from pollster John McLaughlin.

41 Reeves, Thomas, *Twentieth-Century America*, p. 293.

42 Greenberg, *The Two Americas*, p. 179.

43 Heineman, p. 253.

44 Minutaglio, Bill, *First Son*, p. 288.

45 *New York Post*, February 17, 2000.

46 *Wall Street Journal*, March 3, 2000.

47 Ibid.

48 *The Washington Times*, March 6–12, 2000 (weekly edition).

49 *Wall Street Journal*, March 29, 2000.

50 New York *Daily News*, February 28, 2000.

51 Ibid.

52 Ibid.

53 *Wall Street Journal*, February 29, 2000.

54 *National Review*, June 5, 2000.

55 Ibid.

56 *Wall Street Journal*, June 20, 2000.

57 *Wall Street Journal*, June 12, 2000.

58 *Wall Street Journal*, August 11, 2000.

59 *Columbia*, September 2000, pp. 14–16.

60 Ibid.

61 *New York Post*, October 5, 2000.

62 Ibid.

63 *New York Post*, October 24, 2000.

64 Barone, Michael, *The Almanac of American Politics*, p. 28.

65 *Public Interest*, Spring 2001, p. 23.

66 Data supplied by pollster, John McLaughlin.

67 *USA Today*, May 21, 2001.

68 CNN.com, Text of Bush Notre Dame Speech, May 20, 2001.

69 Barone, *The Almanac of American Politics, 2004*, p. 1,349.

70 *The Weekly Standard*, April 5, 2004.

71 Ibid.

72 Greenberg, Stanley, *The Two Americas*, Appendix D.

73 Interview with Dr. Robert Royal, President of Faith and Reason Institute.

74 New York *Daily News*, March 29, 2004.

75 *Human Events*, April 5, 2004.

76 *The Weekly Standard*, April 26, 2004.

77 *Time*, April 5, 2004.

78 *New York Post*, April 16, 2004.

79 *Human Events*, April 5, 2004.

80 *Time*, April 5, 2004.

81 *New York Times*, April 6, 2004.

82 *New York Times*, April 24, 2004.
83 Ibid.
84 Ibid.
85 *New York Times*, May 6, 2004.
86 Ibid.
87 *New York Times*, May 11, 2004.
88 Ibid.
89 Ibid.
90 Robert Novak column, *New York Post*, May 3, 2004.
91 Ibid.
92 *New York Times*, April 20, 2004.
93 *Roll Call,* June 7, 2004.
94 Ibid.
95 *New York Times,* May 24, 2004.
96 *National Review,* May 31, 2004.
97 *New York Times,* June 19, 2004.
98 Ibid.
99 *New York Times,* April 20, 2004.
100 *New York Times*, June 19, 2004.
101 *The New Yorker*, May 16, 2005.
102 *New York Daily News*, August 10, 2004.
103 *First Things*, January, 2005.
104 *The Brooklyn Tablet,* October 23, 2004.
105 *New York Times,* October 22, 2004.
106 *Catalyst* (The Catholic League), July–August, 2004.
107 Ibid.
108 *Kansas City Star,* October 15, 2004.
109 *New York Times,* October 14, 2004.
110 Ibid.
111 *New York Times*, October 25, 2004.
112 *Kansas City Star*, October 15, 2004.
113 *Newsday*, August 4, 2004
114 *New York Times*, August 4, 2004.
115 *New York Times*, October 14, 2004.
116 Statistics compiled by Karl Zinsmeister, *The American Enterprise* Magazine.
117 Ethics and Policy Center forum, Washington, DC, November, 2004.
118 Spreadsheet analysis compiled from 2004 Exit Polls taken in the 50 states.
119 *National Review*, November 29, 2004.
120 NewsMax, June 2005.
121 Ibid.

122 Exit Poll by Edison Media.
123 Associated Press.
124 Spreadsheet analysis compiled from 2004 Exit Polls.
125 *Boston Globe* (Jeff Jacobs' column), November 4, 2004.
126 *New York Times*, November 4, 2004.
127 *Roll Call*, November 17, 2004.
128 *Newsweek*, November 22, 2004.
129 *New York Times*, November 4, 2004.
130 *Washington Times*, November 8, 2004.
131 Ethics and Public Policy Center forum, Washington, DC, November 2004.
132 *New York Times*, February 11, 2005.
133 *National Review*, May 23, 2005.
134 *Catholic World Report*, June 2005.
135 *New York Times*, February 16, 2005.
136 *First Things*, January, 2005.

Selected Bibliography

A Note on Electoral Sources

Unless otherwise noted, all election and population statistics come from the following authoritative sources.

Austin, Erik. *Political Facts of the United States Since 1789*. Columbia University Press, 1986.

Barone, Michael, et al. *The Almanac of American Politics*, published biennially. National Journal Press, 1972–2004.

Burnham, W. Dean. *Presidential Ballots, 1836–1892*. Johns Hopkins University Press, 1955.

Robinson, Edgar E. *The Presidential Vote: 1896–1932*. Stanford University Press, 1934.

————. *They Voted for Roosevelt: The Presidential Vote, 1932–1944*. Stanford University Press, 1947.

McGillivray, Alice, et al. *America at the Polls 1960–1996: A Handbook of American Presidential Election Statistics*. Congressional Quarterly, Inc., 1998.

More, John L. *Congressional Quarterly's Guide to U.S. Elections, Second Edition*. Congressional Quarterly, Inc., 1985.

The New York Red Book. Published annually by the New York State Government. Volumes utilized were published 1898–2002.

Scammon, Richard M. *America Votes*, Vols. 1–10. Congressional Quarterly, Inc., 1956–1972.

Shaughnessy, Gerald. *Has the Immigrant Kept the Faith? A Study of Immigration and Catholic Growth in the United States, 1790–1920*. The Macmillan Company, 1925.

* * * * *

Abell, Aaron I. *American Catholicism and Social Action*. University of Notre Dame Press, 1960.

Adams, James Tuslow. *Dictionary of American History*, Vols. 1–5. Scribners, 1946.

Allen, Oliver E. *The Tiger: The Rise and Fall of Tammany Hall*. Addison-Wesley, 1993.

Allitt, Patrick. *Catholic Intellectuals and Conservative Politics in America, 1950–1985*. Cornell University Press, 1993.

Allsop, Kenneth. *The Bootleggers: The Story of Prohibition*. Arlington House, 1961.

Allswang, John M. *A House for All Peoples*. The University Press of Kentucky, 1971.

————. *The New Deal and American Politics*. John Wiley & Sons, Inc., 1978.

Archdeacon, Thomas J. *Becoming American: An Ethnic History*. Free Press, 1983.

Auchincloss, Louis. *Woodrow Wilson*. Penguin Group, 2000.

Azar, Larry. *Twentieth Century in Crisis: Foundations of Totalitarianism*. University of Iowa Press, 1990.

Baer, Kenneth S. *Reinventing Democrats: The Politics of Liberalism from Reagan to Clinton*. University Press of Kansas, 2000.

Bailey, Harry A., Jr., and Katz, Ellis. *Ethnic Group Politics*. Charles E. Merrill, 1969.

Bailyn, Bernard. *The Ideological Origins of the American Revolution*. Harvard University Press, 1907.

Bannister, Robert C. *Social Darwinism: Science and Myth in Anglo American Social Thought*. Temple University Press, 1979.

Barone, Michael. *The New Americans: How the Melting Pot Can Work Again*. Regnery Publishing, 2001.

————. *Our Country: The Shaping of America from Roosevelt to Reagan*. Free Press, 1990.

Barnard, Harry. *Rutherford B. Hayes and His America*. Russell, 1954.

Barrett, Patricia. *Religious Liberty and the American Presidency*. Herder and Herder, 1963.

Bayor, Ronald H. *Neighbors in Conflict*. Johns Hopkins University Press, 1978.

Bayor, Ronald H., and Meagher, Timothy J. *The New York Irish*. Johns Hopkins University Press, 1996.

Beals, Carleton. *Brass-Knuckle Crusade: The Great Know-Nothing Conspiracy: 1820–1860*. Hastings House Publishers, 1960.

Beatty, Jack. *The Rascal King: The Life and Times of James Michael Curley (1874–1958)*. Addison-Wesley Publishing Company, 1992.

Bell, Jeffrey. *Populism and Elitism*. Regnery, 1992.

Bennett, David H. *Demagogues in the Depression*. Rutgers University Press, 1969.

Benson, Lee. *The Concept of Jacksonian Democracy*. Princeton University Press, 1961.

Bernstein, Carl, and Politi, Marco. *His Holiness*. Doubleday, 1996.

Bernstein, Iver. *The New York City Draft Riots*. Oxford University Press, 1990.

Billington, Ray Allen. *The Protestant Crusade, 1800–1860*. Rinehart & Company, Inc., 1952.

Black, Conrad. *Franklin Delano Roosevelt: Champion of Freedom*. PublicAffairs, 2003.

Blanshard, Paul. *American Freedom and Catholic Power*. Beacon Press, 1949.

Blum, John Morton. *Joe Tumulty and the Wilson Era*. Houghton Mifflin Company, 1951.

————. *Woodrow Wilson and the Politics of Morality*. Little, Brown, 1956.

Boller, Paul F., Jr. *Presidential Campaigns*. Oxford University Press, 1984.

Boorstin, Daniel J. *The Lost World of Thomas Jefferson*. Peter Smith, 1976.

Brands, H.W. *T.R: The Last Romantic*. Basic Books, 1998.

————. *The Reckless Decade: America in the 1890s*. St. Martin's, 1995.

————. *Woodrow Wilson*. Times Books, 2003.

Brant, Irving. *James Madison, 1787–1800*. Bobbs-Merrill, 1950.

Brewer, Mark D. *Relevant No More?* Lexington Books, 2003.

Broderick, Francis L. *Right Reverend New Dealer: John A. Ryan*. The Macmillan Company, 1963.

Brodsky, Alyn. *Grover Cleveland*. St. Martin's, 2000.

Brookhiser, Richard. *The Outside Story*. Doubleday & Company, Inc., 1986.

Brown, Peter. *Minority Party*. Regnery Gateway, 1991.

Buckley, William F., Jr. *The Unmaking of a Mayor*. The Viking Press, 1966.

Burner, David. *The Politics of Provincialism: The Democratic Party in Transition, 1918–1932*. Norton Library, 1967.

Burnham, Walter Dean. *Presidential Ballots, 1836–1892*. Arno Press, 1976.

Burns, James MacGregor. *Roosevelt: The Lion and the Fox, 1882–1940*. Harcourt Brace Jovanovich, 1956.

————. *Roosevelt: The Soldier of Freedom, 1940–1945*. Harcourt Brace Jovanovich, 1970.

Byrnes, Timothy A. *Catholic Bishops in American Politics*. Princeton University Press, 1991.

Calvez, Jean-Yves, and Perrin, Jacques. *The Church and Social Justice*. Henry Regnery Company, 1961.

Campbell, Angus, et al. *The American Voter*. John Wiley & Sons, Inc., 1964.

Cannon, Lou. *President Reagan: The Role of a Lifetime*. Simon & Schuster, 1991.

Carlin, David. *The Decline and Fall of the Catholic Church in America*. Sophia Institute Press, 2003.

Caro, Robert. *The Power Broker*. Alfred A. Knopf, 1974.

Carruth, Gorton. *Encyclopedia of American Facts and Dates*. Crowell, 1956.

Carson, Clarence. *A Basic History of the United States*, Vols. 1–5. ATC Press, 1986.

Carter, Dan T. *The Politics of Rage*. Simon & Schuster, 1995.

Chaffin, Tom. *Pathfinder*. Hill and Wang, 2002.

Clancy, Herbert J. *The Presidential Election of 1880*. Loyola University Press, 1958.

Clark, Dennis. *The Irish in Philadelphia*. Temple University Press, 1973.

Cogley, John. *Catholic America*. Sheed & Ward, 1986.

Cohalan, Rev. Msgr. Florence D. *A Popular History of the Archdiocese of New York*. United States Catholic Historical Society, 1983.

Coleman, Charles H. *The Election of 1868*. Columbia University Press, 1971.

Connelly, James F., *The History of the Archdiocese of Philadelphia*. Archdiocese of Philadelphia, 1976.

Cook, Blanche Wiesen. *Eleanor Roosevelt*. Vol. 2: *1933–1938*. Viking, 1999.

Coughlin, Rev. Charles E. *A Series of Lectures on Social Justice*. Da Capo Press, 1935.

Craycraft, Kenneth R., Jr. *The American Myth of Religious Freedom*. Spence Publishing Company, 1999.

Creedon, Lawrence P., and Falcon, William, D. *United for Separation*. Bruce Publishing Company, 1959.

Croly, Herbert. *Marcus Alonzo Hanna*. Macmillan, 1912.

Crosby, Donald F., S.J. *God, Church, and Flag: Senator Joseph R. McCarthy and the Catholic Church, 1950–1957*. University of North Carolina Press, 1978.

Current, Richard. *The Political Thought of Abraham Lincoln*. Bobbs-Merrill, 1967.

Curtis, Dan T. *The Politics of Rage*. Simon & Schuster, 1995.

Dallek, Robert. *Franklin D. Roosevelt and American Foreign Policy: 1932–1945*. Oxford University Press, 1979.

———. *An Unfinished Life: John F. Kennedy, 1917–1963*. Little, Brown & Company, 2003.

Dalton, Kathleen. *Theodore Roosevelt: A Strenuous Life*. Knopf, 2002.

Daniels, Roger. *Coming to America*. HarperCollins Publishers, 1990.

Davis, Allen F., and Haller, Mark H. *The Peoples of Philadelphia*. Temple University Press, 1973.

Dawidowicz, Lucy S., and Goldstein, Leon J. *Politics in a Pluralist Democracy*. Institute of Human Relations Press, 1963.

Dawson, Christopher. *Dynamics of World History*. Sheed & Ward, 1956.

DeSipio, Louis. *Counting on the Latino Vote*. University Press of Virginia, 1996.

De Tocqueville, Alexis. *Democracy in America*. University of Chicago Press, 2000.

Dohen, Dorothy. *Nationalism and American Catholicism*. Sheed & Ward, 1967.

Dolan, Jay P. *The American Catholic Experience*. Doubleday & Company, Inc. 1985.

———. *The American Catholic Parish*. Paulist Press, 1987

———. *The Immigrant Church*. The Johns Hopkins University Press, 1975.

Donald, David H. *Lincoln*. Simon & Schuster, 1995.

Donovan, Robert J. *Tumultuous Years: The Presidency of Harry S. Truman, 1949–1953*. Norton, 1982.

Dorsett, Lyle W. *Franklin D. Roosevelt and the City Bosses*. Kennikat Press Corp, 1977.

Dubose, Lou, et al. *Boy Genius*. PublicAffairs, 2003.

Dyer, Thomas G. *Theodore Roosevelt and the Idea of Race*. Louisiana State University Press, 1980.

Eaton, Clement. *Henry Clay and the Art of American Politics*. Little Brown, 1957.

Edsall, Thomas Byrne, and Edsall, Mary D. *Chain Reaction*. W.W. Norton & Company, 1991.

Ehrenhalt, Alan. *The Lost City*. Basic Books, 1995.

Ellis, John Tracy. *American Catholicism*. University of Chicago Press, 1969.

―――――. *The Life of James Cardinal Gibbons*. Vol. 1: *Archbishop of Baltimore 1834–1921*. Christian Classics, Inc. 1987.

―――――. *The Life of James Cardinal Gibbons*. Vol. 2: *Archbishop of Baltimore 1834–1921*. Christian Classics, Inc. 1987.

Erie, Steven P. *Rainbow's End*. University of California Press, 1988.

Fanfani, Amintore. *Catechism of Catholic Social Teaching*. The Newman Press, 1960.

Farley, James A. *Jim Farley's Story: The Roosevelt Years*. Whittlesey House, 1948.

Farley, James A., and Conniff, James C.G. *Governor A. Smith*. Vision Books, 1959.

Faulkner, Harold U. *Politics, Reform and Expansion, 1890–1900*. Harold, Underwood Faulkner, 1959.

Feinstein, Otto. *Ethnic Groups in the City*. D.C. Heath and Company, 1971.

Fenton, John H. *The Catholic Vote*. Hauser Printing Co. Inc., 1960.

Fichter, Joseph H., S.J. *Social Relations in the Urban Parish*. University of Chicago Press, 1954.

Finan, Christopher M. *Alfred E. Smith: The Happy Warrior*. Hill and Wang, 2002.

Fischer, David. *The Revolution of American Conservatism*. Harper Torchbooks 1965.

Fleming, Thomas. *The Illusion of Victory: American in World War I*. Basic Books, 2003.

Flynn, George Q. *American Catholics and the Roosevelt Presidency, 1932–1936*. University of Kentucky Press, 1968.

―――――. *Roosevelt and Romanism*. Greenwood Press, 1976.

Foner, Eric. *Reconstruction: America's Unfinished Revolution, 1863–1877*. Harper & Row, 1988.

Formisano, Ronald P. *Boston against Busing*. The University of North Carolina Press, 1991.

Fowler, Robert Booth, et al. *Religion and Politics in America*. Westview Press, 1995.

Fox, Dixon Ryan. *The Decline of Aristocracy in the Politics of New York, 1801–1840*. Harper Torchbooks, 1965.

Fraser, Steve, and Gerstle, Gary. *The Rise and Fall of the New Deal Order, 1930–1980*. Princeton University Press, 1989.

Freedman, Samuel G. *The Inheritance*. Simon and Schuster, 1996.

Freidel, Frank. *Franklin D. Roosevelt: The Apprenticeship*. Little, Brown and Company, 1952.

————. *Franklin D. Roosevelt: The Ordeal*. Little, Brown and Company, 1954.

————. *Franklin D. Roosevelt: A Rendezvous with Destiny*. Little, Brown and Company, 1990.

Fried, Albert. *FDR and His Enemies*. St. Martin's Press, 1999.

Fuchs, Lawrence H. *American Ethnic Politics*. Harper & Row, 1968.

————. *John F. Kennedy and American Catholicism*. Meredith Press, 1967.

Gamm, Gerald H. *The Making of New Deal Democrats: Voting Behavior and Realignment in Boston, 1920–1940*. University of Chicago Press, 1986.

Gammon, Samuel R., Jr. *The Presidential Campaign of 1832*. Da Capo Press, 1969.

Gannon, Robert I. *The Cardinal Spellman Story*. Doubleday & Company, Inc., 1962.

Garrison, Winfred Ernest. *Catholicism and the American Mind*. Willett, Clark & Colby, 1928.

Germond, Jack W., and Witcover, Jules. *Mad as Hell: Revolt at the Ballot Box, 1992*. Warner Books, 1993.

Gibson, Florence E. *The Attitudes of the New York Irish toward State and National Affairs, 1848–1892*. Columbia University Press, 1951.

Gillon, Steven M. *The Democrats' Dilemma*. Columbia University Press, 1992.

Gillis, Chester. *Roman Catholicism in America*. Columbia University Press, 1999.

Glad, Paul W. *The Trumpet Soundeth: Bryan and His Democracy*. University of Nebraska Press, 1960.

Glazer, Nathan, and Moynihan, Daniel Patrick. *Beyond the Melting Pot*. The MIT Press and Harvard University Press, 1963.

Gleason, Philip. *Keeping the Faith: American Catholicism Past and Present.* University of Notre Dame Press, 1987.

Goldman, Peter, and Mathews, Tom. *The Quest for the Presidency: The 1988 Campaign.* Simon and Schuster, 1989.

Goldman, Peter, et al. *Quest for the Presidency 1992.* Texas A&M University Press, 1994.

Goodwin, Doris Kearns. *The Fitzgeralds and the Kennedys: An American Saga.* Simon and Schuster, 1987.

Graft, Henry F. *The Presidents.* Macmillan, 1997.

Grant, George. *Carry a Big Stick: The Uncommon Heroism of Theodore Roosevelt.* Cumberland House Publishing, 1996.

Greeley, Andrew M. *The American Catholic: A Social Portrait.* Basic Books, Inc., 1977.

—————. *The Catholic Experience.* Doubleday & Company, Inc., 1967.

—————. *The Catholic Myth: The Behavior and Beliefs of American Catholics.* Macmillan Publishing Company, 1990.

—————. *The Irish Americans.* Harper & Row Publishers, Inc., 1981.

—————. *Neighborhood.* The Seabury Press, 1977.

—————. *Why Can't They Be Like Us?* E.P. Dutton & Co., Inc., 1971.

Greenberg, Stanley B. *Middle Class Dreams.* Times Books, 1995.

—————. *The Two Americas.* St. Martin's Press, 2004.

Gregg, Gary L. *Patriot Sage.* ISI, 1999.

Grimstead, David, *Notions of the American Culture.* Braziller, 1970.

Guth, James L., and Green, John C. *The Bible and the Ballot Box: Religion and Politics in the 1988 Election.* Westview Press, 1991.

Haldeman, H.R. *The Haldeman Diaries: Inside the Nixon White House* G.P. Putnam's Sons, 1994.

Haller, Mark H. *Eugenics.* Rutgers University Press, 1984.

Halsey, William M. *The Survival of American Innocence.* University of Notre Dame Press, 1980.

Hamby, Alonzo, L. *Man of the People: A Life of Harry S Truman.* Oxford University Press, 1995.

Hamilton, Nigel. *Bill Clinton: An American Journey.* Random House, 2003.

Handlin, Oscar. *Al Smith and His America.* Little, Brown & Company, 1958.

—————. *Race and Nationality in American Life.* Little, Brown & Company, 1957.

————. *The Uprooted*. Grosset & Dunlap, 1951.

Hanna, Mary T. *Catholics and American Politics*. Harvard University Press, 1979.

Harbaugh, William H. *Power and Responsibility: The Life and Times of Theodore Roosevelt*. Farrar, Straus, 1961.

Harris, Louis. *Is There a Republican Majority? Political Trends, 1952–1956*. Harper & Brothers, 1954.

Hart, Jeffrey. *When the Going Was Good*. Crown Publishers, 1982.

Hasian, Marouf A., Jr. *The Rhetoric of Eugenics in Anglo-American Thought*. University of Georgia Press, 1996.

Hawke, David F. *Paine*. Harper & Row, 1976.

Haworth, Paul L. *The Hayes-Tilden Disputed Presidential Election of 1876*. Russell & Russell, 1966.

Heckscher, August. *Woodrow Wilson*. Scribner's, 1991.

Heineman, Kenneth J. *A Catholic New Deal*. Penn State Press, 1999

————. *God Is a Conservative*. New York University Press, 1998.

Henry, William A., III. *Visions of America*. Atlantic Monthly Press, 1985.

Hentoff, Nat. *John Cardinal O'Connor*. Macmillan Publishing Company, 1987.

Herman, Arthur. *Joseph McCarthy*. The Free Press, 2000.

Hernon, Joseph M., Jr. *Celts, Catholics and Copperheads*. Ohio State University Press, 1968.

Hesseltine, William B. *Ulysses S. Grant: Politician*. Ungar, 1957.

Heywood, Steven. *The Age of Reagan*. Forum, 2001.

High, Stanley. *The Church in Politics*. Harper Brothers, 1930.

Higham, John. *Strangers in the Land*. Rutgers University Press, 1988.

Hodgson, Godfrey. *The World Turned Right Side Up*. Houghton Mifflin Company, 1996.

Hofstadter, Richard. *The Age of Reform*. Alfred A. Knopf, 1955.

————. *The American Political Tradition*. Alfred A. Knopf, 1948.

————. *The Paranoid Style of American Politics and Other Essays*. Alfred A. Knopf, 1966.

————. *Social Darwinism in American Thought*. Beacon Press, 1955.

Hollingsworth, J. Rogers. *The Whirligig of Politics: The Democracy of Cleveland and Bryan*. University of Chicago Press, 1963.

Holt, Michael F. *Forging a Majority: The Formation of the Republican Party in Pittsburgh, 1848–1860*. Yale University Press, 1969.

————. *The Rise and Fall of the American Whig Party*. Oxford University Press, 1999.

Howe, Daniel Walker. *The Political Culture of the American Whigs*. University of Chicago Press, 1979.

Hugins, Walter. *Jacksonian Democracy and the Working Class*. Stanford University Press, 1960.

Hurley, Mark J. *The Unholy Ghost: Anti-Catholicism in the American Experience*. Our Sunday Visitor Publishing Division, 1992.

Jackson, Kenneth T. *Crabgrass Frontier*. Oxford University Press, 1985.

————. *The Ku Klux Klan in the City, 1915–1930*. Oxford University Press, 1967.

Jeffers, H. Paul. *An Honest President: Grover Cleveland*. Morrow, 2000.

Johnson, Paul. *A History of the American People*. HarperCollins Publishers, 1997.

Jones, E. Michael. *The Slaughter of Cities: Urban Renewal as Ethnic Cleansing*. St. Augustine's Press, 2004.

Jones, Stanley L. *The Presidential Election of 1896*. University of Wisconsin Press, 1964.

Josephson, Matthew, and Josephson, Hanna. *Al Smith: Hero of the Cities*. Houghton Mifflin Company, 1969.

Judis, John B., and Teixeira, Ruy. *The Emerging Democratic Majority*. Scribner, 2002.

Jung, Patricia Beattie, and Shannon, Thomas A. *Abortion and Catholicism: The American Debate*. Crossroad Publishing Company, 1988.

Kane, John J. *Catholic-Protestant Conflicts in America*. Regnery, 1955.

Kass, Alvin. *Politics in New York State, 1800–1830*. Syracuse University Press, 1965

Katz, Irving. *August Belmont*. Columbia University Press, 1968.

Kelly, Msgr. George A. *The Battle for the American Church*. Doubleday & Company, 1979.

————. *The Crisis of Authority: John Paul II and the American Bishops*. Regnery Gateway, 1982.

————. *Inside My Father's House*. Doubleday, 1989.

————. *Keeping the Church Catholic with John Paul II*. Doubleday, 1990.

Kelly, Robert. *The Cultural Pattern in American Politics*. Knopf, 1979.

Key, V.O. *Politics, Parties and Pressure Groups*. Crumwell, 1967.

King, James. *Facing the Twentieth Century*. Arno Press, 1977.

Kleppner, Paul. *Continuity and Change in Electoral Politics, 1893–1928*. Greenwood Press, 1987.

—————. *The Cross of Culture*. The Free Press, 1970.

—————. *The Third Electoral System, 1853–1892*. University of North Carolina Press, 1979.

Klein, Milton M. *Politics of Diversity*. Kennikat Press Corp., 1974.

Koenig, Louis W. *Bryan: A Political Biography of William Jennings Bryan*. G.P. Putnam's Sons, 1971.

Kramer, Michael, and Roberts, Steve. *I Never Wanted to Be Vice President of Anything*. Basic Books, 1976.

Krason, Stephen M. *Catholic Makers of America*. Christendom Press, 1993.

Kur, Kenneth Franklin. *The Reagan Years A to Z*. RGA Publishing Group, 1996.

Lasky, Victor. *J.F.K.: The Man and the Myth*. Arlington House, 1963.

—————. *Jimmy Carter: The Man and the Myth*. Marek, 1979.

Lay, Shawn. *Hooded Knights on the Niagara*. New York University Press, 1995.

Layman, Geoffrey. *The Great Divide*. Columbia University Press, 2001.

Leckie, Robert. *American and Catholic*. Doubleday, 1970.

Lenski, Gerhard. *The Religious Factor*. Doubleday & Company, Inc., 1961.

Leuchtenburg, William E. *Franklin D. Roosevelt and the New Deal, 1932–1940*. Harper & Row, 1963.

Levine, Edward M. *The Irish and Irish Politicians*. University of Notre Dame Press, 1966.

Levy, Mark R., and Kramer, Michael S. *The Ethnic Factor*. Simon and Schuster, 1972.

Lichtman, Allan, J. *Prejudice and the Old Politics: The Presidential Election of 1928*. University of North Carolina Press, 1979.

Lieberman, Joseph I. *The Power Broker: A Biography of John M. Bailey, Modern Political Boss*. Houghton Mifflin Company, 1966.

Link, Arthur. *Wilson*. Vols. 1–5. Princeton University Press, 1947–1956.

Linkh, Richard M. *American Catholicism and European Immigrants*. The Center for Migration Studies of New York, 1975.

Lipset, Seymour Martin, and Raab, Earl. *The Politics of Unreason: Right-Wing Extremism in America, 1790–1970*. Harper & Row, 1970.

Lipsky, George A. *John Quincy Adams: His Theory and Ideas*. Crowell, 1950.

Liptak, Dolores. *Immigrants and Their Church*. Macmillan Publishing Company, 1989.

Lisio, Donald J. *Hoover, Blacks, and Lily-Whites*. University of North Carolina Press, 1985.

Litt, Edgar. *Ethnic Politics in America*. Scott, Foresman and Company, 1970.

Lockwood, Robert P. *Anti-Catholicism in American Culture*. Our Sunday Visitor Publishing Division, 2000.

Lubell, Samuel. *The Hidden Crisis in American Politics*. Norton, 1970.

————. *The Future of American Politics*. Harper, 1951.

————. *The Future While It Happened*. Norton, 1973.

————. *Revolt of the Moderates*. Harper, 1956.

Luebke, Frederick C. *Ethnic Voters and the Election of Lincoln*. University of Nebraska Press, 1971.

————. *Immigrants and Politics*. University of Nebraska Press, 1969.

Lynch, Margaret. *In the Days of McKinley*. Easton Press, 1986.

MacLean, Nancy. *Behind the Mask of Chivalry*. Oxford University Press, 1994.

Maier, Thomas. *The Kennedys: American's Emerald Kings*. Basic Books, 2003.

Mandelbaum, Seymour J. *Boss Tweed's New York*. John Wiley & Sons, Inc., 1965.

Marino, Anthony J. *The Catholics in America*. Vantage Press, 1960.

Markmann, Charles. *The Buckleys*. Morrow, 1973.

Marlin, George J. *Fighting the Good Fight: A History of the New York Conservative Party*. St. Augustine's Press, 2002.

————. *The Politician's Guide to Assisted Suicide, Cloning, and Other Controversies*. Morley Books, 1998.

Martin, John Bartlow. *Adlai Stevenson and the World: The Life of Adlai E. Stevenson*. Doubleday, 1977.

————. *Adlai Stevenson of Illinois*. Anchor Press, 1977.

Martin, Ralph G. *A Hero for Our Time*. Macmillan Publishing Company, 1983.

Masse, Rev. Benjamin L. *Justice for All*. Bruce Publishing Company, 1964.

Maynard, Theodore. *The Catholic Church and the American Idea*. Appleton-Century-Crofts, Inc., 1953.

————. *The Story of American Catholicism*. The Macmillan Company, 1941.

McAvoy, Thomas T. *The Great Crisis in American Catholic History 1895–1900*. Henry Regnery Company, 1957.

————. *A History of the Catholic Church in the United States*. University of Notre Dame Press, 1969.

————. *Roman Catholicism and the American Way of Life*. University of Notre Dame Press, 1960.

McCullough, David. *John Adams*. Simon & Schuster, 2001.

McDermott, Scott. *Charles Carroll of Carrollton*. Scepter Publishers, Inc., 2002.

McGreevy, John T. *Catholicism and American Freedom*. Norton, 2003.

McKenzie, Richard B. *What Went Right in the 1980s*. Pacific Research Institute for Public Policy, 1994.

McNickle, Chris. *To Be Mayor of New York*. Columbia University Press, 1993.

McPherson, James M. *Battle Cry of Freedom*. Oxford University Press, 1988.

Merrill, Horace S. *Bourbon Leader: Grover Cleveland*. Little, Brown, 1957.

Metzger, Charles H., s.J. *Catholics and the American Revolution*. Loyola University Press, 1962.

Miles, Michael W. *The Odyssey of the American Right*. Oxford University Press, 1980.

Miller, Douglas T. *Jacksonian Aristocracy*. Oxford University Press, 1967.

Miller, John C. *Alexander Hamilton*. Harper & Row, 1959.

Miller, Nathan. *F.D.R.: An Intimate History*. Doubleday & Company, 1983.

Minutaglio, Bill. *First Son: George W. Bush and the Bush Family Dynasty*. Times Books, 1999.

Mitgang, Herbert. *Once Upon a Time in New York*. Free Press, 2000.

Moore, Edmund A. *A Catholic Runs for President: The Campaign of 1928*. Ronald Press Company, 1956.

Moore, James, and Slater, Wayne. *Bush's Brain: How Karl Rove Made George W. Bush Presidential*. John Wiley & Sons, Inc., 2003.

Morgan H. Wayne. *From Hayes to McKinley: National Party Politics 1877–1896*. Syracuse University Press, 1969.

————. *William McKinley and His America*. Syracuse University Press, 1963.

Morris, Charles R. *American Catholic*. Times Books, 1997.

Morris, Roy, Jr. *Fraud of the Century*. Simon and Schuster, 2003.

Moynihan, Daniel P. *Beyond the Melting Pot*. Howard Press, 1963.

————. *Coping*. Random House, 1973.

Muir, William Ker, Jr. *The Bully Pulpit*. Institute for Contemporary Studies, 1992.

Mulkern, John R. *The Know-Nothing Party in Massachusetts*. Northeastern University Press, 1990.

Murray, Robert K. *The 103rd Ballot*. Harper & Row, 1976.

————. *The Politics of Normalcy*. Norton, 1973.

Mushkat, Jerome. *Tammany: The Evolution of a Political Machine 1789–1865*. Syracuse University Press, 1971.

Myers, Gustavus. *History of Bigotry in the United States*. Random House, 1943.

Nelli, Humbert S. *From Immigrants to Ethnics: The Italian Americans*. Oxford University Press, 1983.

Nevins, Albert J. *Builders of Catholic America*. Our Sunday Visitor Publishing, 1985.

Nevins, Allan. *Grover Cleveland: A Study in Courage*. Dodd Mead, 1932.

Newfield, Jack, and Barrett, Wayne. *City for Sale*. Harper & Row, 1988.

Nichols, Roy F. *Franklin Pierce*. University of Pennsylvania Press, 1958.

Nie, Norman H., Verba, Sidney, and Petrocik, John R. *The Changing American Voter*. Harvard University Press, 1976.

Novak, Michael. *The Rise of the Unmeltable Ethnics*. The Macmillan Company, 1971.

O'Brien, David J. *American Catholics and Social Reform*. Oxford University Press, 1968.

————. *Public Catholicism*. Orbis Books, 1996.

O'Connor, Richard. *The First Hurrah: A Biography of Alfred E. Smith*. G.P. Putnam's Sons, 1970.

O'Connor, Thomas H. *Boston Catholics*. Northeastern University Press, 1998.

————. *The Boston Irish*. Northeastern University Press, 1995.

Odegard, Peter H. *Religion and Politics*. Oceana Publications, Inc., 1960.

Olasky, Marvin. *Renewing American Compassion*. The Free Press, 1996.

————. *The Tragedy of American Compassion*. Regnery Gateway, 1992.

Olson, James S. *Catholic Immigrants in America*. Nelson-Hall, 1987.

O'Neill, James M. *Catholicism and American Freedom*. Greenwood Press, 1952.

————. *Catholics in Controversy*. McMullen Books, 1954.

Oulahan, Richard. *The Man Who . . . : The story of the Democratic National Convention of 1932*. The Dial Press, 1971.

Parmet, Herbert S. *The Democrats: The Years after FDR*. Macmillan Publishing, 1976.

————. *George Bush: The Life of a Lone Star Yankee*. Scribner's, 1997.

————. *Nixon and His America*. Little, Brown, 1990.

Pell, Roy V., and Donnelly, Thomas C. *The 1928 Campaign: An Analysis*. Stratford Press, Inc., 1931.

Perko, F. Michael, s.j. *Catholic and American*. Our Sunday Visitor Publishing, 1989.

Perrett, Geoffrey. *America in the Twenties*. Simon & Schuster, 1982.

Peterson, Merrill D. *The Jefferson Image in the American Mind*. Oxford University Press, 1960.

Phillips, Kevin P. *The Emerging Republican Majority*. Arlington House, 1969.

————. *Mediacracy: American Parties and Politics in the Communications Age*. Doubleday & Company, Inc., 1975.

————. *Post-Conservative America*. Random House, 1982.

————. *William McKinley*. Times Books, 2003.

Pickens Donald K. *Eugenics and the Progressives*. Vanderbilt University Press, 1968.

Plunkitt, George Washington. *Plunkitt of Tammany Hall*. Knopf, 1948.

Reedy, George. *From the Ward to the White House*. Scribner's, 1991.

Rieder, Jonathan. *Canarsie: The Jews and Italians of Brooklyn against Liberalism*. Harvard, 1985.

Riordon, William L. *Plunkitt of Tammany Hall*. Alfred A. Knopf, Inc. 1948.

Polsby, Nelson W. *Presidential Elections: Strategies and Structures of American Politics (Presidential Elections)*. Free Press, 1980.

Radosh, Ronald. *Divided They Fell: The Demise of the Democratic Party, 1964–1996*. Free Press, 1996.

Rayback, Robert J. *Millard Fillmore*. Stewart, 1959.

Reagan, Ronald. *Abortion and the Conscience of the Nation*. Thomas Nelson Publishers, 1984.

Reeves, Thomas C. *The Life and Times of Joe McCarthy*. Stein and Day, 1982.

————. *Twentieth-Century America*. Oxford University Press, 2000.

Reisner, Christian F. *Roosevelt's Religion*. Abingdon Press, 1922.

Remini, Robert V. *Daniel Webster*. Norton, 1997.

————. *The Election of Andrew Jackson*. J.P. Lippincott Company, 1963.

————. *Henry Clay*. Norton, 1991.

————. *Martin Van Buren*. Columbia University Press, 1959.

Reuter, Frank T. *Catholic Influence on American Colonial Policies, 1898–1904*. University of Texas Press, 1967.

Richter, Edward. *Religion and the Presidency*. Macmillan, 1962.

Rorabaugh, W.J. *Kennedy and the Promise of the Sixties*. Cambridge University Press, 2002.

Rose, Lisle A. *The Cold War Comes to Main Street America in 1950*. University Press of Kansas, 1999.

Rosenstiel, Tom. *Strange Bedfellows*. Hyperion, 1993.

Ross, Earle Dudley. *The Liberal Republican Movement*. University of Washington Press, 1970.

Rubenstein, Edwin S. *The Right Data*. National Review, Inc., 1994.

Scammon, Richard M., and Wattenberg, Ben J. *The Real Majority*. Coward-McCann, Inc., 1970.

Schlesinger, Arthur. *History of American Presidential Elections*, Vols. 1–10. Chelsea House, 1985.

————. *History of U.S. Political Parties*, Vols. 1–4. Chelsea House, 1973.

Schneider, Rev. Nicholas A. *Religious Views of President John F. Kennedy*. B. Herder Book Co., 1965.

Shanabruch, Charles. *Chicago's Catholics*. University of Notre Dame Press, 1981.

Shannon, William V. *The American Irish*. Macmillan Company, 1963.

Shaw, Richard. *Dagger John*. Paulist Press, 1977.

Sheen, Fulton J. *Communism and the Conscience of the West*. Bobbs-Merrill, 1948.

Sheldon, Garrett Ward. *The Political Philosophy of Thomas Jefferson*. Johns Hopkins University Press, 1991.

Siegel, Fred. *Troubled Journey*. Hill & Wang, 1984.

Silbey, Joel H. *Martin Van Buren and the Emergence of American Popular Politics*. Rowman & Littlefield, 2002.

————. *Political Ideology and Voting Behavior in the Age of Jackson.* Prentice-Hall, Inc., 1973.

Sievers, Harry J. *Benjamin Harrison: Hoosier President: The White House and After.* Bobbs-Merrill, 1968.

Sinclair, Andrew. *Prohibition.* Little, Brown & Company, 1962.

Slayton, Robert A. *Empire Statesman: The Rise and Redemption of Al Smith.* The Free Press, 2001.

Slosser, Bob. *Reagan Inside Out.* Word, Inc., 1984.

Smith, Alfred E. *Campaign Addresses of Governor Alfred E. Smith.* Issued by The Democratic National Committee, 1929.

————. *Progressive Democracy: Addresses and State Papers of Alfred E. Smith.* Harcourt, Brace and Company, 1928.

————. *Up to Now: An Autobiography.* Viking Press, 1929.

Smith, Eric R.A.N. *The Unchanging American Voter.* University of California Press, 1989.

Smith, Jean E. *Grant.* Simon & Schuster, 2001.

Smith, Page. *History of America*, Vol. 12. Easton Press, 1997.

————. *John Adams.* Doubleday, 1962.

Staffer, A.P. "Anti-Catholicism in the United States." Doctoral Thesis, Harvard University.

Stampp, Kenneth M. *America in 1857: A Nation on the Brink.* Oxford University Press, 1990.

Stave, Bruce. *The New Deal and the Last Hurrah.* University of Pittsburgh Press, 1970.

Stephenson, George M. *A History of American Immigration, 1820–1924.* Russell & Russell, Inc., 1964.

Summers, Mark Wahlgren. *Rum, Romanism, and Rebellion: The Making of a President, 1884.* University of North Carolina Press, 2000.

Tarbell, Ida. *The Nationalizing of Business.* Macmillan, 1927.

Taylor, Paul. *See How They Run.* Knopf, 1990.

Tomasi, Silvano M. *Piety and Power.* The Center for Migration Studies of New York, 1975.

Thomas, John L., s.j. *The American Catholic Family.* Prentice-Hall, Inc., 1956.

Thompson, C. Bradley. *John Adams and the Spirit of Liberty.* University Press of Kansas, 1998.

Timberlake, James. *Prohibition and the Progressive Movement*. Harvard University Press, 1963.

Tugwell, Rexford, *The Brains Trust*. Viking Press, 1969.

Tull, Charles J. *Father Coughlin and The New Deal*. Syracuse University Press, 1965.

Turner, Frederick Jackson. *The Frontier in American History*. Henry Holt, reprinted 1990.

Van Deusen, Glyndon G. *The Life of Henry Clay*. Little, Brown and Company, 1937.

Wald, Kenneth D. *Religion and Politics in the United States*. St. Martin's Press, Inc., 1987.

Walsh, George. *Gentleman Jimmy Walker*. Praeger Publishers, 1974.

Walsh, James J. *Education of the Founding Fathers of the Republic*. Fordham University Press, 1935.

Walton, Richard J. *Henry Wallace, Harry Truman, and the Cold War*. Viking Press, 1976.

Ward, Geoffrey C. *A First-Class Temperament*. Harper & Row, 1989.

Ward, John William. *Andrew Jackson – Symbol of an Age*. Oxford University Press, 1955.

Wasson, W.W. *James A. Garfield: His Religion and Education*. University of Tennessee Press, 1952.

Wattenberg, Ben J. *Values Matter Most*. Free Press, 1995.

Weed, Perry L. *The White Ethnic Movement and Ethnic Politics*. Praeger Publishers, 1973.

Weigel, George, and Royal, Robert. *A Century of Catholic Social Thought: Essays on 'Rerum Novarum' and Nine Other Key Documents*. Ethics and Public Policy Center, 1991.

Weisburger, Bernard A. *America Afire: Jefferson, Adams, and the Revolutionary Election of 1800*. Morrow, 2000.

Weiss, Nancy Joan. *Charles Francis Murphy, 1858–1924: Respectability and Responsibility in Tammany Politics*. Smith College, 1968.

Werner, M.R. *Tammany Hall*. Doubleday, Doran & Company, Inc., 1928.

Wesser, Robert F. *A Response to Progressivism: The Democratic Party, New York Politics, 1902–1918*. New York University Press, 1986.

West, John G., Jr. *The Politics of Revelation and Reason*. University Press of Kansas, 1996.

West, Thomas G. *Vindicating the Founders*. Rowman & Littlefield, 1997.

White, John Kenneth. *The New Politics of Old Values*. University Press of New England, 1988.

————. *Still Seeing Red*. Westview Press, 1997.

————. *The Values Divide*. Chatham House Publishers, 2003.

White, Theodore H. *America in Search of Itself: The Making of the President, 1956–1980*. Harper & Row, 1982.

————. *The Making of the President – 1960*. Atheneum Publishers, 1961.

————. *The Making of the President – 1964*. Atheneum Publishers, 1965.

————. *The Making of the President – 1968*. Atheneum Publishers, 1969.

————. *The Making of the President – 1972*. Atheneum Publishers, 1973.

Wicker, Tom. *One of Us*. Random House, 1991.

Will, George F. *The New Season*. Simon and Schuster, 1988.

Williams, Michael. *The Shadow of the Pope*. McGraw-Hill, 1932.

Williams, R. Hal. *Years of Decisions: American Politics in the 1890s*. Wiley, 1978.

Wilson, Charles Morrow. *The Commoner: William Jennings Bryan*. Doubleday and Company, Inc., 1970.

Wilson, James, Q. *The Amateur Democrat*. University of Chicago Press, 1962.

Winter, Paul M. *What Price Tolerance*. All-American Book, Lecture and Research Bureau, 1928.

Witcover, Jules. *Marathon: The Pursuit of the Presidency, 1972–1976*. Viking Press, 1977.

Wittke, Carl. *The Irish in America*. Louisiana State University Press, 1956.

Wytrwal, Joseph A. *Poles in American History and Tradition*. Endurance Press, 1969.

Index

About the Author

George J. Marlin is Chairman and COO of The Philadelphia Trust Company. He served two terms as Executive Director and CEO of the Port Authority of New York and New Jersey. In that capacity he managed thirty-five facilities including the World Trade Center, La Guardia, JFK, and Newark Airports, PATH Subway and the four bridges and two tunnels that connect New York and New Jersey. In 1993, Mr. Marlin was the Conservative Party nominee for mayor of the City of New York, and in 1994 he served on Governor-elect Pataki's transition team. Mr. Marlin is the author of *Fighting the Good Fight: A History of the New York Conservative Party*, *The Politician's Guide to Assisted Suicide, Cloning and Other Current Controversies*, and co-authored with Joe Mysak, *The Guidebook to Municipal Bonds*. He is the editor of the *The Quotable Chesterton, More Quotable Chesterton, Quotable Fulton Sheen, Quotable Paul Johnson*, and *Quotable Ronald Knox*, and the forthcoming *Squandered Opportunities*. Mr. Marlin also serves as general editor of *The Collected Works of G.K. Chesterton*. His articles have appeared in numerous periodicals including *The New York Times*, New York *Post*, *National Review*, *Newsday*, and the New York *Daily News*. A lifelong resident of New York, Mr. Marlin resides with his wife, Barbara, in Nassau County.